SECOND EDITION

SOCIOLOGY
Alive!

18

STEPHEN MOORE

Stanley Thornes Publishers Ltd

First published in 1987 by:
Stanley Thornes (Publishers) Ltd
Ellenborough House
Wellington Street
CHELTENHAM GL50 1YW

Second edition 1996

96 97 98 99 00 / 10 9 8 7 6 5 4 3 2 1

A catalogue record for this book is available from the British Library.

ISBN 0 7487 1531 2

Typeset by P&R Typesetters Ltd, Salisbury
Printed and bound in Great Britain at The Bath Press, Avon

CONTENTS

PREFACE

I have now been teaching sociology and social policy for over 20 years. I still get real pleasure from the subject, and students' opinions and ideas still get me as excited, angry and interested as those first classes all those years ago.

In writing *Sociology Alive!*, I have tried to get some of that excitement over to you. Sociology is not boring, it is not a load of facts to be learned off by heart, it is not irrelevant to your life. The point of sociology is for you to realise that if you start to understand the things 'out there' which seem to control your lives, then that knowledge empowers you (sometimes) to do something about that.

The book is structured to provide you with lots of activities and starting points for discussion – all of them chosen to illustrate or relate to important sociological points. So, please don't regard them as exercises to plod through – they are alive, interesting and challenging, but only if you do your bit and throw yourself enthusiastically into the sociological enterprise. Enjoy yourselves!

Stephen Moore
December 1995

ACKNOWLEDGEMENTS

To the first edition

. . . Sarah and Claudia insist on being thanked too, though I can't for the life of me see why fighting, screaming, falling over, standing on my word-processor, being sick (amongst other things) on the floor of my study, falling down the stairs, ripping my books, stealing my pens, eating page four of *Social Trends*, singing endlessly (out of tune), pestering me to go to Peter Pan's Playground, demanding food and drink at the time of heaviest concentration, and generally making my life sheer hell, deserves thanks. But there you are. . . .

To the second edition

The publishers were somewhat surprised when I asked them to include part of the acknowlegements from the first edition. However, it seems to me today, almost ten years after the first edition, that more people have commented to me on the acknowledgements than the actual book! So for those who teach sociology and read the first edition, I thought I would update you on the Moore family situation, and you might care to compare with the original.

Well, Sarah and Claudia have long since passed being sick and urinating on my study floor, and we have moved away from good old Southend-on-Sea, so I haven't been to Peter Pan's Playground for some years.

I can't give you too much information on Sarah as we rarely actually have a conversation. Returning from school, she flops wearily down for an early evening's diet of *Home and Away*, *Neighbours*, and any other Australian rubbish she can find. This successfully puts her into a catatonic state for a couple of hours, after which she eats and then passes the time before bed in long and intensive phone calls.

Claudia still makes time for me, and after watching the Australian brain-diseased soaps has always got time to talk to me. I worry about Claudia – she is just too nice. I mean, it just can't be *normal* for a 10-year-old girl actually to like talking to her dad. Though, thinking about it, recently she has rather taken to pointing out my defects. Yes, she must be growing up.

Since the first edition, Michael joined our family (no connection between the publication and the birth). I am pleased to say that at 7 years of age he still regards me as the best father, and indeed the most impressive male, in the whole world. I like this, and can see no possible reason why he should ever change his mind.

Finally, one other family thing. I distinctly remember when I had literally just completed the first edition and written the preface, I went downstairs from my 'study' (the spare bedroom) and asked Paola, my wife, if she wanted me to mention her in the acknowledgements. She replied that she didn't mind either way. For the last ten years, whenever we have an argument she always points out that although I mentioned the children in the acknowledgements, I never thanked her. So, listen Paola – thanks! I would also like to thank Stephanie Richards who has now edited both editions of this book and *Social Welfare Alive!* – by nature I am sloppy, lazy and disorganised – I am suitably frightened of Stephanie to do what she tells me.

Stephen Moore

The author and publishers are grateful to the following for permission to reproduce previously published material:

Associated Book Publishers Ltd for extracts from *Coal is our Life* by N. Dennis, F. Henriques and C. Slaughter, (p 140); *The Family* by A. Wilson (p 127); adapted material from *Age and Generation* by M. O'Donnell (p 107) ● Basil Blackwell Ltd for extracts from *The Sociology of Housework* by A. Oakley (pp 73, 142) and adapted material from *Girl Delinquents* by A. Campbell (p 253) ● The British Psychological Society for adapted material from 'Self-reported delinquency among schoolboys and their attitudes to the police' by H. B. Gibson, *British Journal of Social and Clinical Psychology*, 6 (p 253) ● John Calder Ltd for adapted material from *The Assembly Line* by R. Linhart, translated by M. Crossland, 1981, originally published by Editions de Minuit, Paris (p 204) ● Centre for Contemporary Culture for extracts from 'Subcultural conflict and working-class communities' by P. Cohen (p 232) ● Child Poverty Action Group for extracts from *Putting the Treasury First – The truth about child support* by A. Garnham and E. Knights (pp 125, 126, 127, 136), and *Poverty: The facts* by C. Oppenheim (pp 283, 286, 288) ● Collins Publishers for an extract from *The Home and the School* by J. W. B. Douglas (p 185) ● Comedia Publishing Company Ltd for extracts from *The British Media* by M. Grant (pp 308, 316) ● David & Charles for extracts from *View from the Boys* by H. Parker (pp 30, 34) ● *Daily Mail*/Solo for extracts from *The Daily Mail*, © *Daily Mail*/Solo (pp 20, 65, 78–9, 93, 150, 164–5, 273–4, 311, 314, 336, 345) ● *The Economist* for an extract from issue of 1.3.86 (p 317) ● Faber and Faber Ltd, for adapted material from *Married Life in an African Tribe* by I. Shapéra (p 130) ● Gower Publishing Company Ltd for extract from *British Social Attitudes* by P. Jowell and S. Witherspoon (p 33); *Police and People in London* by D. Smith and J. Gray (p 90); and *Sex, Gender and Society* by A. Oakley (p 63) ● Jane Gregory on behalf of Pluto Projects (a division of Visionslide Ltd) for material from *The State of the Nation* by S. Fothergill and J. Vincent, Pan Books (p 88) ● *The Guardian* for extracts from various issues, © *The Guardian* (pp 9, 27, 42, 55, 66, 74, 75, 79–80, 92, 96, 100, 131, 132, 142, 144, 159, 177–8, 195, 207, 222, 246–7, 257, 269, 273, 302, 305, 311, 331, 343) ● *The Health Service Journal* (pp 341, 344) ● William Heinemann Ltd for an extract from *The Grapes of Wrath* by John Steinbeck (p 7) ● Help the Aged for an extract from *People not Pensioners* (p 112) ● David Henke for articles written for *The Guardian*, 10.10.86 and 19.6.86 (pp 124, 127) ● The Controller of Her Majesty's Stationery Office for Crown Copyright material (pp 43, 49, 55, 69, 89, 125, 133, 134, 153, 154, 155, 158, 159, 183, 184, 194, 212, 220, 224, 230, 241, 242, 250, 324, 340, 342, 343, 346, 347, 350) ● Eileen Krige for an extract from *The Realm of a Rain Queen* by J. and J. D. Drige, Juta & Co Ltd, South Africa (p 180) ● Macmillan Publishers Ltd for an extract from *The ABC of Sociology* by M. Slattery (p 239) and for an extract from *Sociology in Context* by J. Nobbs (p 40) ● Mail Newspapers plc for material from *The Mail on Sunday* (p 51) ● Manchester University Press for an extract from *Hightown Grammar* by C. Lacey (p 186) ● William Morrow & Co. Inc. for an extract from *Male and Female* by Margaret Mead, Greenwood Press, 1977 (p 4) ● New Internationalist Publications Ltd for adapted material from *The New Internationalist* (pp 101, 110) ● New Scientist Syndication for adapted material from *New Scientist*, 18.10.84 (p 170) ● *New Society* for material from various editions (pp 130, 137, 144, 164, 210, 219, 254, 277, 319) ● Newspaper Publishing plc for extracts from *The Independent*, © *The Independent* (pp 11, 27, 41, 44, 53, 70, 76, 85, 87, 114, 205, 218, 221, 222, 229, 231, 270, 289, 291–2, 328, 335); and from *The Independent on Sunday*, © *The Independent on Sunday* (pp 20, 104, 108, 111) ● *The Observer* for extracts from various issues, © *The Observer* (pp 44, 86–7, 103) ● Penguin Books Ltd for extracts from *Sociology: A Biographical Approach* by P. L. and B. Berger © 1976 P. & B. Berger (p 209); *Double Identity: The Lives of Working Mothers* by S. Sharpe © 1984 S. Sharpe (p 136); *Just Like a Girl: How Girls Learn to be Women* by S. Sharpe © 1976 S. Sharpe (p 189); and *Working for Ford* by H. Beynon, first published as Penguin Education 1973, © 1973, 1984 H. Beynon (p 214) ● Philip Allan Publishers Ltd for extracts from *Sociology Review* (formerly *Social Studies Review*) (pp 23, 71, 108, 120, 166, 167, 215, 229, 230, 269, 295, 304, 312) ● Laurence Pollinger Ltd on behalf of Colin Turnbull for extracts from *The Mountain People* (pp 1–2, 99) and *The Forest People* (pp 5, 143), Jonathan Cape Ltd ● Routledge and Kegan Paul for extracts from *Family and Class in a London Suburb* by P. Willmott and M. Young (pp 140, 228); *World Revolution and Family Patterns* by W. J. Goode (p 137); *Social Class and the Comprehensive School* by J. Ford (p 175) and *Human Societies* by G. Hurd *et al.* (p 131); and from issue of 20.6.69 of *The British Journal of Sociology* (p 327) ● Sylvia Secker for an extract from *The Ragged Trousered Philanthropists* by R. Tressell, Panther, 1965 (p 322) ● *The Social Science Teacher* for adapted material from 'A new deal for British youth' by D. Finn, Vol. 13, No. 2 (p 179) ● Times Newspapers Ltd for extracts from *The Times*, © *The Times* 1994/5 (pp 163, 252, 311); and *The Times Educational Supplement* (p 183) ● United Newspapers for extracts from the *Daily Express* (pp 74, 127) ● Unwin Hyman Ltd for extracts from *Gender* by E. A. Clarke and T. Lawson (p 68); *Poor Britain* by J. Mack and S. Lansley (pp 281, 284, 300); and *Youth and Leisure* by K. Roberts (p 231)

We are grateful to the following for permission to reproduce illustrations and for providing prints:

● Abbott Mead Vickers – BBDO Ltd for the RSPCA advertisement (p 270) ● Mike Abrahams/Network (pp 156 255 centre left, 325 centre) ● Amnesty International (p 270) ● Martin Argles/*The Observer* (p 44 left) ● Katalin Arkell/Network (p 197 bottom right) ● Associated Press Ltd (p 325 left) ● David Austin/Mail Newspapers plc (p 47) ● Barchester Green Investment (p 13) ● Steve Benbow/Network (p 325 right) ● John Birdsall (pp 203 bottom left, 255 – top two) ● Gary Calton/*The Observer* (p 44 right) ● John Cole/Network (p 225) ● Commission for Racial Equality (p 91) ● Countryside Properties plc (p 113) ● Dateline International (p 12) ● Chris Davies/Network (p 157) ● Department of Social Security (p 212) ● The Elim Pentecostal Churches (p 329) ● Gina Glover/Photo Co-op (p 255 centre right) ● Graphic News (p 70) ● Hill Samuel Investment Services (p 13) ● Institute for Public Policy Research (p 53) ● Mary Evans Picture Library (pp 10, 100 – all except bottom right) ● Edward McLachilan/Punch (p 94) ● Modus Publicity for the Benetton advertisement (p 92) ● New Internationalist (p 93) ● NSPCC (p 124) ● A. D. Peters & Co. Ltd (from Posy Simmonds, *Very Posy*, Jonathan Cape, 1983 (p 73) ● Redferns (p 100 – bottom right) ● Rex Features (pp 197 top right, 198, 203 – all except bottom left) ● J Sainsbury plc (p 11) ● Laurie Sparham/Network (pp 168 left, 197 top left) ● John Sturrock/Network (pp 168 right and centre, 197 bottom left, 255 right, 314 right, 316) ● Topham Picture Library (p 166)

Every attempt has been made to contact copyright holders, but we apologise if any have been overlooked.

INTRODUCTION

Once upon a time there was a mother cauliflower and a baby cauliflower walking down the road. Well, you know what little cauliflowers are like – alway running about, can't keep still. Down the road, driving an enormous tatty old Jaguar came a great big carrot – typical of a carrot, just wasn't paying attention, too busy smoking his fat cigar. Bham!!!! Poor Baby Cauliflower was lying in the road, badly injured it seemed. Carrot was unrepentant – 'not my fault', 'should have kept him under control' – the usual stuff.

Anyway, an onion saw what happened and phoned the emergency services. Within a couple of minutes (you can tell this is fantasy), along came the ambulance driven by a couple of brussels sprouts. 'Looks bad', muttered the senior ambulance-sprout person as they quickly, but carefully, put Baby Cauliflower into the ambulance.

Two hours later at the hospital, Mother Cauliflower has been joined by Father Cauliflower and both are pacing anxiously around the waiting area of the Accident and Emergency Unit. 'What's keeping them so long?', complained Daddy Cauliflower. Just then Doctor Turnip and Nurse Swede emerge through the swing doors of the operating theatre.
'Well?' said Mummy Cauliflower.
'Good news and bad news, 'replied Doctor Turnip, 'which do you want to hear first?'
'The good news.'
'Tell them nurse.'
'Well, we are very pleased to tell you that Baby Cauliflower is going to live.'
'Oh, that's wonderful!', cried Mummy and Daddy Cauliflower in unison.
'But,' said Mummy Cauliflower, 'what's the bad news?'
'Tell them nurse.'
'I am afraid he'll be a cabbage for the rest of his life!'

Well, I know it's not that funny, but there is a point to it. The point about humour is that it provides us with a different way of looking at reality. The humour comes from a different understanding of a situation than the obvious.

That is the aim of sociology, too. It takes the obvious and then it asks us to examine it in a different way. It refuses to take for granted the most obvious day-to-day experiences. With a fresh mind and an outlook unclouded by bias, it pulls apart all those excuses and myths about the world that flow about us. Unfortunately, unlike in the story above, many of the answers, or the understandings, it gives us about our lives upset people, because the truth is not what they would like us to believe.

Chapter 1

SOCIALISATION AND CULTURE

This chapter covers:
- Instinct versus learning
- Culture
- Socialisation
- Social control
- Social roles
- Beliefs, values and norms.

Instinct versus learning

There are two views about what makes us do things. The first of these is the common sense approach that is always being put forward. It is the belief that people are born with natural desires and uncontrollable **instincts**. So when men rape women, it is a result of their uncontrollable sexual desire. When women cuddle babies, it is the response to their natural maternal instinct. When wars are fought, it is the natural result of man's aggressiveness. Theft is the result of our instinct to possess.

Sociologists are very doubtful about this explanation. The first, and major, objection is that if people's behaviour is natural then it ought to be, by and large, the same all over the world, just as their physical abilities are. Most human beings all over the world have the same physical needs such as eating and sleeping, and the same physical abilities such as walking, running and lifting. But *desires*, *attitudes* and *patterns of behaviour* vary tremendously from one society to another.

Culture

Colin Turnbull studied a tribe in the north of Uganda in the 1950s. The Ik tribe had traditionally been hunters. The Ugandan government, however, decided that their hunting lands should become a game reserve and resettled them in a mountainous region, where there were few animals to hunt and inadequate rainfall to grow crops. In effect they had been sentenced to death. The Ik gradually developed a culture to cope with their new and horrifying circumstances.

The quality of life that we hold as necessary for survival, love, the Ik also dismiss as idiotic and highly dangerous. ...

So we should not be surprised when the mother throws her child out at three years old. She has breast-fed it, with some ill humor, and cared for it in some manner for three whole years, and now it is ready to make its own way. I imagine the child must be rather relieved to be thrown out, for in the process of being cared for he or she is carried about in a hide sling wherever the mother goes, and since the mother is not strong herself this is done grudgingly. Whenever the mother finds a spot in which to gather, or if she is at a water hole or in the fields, she loosens the sling and lets the baby to the ground none too slowly, and of course laughs if it is hurt. ... Then she goes about her business, leaving the child there, almost hoping that some predator will come along and carry it off. This happened once while I was there – once that I know of, anyway – and the mother was delighted. She was rid of the child and no longer had to carry it about and feed it, and still further this meant that a leopard was in the vicinity and would be sleeping the child off and thus be an easy kill. The men set off and found the leopard, which had consumed all of the child except part of the skull; they killed the leopard and cooked it and ate it, child and all. ...

Hunger was indeed more severe than I knew, and the children were the next to go. It was all quite impersonal – even to me, in most cases, since I had been immunized by the Ik themselves against sorrow on their behalf. But Adupa was an exception. Her stomach grew more and more distended, and her legs and arms more spindly. Her madness was such that she did not know just how vicious humans could be, particularly her playmates. She was older than they, and more tolerant. That too was a madness in an Icien world. Even worse, she thought that parents were for loving, for giving as well as receiving. Her parents were not given to fantasies, and they had two other children, a boy and a girl who were perfectly normal, so they ignored Adupa, except when she brought them food that she had scrounged from somewhere. They snatched that quickly enough. But when she came for shelter they drove her out, and when she came because she was hungry they laughed that Icien laugh, as if she had made them happy. ...

Finally they took her in, and Adupa was happy and stopped crying. She stopped crying forever, because her parents went away and closed the *asak* [compound] tight behind them, so tight that weak little Adupa could never have moved it if she had tried. But I doubt that she even thought of trying. She waited for them to come back with the food they promised her. When they came back she was still waiting for them. It was a week or ten days later, and her body was already almost too far gone to bury. In an Ik village who would notice the smell? And if she had cried, who would have noticed that? Her parents took what was left of her and threw it out, as one does the riper garbage, a good distance away.

Source: Adapted from C. Turnbull, *The Mountain People* (Picador, 1974)

1 What are the main values of the Ik, do you think?

2 Why did these values develop in your opinion?

3 Why was Adupa different?

4 Do you think the women in the Ik tribe have a maternal instinct? Give a reason for your answer.

5 Sociologists argue that no behaviour is natural to mankind; goodness, evil, love, are all products of society. Having read the extract, what is your opinion? Discuss in small groups then appoint one person to report back to the class.

What is culturally normal in one society may be rather unusual in another

Take the case of language, for example, everyone has the ability to talk, i.e. the ability to make sounds, yet there are thousands of different languages throughout the world. The English language is not 'natural'; it is really just an agreement that certain sounds mean certain things. Language is a **social creation**. But so too are manners. In Bedouin society, for example, it is regarded as polite to 'burp' after a meal, to show that you have found the meal satisfying and tasty. It is regarded as extremely bad manners in Britain. It could be argued in reply that, of course, certain unimportant things are not natural, but all the important ones are, such as sex drives, maternal instinct, the instinct of personal survival, and so on. But this is not true. Society is so powerful that it can swamp these drives with ease. Take the instinct for personal survival; can this explain the actions of Japanese kamikaze pilots at the end of the Second World War (1939–45) who deliberately flew their planes, packed with explosives, into American ships? They were not forced to do it, they were proud to volunteer. In the Japanese culture of that time, it was a wonderful, heroic gesture to die for one's country and emperor. A similar thing happened in Iran in the 1980s, with 'revolutionary guards' who were prepared to go to almost certain death in their country's war with Iraq.

What about people who starve and beat their own children, do they have parental instincts? As for the sex drive, there are countless examples of men and women who choose to become priests or nuns, and so never make love.

The simplest way to prove the importance of **learning** as opposed to instinct is to look at examples of people who have lived their first few years without other human company. The results have always been the same; the person does not have the abilities which we recognise as normal amongst humans. In the case of the 'wild boy of Aveyron' in France, he was found running on all fours and surviving on nuts and berries, living in exactly the same way as the animals with whom he had spent his first formative years. His instinct may have been to survive, but how he behaved was a result of learning.

When people tell us that our actions are the result of nature, they are certainly wrong. Wrong because we know that virtually all human behaviour is the result of learning and, as societies vary in what they consider normal, people learn different things. Sociology says that by understanding the real causes of problems in society, we can learn to control them.

Role models and socialisation

Human beings act in the way they do through copying others around them. The following extract describes how a boy, who had been brought up by wolves, was found.

He heard some squealing, crept up, and saw the boy playing with four or five wolf cubs. He was most emphatic they were wolves.

The boy had very dark skin, finger-nails grown into claws, a tangle of matted hair and callouses on his palms, elbows and knees. He ran rapidly on all fours, yet couldn't keep up with the cubs as they made for cover. The mother wolf was not in sight. The thakur caught the boy and was bitten. But he did manage to truss him up in his towel, lash him to the bicycle and ride home.

At first Shamdev cowered from people and would only play with dogs. He hated the sun and used to curl up in shadowy places. After dark he grew restless and they had to tie him up to stop him following the jackals which howled round the village at night. If anyone cut themselves, he could smell the scent of blood and would scamper towards it. He caught chickens and ate them alive, including the entrails. Later, when he had evolved a sign language of his own, he would cross his thumbs and flap his hands: this meant 'chicken' or 'food'.

Eventually the thakur weaned him off red meat. He forced rice, dal and chappatis down his throat, but these made him sick. He took to eating earth, his chest swelled up and they began to fear for his life. Only gradually did he get used to the new diet. After five months he began to stand: two years later he was doing useful jobs like taking straw to the cows.

Source: *The Sunday Times Magazine*, 30 July 1978

1 When the boy was caught by the thakur what did his behaviour resemble?

2 Could you suggest any reason why he behaved like this?

3 Why did he want to eat only raw red meat?

Culture

As we have just seen, what is regarded as normal behaviour varies from one society to another. This leads us to the concept of **culture**. A culture is the whole set of beliefs and guidelines as to how people ought to behave in any society, which people regard as natural and normal. Each society has a different culture: expectations of behaviour in Britain are very different from those in China, for instance.

Cultures vary over time (the values and expectations of Victorian England compared with today) and by country and area (Tanzania compared with France). Within cultures, groups can vary considerably in their agreement with the main culture; for example many people argue that youth is a period when young people are likely to rebel and to reject the normal values of society. Sociologists call distinctive sets of values within cultures **subcultures**.

The important point to realise is that cultures are made by people in the first place to give a framework and a meaning to life. There is no such thing as 'normal' behaviour or 'abnormal' behaviour for all human beings. Whenever you study another society, rather than thinking how weird/silly/strange their behaviour is, you should realise that it is as sensible and normal as our own seems to us.

Socialisation

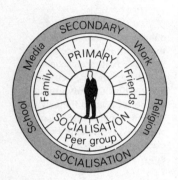

The new-born baby lying in the cot is the centre of attention of her parents and family. They play with her, they smile at her, and eventually she learns to smile back. Months later she learns from tones of voice which actions are not to be done and which actions please her parents. After her parents have constantly repeated words like 'mummy' and 'daddy' to her, she learns that by saying these 'magic' words, she gets a kiss or a drink, or some reward. As time progresses, the child learns more words, and more rules of behaviour. Eventually, the little girl will have learned all the behaviour expected of her in most situations, and of course she will regard this behaviour as perfectly natural. As she grows up, through playing games with her friends, through the example of her parents and later through the official learning at school, the girl will come to learn all the appropriate behaviour expected of girls and women in our society.

Everyone passes through this **socialisation** process and emerges with similar expectations of behaviour. It is only as a result of this that society is possible, otherwise there would be chaos with people doing exactly what they wanted.

In modern societies, sociologists distinguish between **primary** and **secondary socialisation**. Primary socialisation is the learning of social behaviour from those closest to you, such as family and friends. Secondary socialisation is the learning of social rules that takes place in school and at work, and very importantly, in the mass media (television, radio, newspapers).

Socialisation and personality

This extract describes child-rearing in two societies.

The Arapesh treat a baby as a soft vulnerable precious little object, to be protected, fed and cherished. Not only the mother, but the father also must play this over-all protective role. ... When the mother walks about, she carries the child slung beneath her breast ... whenever it is willing to eat even if it does not show hunger, it is fed gently and with attention. Through the long protected infancy, the child is never asked to perform tasks that are difficult or exacting.

The Mundugumor women actively dislike child-bearing and they dislike children. Children are carried in harsh baskets that scratch their skin, high up on their mother's shoulders, well away from the breast. Mothers nurse their children standing up, pushing them away as soon as they are the least bit satisfied. Here we find a character developing that stresses angry, eager greed.

Source: Adapted from M. Mead, *Male and Female* (Penguin, 1962)

1 Suggest two words to describe the Arapesh view of children, and two to summarise the Mundugumor attitude.

2 What sort of personalities do you think the Arapesh children will have when they grow up?

3 What sort of personalities do you think the Mundugumor children will have?

4 What does the extract tell us about the relationship between child-bearing and adult personalities?

Socialisation: Learning the skills

The pygmies were mainly hunters who travelled through the forest, only staying in one place for a short time (nomadic). The extract shows how the children learn the skills necessary to survive as adults in the forest.

Like children everywhere, pygmy children love to imitate their adult idols, and this is the beginning of their schooling, for the adults will always encourage and help them. What else do they have to be taught, except to grow into good adults? So a fond father will make a tiny bow for his son, and arrows of soft wood and with blunt points. He may also give him a strip of a hunting net. The mother will delight herself and her daughter by weaving a miniature carrying basket, and soon boys and girls are 'playing house'. They solemnly collect the sticks and leaves, and while the girl is building a miniature house the boy prowls around with his bow and arrow. He will eventually find a stray plantain or an ear of corn which he will shoot at and proudly carry back. With equal solemnity it is cooked and eaten, and the two may even sleep the sleep of innocence in the hut they have made.

They will also play at hunting, the boys stretching out their little bits of net while the girls beat the ground with bunches of leaves and drive some poor, tired, old frog in towards the boys. If they can't find a frog they go and awaken one of their grand-parents and ask him to play at being an antelope. He is then pursued all over the camp, twisting and dodging amongst the huts and the trees, until finally the young hunters trap their quarry in the net, and with shouts of delight pounce on him, beating him lovingly with their little fists. Then they roll over and over in a tangle with the net until they are exhausted.

For children life is one long frolic interspersed with a healthy sprinkle of spankings and slappings. Sometimes these seem unduly severe, but it is all part of their training. And one day they find that the games they have been playing are not games any longer, but the real thing, for they have become adults. Their hunting is now real hunting, their tree climbing is in earnest search of inaccessible honey, their acrobatics on the swings are repeated almost daily, in other forms, in the pursuit of elusive game, or in avoiding the malicious forest buffalo. It happens so gradually that they hardly notice the change at first, for even when they are proud and famous hunters their life is still full of fun and laughter.

Source: C. Turnbull, *The Forest People* (Picador, 1976)

1 Suggest three skills needed by pygmies to survive in the forest (no jokes about height, please!) and show how they learn these skills through socialisation as described in the extract.

2 How do people learn skills and knowledge in our society today? List five skills all children learn in our society.

Social control

If people act in a way which does not conform to the expectations of society, then they are punished in some way, either by being regarded as odd and perhaps having no friends or, in extreme cases, by being branded as criminals. This is known as **social control**.

There are two types of social control, **formal** and **informal**. Formal social control is when the rules of society are expressed in law and they are backed up by official agencies such as the police and the courts. Informal social control is where there are certain expectations of behaviour which are not formally written down, but most people take for granted. When people break these 'rules', then others show their disapproval.

So, people learn the expectations and values of society (culture) through socialisation and if they do not follow the guidelines of society, then they are punished in some way (social control). (For a more detailed discussion of social control, see pages 234–7.)

Social roles

Do you remember playing with Lego kits as a child, where you put the pieces together to make houses or robots? Each piece of the Lego was fitted together to make the final construction. If the pieces had not fitted, then the house or robot would not have held together.

The situation is exactly the same for society. All society consists of is a number of people acting in predictable ways that fit together into a pattern. The pieces of our 'social Lego' are known as **roles**. A role is a pattern of behaviour that is associated with a particular position (or **status**) in society. For example, the role of father is someone who is supposed to love his children, to teach them manners and punish them when they are naughty, to look after them and to do his best for their future. The same person may also be a teacher and this role involves passing on information to students, being fairly strict, showing an interest in the students, joining in with games after school, and so on.

The important point for society about roles is that the role of father/teacher remains the same even if different people fill those roles. Thus a degree of predictability and order is made possible in society.

Learning the roles

Children play games, and the very first ones are usually of the 'playing at being Mum and Dad' type, and then they develop into playing team games. For sociologists, these games are very important, for they help the children to be aware of how other people see the world, which they need to take into account in order to behave normally themselves. For example, when a group of children play football, each person needs to know just what the other person has to do in order to understand his or her own part in the team. Gradually the child builds up an awareness of what other people expect and how they will react to his or her actions. This process of learning appropriate behaviour continues throughout our lives, although the most important period of learning is in the first five years.

To simplify this incredibly difficult task of having to live in everyone else's mind as well as our own, the number of social roles are restricted. People do not behave just as they wish, they conform to what is generally considered to be the correct behaviour for a particular role. By and large, the behaviour of students is predictable, so is that of teachers, of shop assistants and policemen. We all know what these people ought to do, and it does not matter too much which individual fits into the role, he or she will behave roughly the same. So, I fit my role (for example, at the moment as writer and teacher) to your role (as reader and student).

Role conflict

All of us play more than one role in society. The teacher, for example, may also be a wife, a mother, a best friend, a keen fan of Liverpool Football Club, a member of a church, and a local government councillor. Sometimes, these roles conflict and when they do so then the person has to try to balance one against the other. Generally the culture gives us a 'nudge' to help us to choose which role is more important than another. In the example above it is usually stressed, in our society, that the role of mother is the most important.

Roles

The following extract comes from the classic novel of poverty in the USA of the 1930s, *The Grapes of Wrath* by John Steinbeck. A tractor driver has been sent to destroy the crops of a farmer who is to be evicted with his family. The farmer has no money and nowhere to go. Although it is a novel, it is based upon fact.

The extract illustrates, among other things, the role of sociology in the world. Like the farmer in the extract, we find that the world is far more complicated than we imagine when we try to understand our problems. We give up and just accept that most of the things that happen to us are caused by 'fate' or 'bad luck', and so resign ourselves to accepting our situation. The farmer finally understands that society and its problems, such as crime, unemployment and poverty, are made by people and so if we can truly understand how our situation was created we can strive to change it. This is the whole point of sociology.

'Why, you're Joe Davis's boy!'

'Sure,' the driver said.

'Well, what you doing this kind of work for – against your own people?'

'Three dollars a day. I got damn sick of creeping for my dinner – and not getting it. I got a wife and kids. We got to eat. Three dollars a day, and it comes every day.'

'That's right,' the tenant said. 'But for your three dollars a day fifteen or twenty families can't eat at all. Nearly a hundred people have to go out and wander on the roads for your three dollars a day. Is that right?'

And the driver said: 'Can't think of that. Got to think of my own kids. Three dollars a day, and it comes every day. Times are changing, mister, don't you know? Can't make a living on the land unless you've got two, five, ten thousand acres and a tractor. Crop land isn't for the little guys like us any more. You don't kick up a howl because you can't make Fords, or because you're not the telephone company. Well, crops are like that now. Nothing to do about it. You try to get three dollars a day some place. That's the only way.'

'Nearly a hundred people on the road for your three dollars. Where will we go?'

'And that reminds me,' the driver said, 'you better get out soon. I'm going through the door-yard after dinner.'

'You filled in the well this morning.'

'I know. Had to keep the line straight. But I'm going through the door-yard after dinner. Got to keep the lines straight. And – well you know Joe Davis, my old man, so I'll tell you this. I got orders wherever there's a family not moved out – if I have an accident – you know, get too close and cave the house in a little – well, I might get a couple of dollars. And my youngest kid never had no shoes yet.'

'I built it with my hands. Straightened old nails to put the sheathing on. Rafters are wired to the stringers with baling wire. It's mine. I built it. You bump it down – I'll be in the window with a rifle. You even come too close and I'll pot you like a rabbit.'

'It's not me. There's nothing I can do. I'll lose my job if I don't do it. And look – suppose you kill me? They'll just hang you, but long before you're hung there'll be another guy on the tractor, and he'll bump the house down. You're not killing the right guy.'

'That's so,' the tenant said. 'Who gave you orders? I'll go after him. He's the one to kill.'

'You're wrong. He got his orders from the bank. The bank told him: "Clear those people out or it's your job." '

'Well, there's a president of the bank. There's a board of directors. I'll fill up the magazine of the rifle and go into the bank.'

The driver said: 'Fellow was telling me the bank gets orders from the east. The orders were: "Make the land show profit or we'll close you up." '.

'But where does it stop? Who can we shoot? I don't aim to starve to death before I kill the man that's starving me.'

'I don't know. Maybe there's nobody to shoot. Maybe the thing isn't men at all. Maybe, like you said, the property's doing it. Anyway, I told you my orders.'

'I got to figure,' the tenant said.

'We all got to figure. There's some way to stop this. It's not like lightning or earthquakes. We've got a bad thing made by men, and by God that's something we can change.' The tenant sat in his doorway, and the driver thundered his engine and started off, tracks falling and curving, harrows combing, and the phalli of the seeder slipping into the ground. Across the door-yard the tractor cut, and the hard, foot-beaten ground was seeded field, and the tractor cut through again; the uncut space was ten feet wide. And back he came. The iron guard bit into the house-corner, crumbled the wall, and wrenched the little house from its foundation so that it fell sideways, crushed like a bug. And the driver was goggled and a rubber mask covered his nose and mouth. The tractor cut a straight line on, and the air and the ground vibrated with its thunder. The tenant man stared after it, his rifle in his hand. His wife was beside him, and the quiet children behind. And all of them stared after the tractor.

Source: J. Steinbeck, *The Grapes of Wrath* (Heinemann, 1939)

There are two people in the extract who fill different roles, the tractor driver and the farmer.

1 What behaviour is associated with the role of the driver?

2 What other roles does the driver fill in his life?

3 What behaviour do you think is associated with this?

4 There is evidence of 'role conflict' in the extract. Find this role conflict and describe it.

5 List at least four roles that you play in life. Is there any role conflict?
Take one example and show how you cope with it.

6 Although the two characters in the extract are arguing they share at least one value in common. What is it?

Beliefs, values and norms

Cultures develop in order to make sense of the world around us: they provide us with order and meaning, and as societies' circumstances vary, so do their cultures. The main component parts of cultures are **beliefs**, **values** and **norms**.

Beliefs

These are very vague, general feelings or opinions about the world. They are rarely very clear, or organised, but they provide us with the general framework of our understanding about the world. So most people believe that they are 'free' in our society, exactly what that means is unclear, but it is constantly referred to in newspapers and on the television, 'a free society', the 'freedom of the individual'. This belief in freedom is powerful enough to explain why people ought to go to war – they go to 'defend freedom'.

Values

Values are the ideas about correct and just behaviour that come from beliefs. For example, Western values stress that it is generally wrong to harm or kill others.

Norms

These are normal, expected patterns of behaviour in everyday life. Norms include things like maintaining the correct distance from someone when

Norms are expected patterns of behaviour. Those who differ in some way are treated as 'odd' and face exclusion from 'normal society'

Norms vary over time

talking to them, not asking personal questions of people we do not know too well, and saying thank you. Norms guide us in our everyday existence.

Victorian values

Values change over time. Politicians, particularly from the Conservative Party, praise Victorian values.

The process of industrialisation began in the 18th century and was well underway when Victoria came to the throne in 1837. Society was transformed. However, progress meant riches for some but poverty for others. The elegant clothes of middle-class and upper-class women were made in unhealthy and dangerous conditions by low-paid workers.

The values the Victorians adopted had either to justify or come to terms with this inequality; or to provide arguments for changing it. ...

During the Victorian age values were argued over, as they are now. Queen Victoria was on the throne for 64 years, longer than any other British monarch. In many ways her own firmly held views about morality set the tone for the age. All her life she absolutely hated scandal and what was then known as "fast living", such as swearing, gambling, drinking and smoking.

The idea of "respectability" was born. It is most closely linked with the rising middle classes. Pre-marital sex was considered shameful. At the same time middle-class men were expected to delay marriage until their career had reached the point at which they could afford to keep a wife and family.

Divorce, although legalised in the 1857 Matrimonial Causes Act, brought disgrace with it. (When Edward, Prince of Wales, was involved in a divorce case in 1870 he was hissed on the racecourse at Epsom.) It was rare and generally available only to the wealthy.

Values and practices, as in other periods, did not always mean the same thing. There was a certain tendency throughout the middle classes to do one thing and to preach and give the appearance of another.

The 'self-made man'

The Victorian era was also the period of belief in the "self-made man". The book Self-Help, written by Samuel Smiles in 1859, was a bestseller. According to Smiles, "The spirit of self-help is the root of all genuine growth in the individual and, exhibited in the lives of the many, it constitutes the true source of national vigour and strength."

The family was considered to be the backbone of society and the royal family was held up as the ideal. ...

The lives of the vast majority of people were very different to this.

Friedrich Engels (1820–95), the philosopher and son of a factory owner (and, with Karl Marx, author of the Communist manifesto), painted a grim picture of working-class life in Manchester:

"The cottages are old, dirty and of the smallest sort, the streets uneven, fallen into ruts, and in parts without drains and pavement; masses of refuse, offal and sickening filth lie among standing pools in all directions; the atmosphere is poisoned by the effluvia from these, laden and darkened by the smoke of a dozen tall chimneys. A horde of ragged women and children swarm about here, as filthy as the swine that thrive upon the garbage heaps." (The Condition of the Working Class in England, 1845).

Source: *The Guardian* (Education section), 14 June 1994

1 Are values natural?

2 If they are not, then how do they come about?

3 Does everyone share the same values in a society?

4 What were the values of the upper and middle classes in Victorian Britain?

5 Were values directly related to behaviour?

6 Was it possible for all people to share those values?

7 When politicians say that we should look back to Victorian times and bring back some of their values, what would you say?

Images and reality of Victorian Britain

Values and reality may not be the same for all people in society.

Image – the rich

Reality – the poor

Death of the wolf-men

The writing is on the wall for the British workman's wolf-whistle, as political correctness breaches its last frontier – the building site.

In what is probably Britain's least-sexist construction project, the laying of telephone lines in the East Midlands by an Anglo-American cable company, six men have been fired for wolf-whistling or catcalling at women.

Diamond Cable Communications plc forbids employees from whistling at women as they walk by – or from making suggestive remarks, or even working without a shirt. The penalty is the sack.

Gary Davis, managing director, said: "Wolf-whistling is not something we take lightly.

It is intimidating, not just to women but to people on the street generally. It presents the wrong image to our potential clients."

Four of his own workers and two from subcontracting firms had been dismissed for "conduct unbecoming", Mr Davis said – swearing, catcalling and wolf-whistling in particular, for which the most recent firing

was six weeks ago, involving an employee working for a subcontractor in Nottingham.

"He was wolf-whistling at a woman walking by and making the kind of derogatory comments which usually accompany it," said Paul Niles, Diamond's construction director.

Source: *The Independent*, 1 January 1995

1 Do you agree with what happened to the men?

2 Is wolf-whistling innocent fun or harrassment?

3 Do you think that this would have happened 20 years ago?

4 Ask a selection of men and women over 40 what they think of the article. What views do they express?

Motherhood – still a central value?

Look at the advert on page 11.

1 What feelings does the advert bring out in you? (Serious answers please!)

2 What image and emotions is it meant to bring out?

3 Look at the objects intended as presents. What are they intended to mean and what role do they suggest to you of a 'mother'?

4 Design a culturally appropriate advert for Father's Day. Explain your choice of design.

5 For female students reading this book, is this the image you would like others to have of you when you become a mother (if you are not already one)?

The values of society in Britain today

A

'We met through Dateline'

If you would like a 'love story' of your own, someone to love and care for, and you are beginning to wonder where you can find that special person, come to Dateline.

Seventeen to Seventy...
Many tens of thousands of people of all ages and occupations, from all over the country, join Dateline every year looking for someone to love. These are people who instead of waiting passively to see what life will bring, have decided not to leave their happiness to chance. Every day couples meet who are amazed at how right they are for each other – proof that Dateline works! If you want to meet someone with the same hopes, ambitions and interests as yourself, and are simply not meeting them socially or at work, Dateline, the largest, longest established and most successful computer dating agency in the world combines personal service with the speed and efficiency of modern technology to open up a whole new circle of compatible people for you; interesting, suitable people who could be living very close, people who you might never meet without Dateline's help.

Dateline
The world's largest and most successful agency
WHY LEAVE LOVE TO CHANCE?

■ **FREE** *Compatibility Test matching you to just one of the many Dateline members who could be your 'perfect partner', a full colour guide to Dateline membership and FREE Sphere book "All you need is love."*

START HERE

1. I AM OVER 17
Single ☐ Widowed ☐ Divorced ☐
Your Sex put M or F
Your Height ft. ins.
Your age yrs.
Age you would like to
meet min. max. (BLOCK CAPITALS)
First Name ....
Surname ....
Address ....
....
....
....
.... **Postcode** ....
Occupation ....
Religion ....
LOOK FOR Dateline Magazine – many hundreds of new people to meet – on sale at good newsagents.

2. Tick ✔ which characteristics best describe you.
ARE YOU:
Warmhearted ☐
Serious ☐
Considerate ☐
Shy ☐
Romantic ☐
Fashionwise ☐
Practical ☐
Conventional ☐
Reliable ☐
Adventurous ☐

3. Tick ✔ those activities you enjoy, put an × against those you dislike, and leave blank where you have no preference.
Wining/Dining ☐   Jazz/Folk music ☐
Pubs ☐   Classical music ☐
Sports/Keep Fit ☐   Theatre/Arts ☐
Politics/History ☐   Watching TV ☐
Reading ☐   Smoking ☐
Travelling ☐   Drinking ☐
Science/Tech. ☐   Children ☐
Cinema ☐   Homemaking ☐
Pets/Animals ☐   Gardening ☐
Pop/Rock music ☐   Countryside ☐

Dateline

B

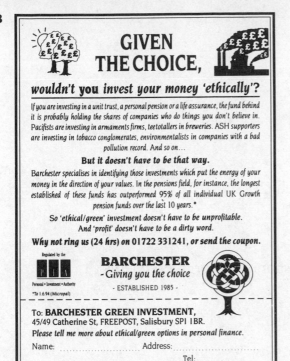

GIVEN THE CHOICE,

wouldn't **you** invest your money 'ethically'?

If you are investing in a unit trust, a personal pension or a life assurance, the fund behind it is probably holding the shares of companies who do things you don't believe in. Pacifists are investing in armaments firms, teetotallers in breweries. ASH supporters are investing in tobacco conglomerates, environmentalists in companies with a bad pollution record. And so on…

But it doesn't have to be that way.

Barchester specialises in identifying those investments which put the energy of your money in the direction of your values. In the pensions field, for instance, the longest established of these funds has outperformed 95% of all individual UK Growth pension funds over the last 10 years.*

So 'ethical/green' investment doesn't have to be unprofitable.
And 'profit' doesn't have to be a dirty word.

Why not ring us (24 hrs) on 01722 331241, or send the coupon.

Regulated by the
P•I•A
Personal • Investment • Authority

BARCHESTER
- Giving you the choice
- ESTABLISHED 1985 -

*To 1.6.94 (Micropal)

To: BARCHESTER GREEN INVESTMENT,
45/49 Catherine St, FREEPOST, Salisbury SP1 1BR.
Please tell me more about ethical/green options in personal finance.

Name: .... Address: ....
Tel: ....

Remember, the price of units can fall as well as rise and past performance is not a guarantee to the future.

C

Do you sincerely want to be rich?

Naturally the answer is yes.

But by saving the conventional way, the chances are your money has not kept pace with inflation.

£1000 invested in 1976 was only worth £854 in real terms by June this year.*

But it could have been working much harder in the City.

Over the last ten years, the Hill Samuel Managed Fund has shown a real gain of over 38%.** With funds easily accessible.

We can't promise to make you rich. But we can promise you friendly, expert advice and no jargon.

So, to find out more, without obligation, simply post the coupon.

*Calculated on the Building Societies historic share account rate enhanced by 1½% per annum, allowing for reinvested income. June 1976 to June 1986.
**Growth in Hill Samuel Managed Fund Series 'S' units on an offer to bid basis from June 1976 to June 1986.

To: David J. Riley, Hill Samuel Investment Services Limited, FREEPOST, Croydon CR9 9EH.
Telephone: 0800 100 100. Anytime. Free of charge.
I'd like to know more about the Hill Samuel Managed Fund.

Name _____

Address _____

_____ Postcode _____

Business Tel: _____ Home Tel: _____

HILLSAMUEL
INVESTMENT SERVICES

YE

Look at advert **A**.

1 What values of British society does it represent? What roles are included?

2 Would you use a dating agency? Explain your reasons.

3 Do you believe in 'love'?

4 The advert seems to imply that there is someone who is made for you. Do you agree?

5 Look at the activities and characteristics mentioned. What are you like?

6 The effects of values and norms is to limit the range of acceptable behaviour so that social life becomes predictable. How does the checklist illustrate this?

Look at adverts **B** and **C**.

7 What values of British society do they represent?

8 Is there any conflict here?

9 How does **B** manage to link two important values?

10 Check through a selection of today's newspapers (both tabloid and 'quality'). What values, norms and roles can you find.

Chapter 2

RESEARCH

This chapter covers:
- The importance of research
- Approaches to research
- Surveys
- Sampling
- Asking questions: Questionnaires and interviews
- Experiments
- Case studies
- Comparative studies
- Primary and secondary sources
- Observational studies
- Accuracy: The problems of reliability, validity and bias
- Which method of research is best?
- Doing a research project.

The importance of research

When people discuss social issues with friends or family, they usually argue from the point of view of their own experience, and back this up with an appeal to common sense. Yet these two methods of making sense of the world are of limited use if we really want to tackle problems in a fresh, accurate and unbiased way. By using our common sense, all we are really doing is applying our prejudices – and, after all, your common sense may not be the same as mine, and who is to say that one is more accurate than the other? The other way of approaching problems, through our own experience, is equally dubious, for everyone's experience is limited and memories or perceptions are distorted. Also my experiences may, like my common sense, be very different from yours.

Properly conducted research can bring out accurate, useful information that provides the basis for well-informed debate. Social science research is widely used by the British government, for example, to allow it to decide how best to provide educational, health and social services, as well as to plan housing and road-building programmes.

Sociology and journalism

The aim of sociology is to uncover the rules of society that govern our everyday lives, which we take for granted. This involves exploring people's experiences, describing their lifestyles and understanding their feelings. But sociologists are not alone in this work: novelists and journalists along with a host of other people do a very similar thing. But there is a difference. Whereas novelists and journalists may embroider their stories, or make their accounts of what happens more exciting in order to sell a few more copies, sociologists must simply, clearly and accurately describe and explain the social world for the sole purpose of advancing our knowledge.

Approaches to research

If you watch an expert craftsperson at work, you will notice that he or she uses the very best tools and follows rules of 'workmanship' that have developed over years of training and experience. If sociologists want to perform their work accurately, then they too must have excellent tools and rules. This chapter is devoted to studying these.

There is a division among sociologists between **positivists** and **subjective sociologists**.

Positivists

Positivists follow, very broadly, the same sorts of research methods as natural scientists (physicists, biologists, etc.) and believe this is the very best way to understand society. The methods used include **surveys**, official published **statistics** (such as the crime rates which are published every year), **historical sources** (such as diaries and war records) and **experiments**.

Subjective sociologists

These sociologists are not convinced that borrowing the methods of the natural sciences is the best way to understand social life. They prefer to try to put themselves in the minds of people whose behaviour we may find unusual or criminal. For instance, to understand why certain young people commit acts of vandalism or fight at football matches, they will join them to try to discover just how they think. This method is known as **observational study**.

The aim of sociology is to go beyond appearances and uncover the reality of social life

Surveys

The most commonly used research method in sociology is the **survey** and the most well-known example of survey is the **opinion poll**, often used to predict the results of elections. A survey is simply a series of questions which are given to a cross-section of the group of people you wish to study (known as a **population** in sociology). For example, when the opinion poll companies want to predict the outcome of a general election, they ask a cross-section of British voters which party they intend to vote for. They add the results together and then make their prediction. Of course sociologists will want to carry out surveys on all different groups on a wide range of opinions.

There are different types of survey which are useful for different sorts of studies. The main problem with the ordinary **cross-sectional survey** just described above is that it only gives people's opinions at the exact time of the survey. It cannot tell you about changes of viewpoint. Sociologists may therefore use **longitudinal surveys**, which are surveys of groups of people lasting a number of years. The main problem with longitudinal surveys is the number of people who decide to drop out of the survey, or who the researchers lose contact with. If too many people are 'lost' it may make the survey unreliable.

A longitudinal study

In the mid1980s, Coffield, Borrill and Marshall conducted a study into the lives and view of young people aged 16–28.

...we carried out two-and-a-half years' fieldwork in a study of 'around fifty' working-class young women and men in the north east of England. ...

Over these early months, we concentrated on building up good relationships with our sample...[later] we kept in touch with them at informal monthly meetings in pubs, cafes or in their homes...the circumstances of their everyday lives (for example, commitments to partners and family ties) affected the attendance of individual members. This drifting in and out highlighted the constantly changing patterns of young adults' lives. ...

Over the following year, however, we maintained regular contact by letter, telephone and with occasional meetings in order to keep up with any changes in their lives. ...

When discussing the size of our sample, we have always referred to 'around fifty' young women and men. ...Unlike most research projects, we are unable to give a simple answer to the question: what is the size of your sample? Some young people, for instance, faithfully turned up to meet us for over a year and then, for a variety of reasons such as...moving home, they stopped seeing us. Others slowly became members of our project because they were the partners or close friends of our original contacts. Again, our sample size varies depending on whether we stress the depth or the regularity of contact established with us. For instance, we met Clara infrequently, but gained as much information about her life and the life of her street in ten minutes as we did from, say, Winnie after hours of monthly meetings. ...

In all, we met far more than fifty young people but we are claiming to have established good relationships for two-and-a-half years with around fifty.

Source: F. Coffield, C. Borrill and S. Marshall, *Growing Up At The Margins* (Open University Press, 1986)

1　Over how long a period was the study carried out?

2　How did the researchers keep in touch with the people they were studying?

3　What was the size of the sample? Explain why they did not claim an exact figure?

4　What is more important, depth of discussion or frequency of meetings?

5　What advantages and disadvantages do you think there are in using a longitudinal study compared with a cross-sectional study?

Pilot surveys

No matter how able the researcher, he/she will not be able to forsee how people are going to interpret the questions asked in the interview or questionnaire, nor what words they may find difficult to understand. Furthermore, the people chosen for interviewing may not be the correct ones for the purpose.

The interview schedule or questionnaire should be given a trial run before being used for the main survey. This testing exercise is called the 'pilot survey'.

1　What is a pilot survey?

2　Give three reasons why sociologists use pilot surveys?

The panel

Sometimes researchers wish to find out the views of a selected group of representative people (a **panel**) about what is happening over a relatively long period. The advantage is that they are able to measure the changing views and ideas of these people and get a clear idea of their habits.

The use of a panel is very similar to the longitudinal survey, and is usually used when examining such things as television viewing habits, radio listening or even eating habits.

RSL – Research Services Limited
Research Services House, Elmgrove Road,
Harrow, Middlesex HA1 2QG England
Telephone: 081-861 6000 International: +44 81 861 6000 Fax: 081-861 5515

January 1994

Mr S. Moore
10 Stanley Road
Thornhill
Cheltenham

Dear Mr Moore

<u>THE RADIO OPINION MONITOR</u>

A few weeks ago we wrote to ask if you would be interested in joining the Radio Opinion Monitor (ROM) which we operate on behalf of the BBC. As we have not heard from you, I wanted to remind you that the invitation is still open.

The ROM panel is a representative group of radio listeners who are asked to give opinions about the programmes they listen to. This helps the BBC to decide which programmes radio listeners would would like to hear.

As a panel member you will receive a questionnaire every four weeks which is easy to complete and won't take up much of your time. Although we cannot pay panel members for their time, being on the panel will not cost you anything as all postage is pre-paid. We do run a weekly prize draw of £25 and send regular newsletters to panel members covering some of the results of our research. Panel members also have the satisfaction of knowing that their views are taken into account by the people who plan BBC radio programmes.

If you are interested in joining the panel, please complete the attached membership form and return it in the pre-paid envelope provided. Please note that this invitation only applies <u>to you personally</u> and cannot be transferred to any other member of your household - it is <u>your</u> opinions that we would like to hear.

I hope you will accept this invitation to join the panel. (If you have already replied we are still processing your application form and you do not need to complete another.)

Yours sincerely,

Richard Windle
PANEL DIRECTOR

IPSOS
company
Registered Office as above.
Registered in England
No. 1640855.

1 What is the person being invited to join?

2 What purpose does this panel have?

3 How does the BBC obtain the information?

4 Why do you think there is a weekly prize draw of £25?

5 The letter insists that the invitation applies only to the person the letter is addressed to. Why?

Sampling

There are about 58 million people in Britain. Finding out everybody's views would be terribly expensive and complicated to do. Only the government has the resources to carry out a survey of every household in Britain (this is the **census**) and there are so many problems that even the government only does it once every ten years. In order to find opinions and get information, sociologists have to rely upon taking an accurate cross-section of people, known as a **sample**, and hope that the opinions of this sample represent the opinions of everyone in the population under study. Clearly, if the sample is not a true cross-section of the people then the whole study will be inaccurate.

The source of the sample

The sample must be taken from some source; it could be every third person walking down the street, or it could be a random selection of names from the electoral roll in a town (this is a list of local voters and can be found in the main library of any town), or a selection from the names of people enrolled in an evening class. Each of these is an example of a **sampling frame**, which can be defined as the source from which a sample can be drawn. If the sampling frame is poor then the sample, and the survey, will be of little use. For instance, it is no use taking names at random from a list of 12-year-olds if the purpose of the survey is to find how people intend to vote in the next election.

Sampling frames

The following is an extract from a leaflet produced by the government research department, the Office of Population Censuses and Surveys (OPCS). The research was intended to give a clear picture of the eating habits of young children and to relate this to their health.

2. Why have we come to your household?
To visit every household in the country would take too long and cost far too much money.

Therefore we selected a sample of addresses from the Postcode Address File. The Postcode Address File is compiled by the Post Office and lists all the addresses to which mail is sent. We sent a letter to each selected address asking for details of the age and sex of everybody living there. We chose those addresses in a way that gave everyone the same chance of being selected. From the replies we were able to tell which households contained a child under 5, and from those we selected a sample to be interviewed. Your household is one of those chosen to be interviewed.

Some people think either that they and their family are not typical enough to be of any help in the survey or that they are very different from other people and they would distort the findings. The important thing to remember is that the community consists of a great many different types of people and families and we need to represent them all in our sample survey. It will therefore be appreciated if everyone we approach agrees to take part.

Source: OPCS, 'The Young Children's Dietary Survey', 1992

1   What is a sampling frame?
2   What was the one used by the OPCS?
3   Why did they ask questions about the age and sex of the people living at each address?
4   Suggest another sampling frame that could be used to interview mothers of young children. (It does not have to be a national sample.)
5   Suggest appropriate sampling frames for a survey of:
    a)   people over 18 years of age
    b)   students in a college
    c)   people who regularly attend night clubs
    d)   Labour Party members
    e)   piano teachers.

Methods of sampling

There are basically two ways in which sociologists ensure that their sample of the population is accurate: through **random sampling** and through **quota sampling**.

Random sampling

This is based on the idea that if you select entirely randomly (as when you throw a dice, the result is random), then you are likely to end up with a sample which is a mirror of the population, as each person has an equal chance of being picked. For example, you could put all the names of the people in your class at school or college in a hat and then select eight at random.

She loves me
She loves me not...

There are some variations on this basic idea. For instance, you may first divide up the population into groups based on some important characteristic, such as social class, and then choose at random within social glass groups. This may give greater accuracy. This is known as **strata sampling**.

Sometimes the population you wish to interview is scattered over a wide area. In this case you could select only a few places at random, and then randomly select a number of people within *these* places. In this way you keep the people you wish to interview within a few clusters. This is known as **multi-stage** or **cluster sampling**.

There are numerous forms of sampling. Some techniques are more accurate than others

Finally, you may wish to go back after your original survey and ask more detailed questions of some of the people. To do this, you choose a few of your original sample at random and interview them. This is known as **multi-phase sampling**.

Quota sampling

This form of sampling is used by most commercial market research companies, as it is accurate and very cheap. Basically, it is the same as strata sampling; each interviewer is told to go out and interview an exact number of particular groups of people in direct proportion to their existence in the population as a whole. For instance, we know that about half the population is female, so half the sample must be female; we also know the proportion of women in each age group, so the interviewers are told to find women in the correct proportion of ages to mirror the population, and so on.

The main problems with this sort of sampling are that firstly, it only works when you know a lot about the population you wish to study, and secondly, it relies upon interviewers correctly spotting the 'right' type of person to fit their quota.

Which sampling method would you choose to use in each of the following situations? Give reasons for your choices.
a) Finding out the views of college students on the use of heroin
b) Finding out the extent of marihuana use by students at one college
c) Finding out the views of a cross-section of people in your town or city about people from ethnic minority groups
d) Finding out the views of football supporters about an increase in entry prices
e) Finding out how people voted in a local election
f) Finding out the patterns of behaviour of the employees of a fast-food chain
g) Predicting the possible voting patterns in a future general election

Example of surveys

Reports of surveys are found almost daily in national newspapers. Here are three examples.

Look through this week's newspapers. How many examples of surveys can *you* find

The perennial teenage complaint – "Our parents don't understand us" – receives dramatic confirmation from a special survey conducted last weekend by National Opinion Polls (NOP) for *The Independent on Sunday*.

Sex, drugs and alcohol provide the most vivid examples. Last year a nationwide survey of people born in 1970 found that 46 per cent of young women and 32 per cent of young men said they had had sexual intercourse before their 16th birthday. A separate survey published two months ago of teenagers in the South-west produced similar figures.

Yet when NOP asked a nationwide sample of 760 parents of 11- to 16-year-olds about their own children, only 5 per cent expected their children to lose their virginity before the age of 16. Among only one group – single parents – did the percentage reach double figures: 14 per cent.

☐ *NOP interviewed a representative quota sample of 760 parents of 11- to 16-year-old children face-to-face at 96 sampling points throughout Great Britain between 19 and 21 July.*

Source: *The Independent on Sunday*, 4 August 1991

This week the Daily Mail is revealing the results of a unique social experiment. In the biggest survey of its kind we commissioned one of Britain's most prestigious polling organisations to find out the truth about life in Britain today.

They crossed every social divide: class, colour and sex. They pulled no punches with the questions they asked. The result is the most remarkable survey you will ever read.

Yesterday we examined British attitudes towards sex and romance. Today we put our attitudes towards morals and family life under the microscope. Some of the findings are comforting; others deeply disturbing. All make compelling reading.

ICM contacted a representative sample of 6,000 people aged 18-plus in 62 randomly selected constituencies countrywide. Each respondent was given one of two questionnaires to complete. In all, 2,000 responses were received. The data is weighted to be representative of the adult population.

Source: *The Daily Mail*, 23 July 1991

It's that Monday feeling, all week
The alarm clock rings and you drag yourself out of bed, as tired as when you crawled into it.

It's a feeling many will suffer today. But for some the lethargy will not disappear once Monday is over.

They are victims of Tired All The Time syndrome, a complaint reaching alarming proportions in Britain. According to new research, almost half the adult population will suffer from TATT at some time. ...

A survey of 1,000 adults by Audience Selection found 48 per cent of the population sometimes feel tired for no reason and four out of ten 'feel exhausted and cannot get up' every day. But only 15 per cent felt able to visit their GP. And only 2 per cent of those who complained were referred to a specialist.

Source: *The Daily Mail*, 1 February 1993

The national survey

The technical note below comes from a national survey of attitudes of British people. The title of the book is *Typically British?* and it claims to portray the views of the British public. MORI is a well-known public opinion company.

Technical Note
MORI interviewed a representative quota sample of 1,230 people aged 15+ in 113 constituency sampling points throughout Great Britain. Interviews were conducted face-to-face, in-home, between 11 April and 2 May 1991. Data are weighted to reflect the known population profile. This size and design of sample we would expect nineteen times in twenty to be accurate to plus or minus three per cent. That is, having a sampling tolerance of ±3%. For example, if we found, as we did, that 57% of our sample said they were married, there would be a 95% probability that the true percentage of married people aged 15 and over throughout Great Britain would be between 54% and 60%, with the greatest probability that the true figure is 57%.

Source: E. Jacobs and R. Worcester, *Typically British?* (Bloomsbury, 1991)

1 What is a quota sample?

2 What is a constituency?

3 Could you suggest why a constituency would provide a good sampling frame?

4 How accurate is the survey believed to be?

5 How many people are in the survey?

6 On what grounds can the authors claim that their results truly reflect the opinions of people of Britain?

Asking questions: Questionnaires and interviews

In order to find out what people actually think, sociologists have to ask them questions. There are two ways of doing this: you can either write down the questions and leave people to answer them by themselves, a **questionnaire**, or you can simply ask them face to face, an **interview**.

Asking questions

When sociologists do research, they have to phrase their questions very carefully – they must be clear and straightforward and have only one possible meaning to the respondent; they must also be expressed in clear English and they ought to 'force' the respondent to give a clear answer. Finally, it must be possible for the researcher to be able to put all of the information obtained into a clear summary.

Here are some questions; imagine you are going to ask them to 20 people. Indicate which are helpful in sociological research and which are not. Give the resons for your answer. Try asking someone these questions.

1 What do you think about racism?

2 How many hours' homework do you do each night?
a) none
b) less than one hour
c) one hour to two hours
d) more than two hours

3 Why do you think people commit crime?

4 Do you agree or disagree with the following statement: 'Religion is in decline in the UK today.'?

5 The internal market has revolutionised health care. What do you think?

6 Which political party do you support?

7 Which party do you vote for?

8 Could you please explain why anybody would possibly vote for the Conservative Party?

9 Wouldn't you agree that private health care is a bad thing?

1 If you only wanted to obtain the views of two people, would it alter your opinion on the usefulness of any of the questions?

2 Sociologists distinguish between open and closed questions. Indicate which of the above are 'open' and which are 'closed' (see the section on Questions on page 24).

Questionnaires

These are usually posted or handed out to people. The essence of a good questionnaire is that it asks exactly the right questions to uncover the information you want to find in as clear and simple a manner as possible and that it is as short as possible.

Questionnaires are very useful for reaching a widely spread group of people (as you can simply put them in the post), and are cheap, as they only need the cost of an envelope and postage stamp. Sometimes people will reply to rather embarrassing questions contained in a questionnaire, which they would not answer if faced by an interviewer.

The disadvantages are that very often people cannot be bothered to send a questionnaire back, so the **response rate** (the number of people who reply) is very low. This can make a survey useless, as you do not know if the few who replied are typical in their views of all those who did not reply. A second problem is that it is difficult to go into depth in a questionnaire, because the questions need to be so clear and simple. Finally, you can never be sure that the person you want to fill in the form actually does so.

Interviews

If the subject of enquiry is complex, or a survey needs to be done quickly, then sociologists generally use interviews. They can be very tightly organised, with the interviewer simply reading out questions from a prepared questionnaire, or they can be very open, with the interviewer being given scope to ask extra questions or rephrase difficult ones. In the first case, the interview is said to be a **structured interview** and in the second case it is described as an **unstructured** or an **in-depth interview**.

Apart from being useful for examining complex issues, the interviewer can compare his or her own observations with the answers of the respondent, to check if they are telling the truth. Also, there is a much higher response rate than when questionnaires are used.

The disadvantages are that the interviewer may influence the replies of the respondent in some way. For instance, a black interviewer asking a white respondent about racial prejudice has been found to receive very different replies than a white interviewer. And, of course, hiring trained interviewers is expensive.

Interviewing

The researcher in the extract below wanted to examine the views of 'feminist mothers'.

Fifty-two women were interviewed for this research – twenty in London, sixteen in Leicester and sixteen in Helsinki. ...The women were found through friends and acquaintances and through various organisations, and a few I knew from previous research contacts.

The interviews lasted up to two hours. The purpose of the interviews was explained to the women as they were contacted; some information was obtained in writing, and the rest of the interview was recorded. All the interviews were transcribed and the transcripts were returned to the interviewees. The interviews were semi-structured, with particular themes I wanted to cover. However, if something in particular was of interest to the interviewee, this was explored at length, and consequently other areas received less coverage.

Source: T. Gordon, *Feminist Mothers* (Macmillan Education, 1990)

1   How did the researcher obtain her sample?

2   How representative of all women is this?

3   How representative of all 'feminist mothers' is this?

4   What is meant by 'semi-structured interviews'? What advantages and disadvantages do they have compared with highly structured interviews?

5   How did she remember what they said?

6   Why did she return the transcripts, do you think?

Interviewing and values

Howard Newby studied the attitudes of farmers and farmworkers in Suffolk. He felt that it was necessary to play different roles with either group.

'With the farmowners this meant convincing them that I was a serious researcher, with the necessary stage props to prove it – briefcase, printed questionnaire and formal manner. Farmers were more difficult to handle than their employees. Some questioned my questions. In addition my own personal dislike of the views of most farmers meant that I was consciously playing a role' [to hide his feelings].

And with the farm workers:

'Here my main concern was to understate the elements of formality and professional-ism...leave the briefcase in the car, appear casually to jot down notes on a piece of paper, laugh, crack jokes.'

Incidentally, Newby wore a suit when interviewing the farmers and took off his jacket and tie when interviewing the farmworkers.

1 Briefly describe the different ways Newby portrayed himself to farmers and farmworkers.

2 Why do you think he acted differently with each group?

3 Do you think the outcome of the research would have been different if he had not hidden his feelings of dislike of the farmers' views?

4 Three interviewers go to ask questions of male, middle-aged, white teachers. One is young and black, a second female and white, a third middle-aged and white. Will the outcomes of the interviews be different, do you think?

5 What if one of the interviewers was much more talkative than the others and expressed his/her opinions forcibly?

6 Now devise a few simple questions on a contentious subject, such as feminism or race, and test whether different types of interviewer influence the sort of responses obtained.

Try this on people outside the classroom using people of different genders and ethnic groups as intervie-wees. Compare the replies you obtain from two different groups of respondents.

Interviewing and values

In order to examine the experiences and attitudes of second-generation Asian Muslim women in Britain I carried out research in Coventry and Bradford. Thirty semi-structured interviews were obtained from both men and women in these areas. All of the informants (15 men and 15 women) were aged between 18 and 30 years. The choice of informants was made to try to obtain a broad cross-section of people in terms of age, gender, marital status, education and occupation. Informants were gained from Youth Centres, Muslim Community Centres and contacts within the two communities. This paper will focus specifically on the experiences of the Muslim women interviewed.

Source: C. Butler, 'Religion and gender' in *Sociology Review*, February 1995

This is an extract from research carried out by Charlotte Butler on the views of second generation Asian Muslims in Britain.

If you assume that Charlotte Butler is not Muslim, what problems or difficulties do you think might emerge in carrying out interviews with a cross-section of Muslim males and females?

Questions...

If you wish to find out people's views in some depth, then you ask **open-ended** questions, for example, 'What is your opinion...?', which requires the respondent to give his or her views on the matter in some detail. If you wish to obtain short, very clear replies then **closed** questions are asked, for example, 'Would you agree or disagree with the following statement...'. In this case the respondent has merely to say yes or no.

Ask two people any open-ended question. What problem do you think emerges if you want to do 50 interviews based on open-ended questions?

And answers

Once the answers are obtained and collected together then there has to be some way of **codifying** them. This involves somebody sitting down and sifting through all the answers and, usually today, putting them into a computer. For example, Do you think sociology is an interesting subject?

Yes, very interesting	1
Quite interesting	2
No, not very interesting	3
Don't know	4

If the answer is 'yes, very interesting', then the number 1 is put into the computer, if 'no, not very interesting', then number 3. The computer then categorises all the replies and prints a summary.

Part of a typical mail question-naire. Notice how clear the questions are and how the answers can be coded very easily.

Thinking now about the amount of talk you can hear on the radio. How much do you like the following?
(PLEASE CROSS ONE BOX FOR EACH)

	Like a lot	Like a little	Neither like nor dislike	Dislike a little	Dislike a lot	Don't know	
Programmes which are <u>mostly</u> music	1	2	3	4	5	0	(68)
Mixture of music and chat/talk	1	2	3	4	5	0	
Programmes which are <u>mostly</u> talk	1	2	3	4	5	0	
Programmes which are all talk	1	2	3	4	5	0	(71)

The construction of sociological information: From question to bar chart

When you read a sociology book, it usually contains a number of tables which summarise people's attitudes or behaviour. Here is an example of how one chart was constructed.

In a recent national study of people's attitudes, one (open) question concerned divorce:

As with our inquiries into why people marry, we did not try to guide our respondents in any particular direction by suggesting reasons why people got divorced. We simply asked: *"What do you think are the main causes of divorce these days?"* Then we noted, grouped and tabulated the answers.

The information was then grouped into categories:

Q18   And what do you think are the main causes of divorce these days? DO NOT PROMPT. MULTICODE OK.

	%
Boredom	5
Children	4
Drink	5
Growing apart	19
In-laws	*
Lack of money/financial problems	43
Lack of respect for each other	8
Poor sex life	2
Unfaithfulness	28
Violence	4
Other (WRITE IN & CODE 'X')	42
Don't know	6

Finally, a bar chart was produced to summarise the information:

10 reasons for divorce

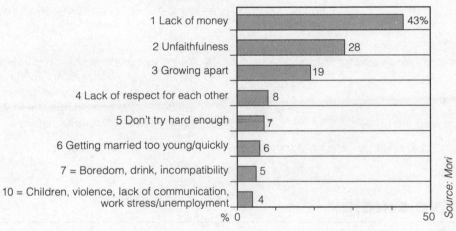

Source: Mori

Source: E. Jacobs and R. Worcester, *Typically British?* (Bloomsbury, 1991)

Reproduce this process. Ask a sample of 20 people the same question. Do not prompt them! Group the answers into the same categories if possible and from that construct a bar chart. Is your information the same as that of the published research?

Experiments

These are not often used by sociologists, because it is the job of sociologists to study people as they behave naturally in their everyday lives. If people were put into an artificial situation in order to see their responses, they would not act naturally. There are also moral objections to do with using people as guinea pigs and possibly harming their relationships with others, or putting them under great stress. Experiments are widely used by psychologists in very controlled circumstances.

Case studies

A case study is a situation when sociologists choose one particular group or situation and carry out an intensive study in order to find out as much information and detail as possible. Generally, a case study is expected to provide information which can be applied to other, similar situations and groups of people. However, the problem is that unlike the survey, it is never certain that the group or situation chosen for the case study really is typical, and as a consequence, the results cannot necessarily be used to produce general explanations.

The uses of case studies

Clearly, case studies can serve a variety of purposes. ...First, they may serve as a simple description. ...The emphasis here is on the *unique* nature of the event or circumstances. Second, such studies although unique can be...interpreted as examples of general patterns. Third, a case study may be chosen in order to develop theory. Then fourth, case studies may be seen as 'plausibility probes' – rather like a pilot study. Finally, there are crucial case studies which allow the investigator to disconfirm some hypothesis or argument or perhaps to support it.

Source: Adapted from R.E. Pahl, *Divisions of Labour* (Blackwell, 1984)

1 In your own words give *five* possible uses of a case study.

2 What is a pilot study?

3 What is a hypothesis?

4 How could a case study help to 'develop a theory'?

5 Give three examples of issues where a case study may be a useful and practical method of research. For example, a case study of bullying in a secondary school. How would you set about doing these suggested case studies?

Comparative studies

Comparative studies are a sociologist's substitute for experiments. Sociologists often compare the behaviour of similar groups in different situations (or different groups of people in similar situations!) to uncover the reasons why there are differences between the behaviour of the two groups. Comparisons are made across age groups, by ethnic group, by gender, by geographical position, by social class, and an enormous range of other **variables**.

Primary and secondary sources

Sociologists must use whatever methods are most appropriate for the situation or group of people they are studying. As a result, they employ a great variety of methods which reflect influences such as how easy it is to obtain access to information, or how up-to-date the information is. The answers to these questions usually determine whether a researcher is going to use **primary** or **secondary sources** of information.

Primary sources include all information that the sociologist has gathered him or herself, irrespective of the method used – from questionnaires, interviews, experiments and observational studies.

Secondary sources include all statistics and information not collected directly by a sociologist engaged in research, but which have been collected by other people. For example: **government statistics** on crime, births, deaths, marriages, etc.; **historical documents** such as diaries, church records, descriptions of important events and court documents; **newspaper and television stories**; **factually-based novels** and **autobiographies**.

Sometimes, research is based entirely on these, particularly if the people being studied are dead, acting illegally or are difficult to trace, but generally sociologists are very wary about using secondary sources. More often sociologists use secondary sources as 'background information' to help them understand their own study better.

The problems with secondary sources are that they have generally been collected for specific reasons, by people who have varying motives. A diary, autobiography or novel may reflect the values and prejudices of the writer. How much therefore can be believed? Statistics on crime are less a reflection on how many crimes are committed a year, more a reflection of how many of the crimes are actually reported to the police (and we know the majority are not) and how many of these the police take seriously.

Official statistics

Although sociologists use a wide variety of published information for their research, they must always be wary of taking the facts as accurate or true.

A The number of accidents reported each year in offices, shops and other businesses is believed to be just one-sixth of the actual number, according to the Institute of Environmental Health Officers.

Source: *The Independent*, 16 March 1992

B Aids or infection by HIV, the Aids virus, has become the most common cause of death among young men in west Central London, according to a survey into the cause of all deaths among men aged between 15 and 64 in the area.

The figures show a marked difference with the numbers of deaths being attributed to Aids or HIV on death certificates, according to a report on the survey today in the British Medical Journal. The Office of Population Censuses and Surveys recorded only six such cases.

It says the fact that certificates are open to public scrutiny may lead to fewer than one in five deaths recorded as being as a result of Aids or HIV.

Source: *The Guardian*, 24 July 1992

C The head of the Government Statistical Service has banned publication of an article commissioned for the 25th anniversary edition of the social statistics bible, *Social Trends*, because it criticises political influence on official statistics in the 1980s.

Muriel Nissel, the first editor of *Social Trends*, wrote an 8,000-word history of the publication, which said that during the Thatcher years the Government drastically cut spending on official statistics; in particular the quality and quantity of politically sensitive social statistics suffered and *Social*

Trends had to "fight for its life".

Statistics on poverty, the growing wealth gap between rich and poor and the North-South divide were either not collected or not analysed. Instead *Social Trends* placed more emphasis on "Mr and Mrs Average" and how well off they were.

Source: 'Attack on bias in official statistics silenced' by Rosie Waterhouse in *The Independent*, 26 January 1995

D One [method of] research was to hang around at leisure centres waiting to talk to people who came in. I soon discovered that whilst most men, whether accompanied by children or not, were there on their own account, many women who accompanied children, were there merely as chauffeurs.

Source: R. Deem, 'Women and leisure – All work and no play?', in *Social Studies Review*, March 1990

Social Trends is the government publication used by many sociologists for their 'facts' about the UK. It has been used extensively in this book.

1 What do extracts **A** and **B** tell us about the published statistics?

2 Can you suggest ways that this could affect sociological trends?

3 Read extract **C**. What happened to the information given in *Social Trends*?

4 Does this make the information less accurate?

5 Extract **D** is from an article in which the researcher argues strongly that men have more leisure than women. This is just a very small extract from the article. Can you suggest any weaknesses and possible bias in this extract?

Accident? Suicide? Murder?

6 Why should we be wary of taking research done by others as fact?

7 Using the cartoon above what comment can you make on the official rates for suicide?

Content analysis

Content analysis is a very common method used by sociologists and consists of searching through newspapers and television (or other forms of media) to find information on a particular topic. This information is then analysed. Research using content analysis has been done on the portrayal of women, on violence, on images of sex, on racial stereotyping and on the reporting of wars.

In 1992, David Morrisson conducted research which:

set out to explore what the viewer considered the role of television ought to be in covering war and to provide an account of how viewers responded to the images they did see and the information they received. ...[As part of his research, he] conducted a massive content analysis of the main evening news and current affairs programmes broadcast during the [Gulf] war on BB1, BBC2, ITV, Channel 4, CNN and BSkyB. In addition, the news on the following foreign channels was also recorded for the purpose of comparative content analysis – Germany (BR2), France (TF1), Italy (RAI1) and Russia (the main service carried on the Gorizont satellite).

Source: D.E. Morrisson, *Television and the Gulf War* (John Libbey & Co., 1992)

Various groups of adults and children were then shown all or part of this material and asked for their views.

1 What does the extract mean when it refers to a 'massive content analysis of the main evening news and current affairs programmes broadcast during the [Gulf] war'?

2 What advantages to the research can be gained by using comparative material?

Observational studies

The methods we have examined so far are generally associated with sociologists who believe that sociology ought, as far as possible, to follow the methods of the natural sciences such as chemistry or physics. The survey is seen as the substitute for the experiment. However, other sociologists argue that the best way to understand people is to try to get as close to them in their daily lives as possible. These sociologists stress the usefulness of **observational methods**.

Sociologists who use the participant observation approach like to blend in unobtrusively with the group under study

Observational techniques are particularly useful for studying people in circumstances where they would not normally reply to a questionnaire or interview. For example, in a study of delinquents or of groups of violent football supporters, it would hardly be possible to ask them to stop fighting for ten minutes while they answered a few questions!

What normally happens in observational studies is that the sociologist joins a group which he or she wishes to study in depth. He or she then has a number of decisions to make.

Does the sociologist become a full member of the group (perhaps the group is engaged in criminal activities)? This is known as **participant observation**. Or does the sociologist follow them around, simply observing, rather like a 'fly on the wall'? This is known as **non-participation observation**.

If the sociologist becomes a full member of the group, the advantage is that he or she will readily get to see things the way the group does, but may be influenced so much by this that the research becomes too biased in favour of the group or prejudiced against them.

If the sociologist acts as a 'fly on the wall', the advantage is that there is far less risk of getting too drawn into the group, so that greater objectivity (seeing things as they really are) results. But there is less chance of fully understanding things as the group under study do, as the researcher is not really one of them.

Whether the researcher engages in participant or non-participant observation, a crucial problem which he or she must solve is the extent to which the mere presence of an observer influences the group's actions. People just do not act naturally, if they know they are being observed.

In certain circumstances sociologists may prefer to pretend to be a member of the group. James Patrick did this in *A Glasgow Gang Observed*, where he joined a violent gang, and pretended to be an active gang member, joining in their fighting and stealing. This has the advantage of really being treated as a full gang member. This is known as **covert observation**.

On the other hand, Howard Parker told the gang of petty criminals in his study, *View from the Boys*, exactly what he was doing. This is known as **overt observation**. Firstly, this was morally better as he was not deceiving anyone. Secondly, he found that gang members would confide things in him that they would be embarrassed to tell other gang members, just because he was a trusted outsider.

Participant observation

Howard Parker decided to study the lives of a group of adolescents in inner Liverpool who were generally regarded as delinquents by the police because they regularly stole car radios. Parker felt that the best way to explain their delinquency was to try to see the world through their eyes. He adopted the method known as participant observation, so he could really get to know and understand them. But the problem was to gain their acceptance – after all, they were 16 years old and he was 22, a middle-class researcher with a degree.

My hanging around 'all the time' period came in the autumn of the second year of my research, when most of the boys were unemployed and were spending their days knocking around the neighbourhood and standing on the corner. The evenings were generally spent in the pubs.

No doubt everyone was aware that I spoke differently and 'posher' than they did. This was not a problem. It was more important to be able to understand 'scouse' than to speak it...as time went on, or when drunk, I found myself swearing a lot more and using local words and phrases – divvy, tart, gear, busies, come'ed, bevvy. ...

My position in relation to theft was well established. I would receive 'knock off' and say nothing. If necessary I would 'keep dixy' [keep watch] but I would not actually get my hands dirty. ...There were occasions when I actually interfered with car-radio theft and suggested to those about to get involved that given the situation and their strategy someone was likely to get caught. My advice was always taken. This reaction on my part could be seen as 'bad' participant observation since it was interfering in normal group behaviour. ...It was during the first half of year three that I found myself as accepted as I ever would be, in the thick of things and at my most functional. Due to my regular court attendance I was regarded as something of an expert in such matters and was able to give advice from time to time.

Source: H. Parker, *View from the Boys* (David and Charles, 1974)

The aim of participant observation is to observe groups as they are naturally and, by becoming accepted and close to the group members, to gain a close understanding of how the group under study really does see the world.

1   There are two major problems which all sociologists who adopt participant observation face: that their presence influences the activities of the group and so they do not act as they would have done without the sociologist and, secondly, that they become so drawn into the group that they lose their ability to describe in a clear and objective way just what is going on. Is there any evidence in the extract that these problems existed for Parker?

2   The advantage of participant observation is that by becoming accepted by the group the researcher can find out far more than any outsider. Do you think that there could have been any other way a researcher could have found out about the lifestyle of 'the Boys'?

Accuracy: The problems of reliability, validity and bias

Reliability

A survey is composed of a number of different interviews or questionnaires which are carried out by one or more interviewers with many different people. The results are added up and at the end of our calculations we can say, for example, that when 100 people were asked about their views on racism and promotion at work:

- 50 people believed there was racial prejudice when it came to promotion
- 30 people said there was not
- 12 people felt that those from ethnic minority backgrounds actually got preference
- 8 people expressed no opinion.

But how do we know that this represents the truth, and that each interview is directly comparable with the others? For example, I am an Afro-Caribbean researcher asking the questions about racism in employment – will I receive the same answers as my white colleague? We can make a reasonable assumption that some people will adjust their views depending upon the perceived ethnic origin of the interviewer.

The point about this example is that we cannot always assume each interview is exactly the same – things may happen to make one interview different from another. This problem is known as the **problem of reliability**.

Validity

Validity is the word used by researchers to describe the problem of making sure that the interview or questionnaire actually gets the information that you want it to. For example, if you wish to find out about violence on television and in the cinema, you might ask a question which says, 'Do you think the media have any effect on people's behaviour?' The respondent may not understand the meaning of the word 'media', but rather than admit this, he or she will reply 'yes' or 'no' in order to say something.

In this case the question and answer do not obtain a measure of the truth – the question is not **valid**.

Bias and values

Everyone has their own views on the world and their own pet theories, but in doing research they need to put those views to one side and be as **objective** or **value-free** as possible. In interviews or questionnaires it is very easy to influence the respondent by putting one's own views into questions, such as '*Wouldn't you agree* that women should be able to terminate their pregnancies if they wish without having to give a reason?'

In observational studies the researcher may interpret the behaviour of people through his or her own values perhaps by being too sympathetic or even intensely disliking the group under study.

Validity: Measuring attitudes

Here is an example of how researchers measure the extent of people's feelings on an issue.

Q22 ASK ALL
SHOWCARD F (R) **Now I'm going to read out some statements, and I'd like you to tell me to what extent you agree or disagree with each?** READ OUT. ALTERNATE ORDER.

TICK START (√)	Strongly agree %	Tend to agree %	Neither agree nor disagree %	Tend to disagree %	Strongly disagree %	No opinion %
a) A woman's place is in the home	7	14	15	29	35	1
b) The law should be changed to make it more difficult for people to get divorced	15	27	14	27	15	3
c) As long as no-one gets hurt, there's nothing wrong with extra-marital affairs	3	10	8	26	51	2
d) Most men do not do enough to share the housework	18	48	12	15	3	3
e) It's a bad idea for women to have children unless they are married	21	29	16	22	10	2
f) It's OK for unmarried people to have sex "just for the fun of it"	8	27	17	24	21	3
g) It is better to get married in a church than a registry office	17	24	32	15	10	2

Source: E. Jacobs and R. Worcester, *Typically British?* (Bloomsbury, 1991)

1 What percentage of people strongly agree that 'A woman's place is in the home'?

2 What percentage tend to disagree?

3 What is the most common view on it being 'OK for unmarried people to have sex "just for the fun of it"'?

4 There is a problem sociologists face called validity. Explain why this may be important in interpreting the information from questionnaires such as this.

5 Try asking any one of these questions to 10 people. Do any problems emerge? How near 'the truth' do you think you come with your finished research?

Which method of research is the best?

None of them!

A sociologist chooses the method which seems most appropriate to the circumstances and aims of the research. Usually surveys are preferred if the aim is to find out opinions of large numbers of people. Secondary sources are used to provide background information or to uncover evidence when there is nobody able or willing to answer questions. Participants observation is used to study small groups and/or deviant groups where simply asking them questions would not uncover the reasons for their behaviour. Comparative methods are used where national or international differences are the focus of research.

Review: The different methods of study

There is no single *best* method of finding the people you want to ask questions of. It depends upon the amount of money available, the size of the group you wish to study (the whole population, or male delinquents in Southend, for example), and the information you wish to find (political attitudes, or number of crimes committed, for example).

The following are very brief summaries of the sampling methods used to cope with the different circumstances of the study.

A A national random cross-sectional survey

In *British Social Attitudes*, Jowell and Witherspoon wanted to find out the views of the whole of the British population. In order to do so they did a national random sample.

The survey was designed to yield a representative sample of people aged over 18 living in Britain. ...

Names were selected from the electoral registers [lists of all the voters in Britain] in 103 of the 552 constituencies in England and Wales, and 11 local authority districts in Scotland. ...

Twenty-two addresses were selected at random in 114 polling districts [a smaller part of the constituencies], which gave 2508 addresses. Interviewers then went to these houses to request an interview with the elector selected.

In all 70 per cent of those selected agreed to be interviewed.

Source: P. Jowell and S. Witherspoon, *British Social Attitudes* (Gower, 1985)

B A longitudinal survey

D.J. West wished to find the reasons why certain working-class youths are more likely than most to engage in delinquent acts. By studying the boys over a number of years (a longitudinal survey), West claimed he could isolate the particular influences which affected the lives of delinquent boys compared to non-delinquent ones. He was able to clearly record all the important influences on a young boy's life.

In order to show that delinquents really are different from their fellows...they must be studied from an early age, using regular interviews...before they begin to appear in court...to show that their delinquency is not due to the effects of police action and court labelling.

The study was based on 411 boys. They represented an unselected sample of local schoolboys living in a traditional working class area of London.

They were intensively studied from eight to ten years and have been subsequently followed up till the age of 19.

Source: D.J. West and D.P. Farrington, *Who becomes delinquent?* (Heinemann, 1974)

C A participant observation study of a group of 'tough' youths

In this second extract from *View from the Boys* (on page 34), Parker describes how he gradually widened his network of connections, known as the **snowball method** – as he 'rolled along' he gained more and more contacts.

It was working as a residential community worker at a country holiday centre for Liverpool 'street kids' that I first encountered The Boys. They came and stayed whenever they could. We went on camping trips and day trips, had parties, discos and arguments. It was only because I got on with and enjoyed being with The Boys and The Girls that this study developed. My acceptance into the network would have been highly unlikely if my credentials hadn't been checked in the highly favourable atmosphere here. By the time I came downtown I was established as OK – that is boozy, suitably dressed and able to play football, as well as 'knowing the score' about theft behaviour and sexual exploits.

Once accepted locally by a few of The Boys, I was able to move slowly into a wider acceptance until I could join any combination of the network when I had the time.

Source: H. Parker, *View from the Boys* (David & Charles, 1974)

D A covert participant observational study of the police

Simon Holdaway decided to study his own colleagues in an attempt to show the way that the police force really operates. However, as other policemen so strongly objected to his research, he had to do it in secret (covert observation), unlike Howard Parker in the earlier extract who explained his situation and aims to The Boys.

I found I was fortunate because I was in a unique position to carry out research: before I studied sociology and during the course of my undergraduate and graduate work I was a police officer.

Source: S. Holdaway, *Inside the British Police* (Blackwell, 1984)

Extract A

1 What is the aim of doing a 'random survey'?

2 What method did the researchers choose to find people over 18?

3 How many people were chosen to be interviewed in all?

4 Do you think that Jowell and Witherspoon did all the interviewing themselves?

5 Can you think of any problems that might occur when you have a large number of interviewers going around collecting information?

6 What percentage of people agreed to be interviewed? If only 25 per cent of people had agreed, would it have been important?

Extract B

7 What is meant by a 'longitudinal survey'?

8 Why did D.J. West think that a longitudinal survey was the best way to explain why certain youths are more likely to commit delinquent acts?

Extract C

9 Howard Parker tried another way of explaining delinquent behaviour. What was this?

10 Why did he do this instead of asking questions like D.J. West?

11 What was the term used to describe the method by which he enlarged his network of delinquent friends?

Extract D

12 In Parker's study all the Boys knew that he was a university researcher, yet Holdaway in his study of the police chose a 'covert' course of study. What does this mean and why did he choose it?

13 Can you suggest another situation in which Holdaway's covert method would be the most appropriate to gain maximum information. Why? Are there any potential dangers in this approach?

14 Which type of research strategy would you use if you were studying:
a) a group of youths engaged in criminal activities?
b) a group of school students' attitudes towards their teachers?
c) the views of the headmaster of a local state school on the existence of private schools?
d) the behaviour of a group of young people at a party?
e) the attitudes of the British population on the extension of pub opening hours?
f) drug-taking behaviour on a local housing development?
g) other students' behaviour in the sociology class?

Doing a research project

Most courses in sociology require students to undertake a piece of research, and in this section we will look at the actual process of doing the research.

Choosing the topic

Choose a topic which is relevant to sociology, which is interesting to you, and which you believe you will actually be able to do some research on. Favourite topics followed by students I have taught are related to areas of gender and race, and less often social class, religion, crime and deviance (usually attitudes to drugs or the behaviour of (male) football supporters). However, I have read excellent pieces of research on nursing, stress, health and illness, the elderly, disability, and part-time employment in a fast-food chain. Each of these research projects had two common characteristics: the students were interested in the issues, and they had some knowledge of them before they started.

Always check with your tutor that your topic is relevant to sociology and that it is feasible, before you start it.

Background reading

Once you have an idea of what you wish to research, ask your tutor for suggestions for background reading, go to your local library (or better still the town central library) and ask for help.

Don't forget the Internet, which has a wide range of information.

Deciding on the most appropriate method

This chapter has explained the different methods of research and the circumstances in which they are normally used, so you should now think carefully about which method would be most useful.

- **Questionnaires** (which are handed out) can provide a lot of information from a range of different people. The major problem will be getting them returned to you.
- **Interviews** will provide more detailed information, but they tend to take a lot of time and so you can only interview a small number of people.
- **Observation** is extremely useful if you wish to look at a group of people that you would normally be a member of, for example your friends' behaviour on your weekly Friday night out. Observation rarely yields much statistical information, although you could follow up observation with questionnaires or interviews.
- **Comparative studies** are very difficult to do, unless you rely upon secondary data for some, if not all, of your information.
- **Experiments** are possible, in a narrow range of situations where you might want to compare how people acted differently in different situations and where you are able to alter and control those situations. An example would be if you wanted to study differences in people's behaviour towards people with disabilities and people without disabilities. You could re-enact the same

situation (person unable to open a door), but somes you would have a person with a disability (or appearing to have a disability) unable to open the door and sometimes a person without a disability.

Remember, you do not have to use just one method – indeed, it is quite normal in contemporary social science research to use a number of different methods together. This is called **triangulation**.

The sample

Having selected your method, you must think about your sample. In some cases the sample selects itself, such as your place of (part-time) employment – although you would need to decide whether this case study is typical of other organisations or not. However, if you are doing a questionnaire or a series of interviews, then you need to think carefully about the effect the sample you have chosen may have on the outcome of your research. Most people use friends, colleagues or family for their interviews, but there are obvious problems with doing this if you are seeking a cross-section of opinion.

Analysing data

Observational studies

You should have already isolated some themes by now that seem particularly interesting or important. You could group your information under these headings.

Questionnaires and interviews

If your school or college has IT facilities, then you can use a spreadsheet. This has particular advantages when it comes to writing up your research project. If you cannot use a computer, or do not have access to one, then a simple way to analyse data is to make a grid like the one below.

Question no.	Response code			
	1	2	3	4
1	~~1111~~ ~~1111~~	~~1111~~	11	11
2				
3				

By coding the answers to the questions, the grid allows you to easily read the types of replies across a large number of questionnaires.

In the above example, there are six questions to which there are four possible replies to each one. The first question was:

1   *In your opinion, which of the four things mentioned below is the single most important cause of crime today:*
    1. unemployment?
    2. breakdown of family life?
    3. drug addition?
    4. lack of discipline at school?

Five more questions followed. Twenty people answered in total, and their replies were as follows:

- five people chose 'breakdown of family life'
- ten people chose 'unemployment'
- two people chose 'drug addition'
- three people chose 'lack of discipline at school'.

Presenting data

Numerical data can be presented in many ways, but the most common are:

- tables
- line graphs
- bar charts (another form of graph really)
- pie charts (another form of graph).

Remember to explain clearly the meaning of the data in your main text.

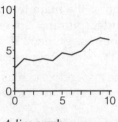

A line graph

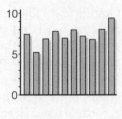

A bar chart

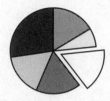

A pie chart

Writing the assignment

Introduction

Start with the background to your study, explaining why you are doing it and what you intend to prove, or what issue you are going to explore. You should include any evidence of background reading or examples of studies which interested you and seem relevant.

The methodology

Explain the methodology you have used, in particular discussing why you used your chosen method(s) rather than any other type. You should always point out the weaknesses of your methodology.

The results

Work through the study and describe what information you have obtained, and how it relates to other published studies.

The discussion

Discuss your study and draw conclusions from it, saying how they do, or do not relate to your original idea.

Conclusion

Go back over the assignment summarising and clarifying the main points as you see them. Criticise yourself and your methodology if you genuinely feel there are weaknesses. Say how you would improve the study if you had to repeat it.

Some simple assignment writing techniques

- Always write in short, clear paragraphs. A paragraph of, say, four to eight lines should consist of *one* point that you are trying to explore.

- Each paragraph should be *linked* to the previous one in some way. Don't leave paragraphs floating by themselves and expect your tutor or the examiner to make sense of the links. Use simple link words or phrases to start a paragraph, for example 'As a result of this', 'Another example of this', 'However', 'So', 'In contrast to', 'Furthermore', 'Also', etc.

- You should insert a paragraph after every page and a half which acts as a signpost to the reader: 'So far we have...' 'And now we will look at... .' This allows the reader to see clearly the argument you have presented and understand what the various relationships are.

- Graphs and tables can either go in the main text in the appropriate place or they can be placed in an **appendix** (plural = appendices) which is a number of pages inserted at the end of your assignment. If you use the appendix, it usually does not form part of the word count of the assignment.

- You can add other things in the appendix such as transcriptions of interviews, copies of the questionnaire, or examples of the replies, photographs, tape recordings and even videos.

Good luck!

Chapter 3

SOCIAL CLASS

This chapter covers:
- Social divisions
- The continuing importance of social class
- The nature of social class
- The measurement of social class
- The class structure in Britain
- The wealthy
- Social mobility.

Social divisions

Divisions other than social class

This chapter explores the **social class** divisions which have an important influence on our lives. However, before we examine social class in detail, we need to look at other types of social divisions.

Divisions in British society today

Oh, working class...
No.. I'm sorry —
through the tradesmen's
entrance..

PEARLY GATES

TRADESMENS ENTRANCE

On meeting someone for the first time, you will notice a number of things about them. Almost certainly, three of these things will be their **sex**, their **ethnic group** and their **age**. The category in which you place the person (for example, middle-aged, Black and male) will influence very strongly how you will behave towards him.

In Britain, although social class remains a very powerful influence on our lives, sociologists have increasingly turned their attention to these forms of social divisions. For example, *within* each social class, people of different sexes, of different ages and of different ethnic backgrounds have very different experiences. Women are more likely to be found in routine office jobs, and rarely in the senior management positions. Blacks are heavily over-represented in manual work. Young people are far more likely to be unemployed than the middle-aged. These divisions have to be looked at alongside social class. As they are so important, each of the divisions of sex, of ethnic group and of age is studied in more detail in Chapters 4, 5 and 6 respectively.

Divisions in the past

There have been two particularly important forms of social divisions in history: **estates** and **caste**.

Estates

In **feudal** societies, which existed in Europe until the late sixteenth century, people were divided into estates, which were based upon ownership of land. Individuals swore allegiance to the king, who rewarded them with land. In turn, followers of these landholders swore allegiance to them and were rewarded with portions of the land. The distribution of land ended with tiny plots being given to peasants, who swore allegiance in exchange for giving a portion of the produce from their land, plus occasional military service. Each level was known as an **estate**. The divisions between the estates were very marked, with great stress laid on the lower estates giving the higher estates higher status. It would have been unthinkable for a person from one estate to marry a person from a higher estate.

Caste

The caste system developed in India. It is based upon the Hindu religion, which preaches that people have more than one life and that they are born into a particular caste in a life according to their behaviour in their previous lives. Someone who has been extremely wicked will be born into the lowest caste and the good person into the highest caste. The fact that one's caste is determined by God means in essence that it is extremely difficult to change caste and move upwards, no matter how much money or land a person acquires. There are rigid lines between the castes and no form of social mixing is allowed, indeed a person of a higher caste who touches a person of a lower caste regards himself as being contaminated. Sociologists describe a situation where one's social position is determined at birth as **ascription**.

The caste system

Castes

Brahmins	priests
Kshatriyas	soldiers
Vaishyas	traders
Shudras	servants and labourers
Harijan (untouchables)	the worst work, refused by others

A man is born into a *jati* [a division of a caste] and this is the only way of acquiring membership. The Hindu doctrine of 'karma' teaches the young Hindu that he is born into a particular sub-caste because that is where he deserves to be born. His life is governed by principles of pollution which rigidly enforce the separation of castes. If a Brahmin, for example, ate food cooked by an untouchable, the resulting pollution would be thought to be so great that he would be thrown out of his caste.

Each caste is traditionally associated with a particular occupation.

Caste membership is linked to status: not only houses, but clothes, customs and manners become symbols of status for those who share a common culture.

1 Which is:
   a) the lowest layer?
   b) the highest layer of the caste system?

2 How does a person enter a particular caste?

3 Would it be possible for members of different castes to be friends?

4 How would people recognise those from a different caste?

5 How would you recognise someone from a different social class in modern Britain?

6 What three differences can you think of between caste and social class?

Source: Adapted from J. Nobbs, *Sociology in Context* (Macmillan Education, 1983)

Caste: A living division

Although people regard caste as something of the past, it remains very important in Indian society.

During the past two months India has come close to a caste war, and the degree of violence, even by Indian standards, is unprecedented. When the government announced in August that it intended to reserve jobs for the backward castes in central and state administrations, the upper caste youth erupted in protest. The police have so far killed more than 50 people. About 30 young people have committed suicide and a couple of irate parents are now talking of assassinating the Prime Minister, V P Singh. As if this is not enough, left-wing extremists, championing the cause of the backward castes, took the law into their own hands last week and killed 47 passengers on a train.

Source: *The Independent*, 1990

Although caste-like structures are common to most societies, including Britain, caste in its classic form is unique to India. Castes are occupationally based, autonomous and hierarchically graded groups marrying and confining their social relations largely to their own members. Members will, in general, eat only with those of the same caste. Some are pan-Indian, others cover one or more states, yet others are confined to small districts. In total, there are just over 6,000 castes incorporating about 500 million Hindu people. The higher castes contain about 20 per cent of the Hindu population, and the middle and lower castes just under 60 per cent.

The "untouchables", now called Scheduled Castes (SC), representing the lowest of the low, contain about 15 per cent. The widely scattered and culturally backward tribal communities, now called Scheduled Tribes (ST), comprise 7.5 per cent.

Source: *The Independent*, 1990

It all started at a crowded cinema in southern India when an Untouchable boy accidentally brushed his leg against an upper-caste youth sitting next to him. A fight broke out, and this eventually led to a massacre this week in which upper-caste farmers hunted down a community of Untouchables and murdered at least 20 people. ...

After the brawl in the cinema, an upper-caste clan known as the Reddis kidnapped the father of the Untouchable boy and forced the son to turn himself over to them. According to press reports, the higher-caste Indians thrashed the boy badly but left him alive.

The Untouchables hit back. When the time came for the Reddis to plant rice in the paddies after the monsoon rains, Untouchables would not work for them. Then the police arrived to protect the Reddis after two farmers were assaulted going to their fields by a gang of outcastes.

A human rights organisation said that on Tuesday police armed with clubs herded the Untouchables out of their mud-hut settlement. In the nearby rice fields, a mob of more than 500 upper-caste farmers awaited the fleeing Untouchables with swords and axes. Riding tractors and buses, the Reddis hunted down the unarmed outcastes.

Survivors said that as many as 20 Untouchables were stabbed and beaten to death in the four-hour carnage.

Source: *The Independent*, 10 August 1991

Social class

Social class is the main form of **social stratification** in British society. People are graded according to economic and status differences. Some people are wealthier than others and some receive greater prestige than others. The differences between social classes are not clearly marked and they merge into one another.

Although many people are in the same social class as their parents, this is not true for everyone. Social class is 'open' and people move up or down the 'ladder' of social prestige. This movement is known as **social mobility**.

Draw a diagram or cartoon which illustrates the differences between estates, caste and social class.

The 30/30/40 society

Society is dividing before our eyes, opening up new social fissures in the working population. The first 30 per cent are the *disadvantaged*. These include the more than four million who are out of work, including those who do not receive benefit or have not looked for work – within official definitions – and so do not count as officially unemployed. It also includes unemployed women, and women who cannot work because the loss of their husband's income support would more than offset their wage. This 30 per cent, under stress and with their children poorly fed, are the absolutely disadvantaged.

The second 30 per cent are made up of the *marginalised* and the *insecure*, a category defined not so much by income as by its relation to the labour market. People in this category have insecure working conditions and have been at the receiving end of the changes blowing through Britain's offices and factories. There are now more than five million people working part-time, 80 per cent of them women. Then there are those with insecure but full-time work, unprotected through the growth of casual employment and fixed-term contracts.

The last category is that of the *privileged* – the just over 40 per cent whose market power has increased since 1979. These are the full-time employees and the self-employed who have held their jobs for over two years, and the part-timers who have held theirs for more than five years. The 31 per cent of the workforce still represented by trade unions generally fall into this category.

It is this segmentation of the labour market that is sculpting the new and ugly shape of British society. The fact that more than half the people in Britain who are eligible to work are living either on poverty incomes or are in insecure work has had dreadful effects on the wider society. Britain has the highest divorce rate and the most deregulated labour market in Europe, and these two facts are closely related. The impact of inequality is pervasive, affecting everything from the vitality of the housing market to the growth of social security spending.

Source: *The Guardian*, 21 January 1995

The continuing importance of social class

- **Birth**   Children of unskilled working-class parents are three times more likely to die within a year of birth than the children of professionals. Working-class women are more likely to be single mothers. Mothers from working-class origins are likely to have children at an earlier age.

- **Health**   Working-class people are three times more likely to have a serious illness than middle-class people. They are six times more likely to get arthritis and rheumatism.

- **Marriage and family life**   Working-class couples tend to have children earlier in marriage, to raise their children in a noticeably different way from the middle class, and are more likely to divorce.

- **Housing**   Eight-five per cent of the upper middle class own their own houses compared to 25 per cent of the unskilled working class.

- **Income**   The higher up the social classes you climb the larger your income.

- **Education**   The middle classes are more successful in the education system and 60 per cent of the upper middle class have been to university or polytechnic.

- **Politics**   The higher your social class, the greater the chance you vote Conservative.

- **Death**   A man with a professional job can expect to live seven years longer on average than a man with a labouring job.

Social class and income

The table below shows the differences in incomes of households in the UK according to the job of the main earner of the households. The households (grouped by their 'social class' on the left) are divided into five equal groups, with 1 standing for households with the highest incomes, down to 5 for households with the lowest incomes.

The column on the far right is headed 'All households'. It shows the proportion of all households which are headed by each 'social class'. For example, professionals form 5 per cent of all households, while skilled manual form 19 per cent of all households.

Differences in household income, by occupation of head of household, UK, 1993

Occupational group of head of household	Percentage of households in each household group (ranked by income)					All households
	1	2	3	4	5	
Professional	–	1	4	7	14	5
Employers and managers	3	4	9	17	34	13
Intermediate and junior non-manual	3	7	14	21	22	13
Skilled manual	10	17	27	26	15	19
Semi-skilled manual	6	10	12	9	2	8
Unskilled manual	3	3	3	2	–	2
Retired	49	44	22	12	7	27
Unoccupied	25	15	9	6	4	12
Other[1]	–	–	1	1	1	1
All occupational groups	100	100	100	100	100	100

[1]Mainly armed forces

Source: *Social Trends 24* (HMSO, 1994) and the Family Expenditure Survey

1 Which occupational group had the highest number of households?

2 Does this alter when you look at it in proportion to all households?

3 Which employed group had the lowest income overall, in proportion to their numbers in the population?

4 We know that the differences in earnings during a person's working life are reflected in his or her pension and savings when retired. What statements could you make about the incomes of households in the 'Retired' group?

5 We know that unskilled and semi-skilled people are the most likely to be unemployed. What comments can you make about the incomes of the 'Unoccupied' group?

6 In what ways can income influence lifestyle? Give three specific examples.

Social class – a personal view

I asked some students to write a personal description of how they perceived divisions where they lived. This is one example:

'I didn't think that social class existed anymore until I moved last year. We used to live in a suburb, where everyone was the same. You know, all the kids who went to the local school were the same, all the members of the brownies and cub packs were the same, and everyone in the pub was the same – similar incomes, similar houses and similar views.

Then I moved to this village and immediately realised that the suburb I had lived in before was a middle-class ghetto. It wasn't that social class is dead, but that we never saw or met working-class (or really rich) people.

This village is split between the "made-its", the "comfortables", the "aspiring" and the "council estate". I'm no sociologist, so how you categorise them, well, I couldn't say.

Now, the "made-its" have the big country houses and their children go to the private schools – we only seem them as they pass by in their Volvos, or

out riding their horses. They ignore us, and we ignore them.

The "comfortables" have the older hourse, you know those pretty cottages with thatched roofs or the converted Victorian cottages. The "comfortables" are all professionals – lecturers at the university, doctors, solicitors – that type. They take their kids to the local school – because they believe in state education. Of course, they all have private tutors for their kids on the quiet!

Next are the "aspiring" – they live in the new developments in modern houses. They commute into town to work in the offices there. They mostly work in the offices in town – they might have grand titles – sales executive or financial adviser – but really they're just selling things. A few are skilled workers with their own small businesses. The "aspiring" want to be like the comfortable, but also despise them with their trendy attitudes, wine-drinking, dinner-party existence. The "aspiring" have very different educational backgrounds which give them, I reckon, a slight sense of inferiority.

Both the "aspiring" and the "comfortable" have an uneasy alliance against the "council house" families. These are poorer than the rest of the people in the village and the men work in the local factories, or increasingly are unemployed. While the women, if they work, are employed by local cleaning contractors. The council houses used to be full of agricultural workers, but only a few old couples remain. The bulk of families living here now have been moved out of the town by the local council. Life here is tougher and faster-moving. There are lots of old cars with wheels removed, resting on bricks in front gardens, and inexplicably lots of pieces of glass, bits of tyres and refrigerators in the roads. Increasingly, single mothers are moving in as the elderly farmworkers die.

Sadly, all these divisions are reflected in the school, where an unwritten code tells children to play with children from their own social class.'

Now you have a go. Write about the divisions (or similarities) in your area.

True or untrue?

Joan Middleton, 58, teaches English to dyslexic children at an independent school in the Winchester area. "Working where I do, I can see that there isn't a class system any more. There is a new class – the moneyed class. This is reflected in British politics. Labour no longer has its cloth cap image. It is a classless party. Blair is the product of the change. Consequently, he appeals both to the middle class and the working class.

Source: 'Can Blair get hold of the middle classes' by Paul Vallely and Ester Oxford in *The Independent*, 5 January 1995

Ask a sample of ten people whether social class still exists. Describe what classes there are according to them.

Is Britain classless?

The poor...and the very rich

Linda Michaels
Age: 31
Job: Unemployed
Status: Single mother
Children: Three
Money: State benefits
Rent: £58 a week (housing benefit)
Money at the end of the week: None

Social life: None
Homes: Maisonette, Mozart estate, north London (soon to be demolished)
Bedrooms: Two
Club: Broadway Project charity centre
Important connections: None
Views on Europe: Never been
Comfort rating (out of 10): 1

Jonathan Aitken
Age: 52
Job: Treasury Chief Secretary
Status: Married to Lolicia
Children: Three
Money: Multi-millionaire
Rent: None
Money at the end of the week: Millions

Social life: Rich, varied
Homes: £1m Georgian house, London; £500,000 house, Kent
Bedrooms: 16
Club: Pratt's
Important connections: Saudi royals
Views on Europe: Anti
Comfort rating (out of 10): 10

Source: *The Observer*, 11 September 1994

The nature of social class

Although it is agreed that social class influences our lives in many ways, there is less agreement about what social class actually is and what its origins are. The two sociologists who first discussed social class in the last century, Max Weber and Karl Marx, have left behind quite distinct sociological traditions. Marxists see society as fundamentally divided into two groups, while those influenced by Weber see society as consisting much more of a 'ladder' of different groups, with only small differences between them.

The Marxist view

The Marxist view of social class is that in every society one group emerges which gains control of the economy (in Britain today, industry and commerce; in the pre-industrial Britain, it was the land). Marx calls these the **bourgeoisie**, and they arrange society to their own benefit using their enormous wealth and power. They are only a tiny fraction of the whole population, no more than 5 per cent. Everyone else in society works for these people, making them richer.

Of course, there are massive differences between those people who work for the bourgeoisie, some are managers earning very high salaries, others may be manual workers who earn very little. However, they all share one fundamental link. They do not own in any significant way the industry or the commercial institutions. These people are called the **proletariat**.

Marxists today stress that there are many superficial distinctions between the various groups in society, but point out the enormous concentration of wealth in the hands of very few people in contemporary Britain. In order to understand our society with its social problems and great differences in wealth and quality of life, Marxists points to the power of the bourgeoisie to manipulate the rest of the population to work for them and to accept this situation as being quite correct.

Critics of Marx have pointed out firstly that it is possible to be socially mobile and to become successful in 'capitalist' society. Secondly, they have pointed to the collapse of communist regimes, such as the USSR, which claimed to follow Marxist ideas, where those in power controlled the population for their own benefit in a far more ruthless way than in capitalist Britain. Thirdly, they have also argued that modern society has developed in a more complex way than Marx foresaw, writing a hundred years ago, and the idea of there being only two classes bourgeoisie and proletariat, is simply inaccurate.

Weber's view

Weber's view of stratification comes from this last criticism. For him, to divide society into two groups on the basis of ownership of the economy or not was just too simple. He suggested instead that social class was based on three elements: **economic factors**, such as how much money a person earned or inherited from parents; **status**, such as the prestige we give to a person based on such things as accent, style of dress and level of education; **power**, the amount of influence a person has to affect important social decisions.

It is by balancing these three elements together that we arrive at our judgement of where a person belongs in society. A scrap metal dealer may earn far more than a doctor, yet it would generally be agreed that in some way the doctor is of a higher social class than the dealer. Weber's view of social class is that it is constantly changing, depending on people's opinions of the worth of a particular occupation. Ownership of property is important, as Marxists argue, but it is only one of a number of elements that link together to form our **life chances**, by which Weber means the chances of being successful in life. In Britain today, for instance, the chances of success for the son of a wealthy banker, who attends public school, are clearly very high.

The great advantage of Weber's model of stratification is that the three distinct elements (economic differences, status or prestige differences, and differences in power) allow a more flexible and detailed way of classifying different people, than Marx's model which is based solely on economic differences. For example, Weber's model lets us see the differences between people with similar jobs which are caused by differences in status.

If two people are doing a similar job, say a shop assistant, where one speaks in a refined accent, and works in an expensive shop, while the other talks with a more 'common' accent and sells cut-price furniture, are there any significant differences, do you think, in how we classify them?

It is unfortunate, but probably true that people are very much aware of issues of race, age and disability in the way they perceive and act towards others. Once again the status and power elements of Weber's analysis allow us to link these with economic differences.

1 Name the two sociologists who first discussed social class.

2 Who are:
a) the bourgeoisie?
b) the proletariat?

3 How many classes are there in the Marxist analysis of the class system? To which do you belong?

4 What do critics of Marx say concerning his division of society into two groups?

5 According to Weber, of what three elements does class consist?

6 What does the term 'life chances' mean?

7 Draw up a table with the following headings; *Economic level*, *Status level*, *Power level*. Beneath each heading, rank (put in order) each occupation/role from the list below. For example, the higher the income, the greater the power or the more prestige or

status an occupation has, the higher up the relevant scale it will appear.

  Secondhand car dealer
  Journalist on local newspaper
  Journalist on national television
  Senior civil servant
  The Queen
  Princess Diana
  A barrister (of Afro-Caribbean origin)
  An MP
  An unemployed 55-year-old man
  An unemployed 16-year-old traveller
  A student
  A managing director of large company
  A nurse (male)
  A nurse (black female)
  A lone (male) parent on state benefit
  A lone (female) parent on state benefit

8 Draw a diagram to summarise Marx's and Weber's divisions of society.

The measurement of social class

In actual research projects, sociologists need to measure social class. Generally, they find the easiest way to do this is to grade people by **occupation**. There are a number of reasons why they do this. First of all, because information on people's occupations is simple and quick to obtain, but also because occupation is related to a number of very important social differences, such as:

- differences in earnings
- differences in the standard of education
- differences in accent and styles of dress, because these in turn reflect differences in education and occupation
- differences in values and patterns of behaviour, again reflecting education
- differences in how people are ranked by others and given prestige, so the doctor receives greater prestige than the estate agent.

How our occupations influence our social class

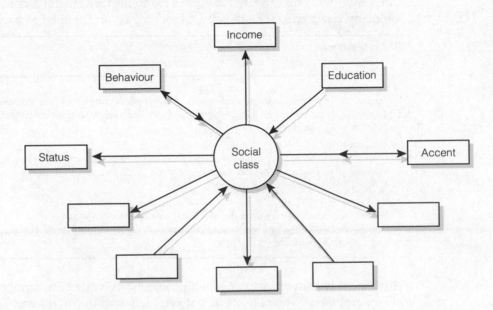

The diagram illustrates how occupations influence, and in turn are influenced by, other aspects of our lives.

Add three more ways in which occupation influences us, and two ways in which occupation is influenced by other factors.

Registrar-General's classification

Source: *The Mail on Sunday*, 11 August 1985

The most commonly used classification is the **Register-General's classification** which groups all jobs into five general categories as follows:

Class	
I	Professional and higher administrative, such as lawyers, architects and doctors
II	Intermediate professionals and administrative personnel, such as shopkeepers, farmers and teachers
III	Skilled i) Non-manual, such as shop assistants and clerical workers in offices ii) Manual, such as electricians and miners
IV	Semi-skilled, such as bus conductors, farm workers
V	Unskilled, such as labourers on building sites

The division of class III between manual and non-manual workers reflects the importance of the differences mentioned earlier, even if earnings are broadly similar.

According to the Registrar-General's model there are no rich people, as class I is mainly composed of professional and managerial workers. Also, self-employed people who have very different opportunities and conditions from employed people are not distinguished as a separate group.

Goldthorpe's classification

In a study of social mobility in the early 1970s, a sociologist at Cambridge University, J. Goldthorpe, decided that the Registrar-General's classification had too many flaws and so he devised a modernised and refined version.

Occupational group	Percentage of workers
Service class	
1 Higher grade professionals, administrators and owners of companies (the 'bosses)	7.7
2 Lower-grade professionals, administrators and managers, high level technical staff (For example, teachers)	6.0
Intermediate class	
3 Clerical, sales and rank and file service workers (sales assistants and clerks)	7.4
4 Owners of very small firms and the self-employed (such as a small builder)	12.6
5 Lower grade technicians and foremen	11.3
Working class	
6 Skilled manual workers in industry (such as an electrician in a factory)	27.2
7 Semi-skilled and unskilled workers in industry (such as assembly line workers) and agricultural workers	27.8

This model has seven groupings with distinctions made between those who give orders and those who take them, between self-employed and employees, and between agricultural workers and industrial workers. Furthermore, the occupations are classified into three classes which enjoy broadly similar life chances.

In sociological research you will see these classifications used to explain differences in earnings, educational success, levels of home ownership, standards of health and a host of other social differences.

Place the following occupations in their groups according to:
a)   the manual/non-manual division;
b)   the Registrar-General's classification;
c)   Goldthorpe's classification.

A teacher
A shopkeeper
The owner of a large manufacturing company
A plumber working for a large building contractor
A self-employed plumber
An agricultural labourer

Measuring the social class of women

One big problem with using occupation as a way of measuring social class is that it tends to give an inaccurate picture of women's class position. This is mainly because the classifications of the Registrar-General and Goldthorpe are designed

Women have criticised the tradi-tional ways of measuring class and have created their own forms of classification

to distinguish the sorts of jobs that men do, and we know that women are generally employed in very different sorts of jobs. Feminist sociologists have, therefore, suggested that classifications need to be developed which incorporate the sorts of job women do. One such measure is that provided by Arber, Dale and Gilchrist:

Class	
I	Higher professionals
II	Employers and managers
III	Lower professionals
IV	Secretarial and clerical staff
V	Supervisors and self-employed workers
VI	Sales and personal services
VII	Skilled manual occupations
VIII	Unskilled occupations

1 What differences are there between this scale and those of Goldthorpe and the Registrar-General?

2 Why do you think the additional categories were added?

The class structure in Britain

We have seen that social class exists in Britain and exerts considerable influence over our lives. It is important to remember, however, that social class divisions are fluid and change over time. The differences between the classes, as shown by the ownership of cars, houses and consumer goods which were so great in the 1950s, have narrowed considerably with the spread of affluence to much of the nation. For instance, almost 70 per cent of the population now own their own homes compared with only 30 per cent in 1945, and whereas less than 10 per cent of the population had cars then, today the figure is over 60 per cent.

Employment patterns

Types of employment, by sex, UK, 1993

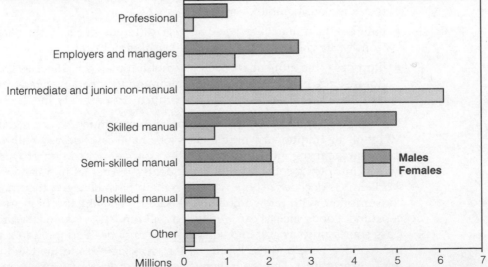
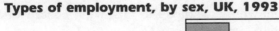

Excludes those on a government scheme and those not in paid employment within the last 10 years.

Source: *Social Trends 24* (HMSO, 1994), Office of Population Censuses and Surveys, General Register Office (Scotland and N. Ireland)

1 What sort of work are the majority of (a) males and (b) females engaged in?

2 When sociologists say that unskilled working-class

people suffer greater relative poverty and ill-health than 30 years ago, it is 'relatively true', but in terms of total numbers it is incorrect! Can you explain this?

A second change has been the move from manual work to white-collar work, this means that today more than half the workforce is engaged in jobs traditionally regarded as middle-class. Whereas a decent education was once only possible for the middle and upper classes today it is possible for most of the population, and this has allowed many children from working-class backgrounds to enter professional jobs, such as medicine and accountancy.

In sum, therefore, there have been considerable changes in the class structure of Britain. Let us look first at the changes using Goldthorpe's division into working, intermediate and service classes, and then move on to examine the extremes of wealth and poverty.

The working class

In the 1950s the working class formed two-thirds of the workforce, and consisted of manual workers in manufacturing industries. Wages were low and so were living standards. Attitudes towards education and the family were very different from the middle class. However, by the 1960s the differences between the middle and working class seemed to be disappearing and some sociologists claimed that a process of **embourgeoisement** (that is, the working class becoming middle class) was taking place. The argument was that the spread of affluence had reached certain higher paid workers, that these were able to afford middle-class standards of living and that they were abandoning their traditional support for the Labour Party.

In a famous research project in the mid-1960s, Goldthorpe and Lockwood studied a group of so called 'affluent workers', mainly production line workers at the Vauxhall factory in Luton, to see if they were becoming middle-class. They concluded that there were still significant differences in terms of:

- income – the affluent workers earned less than white-collar workers unless they did considerable overtime
- values – the affluent workers had very different views on the nature of society from white-collar workers and disliked their jobs far more
- lifestyles – the affluent workers had not adopted middle-class leisure patterns (for instance giving dinner parties) although they had changed from traditional working-class lifestyles by having a much closer family life.

This study was, however, over 25 years ago and much has changed since then. Many of the traditional working-class jobs have disappeared with the decline in the manufacturing industries and so the younger generation of workers have moved into white-collar work. Consequently the actual numbers of manual workers has declined. Those who do remain have changed their patterns of consumption, with foreign holidays, house ownership and high spending on consumer goods such as cars and videos, all funded by credit. Traditional middle-class sports, such as golf and squash, have now been adopted in a large way by the working class and the loyalty of the working class to the Labour Party is under great threat. The result then is not necessarily the disappearance of class, or the embourgeoisement of the working class, but the narrowing of the great gulf of the past.

One more point has been made by researchers into the working class – that more divisions have appeared *within* the working class over the last 25 years. Important divisions have appeared between the employed and the unemployed, those in secure jobs and those in the declining manufacturing industries, between those living in the New Towns and overspill estates and those living in the traditional close-knit working-class communities of the inner cities and the mining villages.

Sociologists now talk about the **new working class** when they describe those living in the prosperous south-east of England, with secure, well-paid jobs, and compare these to the poorer, more traditional working class who are increasingly concentrated in the north.

Another term that is becoming increasingly popular amongst sociologists is the **underclass**. It is argued that there is an increasing number of people, within the working class, who are missing out on the general prosperity and that their plight is worsening. This underclass consists of those groups in society who lack any power, and who receive the worst of everything, compared with the rest of society. Typical groups in the underclass are single-parent families, and many of the ethnic minorities.

Divisions in the working class

Once there was a pecking order within the working class which went from the respectable to the ordinary to the rough. But they all lived in the same areas. Some houses were nicer and better furnished, some families more feckless but it was the same world, with graduations between skills.

It's not that long ago that men learned trades as apprentices. And trades and skills meant unions and working class solidarity. There are still older working class people who belong mentally to this pre-war system. Look at any Sixties realist film and you'll see it – it's another world.

Then the Great Divide started between two new working class types – the people who moved into life's Brooksides, lower middle class-type owner-occupied houses and those who went into the new council estates.

And the children of the former went to grammar school and were sucked up into the new middle class to do the new middle class jobs – teaching, planning and working with computers.

Skills counted for less with more automation. What mattered was whether you were *lucky* or not. Lucky was Southern, employed or self-employed, and owner-occupier. Unlucky was Northern, unemployed, on a council estate.

Imagine the rich 'working class' world of outer East London – taxi-drivers, print workers, self-employed double glazing installers, that kind of job. It's where the husband plays golf and the wife gets the Hansel and Gretel German-style dark wood fitted kitchen costing several thousand, and 13-year-old Jason is asking for a Giorgio Armani sweater for his birthday. They were first in on video and now they have a video camera which they use on holiday in Miami.

The Luckies don't feel working class solidarity, even though there's nothing really planned for Jason's education or career, nothing to push him into the old middle class. They just keep giving him *things*. They think the computer, last year's big thing, will deal with his education.

The Unluckies are out of work in places where there's no moonlighting to be had. There's not much work from Party Planners in Newcastle. Everyone can't clean windows. The unlucky working class lives in the North in decaying Sixties council estates. The estates are class ghettoes. They look it and they feel it. The ones who want to move up and buy their house, and wonder if it will hold its value.

The Unluckies buy in no-frills supermarkets where everything's basic. The Luckies eat from Marks. They have smoked salmon and prawns regularly. It's the difference between, say, Ilford and Kirkby, near Liverpool. There's always been a difference but now it's sharper with not much in between.

Source: *The Mail on Sunday*, 11 August 1985

1 According to the extract, what was working-class life like before the 1960s?

2 What does the author mean when he talks about the 'Great Divide'?

3 'What mattered was whether you were *lucky* or not'? The author (a journalist) suggests that a person's lifestyle was mainly due to luck. As sociology students do you think luck is the only explanation? What other reasons may have caused this division?

4 Sociologists often talk about 'the new working class' and the 'traditional working class' when they analyse the differences between working class people in Britain today. Which names would apply to:
a) the Luckies?
b) the Unluckies?

The intermediate class

The intermediate stratum, or the lower middle-class, has also changed considerably over the last 50 years. The most important change has been the sheer growth in numbers, as there has been a shift in the occupational structure towards service jobs which are usually white-collar.

Clerical work has seen a considerable decline in its status and levels of pay, such that it has been suggested that a process of **proletarianisation** (the move down from the middle to the working class) has taken place.

This argument has not been borne out by research as it has been found that the increase in the low-paid clerical workers is composed mainly of women workers (often employed part-time) and that male clerical workers have generally better prospects of promotion into supervisory positions. Also, clerical workers have better working conditions, receive better fringe benefits such as flexi-hours, sick pay provisions, and some of them have chances of promotion. Possibly most important of all, whereas most manual workers, when asked, describe themselves as working-class, clerical workers describe themselves as middle-class, even though their salaries are rarely higher.

The difference lies, then, in how they *see themselves*.

The service class

The last 50 years has seen a tremendous growth in the professions and to a lesser extent in management. There have been increases in the old established professions such as law, but far more important has been the growth in the new professions of social work and teaching, which have drawn some of their recruits from the working class. This class now comprises almost 15 per cent of the workforce, compared to only about 5 per cent in the 1940s.

It has been argued that a managerial revolution has taken place, in which effective control of all industry has moved away from the owners of large companies to the managers. This is so, it is argued, because the ownership of firms is so widespread that no one person is in control, hence the power of the managers who effectively run the companies. Whatever the truth of this argument, the fact remains that the old idea of the boss owning a company and running it him or herself has become far more rare than in the past.

1 What is meant by the terms:
   a) embourgeoisement?
   b) proletarianisation?

2 Has embourgeoisement taken place? Give three reasons why proletarianisation has not taken place.

3 Name three divisions which have occurred within the working class in the last 20 years.

4 Give two examples of jobs in:
   a) the working class
   b) the intermediate class
   c) the service class.

5 Which two classes have grown in size and which one declined?

Divisions in Britain today: A summary

	Broad social class groupings	Groups within social classes	Divisions other than social class		
			Gender	Ethnic group	Region
The upper class	The rich	The 'establishment' or 'ruling class'	Women concentrated in the lowest-paid jobs in each class	Blacks concentrated in lowest-paid groups/unemployed	The worse-off found in the north and the inner cities
The middle class	• Managers and professionals (mainly men); high pay • Routine white-collar workers in offices, banks, shops and caring services (mainly women); low pay	The 'service class' The 'intermediate groups			
The working class	• Better-paid manual workers in secure employment in newer light industries • The self-employed	} The 'new working class'			
	• Less-skilled, less well-paid manual workers; job increasingly under threat as industry contracts • The poor; the unemployed	The 'traditional working class' The 'underclass'			

A great divide?

The image of Britain as an increasingly polarised society in which the rich get richer and the poor get poorer may be flawed and out of date, Dr Dorling said yesterday. ...

He said that the overall trend was for neighbourhoods to become more socially mixed, with a wider variety of income groups living close together. The place where a person was born and grew up had less impact on his or her chances in life than it did a generation or two generations ago.

Unemployment appeared to have become more evenly distributed in geographical terms and among the different social classes. Ownership of cars and homes and access to higher education had spread to a wider section of the population through the 1980s.

But Dr Dorling conceded that inequalities in earnings and mortality appeared to be still growing. ...Dr Dorling said researchers had a difficult task in assessing trends in inequality because of a dearth of data. The Inland Revenue would not disclose local statistics on income and one of the most authoritative bodies, the Royal Commission on Income and Wealth, was wound up by the incoming Tory government in 1979.

Source: 'Doubt thrown on thesis of polarised UK' by Nicholas Schoon in *The Independent*, 1995

Rising wage inequality in the UK, males

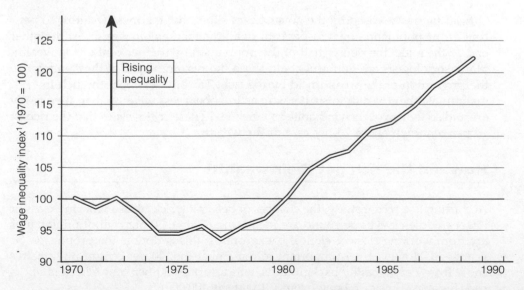

1 Index is log difference between the average weekly wage of the top and bottom decile of adult male wage-earners

Source: E. Balls and P. Gregg, *Work and Welfare* (Institute for Public Policy Research, 1993)

1 In the extract, what is Dr Dorling quoted as saying about the argument that Britain is getting more and more 'polarised'?

2 What arguments does he put forward to support this?

3 What methodological problems does he refer to when it comes to collecting the information?

The graph shows the extent of differences between the earnings of the top 10 per cent of wage earners and the bottom 10 per cent in the UK. The higher the line the greater the differences. Look for the straight line marked 100 – above it there is a move in the direction of inequality and below it there is move towards equality.

4 What does the graph tell us about the differences between the top 10 per cent and the bottom 10 per cent since 1970? You should show any shifts in the trends of equality/inequality and the dates when these took place.

5 Is there any way in which we could reconcile the arguments of Dr Dorling and the information contained in the chart? (Think back to the discussion about the growth of the intermediate class and the splitting of the working class.)

The wealthy

One of the most obvious and taken-for-granted things about British society is the fact that some people have more possessions than others. Some people live in big houses, with smart cars and spend pleasant holidays in exotic places, while others scrape the barest existence from their work. What is not so obvious, however, is the scale of the inequalities in wealth and income, and the ways in which the rich obtain their money.

The meaning of 'wealth'

By wealth, we mean the ownership of goods not for use by a person, but kept for their value and which can be sold at any time. A house bought to live in is not wealth, but a second house bought by someone who already has one is. Wealth is most commonly held in stocks and shares (part-ownership of companies), land and property, though some people invest in works of art, or even rare wines!

The distribution of wealth

Official figures released by the government show that the most wealthy 10 per cent of the population own 51 per cent of all the marketable wealth. At the other end of the scale, the poorer half of the population own 4 per cent of the wealth. Many sociologists are doubtful about these figures, arguing that they understate the proportion of the wealth held by the rich. Tax advisers help the rich to manipulate their wealth in such a way as to appear less wealthy than they really are and so they avoid paying quite as much tax. These critics claim that the richest 10 per cent own about 70 per cent of the wealth.

How did the rich get their wealth?

According to a recent study, the chances of becoming rich from a working-class or lower middle-class background are increasing. Today, 20 per cent of millionaires are from working-class or clerical backgrounds; this is double the proportion 30 years ago. However, it is important to remember that 40 per cent of millionaires come from very wealthy backgrounds, and a further 30 per cent inherited considerable sums of money (from £10 000 to £100 000).

Wealth in Britain today

A

Distribution of income and wealth to the income groups

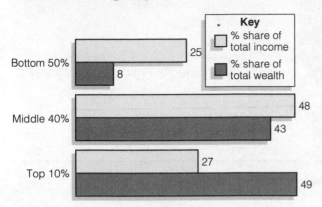

Key
- % share of total income
- % share of total wealth

Bottom 50%: 25, 8

Middle 40%: 48, 43

Top 10%: 27, 49

Source: *The Guardian*, 13 February 1995

B

Cutting the pie – fair shares for all?

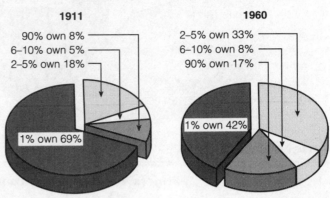
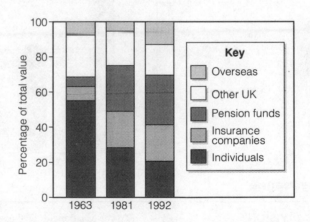

1911
- 90% own 8%
- 6–10% own 5%
- 2–5% own 18%
- 1% own 69%

1960
- 2–5% own 33%
- 6–10% own 8%
- 90% own 17%
- 1% own 42%

C

Shareholders as a percentage of the adult population

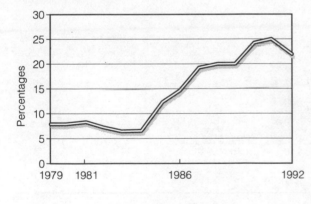

D

Shares held in UK companies, by sector

Key
- Overseas
- Other UK
- Pension funds
- Insurance companies
- Individuals

1963, 1981, 1992

Source (B, C and D): L. Jones, *The Social Context of Health and Health Work* (Macmillan, 1994) and *Social Trends 23* (HMSO, 1993)

A, B and **C** provide information on the changing ownership of wealth in Britain since 1911.

1 Convert **A** into a pie chart.

2 What percentage of wealth was owned by the top 10 per cent in total? (Don't forget to include the figures of the top 1 per cent and 2–5 per cent.)

3 How has this changed since 1911?

4 How has this changed since 1960?

Look at **D**.

5 What proportion of shares are owned by individuals?

6 Which two types of organisation own the majority of shares? What proportion do they own?

7 Can you think of any implications for the future if the majority of shares are going to be owned by these organisations?

Cutting the cake – the share of incomes among the five household income groups (see page 43)

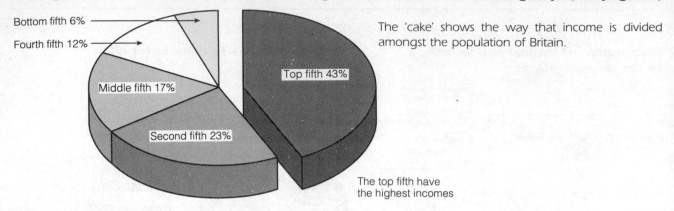

Bottom fifth 6%

Fourth fifth 12%

Middle fifth 17%

Second fifth 23%

Top fifth 43%

The 'cake' shows the way that income is divided amongst the population of Britain.

The top fifth have the highest incomes

Winners and losers

Winners and losers in incomes, 1980–93

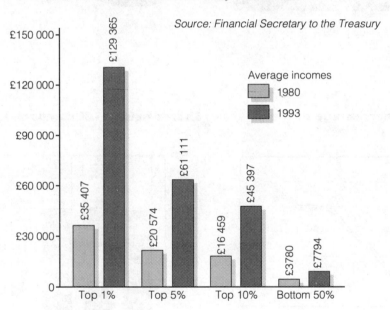

Source: Financial Secretary to the Treasury

Average incomes
1980
1993

£150 000

£120 000

£90 000

£60 000

£30 000

0

£35 407 / £129 365 — Top 1%
£20 574 / £61 111 — Top 5%
£16 459 / £45 397 — Top 10%
£3780 / £7794 — Bottom 50%

The pay league

PREMIER DIVISION	£
Robert Bauman,	
Smith Kline Beecham	1,590,000
Lord Hanson, Hanson Trust	1,350,000
Sir Paul Girolami, Glaxo	1,186,000
Jürgen Klinsmann, Spurs	780,000
Chairman, Schroeders bank	540,9145
Chairman, British Airways	540,915
Michael Aspel, TV presenter	500,000
Top nude photographer	500,000
Page Three model (est.)	200,000

FIRST DIVISION	£
John Birt BBC Director-General	190,000
Editor of The Sun	175,000
Head of top PR firm	150,000
Top foreign exchange trader	150,000
Chairman of British Rail	131,600

	£
Trevor Macdonald, ITN newscaster	120,000
Lord Chancellor	110,940
Law lord	103,790
High Court judge	87,620
Civil Service dep. sec.	64–75,328
City equities trader	50–75,000

SECOND DIVISION	£
Junior Minister	48,815
Archbishop of Canterbury	43,550
GP (national average salary)	40,000
Firm's public relations director	39,900
Police superintendent	36–39,135
Professor (Oxford)	34,984
Top station manager	33,660
Air traffic controller	33,254
Army major (after 8 years)	32,051
MP	31,687

	£
Head of secondary school	30–50,682
Diocesan bishop	23,610
Head of primary school	23–33,789
Classroom teacher (highest)	20,244

THIRD DIVISION	£
Average earnings (April)	17,171
Signalman Grade B (incl. overtime)	14,810
Account executive, PR firm	14,722
Bus driver	13,520
Junior hospital doctor	13–14,900
Police constable	12–21,267
MP's secretary	12–16,000
BBC local radio reporter	12,000
Gravedigger (London)	11,648
First year teacher	11,244
Bus conductor	11,200
Student nurse	6,920–8,020

Source (chart and table): *Sociology Review*, February 1995 and *The Guardian*, 29 August 1994 (table)

The wealthy are composed of:

- the British aristocracy, who own vast tracts of land – the Duke of Westminster, for instance owns 300 acres of some of the richest parts of London in Belgravia, Mayfair and Westminster, amongst his total land ownership of 138 000 acres throughout Britain
- the owners of industry and commerce – only a small proportion of the population, about 10 per cent own *significant* amounts of stocks and shares in companies
- the 'struck lucky' – these are the people who through good fortune (and sometimes, talent) strike it rich. These include sports personalities, entertainers, those who win the National Lottery and those who had one good idea which was successful.

The distribution of income

Income is the flow of money people obtain for their work, from the state, or from their investments. The top 10 per cent of earners take about 27 per cent of all income, compared to the 2.5 per cent earned by the poorest 10 per cent. This is not the full story: the higher up the occupational ladder you climb, the greater the fringe benefits, or 'perks', that go with the job. A manager can expect to receive a company car and possibly free membership of private health schemes, assistance with the mortgage and private school fees for his or her children. The true distribution of income is therefore more favourable to the affluent than the official figures suggest.

Changes in distribution of income and wealth

Over this century there has been a very slow and small decline in the proportion of wealth owned by the rich. This has not gone to the poor, however, but to the better-off, who have become even better off.

In the last 15 years even this small redistribution has stopped.

In terms of income, a very similar process has taken place: a small shift of income from the top 10 per cent to the top 20 per cent and no improvement in the earnings of the bottom 50 per cent, who take exactly the same proportion of earnings as they did 45 years ago. This disguises a very real decline in the earnings of those at the very bottom of the earnings ladder, the huge increase in the numbers of unemployed and aged, living on state benefits, which has taken place in the last 20 years.

1 What is the difference between wealth and income?

2 Ought we to trust official statistics of income and wealth distribution? Explain your answer.

3 'Anybody can be rich if they work hard enough.' What comment do sociologists have to make on this statement?

4 What changes have taken place in the distribution of:
a) wealth?
b) income?

5 What is your view on inherited wealth? Is it right that people should be able to leave all their wealth to their children or do you think that no one ought to be allowed to pass on their wealth, so that each generation could start off more or less equal?

Social mobility

Probably the major difference between social class and other forms of stratification, such as caste, is the ability to move up or down the ladder of social class. This movement is called **social mobility**. The amount of movement in society is the evidence to prove (or disprove) the claim that Britain is an 'open' society where people arrive in positions of social esteem depending upon their ability. High rates of mobility mean that the most able members of the working class can move up in the class system and the less able of the middle class move aside for them.

There are two measures of mobility: **intergenerational** and **intragenerational**. Intergenerational mobility is the comparison of a person's occupation with that of his or her father. Intragenerational mobility is the comparison of a person's present occupation with his or her first occupation. We normally call this a person's 'career'.

The extent of mobility in Britain

The Oxford Mobility Study is a major investigation of patterns of inter-generational social mobility in Britain. It was based on a survey of 10 000 males aged 20–64, who were divided into seven social classes (see Goldthorpe's classification, page 48).

Overall, the authors concluded that 30 per cent of the men had moved up and 18 per cent had moved down the class structure. However most of the mobility was 'short-range' (that is, no more than two occupational groups up or down), and only 7 per cent of those from social class 7 backgrounds (the lowest group) had reached class 1. On the other hand almost half of those in social class 1 occupations had come from social class 1 backgrounds.

We can say that it is possible for people to move up the class structure, but it is a lot easier for those from the top to stay there.

The social class escalator

A shows mobility in the 1950s and 1970s according to the Oxford Mobility Study. **B** shows social class mobility for males and females between 1971 and 1991. **C** shows the rate of mobility for women.

A

Your chance of ending up in service class

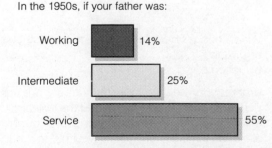

In the 1950s, if your father was:

Working 14%

Intermediate 25%

Service 55%

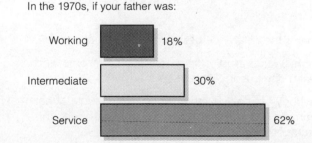

In the 1970s, if your father was:

Working 18%

Intermediate 30%

Service 62%

Source: Adapted from Haralambos *et al.*, *Sociology: A New Approach* (Causeway Press) and *The Sunday Times*, 13 January 1980

B

Social class mobility, by sex

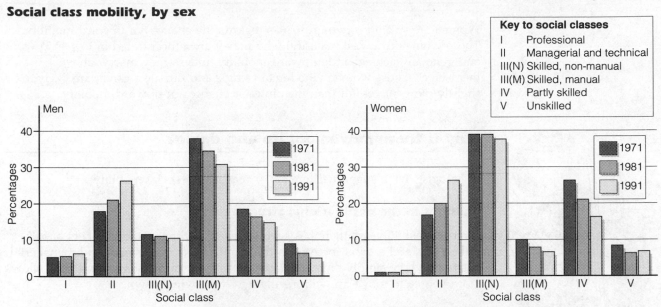

| **Key to social classes** |
| I   Professional |
| II   Managerial and technical |
| III(N) Skilled, non-manual |
| III(M) Skilled, manual |
| IV   Partly skilled |
| V   Unskilled |

Source: *The Guardian*, 25 February 1995 and the Office of Population Censuses and Surveys

C

Female social mobility (compared with fathers' occupational class)

Fathers' occupational class	Respondents' occupational class			
	Service	Intermediate	Manual	Total
Service	82	114	47	243
Intermediate	68	134	137	339
Manual	64	211	347	622
Total	214	459	531	1204

Source: R.G. Burgess, *Investigating Society* (Longman), adapted from Goldthorpe and Payne (1986)

Look at **A**.

1 Which group has the highest chance of entering the service class?

2 Which group has the lowest?

3 Would it be true to say that the class structure has become more open?

Look at **B**.

4 What one clear trend for men is noticeable between 1971 and 1991?

5 What differences are there in social mobility between men and women?

6 Looking at **B** and the answers you gave earlier, suggest one major reason for the apparent increase in mobility.

Look at **C**.

7 Which group are the daughers of men working in service and intermediate occupations most likely to enter?

8 What comments could you make about the mobility pattern of the daughters of manual workers?

9 Although it is difficult to compare male and female mobility, can you see any differences in the patterns of social mobility between the sexes? Can you give any evidence to support your argument?

Women and social mobility

Women are split into two groups as regards the chances of upward mobility. Those women (the vast majority) who marry are concentrated in low-paid work and generally achieve little upward mobility, unless they marry 'above' themselves. Those women who remain single and pursue a career are likely to be slightly more successful than men in their chances of upward mobility.

Why is there movement up and down?

Sociologists have suggested five major reasons for social mobility.

Changes in the occupational structure

Over the last 40 years there has been a steady decline in the numbers of low-skilled jobs and a great increase in the numbers of professional and managerial positions. Quite simply there are many more high status jobs around. This allows more people to move up, with relatively few moving down.

Changes in fertility

The higher status groups in society have consistently had fewer children than the increase in the number of top jobs. This creates space at the top as the children of the highest group cannot fill all the vacancies.

Education

The education system has been expanded and improved to give intelligent working-class children greater chance of success. Combined with the expansion of the numbers of top jobs, this has allowed considerable numbers of working-class children into higher status jobs. Twenty-five per cent of men in the professions are from working-class backgrounds of one sort or another.

Environment

A person's background, parental encouragement and peer group support can create a determination to succeed, as well as giving the individual the 'correct' social attributes. The child from a privileged background may have the right manners and accent to pluck a plum job. However a determined, intelligent working-class child, given the right circumstances may well be equipped to succeed.

Marriage

Generally, people marry others from similar backgrounds to themselves. However, if women marry outside their class this usually means them taking the class position of the husband, as it is he who will generally be the main earner throughout their married lives.

1 A **meritocracy** is a society where people's jobs and incomes are a result of ability, not friendship or family connections. Is Britain a meritocracy?

2 Find out and compare your parents' occupation with those of your grandparents. What social mobility (if any) has taken place?

Social mobility and education

While direct discrimination against women, blacks and, probably, the working class still exists, such evidence that we have suggests that it may be on the wane, but at the same time indirect influence via the educational system has increased as family background has become more closely linked to educational success and failure.

As society tries to become fairer with equal pay legislation and so on, new 'unfairnesses' may arise as the better off try to find new ways of keeping their privileged position. It would not be surprising if the better off sections of society found that private schools could best defend their privileges, while within the State system, neighbourhood comprehensive schools develop to satisfy the ambitions of the middle class (who live in separate residential areas from the working class). Direct discrimination may decline, but new ways of ensuring that the middle and upper classes keep ahead in the education system and therefore in the race for the better jobs, will develop.

1 What is taking over from 'direct discrimination' as the most important influence on occupational attainment?

2 How does this work in practice?

3 What ways could you suggest that would ensure equal opportunities for all?

Chapter 4

GENDER AND SEXUALITY

This chapter covers:
- Men and women: Gender divisions in society
- Childhood
- School
- Work
- Parenthood
- Leisure
- Divisions between women
- Sexuality
- Women and violence.

Men and women: Gender divisions in society

Nowhere is the power of socialisation so clearly illustrated as in the creation of **gender roles**, that is in the different expectations we have of the proper behaviour for men and women. No one disputes that men and women are *physically* different (the division by sex) but sociologists argue that the differences in *behaviour* between men and women are not a result of these physical differences at all, they are learned (the division by gender).

Males and females: Occupations

On the right is a sample list of jobs. In each case over 75 per cent of the people involved are either male or female. Trace or copy out the list and indicate which sex you think dominates each job.

1 What reasons can you suggest for some jobs being done mainly by males and other jobs mainly by females?

2 Apart from physical differences, in what ways are females 'naturally' different from males?

3 Now leave your answers, without discussing them. Wait until the end of the chapter and then compare your views. Have they changed?

Occupation	Male	Female
Miners		
Butchers		
Nurses		
Typists		
Drivers		
Administrators and managers		
Postal workers		
Shop assistants		
Telephonists		
Cleaners		
Painters and decorators		

Learning the gender roles begins as a baby in the family, and every experience that a person has after that reinforces a few clear messages: that males and females ought to act differently; that these differences in behaviour are the result of biology and are therefore natural; that those who do not wish to fit in to the expected patterns of behaviour are 'deviants' (or freaks).

The roles themselves are fairly clear: women are expected to be physically weaker, more emotional, have motherly and homely instincts, and do not have strong sexual desires. On the other hand, men are stronger, less emotional, more aggressive and have powerful sexual drives. In order to understand how these roles are learned and how they influence the lives of women in particular, let us follow the lives of women through childhood, school, work, parenthood, leisure.

Are gender roles natural?

Sociologists argue that the expectations we have of males and females are not based on any natural, biological differences between them, but are the result of different upbringing in different cultures.
...

In *Sex and Temperament in Three Primitive Societies*, Margaret Mead describes three New Guinea tribes: the Arapesh, the Mundugumor and the Tchambuli. Among the Arapesh, the ideal adult has a gentle passive, cherishing nature and resembles the feminine type in our culture. In relationships between the sexes, including the sexual, the Arapesh recognise no temperament between men and women. The main work of both adult men and women is child bearing and child rearing – indeed they call sexual intercourse 'work' when the object is to make the woman pregnant! The verb 'to give birth' is used for both of the sexes. Mead observed that if one comments on a middle aged man as good looking the people answer 'Good-looking? Yes. But you should have seen him before he gave birth to all those children!'

Amongst the Mundugumor the opposite of the Arapesh holds true, where both sexes follow our idea of the 'masculine' pattern. The women are as forceful and vigorous as the men, they detest bearing and rearing children, and men in turn detest pregnancy in their wives. Both sexes are reared to be independent and hostile and boys and girls have similar personalities.

In the third tribe, the Tchambuli, there was a great difference between the sexes. However, the males showed what we would say are 'female' characteristics and the women showed 'masculine' characteristics. Women are self-assertive, practical and manage all the affairs of the household. Men are 'skittish, wary of each other, interested in art, in theatre, in a thousand petty bits of insult and gossip. Hurt feelings are rampant...the pettishness of those who feel themselves weak and isolated, the men wear lovely ornaments (the women shave their heads and are unadorned), they do the shopping they carve and paint and dance.'

A similar pattern of sex differences occurs in a South-west Pacific society studied by William Davenport.

'Only men wear flowers in their hair and scented leaves tucked into their belts or arm bands. At formal dances it is the man who dresses in the most elegant finery and...when these young men are fully made up and costumed for the dance they are not allowed to be alone even for a moment, for fear some women will seduce them.'

Source: A. Oakley, *Sex, Gender and Society* (M.T. Smith, 1972)

1 Describe the typical characteristics of males amongst:
 a) the Arapesh
 b) the Mundugumor
 c) the Tchambuli.

2 What does the information provided in the extract tell us about gender roles in our own society?

3 Can you provide three examples from your own experience when you have been treated differently solely on the basis of your sex?

Gender roles are learned in childhood

Childhood

Gender socialisation begins as soon as the baby is born. Midwives ask 'Which do you prefer boy or girl?', indicating the different expectations we have. The adjectives used to describe children of different sexes indicate just what these expectations are. Boys are described as strong, tough, 'a little rascal'. Girls are described as sweet, pretty or angelic. Later on, as the child grows we have terms which are used to describe children who do not quite fit into the patterns of behaviour expected of their sex, for example 'tomboy' or 'cissy'.

Parents' expectations

Parents' expectations of children lead them to encourage different forms of behaviour. For instance, girls are expected to be neat and tidy, to appreciate wearing attractive dresses and so to be very aware of their appearance. The toys they are given and the games they are encouraged to play are very different from those of boys. Girls play at cooking, washing up, being mother with dolls. Boys play with balls, and building things, so that by an early age children have learned what behaviour, even in games, are expected of them.

Imitation

It is rare for the main characters of an action story to be female

The children **imitate** adults, and are encouraged to do so. So the son imitates his father, and in so doing learns traditional view of what manliness is. The girl imitates her mother, so games might involve dressing up in mum's clothes, wearing her high-heeled shoes and putting on her make-up.

Identification

Identification also takes place, with children seeing themselves as their parents, or as heroes/heroines from comics and television. So as well as imitating parents' behaviour, they also play at being their parents/hero figures.

Group pressure

This is applied to children by their friends (peer group) if they fail to act in the right way. Friendships develop along sex lines with separate groups of boys and groups of girls, both playing different sorts of games.

Are there differences in the ways that parents treat their sons and daughters concerning:
a) time to be in at night?
b) places to go to?
c) type of clothes?
Why do they say they do this?

A bedtime story (and a lesson in life)

Combatting sexism or interference?

The Rev W.V. Awdry was as cross as Gordon the Big Engine on a particularly bad day.

At 83, the creator of Thomas the Tank Engine had just heard news that left him feeling far from chuffed.

The people who once paid him £50,000 to put his railway series on TV were mucking about with the storylines again. In particular, they were elevating lesser-known female characters to starlet status to meet the politically correct demands of the Nineties.

Mavis, a diesel engine belonging to the Ffarquhar Quarry Company when Mr Awdry invented her in 1972, was to have a leading role.

Caroline, a rickety old car who featured briefly in one story, was also to get the star treatment as Caroline the Clapped Out Car. Even Nancy, the Guard's pony-tailed daughter, and the Refreshment Lady, who had only ever been seen from behind, were getting their names in lights. ...

Britt Allcroft, the Southampton mother of two behind the TV series and other money-spinning ideas, was unashamed that Thomas's chauvinist world was being turned upside down for a new series of 26 stories being filmed at Shepperton Studios in London.

'Ideally I would like to have far more female engines, but the problem is that they don't feature in Wilbert Awdry's work,' she said. 'However, I'm specifically using stories that have female characters.'

Last night, the gossip in the engine shed was over how Edward the Blue Engine had narrowly escaped a sex change to become, possibly, Alice, the Pink Engine. 'Phew!' said Edward.

Source: *The Daily Mail*, 1994

Do you agree that plots and characters of children's books and videos should reflect a 'politically correct' view of the world?

School

In terms of academic attainment girls have significantly higher levels of achievement than boys, although about the same proportion of males and females eventually go to university. But success in education, as we will see later, is not necessarily linked to success in careers later in life.

As soon as males and females are given choices of subjects to study, they choose quite different ones. Girls are less likely to take Maths, Computing and the natural sciences, more likely to study English, Human Biology and foreign languages. This is even more pronounced at A-level. Those girls who do go on to further education are most likely to be following vocational courses in clerical and caring skills.

There is some evidence that the intellectual abilities of girls and boys are slightly different, with girls being superior in the use of language, and in early adolescence boys develop greater ability in Maths. Even if these differences are natural, however, sociologists still argue that the more important influences on educational attainment of boys and girls are the social ones.

Gender divisions: From school to work

Secondary and higher education

English, maths and history are fairly evenly studied by both sexes, but more girls than boys study biology, French, music and drama, whereas more boys study physics.

Figures from the Department of Education and Science show that girls have a higher pass rate than boys in all GCSE subjects, with the exception of biology and maths.

In higher education, seven times more men than women study computing at university and fewer young women are undergraduates in mathematics, physics and chemistry. However, as traditional jobs decline, boys face restricted prospects through relatively lower percentage success than girls in arts subjects.

Training

The Equal Opportunities Commission says that more boys go into job-related youth training schemes. More than 60 per cent of trainees in Employment training are male.

Young women leaving school are opting for 'traditional female occupations', according to a survey of inner-city schools by the Policy Studies Institute.

It found that of 16-year-old girls who left school for work or training, 40 per cent went into office work, 17 per cent into 'caring' jobs and 16 per cent into hairdressing.

The survey looked at more than 2,500 young people from 34 schools in east and south London, Birmingham, Leeds, Manchester and Merseyside.

Young men who left school went into a broader range of jobs. But more than half went into 'traditionally' male areas: construction, vehicle engineering and joinery or carpentry.

Source: *The Guardian*, 12 September 1994

Work

More men than women go into these jobs: agriculture, forestry, fishing, engineering and construction.

More women than men go into these jobs: education, welfare, health services, clerical work, catering, and many service jobs.

Family

Women with young children tend to take a break from work or work part-time. But having children does not affect the working patterns of men so dramatically.

Only 8 per cent of mothers with children aged 0–4 years are in full-time work and 21 per cent in part-time work.

Eighty-three per cent of fathers with young children are in full-time work and 1 per cent in part-time work.

It has also been found that teachers, like parents, have different expectations of behaviour for boys and girls. Boys are expected to be more boisterous, girls to be quieter and more obedient. As a result, teachers are likely to treat the children differently according to their sex.

The way that teachers act towards girls, and expect different behaviour and academic standards from them, has been called the **hidden curriculum** (a curriculum means the information taught at school). In effect boys and girls are taught different things at school, although it is not officially organised that way.

Pupils' expectations

In education, one of the more important factors which motivates pupils and students is an idea of what future career prospects they may have. These ideas are a result of the wider culture, peer group influence, teachers' views and finally the individual's own desires.

There has been a very significant shift in attitudes over the last 20 years regarding the jobs which are perceived as appropriate to males and females. So females now stay on at school and enter higher education in equal numbers to males. They no longer see marriage and motherhood as the most important 'career' for them. However, women are still concentrated in a narrow range of jobs which reflect the female role in our society, and which they actively *choose*.

At school males and females study different subjects, with females studying languages and social sciences, and males more likely to follow sciences. This relates to future careers where women are concentrated in caring work (teaching, social work, nursing) or in a range of office jobs.

The glass ceiling – role models

Men continue to hold the most highly-paid and influential positions within government and industry. Over 70 per cent of working women hold the lowest-paid jobs. By contrast only 10 per cent of senior managers are female.

The Hansard Society, an educational charity, recently held an inquiry into the problems faced by women seeking promotion to top jobs. It concluded: "For too many women there is a glass ceiling over their aspirations – it allows them to see where they might go, but stops them getting there."

Source: *The Guardian*, 26 March 1991

1   What is the 'glass ceiling'?

2   How can this influence pupils' performance at school, do you think?

Work

Women form about half the workforce today, yet they are seriously under-represented in management and the higher levels of the professions (such as medicine and the law). They earn on average less than 80 per cent of men's wages, and are far more likely to be in part-time work than men. Finally, as we saw earlier, they are more likely to be concentrated in a few areas of employment, particularly clerical and caring work, and the service industries.

The main reason is that women are still expected to be responsible for their children, unlike their husbands who must first have a career and second be a father. This means that women leave work in order to bear children and then care for them. They are then likely to return to work, but will have missed out on the chances of promotion. A second reason was given earlier: women learn at an early age that their main role is to be mothers. School and career choice are less important than marriage and a home. They may later regret this but they initially make this choice.

Male dominance and prejudice against women is also important. Some men like to believe that women are less intelligent, and that really their place is in the home. The result is that women are less likely to be promoted.

Women at work

The 1970 Equal Pay Act promised equal pay for equal work in 1975. ...However, employers have devised a variety of techniques to avoid increasing their wages bills unduly. Strategies like the separation of male and female workers, the attachment of extra 'responsibilities' to male employees (such as heavy lifting), ensures that the differences are maintained.

If the employer does not want a life-long worker, he may choose a woman because it is 'well-known' that they have a higher labour turnover, and are less likely to join a trade union and therefore are easier to dismiss if the necessity arises. ...Employers, along with many others, seem to believe that women do not mind doing boring, routine jobs, because that is where they have traditionally worked. Therefore they tend to choose women for routinely fiddly jobs, because they have 'naturally nimble fingers'.

Source: E.A. Clarke and T. Lawson, *Gender* (Bell & Hyman, 1985)

Employment and gender

Employees and self-employed, by gender and occupation, UK, Spring 1994

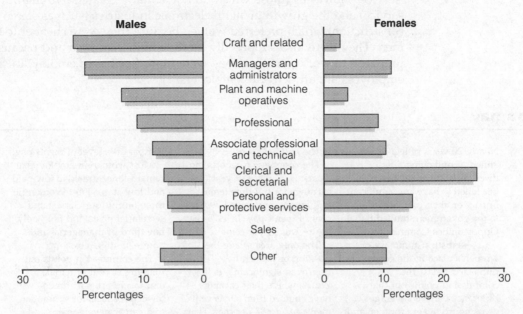

Source: *Social Trends 25* (HMSO, 1995) and Employment Department

1 How have employers managed to overcome the laws relating to equal pay?

2 Why do you think women are more likely to accept repetitive and low-paid employment?

3 Do you agree that women are 'more naturally nimble' than men?

4 According to the chart, what is the most common type of occupation for women?

5 What is the most common type of occupation for men?

6 Which sex has proportionately more jobs in management?

Women and the employment market

Two hundred years ago, women were regarded very much as the equal of men – they worked alongside them in all sorts of labouring work, for instance. However, as the industrial revolution began to require fewer workers, gradually women were pushed out of the industrial workforce and the belief grew that the proper place for a woman was in the home. Feminist sociologists have argued that what was happening here was really a battle of the sexes and the males won, banishing women to the home.

At the turn of the century, less than 30 per cent of the workforce was female. However, the First World War (1914–18) took away the bulk of young men to fight. Women were recalled to the factories where they did all the work men had done. But, with the war over, the jobs were returned to the men. The same thing occurred in the Second World War.

In the 1960s, however, the numbers of women in the workforce began to increase quite noticeably. This reflected the changing attitudes of women themselves. They began to fight against the idea that once they had children they ought not to return to work, instead they began to seek work as soon as the youngest child attended school. Allied to the changing attitudes of women was the growth in 'service' industries (those which do not actually create anything but provide a service) and the growth in 'light' electronic industries (such as stereo or computer construction) which preferred women because they were cheaper to employ than men. They were also supposedly more nimble than men and because they were prepared to work part-time they were more flexible to employ. In short, female employees are attractive to employers.

Women's pay

Nearly 20 years of legislation aimed at outlawing discrimination against women has failed to have any significant impact on their pay, according to the government-funded Equal Opportunities Commission.

In a statistical summary of women's place in the economy published today, the commission points out that the difference between average gross hourly wages for men and women has improved little since equality laws were introduced in the mid-Seventies. ...

The commission reports the "stark fact" that last year earnings for full-time female employees represented 79 per cent of men's pay. In 1975 the figure was 71 per cent.

The only area where the position of women has improved significantly is in Wales, where their earnings have climbed from 69 per cent of men's pay to 84 per cent. That increase, however, mainly reflects a drop in the comparative level of men's pay.

Most women in employment remain concentrated in low-paid and low-status jobs. Women fill three out of four clerical and secretarial posts, but hold only one third of managerial and administrative jobs.

The commission points out that 45 per cent of female employees are part-timers, with fewer prospects for promotion and career development and inferior benefits.

Source: 'Equality laws have failed to close gap in wages' by B. clement in *The Independent*, 3 October 1994

Comparing men and women's earnings

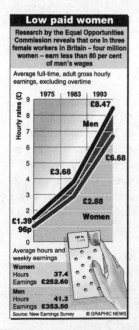

Source: *Cambridge Evening News*, 28 November 1994

1 Has the Equal Pay legislation worked?

2 What proportion of male pay do women receive on average?

3 What sort of work do women perform?

4 Why are women more likely to go into part-time employment?

5 In 1993, what was the average difference between what a man and a woman earned each hour?

6 What differences are there in the number of hours worked for males and females?

7 What effect did this have on the weekly income, according to the information provided?

8 What could be done, in your opinion to combat the differences you have found?

The long route to the top

[The diagram below] shows women's restricted access to higher management grades, with successive steps in the hierarchy having fewer places for women; access to the highest grades has improved in the last 20 years: an increase in the proportion of directors from 1% to 3% is a three-fold increase, but still puts a tiny minority at the top! Almost throughout the professions women are concentrated at lower levels. Women solicitors in private practice are more likely to be assistants, while male solicitors are more likely to be partners. Women are especially under-represented in the judiciary: in 1993 there were 5 women High Court Judges out of 91 and 28 women circuit judges out of 496. ...

The Hansard Society's report on *Women at the Top* found that: 'in any given occupation, and in any given public office, the higher the rank, prestige or influence, the smaller the proportion of women' (Hansard Society 1990:2). Stereotypically, girls leaving school in the 1960s expected a short 'career' in nursing or secretarial jobs, after which motherhood led to a new 'career' as a housewife. These expectations have been confounded as women now in their forties have found themselves drawn back to paid work; the lack of qualifications, confidence, contacts, has often made the route back a hard if exciting one through education, ACCESS courses, degrees. ...

To understand women's working lives, it may be better to rethink career as a lifetime path trodden between paid work in the labour market and unpaid work in the family.

The female share of management, by grade, UK 1974–93

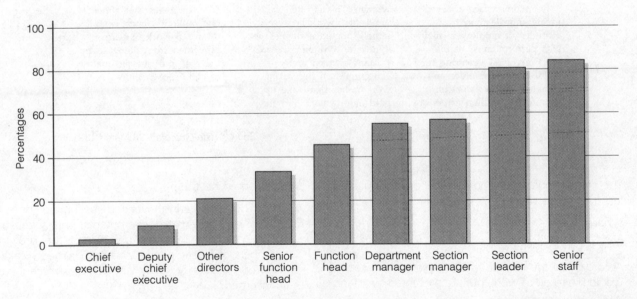

Source: G. Pascall, 'Women on top?' in *Sociology Review*, February 1995

1 What proportion of all chief executives are female?

2 Complete the statement, 'The higher the level of management, ...'

3 What proportion of high court judges are women?

4 How have the expectations of the 1960s been confounded?

5 What are the implications for education?

6 According to the author, what is the best way to understand women's careers?

7 Interview people at your local college on the ACCESS course or, if you can, mature female students at your local university. Is this description accurate?

Domestic labour

Ask anyone what work is and they will probably reply with a description of paid employment, possibly giving the example of a clerk or manual worker. Few people would define housework as 'work'. Yet each day in Britain, millions of women spend a full day in the house, cooking, cleaning, washing and childminding. Each of these tasks by themselves if performed outside the home and paid would be considered a 'job'. In one famous study, *The Sociology of Housework*, Ann Oakley compared the work of housewives to that of car production line workers. She found the two 'jobs' very similar indeed. She concluded that the housewife worked as long as 72 hours each week, far longer than any worker in a factory; that housewives found their jobs very boring; that the amount of physical effort was certainly as great as the manual workers'; that the housewives felt very isolated, having no one to talk to very often, except for young children. The biggest difference, however, was that at the end of the week, the housewife received no wage and her work was not even rewarded by others with the *status* of work.

The invisible work of caring

But women face an even greater hurdle than the attitudes of employers: they also perform most of the work involved in caring for children and for older and disabled people. Most of Britain's six million carers are women. This is often called "invisible" work because it is largely unpaid and does not appear on economic records.

Many women prefer to concentrate on this caring work rather than take up paid employment. But the EOC estimates that almost one million women want to return to work but are prevented from doing so by the cost and uneven quality of child-care facilities.

Source: *The Guardian*, 26 March 1991

1 The official hours that women work are considerably less than those of men. Why is this?

2 What is 'caring' work?

3 Why is caring 'invisible' work?

4 According to the extract what proportion of women would like to go to work; but are prevented by 'caring work'?

5 What prevents them?

6 The issue of caring work is becoming one of increasing concern to governments. This is because of the increase in single parents, of the growing numbers of elderly people and the claimed weakening of the family. Why should governments be concerned?

Parenthood

Once married, a woman finds that she is expected to do the housework and to 'look after' her husband. His career becomes the important one and her role is to have children and be a good mother. A woman who does not want children is regarded as 'odd' and if the house is untidy or dirty, then comments are made concerning *her* laziness.

When a couple has children, it is expected that the woman ought to put the child first, and for the pre-school years she should give up work, or work part-time. People refer to the **maternal instinct** which it is assumed that all women have. However, there is absolutely no evidence to prove that this exists.

Some sociologists have argued that there is increasing equality in the family and that today men and women are equal. But feminists reply that men are still in control and that the family is really a trap for women.

(For a more detailed discussion on relationships in the family, please turn to Chapter 7.)

Housework, image and reality

The media have created an image of what the perfect housewife ought to be like. In a study of magazine advertisements, Millum found that the picture of the ideal woman was of a hardworking housewife who was calm, satisfied with her life, attractive, enjoying doing the housework, with never a hair out of place. The problem is that if a women did not feel this, then she feels guilty, as there has to be something wrong with her. Of course, this view of housework is also taken by all others not directly involved.

'I always say housework's harder work, but my husband doesn't say that at all. I think he's wrong, because I'm going all the time – when his job is finished, it's finished...Sunday he can lie in bed till twelve, get up, get dressed and go for a drink, but my job never changes.'

Source: A. Oakley,
The Sociology of Housework
(Martin Robertson, 1974)

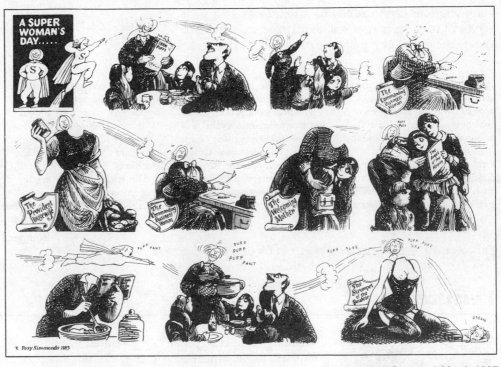

Source: *New Society*, 6 March 1987

1 Look at the cartoon above, what are the images of women portrayed?

2 Do you think that the cartoon presents an accurate picture of the housewife's life, according to your own experience?

3 According to the extract, what happens when women do not achieve this ideal?

4 Is the work of women in the home appreciated as work according to the extract?

5 Do you think this would have any effect on the relationship between husband and wife?

Laws work both ways

Complaints by women about sexual harassment at work have soared to a record high in the past year.

And bosses are having to fork out much more in compensation as the victims take the office pests to courts or tribunals.

There was also a big rise in claims by women for equal pay, the annual report of the Equal Opportunities Commission revealed yesterday.

Chairwoman Kamlesh Bahl

called for new initiatives to tackle "far-reaching and deep-rooted" discrimination against women in many firms.

She said a sustained effort was needed to check the running-down of females in the workplace and in society as a whole.

The report says there was a 58 per cent rise in sexual harassment complaints investigated by the commission last year. Ms Bahl said the

increase – the total went up by 300 to 793 – was largely due to a growing awareness that women can challenge such behaviour and take legal action.

The commission was particularly successful in settling claims by ex-servicewomen dismissed when they became pregnant.

Other victories included:

■ £15,000 was awarded to women clerks at a Ford dealer in Manchester who claimed they

were paid less than male sales staff despite doing similar jobs.

■ £750 compensation was agreed with a woman who was told by a firm that plans for her new kitchen could not be discussed unless her husband was present.

■ £8,500 was paid out to Britain's first female boxing master of ceremonies Lisa Trayler, who was told being an MC was not a job that should be done by a woman.

Source: *The Daily Express*, 23 June 1994

Have you ever been sexually harassed? Conduct a small survey of students and/or staff (both male and female) to gauge the extent of the problem and its consequences.

A woman's right to be fitted for a bra or corset by another woman, without men present, was at issue at an industrial tribunal in Reading yesterday.

In what the Equal Opportunities Commission is funding as a test case, a man took the lingerie chain Contessa to the tribunal for alleged sexual

discrimination in refusing him a job as a regional manager.

The firm said its policy was not to employ men in the post because managers often had to help out as branch assistants. ...

But the man, Leslie Rowson, aged 46, formerly a regional sales manager for another company, earning £32,000 a

year, had been out of work nearly three years and had applied for more than 400 jobs. After being refused by Contessa, alongside 12 other male applicants, he investigated the decision.

This enabled him to argue that managers were never required to work as assistants in

at least one Contessa shop or in the rival Marks and Spencer chain. Then he complained to the commission.

Single-sex job recruitment is allowed by an exemption to the Sex Discrimination Act if it can be shown to be essential for "privacy and decency".

Source: *The Guardian*, 25 September 1994

Do you think Leslie Rowson should win his case?

Leisure

Virtually all leisure pursuits are related to gender roles. How many girls play football, for instance? And if they do, what sort of jokes are made about them? The gender roles of our society mean that men ought to be interested in 'tough' games (rugby) or those linked to pubs (snooker), and women ought to be interested in 'feminine' activities such as the caring ones of knitting or cooking, or the 'attractive' one of dancing.

Even in relationships, the girls are supposed to attract the boys to them, not to be the aggressive ones who introduce themselves to the boys and 'pick them up'. A girl who does this is seen as a bit pushy. When it comes to sexual relationships, girls have to be careful about their reputation. Those who have sexual relations with lots of boys are seen as 'scrubbers' or sluts, whereas boys who go with lots of girls are universally admired (or envied).

1 Choose any one of tonight's television programmes. Watch it carefully and write a brief description of the characters and roles of the main male and female characters. In class compare the types of parts females and males typically play.

2 Compare the contents and stories of comics/magazines for males and females. What happens to the stories if you change the sex of the main characters?

3 Find out the proportion of male to female teachers/lecturers in your school/college, who are in the senior posts, such as heads of department and principal/headteacher.

4 Conduct a survey of the careers that people in your school/college year would like to follow. Do clear sex differences emerge?

5 Find out the proportions of males to females doing science subjects, sociology and office skills. What differences, if any, are there by sex?

6 Draw a diagram summarising the experience of gender for women.

7 Write a paragraph, or sketch a diagram to show how you see your future.

8 Comparing them in class, can you tell which are written by males and which by females – without reading out the names?

Divisions between women

When we discuss the situation of women, we have implied that all women share a common situation. This is not completely true, however, for there are many divisions between women based on race, religion, nationality and social class.

Women across the world

It is not just in the developed world that women provide a massive contribution to the economic and social life of society. However, if western women have gradually begun to change attitudes and to challenge their economic exploitation, their gains may not have been shared with women from other, less well-developed nations.

According to the United Nations, women grow more than half the food produced by developing nations: over 80 per cent of the food for sub-Saharan Africa and almost 60 per cent of that for Asia. Women also collect most of the water needed to keep families and crops in these countries alive.

In some families, women are in charge of all the farming work because the men have migrated to towns in search of paid jobs. The Food and Agriculture Organisation of the United Nations estimates that a third of rural households in developing countries are headed by women. ...

There is also a growing trend for women to migrate to towns in search of factory work. These factories produce goods for export to Britain and other western countries. Many developing countries are trying to expand their industrial base as a means of earning much-needed foreign currency.

For example, much of the cheap clothing sold in British shops comes from countries such as the Philippines, Taiwan, Indonesia and Bangladesh. The clothes are made in factories which employ up to 90 per cent female labour.

The goods produced are cheap because rates of pay in countries such as the Philippines are lower than in Britain and because female labour is even cheaper than male. ...

Most women work for only two to three years in these factories, partly because the work is so wearing. For instance, many South Korean women are employed to put together the component parts of hi-fi stereos and other electrical goods. They have to spend long hours looking through microscopes, which can lead to eye problems.

Source: *The Guardian*, 26 March 1991

Race divisions

About 17 per cent of women from ethnic minorities are out of work, compared with 7 per cent among white females. The highest jobless rate is 28 per cent for Pakistani and Bangladeshi women.

Social class divisions

Jane Anderson, 24, is on an access course studying fashion and textiles at City and Islington College, north London. She was born in Linwood, near Glasgow, and left school at 16. Her parents are divorced. Both are unemployed.

I left school in 1987, age 16, with three O-levels: art, secretarial studies and home economics. My parents were divorcing, and school was hard. I went on to do a couple of YTS jobs, one as a dental assistant and one giving car insurance quotes. I stayed there for about three years but I was treated like a dog's-body; in the end, I resigned. ...

When I was 20, I moved to London. I still had no job. I must have lived in about six or seven places, with friends. What did I do all day? Not much. Sat around and watched telly. I became a bit of a soap addict. In the evenings we saw bands. I thought I was having fun.

Gradually, my attitude changed. I got bored; I was broke. Nothing was going on for me at all, but I couldn't find a way out. When you're out of work, you've no way of getting experience. ...

Because I'd been unemployed for so long, the employment office put me on a Restart course; out of 15 people on the course, I was the only one accepted into college.

I started at City and London last year. Next year, I'm intending to do a degree course in theatrical costume at the London College of Fashion. ...

I know what I want to do, and I'm going to do it. I have enormous drive, I want to better myself, and I'm ambitious. I'm going to have to study a lot when I get to the London College of Fashion, but that doesn't put me off. I couldn't be without an aim, not after being unemployed for so long. If I had all the money in the world, I'd still want to have a job.

I'm still skint and I still wear clothes from charity shops, but I know I'll own a house one day, and I know I'll be a success. I feel so proud of what I've achieved.

I'll show people how serious I am about my career. I'll have kids, but not until I'm established. Of course I want to make money. Who doesn't? Am I a product of the Thatcher years? I don't take any interest in politics whatsoever. I've simply found out what I really want to do with my life. I don't want to end up like all my girlfriends back in Linwood have ended up, pushing babies around.

Bryony Gibbins will be 20 next month. She was educated at Roedean, a girl's private boarding school in East Sussex. She has nine GCSEs, two A-levels and an A/S-level (equivalent to half an A-level). She lives in her own flat in Kingston and attends St James's secretarial college in Kensington. Her parents are divorced. Her mother works for a travel PR agency, her father is a chartered accountant at KPMG.

I was at Roedean for seven years. I loved it. I suppose I didn't know anything different. I wanted to teach primary science, so when I left Roedean I went straight on to study for a degree in education at Kingston University. I left after two weeks. It wasn't for me. It was all about how to teach kids English or geography. When I left, I was a bit worried about what my parents might say, particularly my father. He was fine about it.

I changed to a degree in applied biology and chemistry, with the intention of doing a PGCE [post-graduate certificate in teaching] at the end. I failed the end-of-year exams, so I had to leave the course. I failed them accidentally-on-purpose. I didn't know what I wanted to do, but I did know that I didn't want to be at university. I didn't like being a student. I was lost. No one knew my name. I felt like I was simply a student identity number.

My father has bought me this flat in Kingston, where I live with my boyfriend and a tenant. It cost about £60,000. My father set up a trust fund for me when I was born, which gives me an allowance of £500 a month.

I know that's quite a lot, but I still have an overdraft. The fund pays for things like my car, which cost £6,000. It's a J-reg Renault Clio. I'm half way through my secretarial course in Kensington.

The fees are £2,000 a term, which my father also pays for. You learn shorthand and typing and word processing. It's quite a smart place. You have to wear skirts. I think it will give me a good start.

I don't worry about not having a degree. So many graduates can't find jobs anyway. I think secretarial skills will get me a good job.

Until then I can live off my trust fund. Hopefully, it'll go on until I can find a job. I can't get my hands on all the money until I'm 25 – my father knows me too well!

Ambitions? Well, I don't want to be the chairman of ICI. I'd be quite happy to plod along. I want to do something in the City, like being a PA to someone in finance or banking. That's where the money is. I don't know very much about finance or banking. I don't know if that matters very much.

I am pretty optimistic about the future. I expect I'll get married when I'm in my late twenties, and have kids.

I don't think I'll work when I have kids – at first. I'll have a nanny and I'll probably pack them off to boarding school. Then I might go back to work. I'll live in a nice London town house.

No, I can't ever see a time when I'll be hard up.

What do I think if people might criticise me for having an easy life? Mind your own business.

Source: *The Independent*, 26 January 1995

You can see from reading the above extracts that there are major differences between women, as well as shared problems.

1 Some sociologists have suggested that the divisions of race, religion, nationality and social class may be more important than gender. What do you think?

2 Write down a list of similarities and differences.

3 Do you think class is as important as ever, reading this? Or do women 'share' a distinct social position?

Women and violence

Sexual assaults

Most people believe that sexual attacks are performed by strangers at night in deserted streets, yet this is not the case. The majority of sexual attacks involve people who are known to each other, including family members, and about one third of rapes take place in the homes of the victims.

Smart suggests that rape should not be seen as being performed by disturbed men, but instead suggests that rape is merely an *extension* of normal sexual bargaining which occurs in UK society. Socialisation of women is to stress their allure to men. On the other hand, men are expected to initiate sexual encounters and women to at least make a show of 'resistance'. Therefore rape can be seen not as in opposition to the values of our society, but as an extension of them.

Domestic violence

This is the use of violence against women by their partners within the home and, just like rape, there is assumed to be huge under-reporting in the official statistics. This seems to be caused partly by female partners feeling reluctant to report crime and, when there is a complaint, the police may be reluctant to arrest unless the violence seems to be quite 'serious'.

Domestic violence – The reality

Anyway, I was very tired that night and I went to bed early. Then he came to bed, and my little girl woke up, because she'd wet the bed. Anyway I went to see to her and I took the sheet and I moved it round so that I moved her off the wet part. And I went back to bed. Anyway she cried again and he went out to see to her. And I didn't know what had hit me.

He came in and he ripped the clothes off me and grabbed me by the feet, and dragged me out of bed. And he kicked me out into the hall and he called me all these names, and he said, "How dare you leave that child with a wet sheet on the bed." And he threw me into her bedroom. So I did the little girl, changed bed all right round again, and then I went into the bathroom and

locked the door, because I was so upset. He came and knocked the bolt off and he dragged me back to our bedroom to make the bed. And I remember I had my dressing gown on and he threw me all the way down the hall and he ripped my dressing gown and then he threw me on the floor and he was kicking me and I was sitting there screaming. And then he said

he'd give me half an hour and then I was to go back into the bedroom and I was to apologise and he meant apologise properly. He put one arm round my throat, and he slapped me and punched me and he said, "How dare you look at me as if I'm repulsive to you. You're my wife, and I'll do what the bloody hell I like to you".

Source: Pahl, *Marital Violence and Public Policy* (Routledge & Kegan Paul, 1985)

Explanations for violence and sexual assaults

Sociologists have similar types of explanation for violence and sexual assault. Basically they argue that these are not performed by abnormal men as generally assumed, but that they are simple *extremes* of behaviour that occur very often. In the case of sexual assault (remember this is often between people who know each other), men are constantly exhorted to see women in sexual terms by the media and to belive that they know 'what women really want', and it is claimed that males may very often use forms of 'coercion' to obtain sex from partners.

When it comes to violence, sociologists argue that violence against female partners is deep in our culture. Historically, the use of a limited degree of violence by husbands has been culturally and legally acceptable, and it is only very slowly that this is being challenged.

Sexuality

Beauty

What is considered to be attractiveness varies across societies and time, with some societies stressing slimness, others weight. Sexual attraction is also attributed to different part of the body, so that the breasts can be regarded as highly sexual or as of no interest whatsoever, yet other societies have stressed ankles, necks and ears.

Normality and abnormality

The traditional assumptions regarding the 'natural' nature of our sexuality have come to be questioned in recent years, and those who have different sexual orientations from heterosexuals, such as gays and lesbians, have used the successful feminist attack upon traditional male attitudes as their model of how to change our assumptions regarding the 'normality' of heterosexuality.

Gays and lesbians claim that anything up to about 10 per cent of the population share their sexual orientations. In a series of studies of sexuality in the USA during the 1950s, Kinsey found that 37 per cent of men had engaged in homosexual acts, and 15 per cent of women. The idea that there is any normal form of sexuality has been challenged by cross-cultural studies, with virtually any form of sexual activity being regarded as normal, or at least 'acceptable' in one society or another.

The idea that there are quite distinctive sexual 'types' of people, such as heterosexuals and homosexuals and lesbians, seems to be a relatively modern phenomenon in Europe. For although various acts were condemned or thought of as illegal, it was the *acts* which were condemned. The term 'homosexual', for example, was not used until the mid-nineteenth century and it is only since then that there has developed the belief that people are *either* homosexual or heterosexual. Today, in many non-Western cultures this clear cut division does not exist. For example, among the Butak people of Sumatra, homosexual activity is seen as the normal form of sexuality for young males before they marry when they take on a predominantly heterosexual role.

Gay rights?

A lesbian who gave birth to a daughter after a do-it-yourself pregnancy said yesterday: 'It's time people stopped talking about traditional families. They are in the minority now.'

Natalie Wilson, 24, conceived her child after a gay man provided sperm which her lover implanted with an hypodermic needle.

In effect, this means the mother of a 6lb 10oz baby remains a virgin. She has changed her surname by deed poll so it is the same as her lover Denise Wilson, 26, and they plan to act as the baby's parents.

The biological father has abdicated any rights or responsibilities to the three-day-old girl, named Ellesse Denise, and they intend to preserve his anonymity to prevent the Child Support Agency demanding maintenance from him.

Cuddling her daughter at home near Cannock, Staffordshire, Natalie looked drawn but elated after a 17-hour labour. She said: 'We feel like a real family now. This has made my life complete.

Natalie said: 'We just want people to accept us for what we are and leave us alone. They should give us a chance to give Ellesse a good life. Really, I am no different to a single mother – and there were more single mums at the hospital than married women.'

Natalie was 15 when she met Denise, then 17, as they socialised with friends. Natalie had fledgling relationships with a couple of boys 'but I never felt comfortable with them'.

Several months after they first met, Natalie and Denise kissed for the first time. Six months later, they were living together in a bedsit. Nearly a year later, Natalie told her parents of her true feelings. She said: 'They had probably guessed anyway.'

They are drawing up legal documents so that Denise can be formally recognised as a 'legal guardian'. The father has signed forms to say he will not demand access as long as they do not demand maintenance.

They plan to tell the infant her history when they think she is able to comprehend it. Natalie said: 'We will always reinforce the idea to her that she is a special child. We will look after her properly. She has got uncles. I have lots of straight male friends.

'What's so good about ordinary families? Those parents often abuse their children and society doesn't condemn them as it should.

'Frankly, I hope she grows up straight rather than gay. Gay people have too many problems but maybe people will be less prejudiced by the time she's an adult.

'Come back when she is 18. I'm sure people will be pleased.

Source: *The Daily Mail*, 19 January 1995

1 Do you agree that the couple should have a child?

2 Do you think that their sexual orientation will influence the child's?

3 Do you think it matters anyway?

4 Why do you think Natalie said that she hoped her daughter would grow up to be 'straight'?

5 Is Natalie right when she says 'traditional families are in the minority now'?

These charts show some of the results of a national opinion poll.

According to a 1992 Harris poll, public opinion is moving towards equal treatment for homosexuals.

Age of consent

Should the age of consent be the same for everyone irrespective of their gender or sexual orientation, or not?

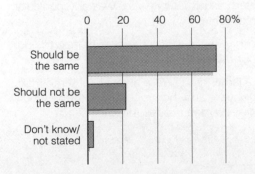

Rights

Should gay men and lesbians have the same rights under the law as everyone else?

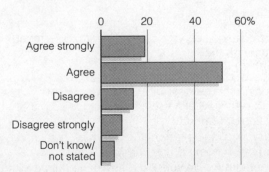

Child care

However, over 40% of those interviewed believed that gay men and lesbians who are suitably qualified in every other way should not be allowed to foster or adopt children.

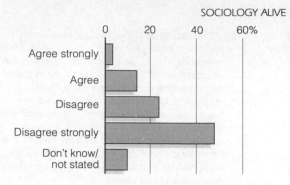

Source: *The Guardian* (Education section), 29 June 1993

1 What percentage of people think every sexual orientation should have the same age of consent?

2 What percentage agree that gays and lesbians should have the same rights as everyone else?

3 How does the chart of results about child care appear to contradict the other charts?

Intolerance and harassment of homosexuals are rife, and most believe they receive less favourable treatment by the police and that the courts are biased against them, according to a survey published today.

Nearly half of the homosexual men and women questioned in the study, by Social & Community Planning Research, an independent research institute, said insults had been shouted at them in public. One quarter had been physically threatened or attacked, and 21 per cent had been harassed at work.

Many were forced to hide their sexuality because of discrimination.

The study is the first to examine attitudes towards homosexuality using a random national sample of homosexual and heterosexual people instead of relying on the experience of activists....

The report finds that society is more tolerant of lesbians than of male homosexuals. While 54 per cent of the lesbians had never encountered discrimination, only 38 per cent of them could say that.

The researchers believe this is because lesbians are seen as less of a threat to society.

At work, 53 per cent of those surveyed said they kept their sexual identity secret from colleagues, and 44 per cent said they concealed it when applying for jobs.

Almost all of the 116 male homosexuals and lesbians believed employers would refuse job applications from gay candidates, and 96 per cent worried that they would lose their job if their employer discovered their sexual preference. ...

Although more than half of the heterosexual sample agreed that homosexuals made excellent teachers and youth leaders, one-quarter thought they should be banned from working with children.

There was particular concern about homosexuals working with young children. More than 45 per cent thought it was never acceptable for a male homosexual to be a primary school teacher, and 34 per cent believed lesbians should never be allowed to teach in primary schools.

Source: *The Guardian*, 22 May 1995

1 What percentage of homosexual men and women had been:
   a) physically threatened?
   b) shouted at?

2 What percentage keep their sexual identity a secret at work? Why do they do so?

3 a) Describe the methodology used in this study, including the number of people questioned.
   b) Are there any weaknesses in the methodology that you could suggest?
   c) Can you suggest alternative ways of gathering information from homosexuals and lesbians? What advantages would your alternative methods have?

4 Who believed they had suffered more discrimination – males or females? Can you suggest a reason for this?

5 Of the heterosexuals interviewed, was any particular concern highlighted?

6 Explain your view on this to the person next to you. Explain your reasons.

7 Report to a larger group. Take a vote in order to make a group decision, and then report back to the whole group. What do most groups think?

The growth of a gay culture

In recent years, gay men and lesbians have increasingly developed an alternative culture, which rejects the negative images of them in the wider society.

The National Newspaper for Lesbians and Gay Men

The PINK Paper

29 Apr 1994   Issue 325

Gay men in Manchester demonstrate after officers drag half-dressed men into police vans during raid

Police arrest 13 in club swoop

Gay men in Manchester are in uproar over a police raid on the city's Mineshaft club on Saturday night. After two weeks of undercover surveillance at the club, uniformed and plain clothes officers raided the Mineshaft at about 1.30am. Armed with warrants, they arrested 13 men.

Within hours, activists had called a public meeting which attracted 100 people and over 200 joined a protest rally on Tuesday lunchtime this week.

Police said they carried out the operation after allegations that men were having sex in a backroom at the club and customers were smoking cannabis. One man was charged with a public order offence, another was cautioned for obstruction, another cautioned under the public order laws and eight men accepted cautions for gross indecency. Two others were released without charge from the city's Bootle Street police station later on Sunday morning.

But the circumstances of the arrests have prompted uproar in the city with gay campaigners and activists insisting that the incident has damaged relations with the police after what had been acknowledged as a steadily improving situation since the retirement of Chief Constable James Anderton.

Paul Fairweather, Chair of the Greater Manchester Lesbian and Gay Police Consultation Group described the police action as "completely over the top. I had been led to believe by the current Chief Constable that heavy-handed policing of the lesbian and gay community had gone out with Anderton. I call upon David Wilmot to publicly re-affirm his personal commitment to the equal treatment of lesbians and gay men."

Greater Manchester Police declined to issue any further comment on the raid. But police are considering prosecuting the Mineshaft's owner, Michael Snailham, for running a disorderly house.

Eyewitnesses described the police raid as frantic. One man who was cautioned for gross indecency said officers shouted "Cuff 'em, cuff 'em" as they invaded the backroom.

"One man was even dragged out with his trousers round his ankles and we were all bundled into vans before being taken away. It was shocking and disgraceful," the eyewitness said.

Other men were not allowed to retrieve their clothes from the club before being taken out in handcuffs. Other customers said police wore protective clothing and were told over their radios to "watch out for disease."

Michael Snailham was in the club during the raid and flew to Tenerife the following day. He was unavailable for comment as the Pink Paper went to press. In his absence, detectives were interviewing the club's manager, Phil Burke, about the incident.

Paul Fairweather said he expected councillors from the Labour-controlled city council, which has a good relationship with the gay community, to attend Tuesday's demonstration. There were fears, he said, that the arrests might mark a change in police attitudes towards lesbians and gay men in Manchester.

Inspector Tom Cross, Manchester police's lesbian and gay liaison officer admitted that the raid "could only damage relations. There's no doubt the incident is a setback and no-one could deny that." He denied there had been an increase in police presence in the city's pubs and clubs.

Spaced out and proud: Two cybermen from the Sisterhood of Karn lesbian and gay Dr. Who fan club landed at St. Paul's Passage in London on Sunday. Wearing originals from the BBC series they were joined by K9 and a Sea-Devil. The club hopes to find earthlings to donate material for their Pride costumes.

PIC ANTONIO CARRASO

Chapter 5

RACE AND ETHNICITY

This chapter covers:
- Race – myth and reality
- Immigration to Britain
- Race and life chances
- Explanations for racial prejudice
- Combatting discrimination.

Race – myth and reality

The whole topic of race and immigration is a minefield of passions and prejudices where even the language used is dangerous if not handled properly. The term 'race' has a long history of abuse. The idea that such a thing as a pure racial group exists is dangerous nonsense. There is a very general division of people into three broad and overlapping groups – negroid, mongoloid and caucasoid. However, in practice it is very hard to distinguish these groups from one another. The attempts of the Nazis to distinguish 'Aryan' people from other 'races' was a failure.

Sociologists tend to use the terms **ethnic groups** or **ethnic minorities** to distinguish people from each other. By these terms they mean groups of people who share distinctive cultures which are usually different from the culture of the majority of the people living in that society. If they use the term 'race', it has this meaning rather than any biological one.

In Britain there are very many ethnic groups, but some groups have drawn very little attention at all; the many thousands of Italians for instance, who settled in Bedfordshire during the 1950s. While other groups, particularly people of Afro-Caribbean origin, Indians, Pakistanis and Bangladeshis, have been paid great attention. The common characteristic of those groups who have attracted much attention is their skin colour. So sociologists, following the lead of the leaders of these ethnic groups, commonly refer to all of them under the terms 'Blacks' and/or 'Asians'. Clearly this glosses over the large differences between different ethnic groups, but it does allow us to talk about the common problems resulting from the prejudice that they all face.

Immigration to Britain

The historical background

Britain has always had a steady inflow and outflow of people. In the last century, Jews came here fleeing from the persecution they faced in central Europe, while the Irish came in to escape from the terrible poverty there. Incidentally, the single largest immigrant group today remains the Irish.

The immigration which led to the presence of people of Afro-Caribbean origin, Indians and Pakistanis in Britain can be divided into three phases.

From the end of the Second World War until 1961

Afro-Caribbean people were the first to come to Britain, and then from the mid-1950s they were joined in ever-increasing numbers by Indians and Pakistanis.

Why? Britain experienced a period of great prosperity in the 1950s; in fact there were too many jobs for the workers available. Afro-Caribbean people and then Asians were encouraged to come here to take the jobs that the British did not want. The people of Afro-Caribbean origin, in particular, thought of Britain as their 'motherland' where they would be very welcome.

From 1961 to 1972

There was a sharp decrease in the numbers of immigrants from the West Indies, but the numbers of Indian and Pakistani immigrants remained fairly high. However, to get the scale of immigration in proportion, by 1962 only 0.5 per cent of the population were non-white immigrants.

Why? In 1962 an Act of Parliament limited the numbers of immigrants allowed in. Effectively only those with jobs who had skills we wanted were allowed to enter Britain. Because Indians tended to be more educated, a greater number of them continued to come. Also, the wives and dependants of immigrants already settled here were allowed to join them.

From 1972 to the present

Immigration from the West Indies was extremely low. Indian, Pakistani and Bangladeshi immigration fell overall.

Why? The relatives of Asian immigrants already here continued to come, though in small and decreasing numbers. Sudden rises in 1972 and 1976 were caused by African governments throwing Asians out; as they held British passports, the British government reluctantly accepted them.

Today, only about 4500 Asians are allowed to settle here each year, and only about 5 per cent of the population are black immigrants or their British children/ grandchildren.

Why did immigrants want to come to Britain?

Apart from a short period of about seven years, there has always been a greater number of people leaving Britain to live abroad than entering. Those who came did so for a combination of the following reasons.

Push reasons

They may have experienced dreadful poverty in their original country and hoped to find a better life in Britain. This is the main reason for most West Indian and Pakistani immigration. They may have suffered persecution and been forced to leave, such as the Asians who were thrown out of Uganda.

Pull reasons

Because of labour shortages in the 1950s, immigrants from the Commonwealth were encouraged to come to Britain. The British textile industry, for example, has relied upon cheap immigrant labour to survive. The strong family ties amongst Asian immigrants meant that close relatives have been brought to Britain wherever possible. Over two-thirds of Indian, Pakistani and Bangladeshi immigrants come to join relatives already settled here.

Citizens

It may have been useful once to examine the problems faced by the ethnic minorities in terms of them being 'immigrants', but this is no longer so. The majority of all Blacks and Asians living in Britain are British-born citizens; they are not immigrants, and indeed they are now second or third generation citizens.

- **Racial prejudice:** when people are disliked simply because they belong to a particular ethnic group
- **Racism:** the belief in the idea of the existence of distinctive 'races' and that some races are superior to others
- **Racial discrimination (racialism):** when people are treated unequally simply because they belong to a particular ethnic group

1 Are you racially prejudiced?

2 Would you go out with an Indian boy/girl?
      with a Pakistani boy/girl?
      with a West Indian boy/girl?
      with a White boy/girl?
   If the answer to any of these is 'No', give your reasons.

3 In a recent survey, the majority of those questioned believed that there is racism in Britain today. In a different survey, 35 per cent admitted to being prejudiced themselves in some way.

As an exercise, choose ten people outside your class and ask them to categorise themselves by 'ethnic group' and ask them the questions above. Compare the results. Do any patterns emerge?

Views on race and racism

A national study by *The Independent* and National Opinion Poll (NOP) found the following results. (All figures are percentages.)

Racism in Britain

Do you think Britain as a society is:	Whites	Responses by Afro-Caribbean	Asians
Very racist	10	26	6
Fairly racist	57	53	50
Fairly non-racist	26	14	28
Completely non-racist	4	3	6

Compared with ten years ago, do you think Britain today is:			
Much more racist	11	9	9
A little more racist	17	10	18
About the same	28	25	20
A little less racist	33	39	28
Much less racist	6	9	8

Treatment by authorities

Do you think non-whites are treated better, worse or the same as whites by:	Whites	Responses by Afro-Caribbeans	Asians
Employers			
Better	9	1	3
Worse	39	67	42
Same	44	22	44
The police			
Better	7	0	2
Worse	48	75	45
Same	36	16	40
Schools			
Better	14	1	2
Worse	13	38	15
Same	61	48	74
The courts			
Better	10	1	2
Worse	24	57	19
Same	55	26	53

Race relations

Do you agree or disagree with the following statements:

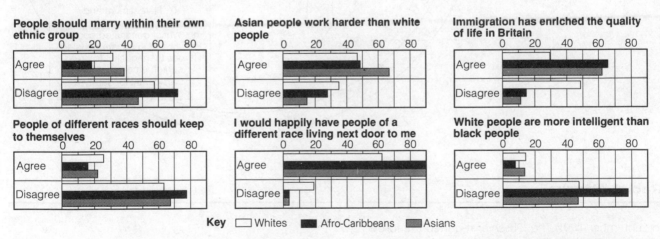

Key ☐ Whites ■ Afro-Caribbeans ▨ Asians

Source: *The Independent*, 7 July 1991

1 What proportion of each group believe that Britain is 'very' or 'fairly' racist?

2 Are there any differences between the three groups?

3 Do you think Britain is a racist society? Explain your answers.

4 Overall, is there a belief that Britain is becoming less racist?

5 Which group is more likely to believe that 'non-whites' receive worse treatment from employers, the police, schools and the courts?

6 Look at the questions under the section on race relations. Describe the patterns that emerge.

7 You might consider conducting a small-scale study asking the questions in the extract. This is a sensitive issue, so discuss whether you wish to do it first. If you do, see if black and Asian students asking white people get different replies from white students.

Ethnic ghettos?

Although Black and Asian people form only 5 per cent of the total British population, they are concentrated in a relatively few areas of a few major conurbations, in particular the Midlands, London and its surroundings, and West Yorkshire.

What influences the pattern of settlement of the ethnic minorities?

The formation of ghettos in British cities

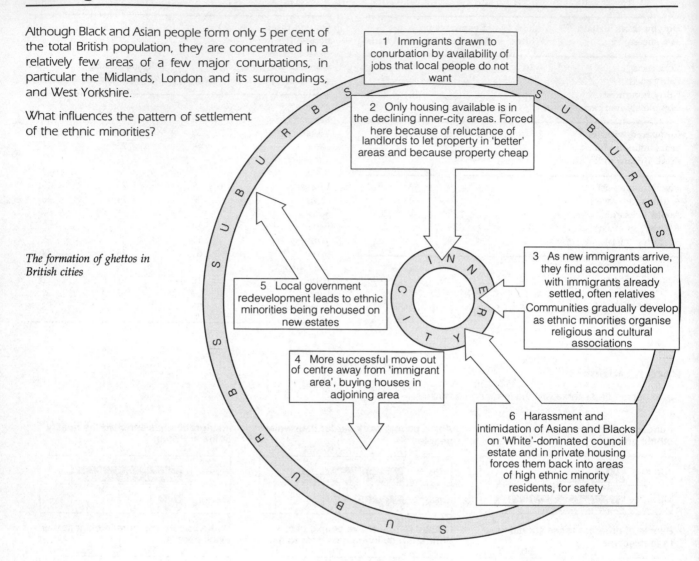

1 Immigrants drawn to conurbation by availability of jobs that local people do not want

2 Only housing available is in the declining inner-city areas. Forced here because of reluctance of landlords to let property in 'better' areas and because property cheap

3 As new immigrants arrive, they find accommodation with immigrants already settled, often relatives
Communities gradually develop as ethnic minorities organise religious and cultural associations

5 Local government redevelopment leads to ethnic minorities being rehoused on new estates

4 More successful move out of centre away from 'immigrant area', buying houses in adjoining area

6 Harassment and intimidation of Asians and Blacks on 'White'-dominated council estate and in private housing forces them back into areas of high ethnic minority residents, for safety

Racial attacks

In September 1992 *The Observer* reported the following incidents of racist violence that occurred over a period of just a few months that year.

West London: Iranian refugee beaten up by white youths. Required plastic surgery; White youths hurl 13-year-old black boy off estate walkway.
Euston: Series of assaults on black people by white youths in cars.
Norbury: Afghan refugee Ruhullah Aramesh murdered

after attack by 15 white youths wielding iron bars and clubs.
Eltham: Asian youth, Rohit Duggal, 16, stabbed to death by white youth.
Plumstead: Asian man, a Mosque elder aged 60, seriously assaulted outside his front door.
Charlton: Mosque set on fire,

second time in two years.
Tower Hamlets: Murder of Tamil refugee Panchadcharam Sahitharan after attack four days earlier by white youths wielding baseball bats.
Newham: Somali boy stabbed; Bengali family fired at by white neighbour armed with sawn-off shotgun; Nigerian refugee

woman, 24, punched and kicked. Graffiti sprayed on car; Ugandan woman, single parent, verbally abused and battery acid poured on home; Black African refugee man punched, kicked, beaten, abused after speaking out at a tenants' meeting; Single mother from Uganda attacked by neighbours. Repeatedly beaten on head with milk bottles. Boyfriend, also Ugandan, helps but arrested by police. Assailants not arrested. No charges laid; Refugee from Mauritius beaten and threatened every Wednesday; Refugee family from Zaire moved out of home after repeated harassment. During first day in new home, neighbours forced way into back garden and dug grave, saying children would be killed and put into it; Somali woman repeatedly harassed by gang of white youths. Mooned at, verbally threatened, constantly

called 'Somali cunt'. Excrement put through windows.
Forest Gate: Ugandan man, aged 28, repeatedly assaulted inside and outside a pub by 10–15 white men. Forced to drink own urine. Dislocated jaw, severe concussion, ripped lip and nostrils. Saved by passing bus driver.
Ilford: Asian woman, aged 40, set on fire waiting for a bus.
Greenwich: Arson attack on Sikh Temple; Ceremonial flag of Hindu Temple burnt.
Hounslow: Somali family, the Kahins, moved out of house following serious arson attack while inside; Somali family —

single mother, four boys and a girl — attacked inside their home by gang of four white men armed with knives and iron bars. Eleven-year-old boy, Abderahman Dahir, needed 23 stitches after stabbing; disabled Somali man, Suliman Farah, 21, savagely beaten, first in supermarket, then in High Street, by three white men. No one helped him.
Manchester: Asian taxi driver and shopkeeper Mohammed Sarwar and Siddik Dada murdered by whites; Councillors sent abusive Ku-Klux-Klan literature through the post. Describes gay people

as 'human maggots'.
Rochdale: Nine people found guilty after 10-hour attack on Pakistani shop; Asian taxi driver escapes from house after arson attack on home.
Birmingham: Racist playground bullies 'hang' Asian youth from basketball net; Asian cabbie Ashiq Hussain, 21, stabbed to death.
Walsall: Hooded Ku-Klux-Klan men hold cross-burning ceremony.
Sheffield: Somali man, aged 22, stabbed by four white youths; Somali child, aged 14, badly beaten.

Source: *The Observer*, 13 September 1992

A rising tide of race attacks and racial hatred is threatening the fabric of British society, an all-party committee of MPs reported yesterday.

The Common Home Affairs Select Committee said in a report on racism that urgent action, including new laws, was needed to combat the growing problem. ...

There were an estimated 140,000 incidents in 1992, of which only 7,000 or 8,000 were reported to the police. However racist attacks and harassment represented less than 2 per cent of all crime. The low level of reporting was partly because

some black people believe the police are racist and fail to take complaints seriously, said the committee, which is chaired by the Conservative MP Sir Ivan Lawrence.

The police service, however, had taken "considerable steps" to combat racism in its ranks, the report said. But the committee emphasised that more should be done to encourage black people to join the police. Only 1.53 per cent of the officers in England and Wales were black — less than a quarter of the proportion of the country's ethnic population. In Kent there are only 11 black officers out of

3,171. ...

The report follows a court case on Monday in which three men were jailed for a total of more than 11 years for beating, stabbing and running over a black man with a car in east London because he was with a white woman.

In another recent case, which was criticised for its leniency by anti-racist groups, an official of the British National Party was given a three-month jail sentence after being convicted for his part in a savage attack on a black man.

Source: 'MPs call for new laws to tackle wave of violence' by J. Bennetts in *The Independent*, 23 June 1994

1 What was the estimated number of racially-motivated 'incidents' in 1992?

2 Were these generally reported to the police? Give reasons to support your answer.

3 What proportion of police officers are drawn from the black and Asian communities?

4 Does this reflect their proportion of the population as a whole?

5 Part of the original article in *The Independent* said that the MPs recommended that a new offence be created for racially-motivated violence carrying a maximum five year jail sentence, and that racial harassment should carry a maximum of 12 months instead of the current £1000 fine. Both of these recommendations were turned down by the government at the time.
What is your opinion? Should there be a special offence for racially-motivated attacks? If so, will it help to stop racially-motivated attacks?

Race and life chances

- **Life chances:** refers to the possibilities a person has at birth of obtaining a high standard of living and general success in life

Being Black or Asian can powerfully influence the course and quality of a person's life in our society.

Work

Black and Asian workers are likely to be in semi-skilled and unskilled manual occupations. They are heavily under-represented in the professions (such as law and medicine) and in management posts. They are less likely to get promoted. They are more likely to have jobs involving shift work. They have higher unemployment rates than Whites. The most successful groups are those from African Asian backgrounds who are usually well-educated. Where Asians do break out of manual work, they tend to run small, family-based businesses requiring long hours of work, such as grocers' shops.

Why? A major reason is racial discrimination, but also because older immigrants with their poorer educational standards and lack of English were prepared to take the worst jobs. Also, certain industries, such as textiles deliberately recruited Pakistani and Bangladeshi workers because they accepted low wages and were prepared to work long shifts; these workers were then trapped in this industry. The younger generation of British-born Blacks and Asians are unlikely to accept this situation. Higher rates of unemployment exist amongst Blacks in particular because the type of semi-skilled jobs which they tend to do are the ones hardest hit by the recession.

Race and life chances

In most parts of the country, Black and Asian communities were unknown until the 1950s and 60s when West Indians, Indians, Pakistanis and others were encouraged to come here to work. Britain was then suffering from a shortage of labour.

London and Birmingham were favourite destinations, since that was where many of the unfilled vacancies were.

The few areas of unemployment – the North East for example – attracted limited numbers. The textile towns of Lancashire, West Yorkshire and the East Midlands also drew in Black and Asian workers, because the local population seized the opportunity to opt out of the poorly paid shift work in the mills. Also, cheap and dilapidated housing in

industrial and inner city areas became available to immigrants as many whites moved out.

The Black and Asian population remains small in relation to the total. It continues to be concentrated in low status, low-paid work, in inner city areas and, increasingly, in the dole queues. This is partly because of widespread prejudice, and

discrimination that is illegal but hard to prove.

The Black and Asian population is made up of a number of communities, fragmented along ethnic and linguistic lines. But this is changing: the majority of the younger generation were born in Britain.

Source: Adapted from S. Fothergill and J. Vincent, *The State of the Nation* (Pluto Press, 1985)

1   In which areas did immigrants settle? Why?

2   Did they take work from the local people?

3   What sort of housing did the immigrants move into?

People's occupations by ethnic origin, Great Britain, 1987–9

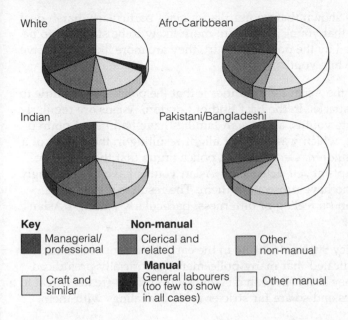

White

Afro-Caribbean

Indian

Pakistani/Bangladeshi

Key

Non-manual

■ Managerial/ professional

▨ Clerical and related

▨ Other non-manual

Manual

▨ Craft and similar

■ General labourers (too few to show in all cases)

□ Other manual

Unemployment rates, by ethnic group, Great Britain, Spring 1994

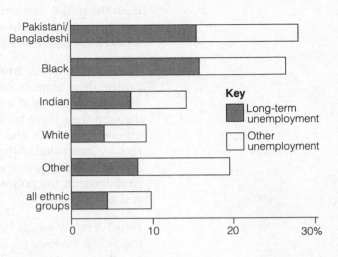

Pakistani/ Bangladeshi

Black

Indian

White

Other

all ethnic groups

Key

■ Long-term unemployment

□ Other unemployment

0   10   20   30%

Source: *Social Trends 25* (HMSO, 1995) and Employment Department

With the exception of racial discrimination, the disadvantages suffered by Britain's ethnic minorities are shared in varying degrees by the rest of the community. Bad housing, unemployment, educational underachievement, a deprived physical environment, social tensions – none of these are the exclusive preserve of ethnic minorities. ...But the ethnic minorities suffer such disadvantages more than the rest of the population, and more than they would if they were white.

Source: Report on Racial Disadvantage, House of Commons Home Affairs Committee, 1980–1

1 Which group had the largest percentage of people in managerial and professional employment?

2 Which group had the fewest?

3 Which group had the largest number of workers in 'other manual'?

4 Which groups are the most likely to be unemployed?

5 What reasons would you put forward for these statistics?

6 Summarise the information contained in the tables in one paragraph.

Housing

There are clear differences in the types of housing in which different ethnic groups live. Asians have the highest levels of home ownership (more than Whites), but overall these are poorer quality homes in the 'less desirable' districts of the large cities, compared to the Whites who overall own homes in the suburbs. Blacks have similar levels of ownership to Whites, but are more likely to live in flats in overcrowded conditions.

Why? Because of prejudice again, with Whites reluctant to sell to Asian and black families, but also because of the different income levels of the various ethnic groups.

The police

Government research has shown that young Blacks get a particularly harsh deal from the police. It seems that young Blacks are more likely to be stopped, to be searched and to be arrested by the police. In court, they are more likely to receive a heavier sentence than white youths.

The main complaint from the Asian communities is that the police do very little to protect them from racist attacks. In the East End of London, Asians are regularly attacked by gangs of white youths, and Asian families have had petrol poured through their letter boxes, which was then set alight resulting in the deaths of a number of women and children. Generally the police argue that these are not racially-motivated. Attempts at self-defence by Asian youths have been strongly opposed by the police who have prosecuted them. The result is a lack of confidence in the police and a feeling of bitterness, particularly amongst Asian and black youth.

Why? A study by the Policy Studies Institute in the early 1980s, commissioned by the police themselves, indicated that many policemen were racially prejudiced (see the extract below). They also believe that black youths offer a greater threat to law and order than whites and so are far stricter in their dealings with them.

Racism in the police force

In the early 1980s the Metropolitan Police asked a group of researchers to investigate policing practices 'on the beat'. The results were often rather shocking.

Similarly, racialist language is quite commonly used over the personal radio. For example JG (a researcher) heard the inspector of the relief with which he was working say over the personal radio 'Look, I've got a bunch of coons in sight'. The inspector was standing in a public place at the time and of course this message came up over the radios of all the police offers in the Division, many of whom would have been in public places at the time.

On one occasion DJS was with two officers who were dealing with a suspected bomb in a mailbag. Of the two postmen who noticed a sound coming from the bag in the back of their van, one was black and the other white. The black man was the driver, and the white man saw him as the boss; if for example he was asked a question, he often said 'I don't know about that, you'll have to ask my driver'. Later the police questioned the black man in a friendly manner and the answers were given with clarity, common sense and courtesy.

As they got back into the police car afterwards, one of the officers, checking through his notes, said to the other, 'Was it the coon who called us out?' The other replied 'Yes, believe it or not, it was the coon that was the driver.'

Source: D. Smith and J. Gray, *Police and People in London* (Gower, 1985)

Since this research was published in 1985, the police report that they have been tackling racism in the force through training programmes and that reports of racist attacks are being monitored in London.

1 What does the extract tell you about the taken-for-granted attitudes of the police officers about black people? Give an example to illustrate your answer.

2 Do you think the police officers were deliberately being racialist in the language they used referring to black people?

3 Some people have argued that passing laws against racial discrimination has little effect in combatting racism. How does this extract illustrate this argument?

4 Some sociologists have argued that 'racism is deep in our culture' and that our language contains many words and phrases which we commonly use, which strengthen this racism.
   a) What does the phrase 'deep in our culture' mean?
   b) Can you suggest any commonly used words or phrases that we use, which, if we think about it, are racist?

Education

Overall, Blacks and Asians do badly in our education system, although there are considerable variations, with Indian girls doing particularly well and West Indian boys doing particularly badly.

Why? One argument is that the education given to children in our schools is predominantly 'white' in its content – the history of Africa or India is seen through the exploits of British explorers, and the culture and civilisation of Africans and Asians is ignored. To combat this, programmes of multi-cultural education have been developed which stress the positive contributions of Blacks and Asians. A second explanation is that educational attainment reflects social position – and we know that ethnic minorities are more likely to be poor and disadvantaged.

Explanations for racial prejudice

There are two basic types of explanation of why people are racially prejudiced. The first type stresses the **individual** and the second stresses **cultural** reasons.

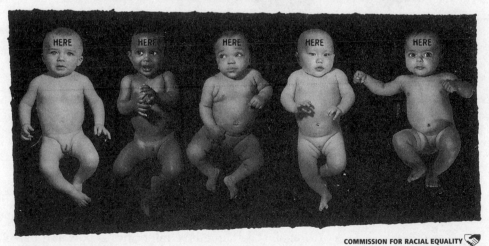

If racism is not natural, then there are social reasons for its development

The individual

Individuals who tend to 'bottle up' their frustrations and problems find an outlet for them in hostility against certain easily identifiable groups, such as immigrants. This is often linked to an 'authoritarian personality' which is very rigid and conventional.

Critics of this explanation argue that if 35 per cent of the population admit to being racially prejudiced, can so many people be unable to express their feelings, and suffer from an authoritarian personality?

Challenging perceptions of race

Not amused...Benetton's computer-altered image of the Queen, which makes her appear black

Source: *The Guardian*, 27 March 1993

Buckingham Palace yesterday expressed its disapproval at the latest in a series of controversial advertising campaigns by the Italian clothing manufacturer Benetton, which shows a photograph of the Queen depicted as a black woman in its April catalogue.

Her Majesty's nose and lips have been broadened in the computer-aided photograph, which will appear with the words "What if?" A spokesman for Buckingham Palace said: "We don't like members of the Royal Family being used in this way. Specific guidelines have been laid down to prevent them from being used for commercial purposes. They shouldn't be used to promote any product."

The black Queen, in a formal pose wearing a crown, is part of an advertising campaign designed to challenge perceptions on race. Other photographs due to appear in Colours, the monthly Benetton catalogue, will depict the Pope as Chinese, Arnold Schwarzenegger as black and Michael Jackson and Spike Lee as white.

Royalty, it is claimed, embody the values of British society. Yet the idea that one of the royals might marry a black or Asian citizen has never even been suggested. Look at the picture, why should there be any objection to the computer-altered image of the Queen, do you think?

The culture

This second approach, taken by most sociologists today, argues that prejudice against certain ethnic minorities is part and parcel of our culture. People are socialised into thinking in racial terms, through the history we learn at school, through the media and in some cases through the family. The reason why our culture contains so much prejudice is explained in two main ways.

Scapegoating

The real explanations for social problems such as unemployment or poor housing may be too complex for people to understand. A simple, easily understood explanation is that it is the fault of 'outsiders', such as the ethnic minorities; they are taking the jobs or the housing. The fact that this is not true is ignored.

More radical sociologists have gone a stage further and argued that blaming the Blacks and Asians for society's problems draws attention away from the root cause which is the great differences in wealth in our society. To them, both Blacks and Whites are being exploited, but they are blinded to this, preferring instead to blame the other group.

Stereotyping

This explanation goes hand in hand with scapegoating. When Britain was a colonial power, invading other countries (or 'tribes') and then exploiting them for its own good, it was necessary to *depersonalise* the people being oppressed, that is to make people believe that the conquered are somehow inferior to the conquerers. Africans were seen as 'children' who needed Whites to keep control over them, for example. Blacks and Asians, therefore, came to be seen as inferior and this view of them entered into our culture.

Racism in action

I GET ON FINE WITH ASIANS — THERE'S ONE IN THE SHOP DOWN THE ROAD AND HE'S ALWAYS CHARMING TO ME.

I'D BE ALL IN FAVOUR OF MY DAUGHTER GETTING MARRIED TO A BLACK MAN IF IT WEREN'T FOR THE PROBLEMS THE CHILDREN WOULD FACE.

NEGROES HAVE A ROUGH TIME OF IT. BUT THEY DO SEEM TO GET A CHIP ON THEIR SHOULDERS SO EASILY AND IT DOESN'T DO THEM ANY GOOD AT ALL.

OF COURSE I THINK THEY SHOULD BE TAUGHT SOMETHING ABOUT THEIR OWN CULTURES. BUT BY THE SAME TOKEN THEY OUGHT TO BE MAKING MORE OF AN EFFORT TO LEARN ENGLISH AND FIT IN HERE.

Source: *New Internationalist*, March 1985

1 The statements above are frequently heard. Do you agree, or disagree, with them?

2 What, do you think, are the real feelings of each speaker? (Explain each one separately.)

3 In each case, what would you do, or say, if you were the person being addressed?

4 The young man on the right says, '...they should be taught something about their own cultures, 'What do schools teach about Africa or India? What attitude does this create?

Reading racism

BERNIE GRANT IN SECOND DIVORCE
Left-wing MP Bernie Grant has finally divorced Anna Maria, his British-born wife of 16 years.

The couple, who have three young sons, were granted a decree absolute last week after living apart since 1985.

It is the second failed marriage for Guyana-born Mr Grant, 49, Labour MP for Tottenham, North London. The divorce comes two weeks after Left-winger Diane Abbott, Britain's first black woman MP, revealed that her marriage had collapsed.

Source: *The Daily Mail*, 13 September 1993

The mainstream media rejects the view that they are racist, and it is hard to find obvious racism. However, many critics say that the methods of reporting, the style of words used, and the content of stories can often, if unintentionally, be racist. I saw this small story in *The Daily Mail*.

What is your view? Do you think that readers can easily 'read in' a racist message?

Immigration laws

- **1948 British Nationality Act:** encouraged Commonwealth citizens to settle in Britain and work here
- **1962 Commonwealth Immigrants Act:** entry restricted to those with special skills that were required. Controls were placed on the right of entry of family of those already living here. In 1969 a special certificate was introduced which family members had to have before they could enter Britain. These are very difficult to obtain
- **1971 Immigration Act:** entry further restricted. A special group of privileged immigrants was created called 'patrials', those with British grandparents. Many saw this as a way of allowing white immigrants but not Blacks
- **1981 British Nationality Act:** changed the basis of British citizenship to exclude certain groups, in effect Chinese from Hong Kong and African Asians holding British passports, from ever   settling here

Racism and job opportunities

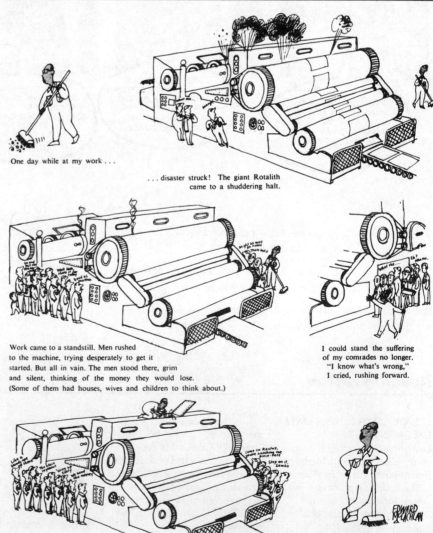

One day while at my work . . .

. . . disaster struck! The giant Rotalith came to a shuddering halt.

Work came to a standstill. Men rushed to the machine, trying desperately to get it started. But all in vain. The men stood there, grim and silent, thinking of the money they would lose. (Some of them had houses, wives and children to think about.)

I could stand the suffering of my comrades no longer. "I know what's wrong," I cried, rushing forward.

Source: *New Internationalist*

I worked in a silence broken only by the encouraging shouts of my workmates. A few minutes later, the mighty machine started. The day's production was saved!

Yes, it's certainly an exciting life as a factory sweeper—especially when occasionally you get a chance to use your higher degrees in science and engineering.

1 Why is the black worker sweeping the floor if he can repair the machine and has a degree?

2 How do the white workers respond to his help: are they grateful, for instance?

3 The black worker does not appear to be resentful of his treatment; how would you feel in his situation?

Combatting discrimination

Are laws an adequate way of fighting racial prejudice?

Legal changes

1965 Race Relations Act

Racial discrimination was made illegal in employment, housing and the provision of goods and services to the public. It became an offence to 'incite racial hatred', for instance by publishing newspapers with racialist propaganda. Two Boards were set up to investigate accusations of racial discrimination and to promote racial harmony.

1976 The Commission for Racial Equality

This was set up, with stronger powers, to replace the two Boards formed by the 1965 Act.

Education

Programmes of multi-cultural education have been set up to show how to teach the history and cultures of the ethnic minorities.

How effective have these measures been?

Prejudice still exists, though it is more difficult to find out if discrimination does (because it is illegal, people will not admit to it). However, some changes have taken place; in 1984 whereas two-thirds of Whites over 55 objected to the idea of an Asian marrying into the family, only one-third of those aged 18–34 did. Indeed overall, the survey found young people to be less prejudiced than older people and more aware of discrimination against ethnic minorities.

Laws can prevent obvious discrimination but only a change in people's attitudes can really eradicate it.

Cards in the equality pack

Education

Children at school are protected by a network of laws, guidelines and policies relating to multi-cultural education which:
● Make it unlawful to refuse a child entry to a school because of his or her colour.
● Encourage children to understand that Britain is made up of different minority groups, many of whom speak different languages and wear different clothes. All should have equal rights and opportunities.
● Make it unlawful to discriminate against children because of their language or their dress – for example, a requirement to wear a cap could discriminate against Sikh boys, whose religion requires them to wear a turban.

Employment

Many employers have adopted equal opportunities policies, which means they carry out ethnic monitoring, among other practices. Ethnic monitoring involves finding out how many people from ethnic minorities are employed. The aim is to ensure that everyone gets an equal chance.

Public places

It is unlawful for pubs, restaurants, shops or clubs with more than 25 members to refuse entry or service to anyone on racial grounds or to provide an inferior service.

Housing

It is unlawful for estate agents or anyone letting property to discriminate against ethnic minorities. There is a Code of Practice for estate agents and providers of rented housing to follow. They should not undervalue a property because it is in an area with a large ethnic minority population.

Service industries

It is unlawful for building societies, doctors, government departments, car-hire firms, etc. to discriminate on grounds of race.

Public order

It is an offence under the Public Order Act to behave in any way which is likely to incite racial hatred. Such behaviour might include distributing racially inflammatory books or leaflets and joining some forms of demonstrations.

But if there is a complaint...

Many prosecutions for racial discrimination are made on behalf of individuals by the Commission for Racial Equality. It will examine the case to see if there is enough evidence as discrimination is very hard to prove. In the case of an employer being accused of discrimination, the case goes before an industrial tribunal. Non-employment cases end up in court. People can also go to a trade union, the Citizen's Advice Bureaux, the local law centre or the local Racial Equality Council.

The 1990 CRE annual report showed that:
1,381 applications were made, of which:
● 53 employment cases and 6 non-employment cases were settled without going to court;
● 24 employment cases and 2 non-employment cases were successful after a hearing;
● 22 employment cases and 2 non-employment cases were dismissed after a hearing;
● £40,612 was awarded by tribunals to people who had been discrimated against;
● £121,472 was paid in out-of-court settlements.

Individual complaint
↓
CRE assesses case: brings prosecution or advises against doing so
↓
If the CRE decides to act:
↓
Employment cases:
Case goes before an industrial tribunal.
↓
Non-employment cases:
Case goes to court.

Source: *The Guardian* (Education section), 19 May 1992; CRE and *Employment Gazette*

Chapter 6

AGE

This chapter covers:
- Ageing as a social process
- Childhood
- The age of youth
- The origins of youth culture
- The purpose of youth culture
- The peer group
- The varieties of youth culture
- Commercialism and youth culture
- The generation gap
- The elderly.

Ageing as a social process

Ageing is, of course, a natural process that happens to us all and it can be seen in the physical changes that occur. For sociologists, the fascination with age comes from the fact that we *treat people differently* according to their age, and have very *different expectations* of what they ought to do. A 40-year-old man skipping down a

Certain forms of behaviour are related to age

High Street on a Saturday afternoon would be a ridiculous sight. He would be told to 'act his age', and onlookers would think he was either mad or drunk. But what if a four-year-old boy was skipping along? There would be absolutely no comment. Age has a social as well as a biological element.

The major age divisions which are recognised are **childhood**, **youth**, **adulthood** and **old age**. As most of the contents of this book are about the lives and experiences of adults, in this chapter we will concentrate on the significance of the other three divisions.

Childhood

We think of children as being 'precious', delicate creatures who are in need of protection, and we have special laws to protect them. It has not always been this way. It was only with the coming of industrialisation with its increase in wealth for the middle classes and the greater chances of children surviving at birth, that the idea of the 'precious' modern child was born. Before that (and amongst the working class, long after that) the child was seen as a miniature adult as soon as he or she emerged from infancy. So children worked for long hours in agriculture and then in factories, until the reforms of the 1820s. In the last century children were divided into two groups: the children of the middle and upper classes who were regarded as delicate creatures in need of protection, and the children of the working class who were seen as far tougher and capable of looking after themselves. Both groups of children were strictly controlled by parents and, if they were disobedient, they were harshly punished.

Throughout this century, however, there has been a general acceptance that children of all kinds are in need of protection and guidance, but that blind obedience reinforced by violence is wrong. Normal 'beatings' by parents at the beginning of this century would now be regarded as a crime. In the modern family, the views of children are generally regarded as being worth taking into account and the relationship between the majority of parents and children is (ideally) one of partnership.

We ought to note though, that there is still much violence against children and the fact that social workers and the National Society for the Prevention of Cruelty to Children (NSPCC) still exist, indicate just how great the problem is.

Damned kids!

Young bar
Does the Government's proposal to change the law to allow children to go into pubs mean that our pubs will be inundated by small children running around screaming, shouting, playing the gaming machines and generally getting in the way of everyone?

I am not against children in their place, but a pub is not one of those.

Mrs M, Clywd

This is a letter written to *The Daily Mail*.

1 What does the letter tell us about attitudes to children in Britain?

2 Do you agree with the letter writer?

3 The writer says she is not against 'children in their place'. What do you think she means by this?

Source: *The Daily Mail*, 24 March 1993

Childhood amongst the Ik

The Ik were a small tribe who lived in northern Uganda. The Ik regarded children as a great nuisance. So much so, that they were thrown out by their mothers at the age of three and expected to look after themselves.

In this environment, a child stands no chance of survival on his own until he is about 13 years old, so children form themselves into two age bands, the first from 3 to 7.

For the most part they ate figs that had been partially eaten by baboons, a few cherries, bark from trees, and when they were really hungry they swallowed earth or even pebbles.

Source: Adapted from C. Turnbull, *The Mountain People* (Picador, 1974)

1 At what age does the mother regard the child as old enough to care for itself?

2 Would a child in Britain be capable of looking after itself at this age?

3 Some people argue that our abilities are completely controlled by our age and that our development is 'natural'. Does this extract tell us anything about our ideas of what children are capable of?

4 What does the extract tell us of the relationship between mother and child?

The changing attitudes towards childhood

Up to the eighteenth century	ARISTOCRACY	PEASANTS
	**Boys** were treated as 'little men', trained in the art of war, and possibly learned some some reading and writing **Girls** were educated to be mothers and wives; no formal schooling; household skills learned	**Boys** were expected to work in the fields as soon as able; no such thing as childhood; treated roughly **Girls** had no childhood; worked from earliest age; trained to be a farm-worker first and a mother/wife second

Industrialisation 1700	RICH	WORKING CLASS
	**Boys** were treated as little creatures who were to be strictly brought up to learn how to be 'gentlemen'; often attended public schools; children wore special clothes and were regarded as inferior to adults **Girls** were seen as being less important than boys; taught that they had to make perfect wives and run the household while men got on with business; rarely attended school; treated strictly; special clothes for girls introduced	**Boys** worked from very early age in factories; very often treated with brutality by parents; little time for childhood, never had time to play; strict discipline; no special clothes **Girls** treated as boys; worked from a very early age; no special clothes; not regarded as being very different from boys; treated strictly and punished with violence

Twentieth century 1900–49	MIDDLE CLASS	WORKING CLASS
	**Boys** began to be treated with love and affection; encouraged to do well at school and in sports; children seen as in need of care and protection; if parents fail, state takes over; higher expectation of boys than girls **Girls** treated with love and affection; stress on being pretty and learning to be a successful wife and mother; as century progresses increasing stress on education and career For boys and girls: close family life	**Boys** By middle of century, the working class had adopted idea of the innocence of children and it was normal to treat children with love and affection. Diminishing use of violence in discipline **Girls** As boys above, but less stress on on educational achievement and career prospects; close family life

1950–

Differences in social classes have declined, though divisions in income remain, which lead to different opportunities for sport, leisure and education. Ethos of parenting is now strongly on love and affection, and the importance of encouraging success. Smaller families allow deeper relationships with parents. Gender differences remain, but are becoming less important as education is seen as equally important for females as well as for males.

Main differences lie in the shortening of childhood and the extension of youth.

A moving image of young people

Mid-19th century: children and young people were increasingly seen as delinquents. Many adults felt that precocious children needed curbing.

Late 19th century: society strove to impose strict moral and religious codes. The use of children as wage-earners was seen as wrong; children and young people were considered at risk of delinquency if not given care and protection. Their inability to survive independently of parents was regarded as further proof of their 'moral weakness'. Education was a remedy for this; it became compulsory from 1870.

1900s: Children and young people were seen as innocent, incompetent, undisciplined things to be acted upon and 'improved' by adults. The start of the Edwardian social-service state ensured children were given new prominence – for instance, they were provided with school meals. The welfare of the child began to be seen as vital to the welfare of the state.

1890s: young people were seen as worthy of academic study with the birth of the Child-Study movement.

1930s–40s: understanding children's relationship to the family and their environment was seen as an important factor in creating a socially stable individual.

1960s to present: children and young people are still viewed with some ambivalence; adults see them representing both innocence and corruption. New teenage affluence has led to new kinds of youth sub-culture – such as mods and rockers, teddy boys, punks and, more recently, ravers. Many adults disapprove of these trends.

Source: *The Guardian* (Education section), 30 March 1993

A rite of passage

The **bar mitzvah** is a ceremony (a rite of passage) which each boy goes through in the Jewish religion at the age of 13. It means that a boy has entered the adult Jewish community: has become a man, ready to fulfil the commandments gleaned from the Talmud, the book that codifies ancient Jewish laws and traditions. Many girls now participate in a parallel ceremony at the age of 12 called a **bat mitzvah** ('bat' means daughter).

Traditionally, the first public declaration of a child's new acceptance into adulthood takes place on the first Saturday after the boy's thirteenth birthday. This ceremony closes with the boy's father reciting the Hebrew blessing, 'Blessed are you who releases us from the responsibility of this child'. The blessing makes clear the boy's new responsibility to himself and the community's recognition of their altered responsibility to him.

So the social impact of the bar mitzvah is profound. It draws into consciousness a clear line between childhood and adulthood.

Source: *New Internationalist*, August 1984

But rites of passage are not just for youth

Everybody working in the offices came over to the Special Features Room as work finished that day. Even the Managing Director, a rarely-seen figure, turned up (late) especially for the ceremony. At exactly 4.30 p.m. one bitter February day, my father became the centre of interest. Speeches were made on his 35 years of service, broken only by time in the armed forces...'Never missed a day's work in all that time.' ...'An example of hard work and commitment to the interests of Oakalls newspapers.' ...'a popular figure in the office'. My mum looked on proudly, her hair specially permed for the occasion, dressed in a brand new outfit. The office presents were given – a set of silver plated goblets and a copy of the front page of the paper on the day my dad first started work. For an hour the drink flowed and photographs were taken. Then my mum and dad caught the bus home, just like he had done for 35 years ('broken only by time in the armed forces'). And when he arrived home he was a pensioner.

1 What is a 'rite of passage'?

2 Give three examples of rites of passage which people go through in contemporary society.

3 In both extracts, the person had a new 'social status' after the rite of passage. What was this new status?

4 Compare the social status of the person in the second extract before and after the rite of passage.

5 What purpose does a rite of passage serve for the individual and society?

6 Is there a clear rite of passage in modern society to indicate the move from childhood to adulthood? Might this have any repercussions for young people?

The age of youth

We use the term 'youth' in normal conversation without a very precise notion of the age at which we enter and leave it. Does youth finish at 16 when you can leave school? Or 17 when you can drive a car? Or maybe at 18 when you can vote and legally purchase alcohol. Perhaps youth is not directly restricted to any age but is over when you marry? Clearly the notion is confusing and perhaps that is the very core of the meaning of youth – it is a period of *transition* between childhood, when we are bossed around and regarded as having little to contribute to discussions on matters of importance, and adulthood, when we are weighed down with domestic concerns, the mortgage, and the rearing of children.

Many societies have very clear **social markers** which tell other people what a person's status is, either child or adult, as there is no 'in-between' stage. For example, in Jewish society there is the *bar mitzvah*, which is a ceremony that marks the break between boyhood and manhood. Today, it is largely ceremonial, but once signalled an important change in a person's life.

The ceremonies which act as social markers of status are known as **rites of passage** and, although less common than they were, we still have some left. Soon after birth, for instance, we celebrate with baptism, and our countdown to death begins with our retirement.

There is no form of rite of passage into adulthood in British society, where entry into adulthood is rather confused and unclear. Although we are 'of age' officially at 18, a large proportion of young people continue to be economically dependent on their parents and continue to live in their parents' house. The period of change from childhood to adulthood is elastic in length, and may be lengthening as young people's unemployment grows. The term *youth* then refers to the period of transition, however long that may be.

The values of youth

The development of the age of youth has been associated with the growth of distinctive values which young people hold. These values serve to distinguish them from the older generation. *Subculture* is the correct term to describe these noticeably different sets of values. However, instead *youth culture* has become the most commonly used term.

- **Culture:** a whole way of life that guides our way of thinking and acting. People within a culture regard it as somehow natural, for example, the difference between British values and Italian values
- **Subculture:** exists within a culture and is a distinctive set of values that marks off the members of the subculture from the rest of society, for example, youth (sub)culture
- **Contraculture:** a form of subculture which actively opposes the dominant culture of society; for example, terrorist groups

The origins of youth culture

Youth and youth culture are relatively new. It was not until the 1950s that the distinct identity of a (sub) culture of youth was recognised. Although British youth culture has always been very different from US youth culture, its origins come from there and it has always been strongly influenced by it musically and artistically. This can be seen in the popularity of American films and records here.

Three closely related facts are crucially important in understanding the birth of British youth culture. The first is the growth in affluence of young people in the 1950s. The second is the development of new means of recording and transmitting music and entertainment, which led to mass culture. The third is the speed of social change.

Affluence

The 1950s was a period when there was an unlimited number of jobs and wages were increasing rapidly. The result was more money in people's pockets. Most importantly, young people shared in this prosperity but were not bogged down with mortgages and heavy household bills. What they earned, they were able to spend.

Mass culture

The 1930s had seen the development of the record industry, the film industry and the rise of radio. The 1950s added television to this and technical advances in record players. The adult market had reached saturation, so the commercial companies turned their sights on the newly affluent youth.

Social change

The increasing speed of technological change (think of the advances in computing for instance in the last 10 years) has influenced patterns of behaviour and meant that the expectations and behaviour of one generation is not relevant to the next. This has meant that youth has had to develop its own ways of acting.

The spread of youth culture

At first the main consumers of the clothes and music were the working class; after all they left school first and had money of their own to spend. Gradually, however, the youth culture of music and distinctive clothes spread to the middle class. The form it took was different though, as the middle-class youth were (and still are) more likely to be in full-time education until 18 or even 21.

Time to wake up from the youth dream

The very idea that acned people represent some kind of unique and unified culture divided from the real world by the single fact of age is ridiculous. The whole generation gap game died a final death a decade ago. The cult of us against them teendom was a historical freak which was a result of all the social disruption caused by World War II. It brought in a new set of values and vices in the mid-1950s. But 20 years on everybody knew how to spend money and how to disco dance and the youth thing was no longer a rebellion but a tradition. Punk rock and all that was the theatrical death rite of the beast of teenage. Now there's just people again.

But yesterday's teen producers turned today's media product producers have simply moved from acned to hackeneyed in their desire to cater for this supposed golden age group. So, instead of producing good movies, people try to make young ones, saddled with awful rock tracks. They also make young people's television where discos, gender bending and unemployment are substituted for character, plot and intelligence. ...And all this is baded on the one ridiculous assumption that all young people want the same things – they want young things.

The current obsession with youth is actually a sign of a culture come of age. Before the teen explosion, young people were simply old people in smaller sizes. Now it is the other way around, nobody is a teenager anymore because everybody is.

Source: Adapted from *The Observer*, 1985

The writer thinks that there is no longer a youth culture.

1 When does he or she see youth culture beginning and ending?

2 Is the music and entertainment for youth today created by them, according to the writer?

3 Who are yesterday's 'teenagers' now?

4 What is your opinion of the writer's argument? Give reasons for your conclusions.

5 One way to test the author's argument would be to contrast the style of clothes worn by youth and that worn by the over 25s. Are there significant differences? Now, suggest two other ways and then check to see if they confirm or reject the writer's opinion.

The decline in class differences in childhood and youth

In most respects, middle-class children have – unsurprisingly – more possessions than working-class children; although among the items on our list the differences are not great. But in one important respect the pattern is reversed. Sixty per cent of 11- to 16-year-olds in working-class families have their own television compared with only 49 per cent of middle-class children. But overall the poll demolishes myths about families and class. Respondents were almost evenly divided between middle-class (ABC1) and working-class (C2DE) parents. ...

● It is *not* true that middle-class children are more likely to grow up without being slapped. Almost equal numbers among both classes say they have never hit their child.

● Working-class parents are *not* more likely to leave young children at home without adult supervision: 6 per cent of working-class parents say they first left their child at home for more than 30 minutes before he or she was 10; the figure among middle-class families is identical.

● It is *not* true that working-class parents shower their children with more large presents: 89 per cent of middle-class children aged 11–16 have a personal stereo, 86 per cent a bicycle and 67 per cent a camera; the figures for working-class children are 75, 75 and 48 respectively. ...

However, some stereotypes do receive support in the survey.

● Working-class parents hold slightly more traditional views about the role of women.

● A large minority of working-class parents say they would allow their children to smoke.

● The tiny minority that admit to slapping their child frequently is found more among working-class parents (4 per cent) than middle-class (1 per cent').

Source: 'Back to the generation gap' by P. Kellner in *The Independent on Sunday*, 4 August 1991

1 Does the extract support the argument that youth have very different experiences of life depending on their social class? Explain your answer and provide evidence to support it.

2 If you read the extract carefully, you can work out the questions asked which gave the information provided in the extract. Reconstruct the questions and see if you can replicate the research, on a very small scale. How do your findings compare?

The purpose of youth culture

We know why youth culture developed in the 1950s in Britain. But sociologists have asked what, if anything, does youth culture actually do for youth? The answer seems to be that youth culture helps solve the specific problems faced by young people. The trouble is, however, that sociologists disagree over exactly what these specific problems are.

The first approach, that all young people face similar problems, claims that young people are unsure of themselves in the difficult period of transition from childhood, when a person has no responsibilities, to adulthood, when a person is absolutely loaded down with them. In order to cope with this period of uncertainty, youth develop a culture which provides them with a clear way of behaving and looking. The **peer group** becomes all important and young people can feel safe in the security of their group. The differences between young people are not seen as being very important.

The second approach, that young people face very different problems according to class, gender and colour, argues that the different problems faced by different sections of youth are so great that they develop their own 'responses'. For instance the black working-class youth in the inner city grows up in very different circumstances from the white middle-class youth in the suburb. The results are the very distinctive black subcultures which have developed, with their particular types of language and music.

The peer group

Before we go on to look at the different sorts of youth styles, we must briefly glance at a key group for young people, the peer group. As children, most of us are brought up in families which, ideally, provide us with protection, emotional security and a sense of belonging. As we grow up the constraining bonds of the family prove too tight, we need more freedom but without losing that sense of security. It seems that the role of the peer group is to do just that; it gives independence and security. The peer group consists of other people of the same age who are seen as the correct people to judge our behaviour against.

The peer group can be a decisive influence on a young person's lifestyle. We have all heard of someone in trouble with the law having 'got in with the wrong crowd', and it is true that status within the peer group partially comes to replace loyalties outside.

The influence of the peer group

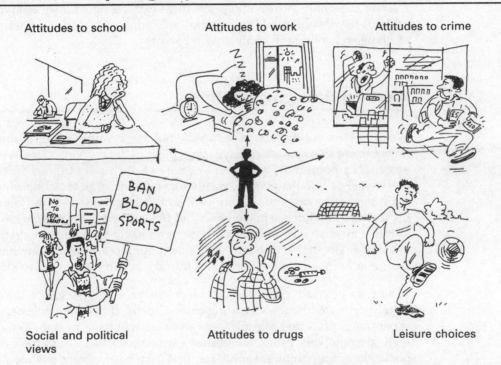

Attitudes to school

Attitudes to work

Attitudes to crime

BAN BLOOD SPORTS

Social and political views

Attitudes to drugs

Leisure choices

1 Give an example of the importance of the peer group in attitudes to school.

2 How important do you think the peer group is in attitudes to drug use?

The varieties of youth culture

There is a wide variety of youth cultures which reflect the range of problems faced by youth. As mentioned earlier, black inner-city youths have very different experiences of life than do white, suburban youth. These differences are reflected in the styles of clothes, the choice of music and the forms of expression of the different groups.

Before we examine these different forms of youth culture, it is important to remember that all young people seek as much enjoyment as possible from life and they are not too concerned with long-term planning. This, combined with the fact that most adolescents are free from major worries over household bills and family responsibilities, means that they are more able to plunge themselves into wholehearted enjoyment than most adults.

- **Style:** a term to summarise a way of dressing, appreciation of a certain type of music, use of particular speech expressions and a whole set of likes and dislikes which mark off a particular group as different.

Middle-class youth culture

As middle-class youth are more likely to stay in the education system to take A-levels or a degree, their form of youth culture is likely to be based on student life and often linked to some form of protest politics. Isolation from the 'real world' in tolerant university surroundings lets them explore new lifestyles and attitudes without the possibility of being disciplined, unlike the working-class youth living at home and coming in conflict with parents.

Working-class youth culture

Working-class youths have developed a number of styles which sociologists have linked to the changes which have taken place in the working class over the last 20 years. They point out the different extremes which reflect the splintering of the working class into the poorer, usually inner city or large social housing estates on the fringes of towns, and the more affluent children of those who benefitted from the increase in affluence in the 1980s and 1990s. The poorer groups have appeared to move more to use of drugs and are more likely to engage in aggressive behaviour. On the other hand, the affluent are more likely to purchase their leisure in terms of clubs, sports, and through relatively expensive clothes.

The future of youth cultural styles amongst the working class will depend very largely upon the chances of getting work. Clearly, if there are no jobs, then buying expensive clothes, stereo equipment and cars will have to stop. Yet against this there are now very firmly established expectations that youth have concerning possessions; they think it is only fair that they have decent clothes and stereo equipment. With less money to spend, but the same amount of advertising and commercial pressures to buy goods, plus high expectations, the future looks gloomy for youth.

1 Why are there different styles amongst youth?

2 Name four types of youth style today. Which groups (class, race, etc.) are they generally associated with?

3 Do you think you associate yourself with any particular style? If so, what is it? Briefly describe it.

4 Now construct a chart of all the current youth styles, with a description of each. You may want to use a number of headings, such as clothes, music, etc.

5 Write a brief description of how you see the future of youth. Alternatively, you could draw a sketch of the future fashions as you imagine them.

Black youth culture

Any survey of job opportunities and living conditions finds black youths of Afro-Caribbean descent at the bottom of the pile. On top of this black youth faces racist attitudes amongst large sections of the white community. Sociologists have suggested that in order to cope with their problems and low status in British society, black youth have 'turned to their roots', adopting a culture which is based on some imagined version of black or West Indian culture. By adopting 'reggae' music and 'Rasta' styles, the black youth escapes the white society and gives itself status.

Youth culture – a solution to the problems of youth?

Some sociologists now suggest that the pace of change of new youth cultures is so rapid that they cannot reflect a 'solution' to the problems youths face, but instead are a mixture of genuine response by young people, trying to make sense of the world, and a manufactured culture created by the music and fashion industries.

Previous theorists of postwar popular music, youth culture and deviance ... have tended to look beneath or behind the surfaces of the shimmery mediascape in order to discover the 'real', authentic subculture, apparently always distorted by the manufactured press and television image, which in turn becomes 'real' as more and more participants act out the media stereotypes. This 'depth model' is no longer appropriate – if it ever was – for analysing the surfaces of the (post) modern world, a culture characterised by shallowness, flatness and 'hyperreality'. .....

For youth subculture prior to the early 1970s, there was generally thought to be an 'authenticity' about their street-generated style. Thus, teds, beats, rockers, mods, skins, hippies, rudies and rastas [were] largely applauded for their much-flaunted 'signs' of resistance and rebellion to contemporary society ... After 1970, however, 'manufactured' subcultures were constantly spotted as first 'glam' (Bowie, T Rex, Gary Glitter) and later disco took over the night-time economy of many cities and towns. Punk was always going to be a hybrid of manufacture/authenticity, explaining the rigorous debate which has raged ever since about the subculture's origins in the art school or dole queue. Whatever the accuracy of the various positions in this argument, post-punk subcultures have been characterised by a speeding up of the time between points of 'authenticity' and 'manufacture'.

Source: S. Redhead, 'Rave off: Youth subcultures and the law' in *Social Studies Review*, January 1991

1 What did the early theorists of post-war youth culture believe?

2 What does the author mean when he refers to a post-modern world?

3 Why does he think that contemporary subcultures are manufactured and that the original ones were 'authentic'?

4 What current fashions/youth subcultures are there? Use the following headings to try to analyse them:

Name
Style of clothes/hair
Key words
Use of drugs
Type of music
Origin

Appeal to a particular race/ethnic group, age or social class
National/international
Most famous personalities

Asian youth culture

One group who rarely receive any publicity are the youth of Asian origin. It seems that the family remains centrally important in their lives and they are far more conformist than most other youth. Girls are particularly sheltered, and traditional Asian views on the role of the female mean that they are strictly controlled. There is recent evidence that the influence of British culture is starting to weaken the control of Asian parents and that some sections of Asian youth are attracted to British youth cultural styles. So it is now common to see Asian girls dressed in fashionable western-style clothes. However, the influence of Muslim values is growing again, so that second generation (Muslim) Asians may be taking certain western cultural styles, but retaining many Islamic values.

Second-generation Muslim women – constructing their own culture

The following is an extract from a piece of research about second-generation females of Asian Muslim origins.

What the findings from the research show is that second-generation Muslim women are in the process of actively creating a new role for themselves in British society, using established belief and traditions from both British and Asian cultures. There are aspects from both cultures that they can use to construct appropriate roles for themselves as Muslims in Britain. For most Muslim women, maintaining a distinct Muslim identity is [very important.]...

Following the beliefs and practices of Islam enables second-generation Muslims to establish identities appropriate to their lives in Britain. They choose which elements from other British or Asian cultures they can utilise. ...Thus inconsistencies with Islam and Asian culture, such as dowry giving and the arranged marriage system, and with British culture, such as gambling and drinking, can be eliminated from their various lifestyles.

Source: C. Butcher, 'Religion and gender' in *Sociology Review*, February 1995

1 The extract is extremely interesting in what it says about the way that people manage to construct their own subcultures. Explain in your own words what the extract says.

2 Do you think that the argument holds for other people who were born in Britain, but whose parents were born elsewhere?

Girls in youth culture

Studies of female youth cultures show that they have changed significantly over the last ten years. Previous research had shown that females were generally peripheral and that the subcultures were male-focused. They also showed that females were most likely to spend time in their homes, in a so-called bedroom culture. However, the female youth culture has changed to reflect the more outward and assertive role which young women have taken on. So young females are more likely to go out than previously, and to have much greater freedom. But this freedom is still less than that which males have and there is still much greater social control placed upon them by parents.

If you go out to a club (or pub?) this weekend, closely observe the way girls and boys act, bearing in mind the information above. Report back to the class at your next meeting on what you have observed.

Gender differences

Adolescence: What parents allow before 18

	All	Girls	Boys
Drinking	14	13	16
Smoking	14	12	16
Girl/boyfriend stay	11	12	10
Stay out all night	29	23	34
Party at home	32	36	28
None of these	35	37	34

All figures are percentages

Source: 'Back to the generation gap' by P. Kellner in
The Independent on Sunday, 4 August 1991

What differences emerge in the way that young males and females are treated by their parents?

What causes the differences in subcultural styles?

Youth

Youth culture occurs in the period of relative freedom from childhood constraint and adult responsibilities.

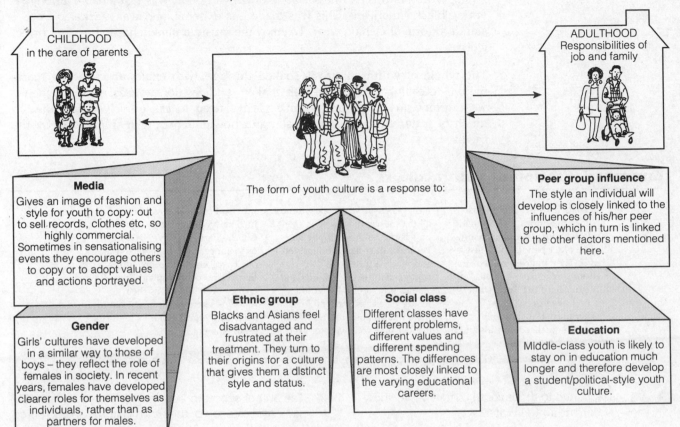

CHILDHOOD
in the care of parents

ADULTHOOD
Responsibilities of
job and family

The form of youth culture is a response to:

Media
Gives an image of fashion and style for youth to copy: out to sell records, clothes etc, so highly commercial. Sometimes in sensationalising events they encourage others to copy or to adopt values and actions portrayed.

Peer group influence
The style an individual will develop is closely linked to the influences of his/her peer group, which in turn is linked to the other factors mentioned here.

Gender
Girls' cultures have developed in a similar way to those of boys – they reflect the role of females in society. In recent years, females have developed clearer roles for themselves as individuals, rather than as partners for males.

Ethnic group
Blacks and Asians feel disadvantaged and frustrated at their treatment. They turn to their origins for a culture that gives them a distinct style and status.

Social class
Different classes have different problems, different values and different spending patterns. The differences are most closely linked to the varying educational careers.

Education
Middle-class youth is likely to stay on in education much longer and therefore develop a student/political-style youth culture.

Take a selection of the current youth styles plus some older ones such as teddy boys, skinheads, Rastafarians, hippies, etc. and analyse them using the headings of the boxes above.

You will need to do some research on past youth cultures–at the library and from old films/videos. You could also ask older relatives about their youth.

Commercialism and youth culture

Youth culture developed in Britain first amongst the working class. It was not entirely accidental; working-class youth had money to spend. Recording and clothing companies saw this, as did the advertisers. Soon a whole industry developed to cater for (or perhaps create) the changing fashions of youth. As soon as a new style emerges it is taken, cleaned up, standardised and marketed. An example of this is what happened to Black American 'protest' music in its various forms. 'Rap' music originally developed from Black Americans' attempts to create their own music reflecting their situation. It accurately reflected life for the poor

Blacks in the USA. The lyrics of the music were often violent, highly sexist and often supported drug use and criminality. However, as it moved into the mainstream and became commercial, it was toned down so that it remained slightly dangerous – at least dangerous to appear to be protest, but not so threatening that it could not be sold commercially to white audiences.

Along with the music came the style of dressing that was fashionable among young black Americans. This was made less extreme, and was marketed as a standard form of fashion wear. To enjoy the music, a person has to buy the correct clothes.

The whole of youth culture is soaked through with exploitation by the mass media, recording companies, film makers and fashion houses, so that when we examine any particular youth style we need to ask ourselves just how much of it derives from youth itself and how much from manipulation by the media.

Commercialisation of youth culture

Teenagers didn't really exist before the Fifties. Before that decade young people consumed what older people did – just less of it. They danced to the same bands as their parents, kissed to the music of the same singers, didn't even dress very differently. But suddenly someone realised that although teenagers have less money, almost all the money they have is spent on leisure. So they supplied a leisure culture based on fashion – and made a fortune. It's a commercial dream. Records and clothes go out of date within a matter of weeks and you buy more not because you need it, but just because you want to 'keep up'. You can take this point further, 'youth culture', critics like Charlie Parker believe, 'is a form of social control'. In other words, one by-product of youth culture is that young people spend their energy on it as well as their money – energy that might have been dangerous to the establishment.

Source: C. Brazier, 'Cashing in on the youth revolution' in *New Internationalist*, August 1984

1 What happened to make youth culture as we know it now, according to the writer?

2 Why is youth culture the perfect dream?

3 What is the 'by-product' of youth culture?

4 The author seems to be arguing that youth have no say in the creation of their own culture. Do you agree with him?

The generation gap

So far, I have stressed the differences between youth and adults. Some sociologists have gone so far as to say that the division of people into age groups is actually more important than the division into social classes. Is this so?

Probably the differences between the generations have been overstressed and the similarities remain unappreciated. This is probably no comfort to those students reading this book in the middle of a dispute with their parents on just how much freedom they ought to have! However the fact remains that all surveys indicate that youth is only marginally rebellious and soon 'returns to the fold' of conformity.

Most surveys of younger people indicate not how radical they are, but just how conformist they tend to be. Attitudes towards drugs, and even sex, were quite conservative. Most were politically apathetic rather than radical. Most wanted jobs and the spending power that went with them. Most believed in marriage and disapproved of adultery. Unfortunately, like the older generation, many of the younger generation shared feelings of racial prejudice.

Speaking for ourselves

ANDREA, 13, from Finchley, north-west London: My mum let me out on my own when I was about 10 – I could go anywhere really, as long as I let her know. I always had to be back by about 7 pm. My mum will slap me across the face if I am rude to her. I am allowed to watch sex and horror movies now but when I was younger my mum used to say "Shut your eyes" when a sex scene came on the TV. I used to do that but when I was nine I knew all about sex, I learnt about it from my friends and at school.

Two of my friends have had sex. I think a lot of young people have sex before they are 16, but they would never tell their parents. I certainly wouldn't. I am at a good school and learnt all about sex and Aids in my science lessons. My mum only told me about periods.

KIRSTY, aged 17, from York: I think years ago there were so many restrictions and my mum was brought up really badly. She's 37 now. She was not allowed to go anywhere or do anything, which is why she got married at 16, just to get away. I go to nightclubs and pubs, even though I shouldn't. My mum likes me to be in by about one o'clock in the morning and she never goes to sleep before I am in. She doesn't say I have to be in by then, but I am. I know all about sexual matters but I have learned from my friends rather than my parents. I would never take drugs or anything like that and basically my mum trusts me. With my own children I think it will be different, particularly knowing about life. I would rather have known more from my mum.

HANNAH, 14, Golders Green, north-west London: When I was eight I was allowed out on my own as long as it was not far and my parents knew where I was. Normally I was allowed to stay out until dark. My parents have never hit me.

If I am naughty they sit me down and explain why I was wrong and ask why I did it.

KARIN, 14, Golders Green: My mother has tried to talk to me about sex. Aids and babies but she treats me like a little girl and explains really simply. I know she is embarrassed but the things she tells me I already know about.

TARIQ, 15, Barnet, Hertfordshire: My mum went mad at me last weekend when I came home at 7.30 am after being at a rave. I should have told her what time I was going to be in. When I was 14 I started going to parties and my mum worried at first, but now I can stay out all night – as long as I tell her.

I had sex when I was 14 with this girl who was also 14. I think that most people I know will have done it before they are 16. None of our parents knows anything about it. Mine don't even know that I have got a girlfriend. I dread to think what they would say if they knew that I had sex when I was 14. I learnt all about sex at school and from the TV.

JON, 16, from Bristol: Friends of mine are having sex with their girlfriends but I admit I'm a virgin. I'm not just going to have sex so I can boast about it. I think it will be an interesting experience when the time comes. If I had a big emotional problem or needed somebody to turn to it wouldn't be my parents. But my parents are very good. I always tell them where I am going and what time I will be back and because I haven't let them down they don't mind me staying out late and going to pubs and clubs.

Although I drink I rarely get drunk. I smoke joints but I think that should be made legal – it's certainly not as bad as alcohol. If people smoked dope rather than drank there would be less violence. Bristol city centre is really dangerous with fighting late at night.

Source: *The Independent on Sunday*, 4 August 1991

1 What is the general attitude to sex given by:
a) the females?
b) the males?

2 Do these reflect your attitudes?

3 Is there a generation gap, do you think?

4 One way of finding out if a generation gap has opened up is to look at attitudes to drug use. Carry out a small-scale survey to compare attitudes to cannabis, alcohol and ecstacy use by age.

The elderly

Today, 20 per cent of the population is above retirement age and that figure is going to continue increasing until the end of this century. Improvements in hygiene, in standards of living and, to a lesser extent, in medical care have caused this rapid expansion in life expectation. Here we will concentrate on changing attitudes to the elderly and the problems they face.

Old people feel trapped by the attitudes of young people

Never before in history have there been so many elderly people. A time traveller from the seventeenth century would be just as shocked to see all the old faces around as by the changes in technology. Indeed he would be shocked by the numbers of people over the age of 40, never mind 60! In most societies, old people would be of enough rarity to guarantee them some degree of status. Furthermore, in societies based on agriculture there is little change, each generation learns from the previous one. It was true to say that old people may well have had relevant advice to give to younger generations. The pace of change in advanced technological societies like our own means that the experience of one generation is not really useful to the next. The result is that the old in our society have low status. For many, old age is a time to be feared, a time of decline preceding death.

But it is not all bad. First of all, people do not just live longer, they remain active and healthy longer. It is claimed that the most affluent and relaxed period of people's lives now is the first eight years after retirement. Secondly, there is no real evidence that the elderly were treated with any great respect in the past. The elderly of today remember being respectful to the elderly when they were young, but they would say that, wouldn't they!

Variations among the elderly

The underlying assumption is that the elderly are a problem for society. The growing proportion of the population who are elderly is emphasised, and particularly the burden of the 'old' elderly (i.e. over seventy-five years old) and the 'very old' elderly (over eight-five). These two groups are [seen] as a burden on the State because they are high users of health and welfare services. They are also seen as a burden on women because policies of community care mean that most...care of the elderly is done by women.

The elderly are primarily seen as a homogeneous [single group with similar characteristics] group and attention is given to age relations, rather than class or gender differences among the elderly.

...[They are also seen]...as of low moral worth—evident from the 'social problem' focus and from the more general image of the elderly as poor, disabled, dependent and passive.

But how does social class influence these age relations? We have only to consider the Queen Mother, the House of Lords and many elderly judges and politicians to realise the sharp contrast they provide to the more general image of the elderly.

Source: S. Arber, 'Class and the Elderly' in *Social Studies Review*, 1989

1 What is the assumption when talking about the elderly?

2 What two groups of the elderly are seen as particularly burdensome?

3 Why is it incorrect to talk about the elderly as a homogeneous group?

4 Is it true, as the writer argues, that we hold the elderly in 'low moral worth'? Why do you think we hold some elderly in respect, as indicated in the extract, and the majority of the elderly as of 'low moral worth'?

5 At present, in your family, are the oldest generation contributing positively to the quality of life of the younger members of the family or you personally?

6 Make a list of the costs and benefits of the elderly in your family and your community.

7 Within your group or class, how many of you would be prepared (or are doing so now) to look after your parents should they become unable to look after themselves?

8 Whose responsibility are the elderly?

The supercentenarians of Abkhazi

In a few parts of the world, remote from the hustle and bustle of Western life, there are people today who are living extraordinarily long lives. One such place is Abkhazi in the Southern USSR.

In Britain the number of supercentenarians (people over 100) is estimated at 1 in 4000 of the population. In this area of Russia, the number is 204 in 4000. Perhaps the most important reason for long life is the attitude of these people to growing old and in the way their society is organised. At an age when most people in this country are thinking of drawing their pension, Abkhazians think of themselves as in their prime. They are not obsessed by age as we are. No one is forced to retire at 60 or 65 and older people go on working in the fields, caring for the flocks of sheep, doing housework and looking after their grandchildren and are involved in everything that goes on in the community.

Source: *People not Pensioners* (Help the Aged, 1978)

1 What is the main reason for the long life span?

2 What are the main differences between the way old people in Abkhzai act and the way old people act in our society?

3 Give three examples of how you treat old people differently from people your own age. Coule you imagine treating old people in the same way as those of your age?

Family life and the changing life styles of the elderly

A big house used to be a good idea with a family.

But now that you are alone again it may seem more of a burden than an asset.

The upkeep of a large, near empty home can be an expensive liability, as well as a quiet and lonely place. The rooms you rarely use, repairs that are never done, and a garden which seems to grow bigger by the year. Isn't it time you took a closer look at *Countryside's* exciting range of luxurious apartments.

Created with you in mind, the care and dedication applied to the design and construction of these exclusive apartments is the hallmark of *Countryside's* reputation for building quality homes of character and elegance.

Any essential repair and maintenance jobs are taken care of, and with a residential housekeeper, it's nice to know someone is there to cope with any emergencies.

Strolling in the beautifully landscaped garden, relaxing in the friendly atmosphere of the residents lounge, or the comfort of your own apartment. Whichever you choose, you can be sure that *Countryside's* unique blend of complete privacy when you want it, or a shared environment when you don't, allows you the privilege of enjoying the retirement you deserve.

If you live in Essex or East Anglia and would like to visit one of our luxury retirement apartments but find it difficult to do so, we will be happy to collect you, show you round and take you home again.

For further details please complete the coupon or telephone **Eve Bayley** on **(0277) 234136.**

Countryside

Advertisements like this are becoming increasingly common.

1 Which group are they aimed at?

2 Why are builders finding this group a worthwhile target for advertising?

3 What is the 'family life cycle' (see page 146)? Why is it relevant to the advert?

4 What does the advert tell us about old age in Britain?

The third age

In spite of the "halo" effect of nostalgia, 38 per cent of the over-50s now think that life is more satisfying than when they were younger, compared with 33 per cent in 1988. Among those aged 50–54, the figure rises to 47 per cent, much higher than for people aged 15–34. Even among the over-70s, satisfaction levels are rising – from 24 per cent in 1988 to 28 per cent now.

A Mintel study on the "third age" – those over 50 – says that their influence, demographically and on the marketplace, will rise dramatically in the 1990s as the baby-boom generation turns grey.

During the 1990s the number of over-50s will increase by 9 per cent, compared with a 3 per cent growth in total population. By 2001 there will be a "staggering" 31 per cent increase in the number of adults in their early 50s and a 15 per cent rise in people in their late 50s.

"Third-agers", the study says, have more surplus income and leisure time. They spend it on holidays, visits, pets, gardening, reading books and newspapers, eating out and watching videos. The 55–64 age group is also the keenest on gambling.

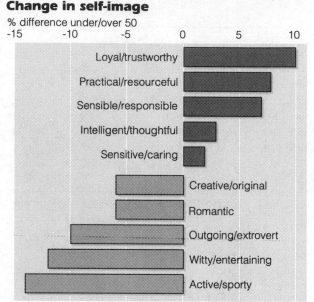

Change in self-image

Source: 'Baby boom generation is "glad to be grey"' by D. Nicholson-Lord in *The Independent*, 9 November 1993

Is life better now?

	% more satisfied now than when they were younger	
	1988	1992
All 50+	33	38
Men	34	43
Women	31	34
50–54	46	47
55–59	40	47
60–64	29	39
65–69	23	38
70+	24	28
AB	37	47
C1	30	40
C2	36	41
D	37	32
E	26	28
Married	38	43
Not married	22	28

Source: 'Back to the generation gap' by P. Kellner in *The Independent on Sunday*, 4 August 1991

1 Explain what the term 'third age' means.

2 The general belief is that the older you get the less happy you are. What does this extract say?

3 What increase will there be in the number of people in their early fifties in the year 2001?

4 Can you think of any effects this might have on society (patterns of consumption, holidays, the media, etc.)?

5 Look at the chart showing changes in self-image. Which self-images decline?

6 What self-images increase?

7 Design a simple questionnaire to ask a sample of three 'third agers' how they would rank these attributes gained and lost.

8 Look at the table 'Is life better now?'. What differences are there by:
a) sex?
b) age?
c) social class?

The last word

The following piece was given to me by my 93-year-old aunt, who thought I might like it for the book – I did, thanks Auntie Chris!

Some thoughts of a 'senior citizen'

Since my retirement I have had plenty of time to contemplate. Lately, I have been contemplating the Hereafter. Several times, having passed from one room to another, I pause and say, 'What on earth am I here after?' However, growing old has its compensations. I now have silver in my hair, gold in my teeth, lead in my limbs, stones in my kidneys and natural gas in my stomach. I'm rich!

Just think, we Senior Citizens were here before video, television, frozen foods, credit cards, ball-point pens, plastic, polio vaccinations and contact lenses. When we 'mugged' a person, we did so by settling their bill (usually drinks). For us, time-sharing meant togetherness. We wound up our watches daily and had no calculators other than the brain God gave us. A chip was either a piece of wood for fire lighting or a piece of fried potato. Hardware meant something from the chandler's and software wasn't even in the dictionary. Jeans were any property belonging to a girl of that name.

We had no dishwashers, tumble driers or central heating. Fast food was what we ate during Lent. We married first and then lived together (how quaint!), but how nice! Divorce was a pastime exclusive to film stars, and girls thought that 'cleavage' was what a butcher did. Bunnies were little rabbits and dishes were for eating off, not for receiving signals from outer space. We smoked cigarettes. Pot was for cooking in and grass was for mowing. Rock music was a lullaby and AIDS were for people hard of hearing. We used manual typewriters and carbons for copying. FAX was what we looked up in an encyclopedia. We were before: vitamin pills, disposable nappies, Macdonalds and pizzas. Instant coffee and Chinese takeaways were unknown. 'Made in Japan' meant poor quality.

How in God's name did we exist? We must have been a tough bunch!

Chapter

7

FAMILIES, PARTNERSHIPS AND MARRIAGE

This chapter covers:
- Types of family
- The changing form of the family
- The role of the family in society
- Lone parents
- Alternatives to the family
- Love and marriage
- Marriage
- Divorce
- Family relationships.

Types of family

A family is best described as a group of people living with or near each other, who are closely related by marriage or blood. (Unrelated people who live together and give each other help are usually known as a 'commune'.) 'Kin' means a wider circle of people who are related to one another and who generally give each other help. However, the contact is not as close as between the family.

There are four main types of family organisation: the **extended family**, the **nuclear family**, the **lone-parent family** (also known as the **single-parent family**) and the **reconstituted family**.

The extended family

This generally consists of three generations of people, that is grandparents, parents and children, who all live very close to each other and maintain close contact.

The extended family is usually found in societies where a large group of people living together can be of real use. For example, in an agricultural society where people live off the produce of the land, a large group of people can sow, reap and care for the animals most efficiently. Or in an industrial society, where there is a great poverty, the mutual aid provided by a large group of workers is most useful in surviving in periods of crisis. There is clear evidence for it amongst the working class in Britain until the 1950s and it exists today amongst Asian immigrants in Britain.

The nuclear family

This is much smaller than the extended family and generally consists only of parents and their children, of which there is usually a maximum of three. Contact with the wider kin is much weaker and less frequent than amongst members of the extended family.

The nuclear family is usually found where a large group would be more of a hindrance than a help. In some simple societies based on hunting, food is in short supply and a small, fast moving group is more likely to survive. Nuclear families are also found in advanced industrial societies, such as our own, where there is less need to rely upon the family for help. This appears to be the most common form of family in Britain today.

The lone-parent family

This consists of a single parent plus his or her dependent children. It is *usually* headed by a female. In Britain, the single parent reflects the rise in the divorce rate and, to a lesser degree, pregnancy outside marriage or death of a partner.

Reconstituted families

As the number of divorces and remarriages increase, and there is a parallel increase in the number of people who change from cohabiting with one partner to another, there is a consequent increase in the numbers of families which are headed by step-mothers and step-fathers, each of whom may bring their own children to live together.

Being a divorcee or the head of a lone-parent family is usually a temporary condition as nearly three-quarters of men who divorce, and a slightly smaller percentage of women, remarry within five years. It is estimated that about six million people live in reconstituted families of one type or another, and 1 in 10 children are currently living with step-parents.

As soon as a 'nuclear family' mould is broken the nature of the relationships that constitute 'family' are opened to question. If a man comes to live with a divorced woman who has three children, does his mother become their grandmother? Can he, himself, be their stepfather if there is no marriage? If so, how long must he be in residence before he graduates into that role from being the mother's lover? And if there is a marriage, does he, the step-father, remain part of the children's family if their mother divorces him? Policies based on the old, neat categories of 'marriage' and 'divorce' simply do not fit today's world.

Source: P. Hewitt and P. Leach, *Social Justice, Children and Families* (Commission on Social Justice)

Defining the family is not as simple as it might once have been.

Changing form of the family

Before industrialisation, when most people obtained their living from the land, people lived for a relatively short time (a typical person in seventeenth-century England would expect to die in their early 40s). They apparently married and had children fairly late in their lives. The result was that it was unusual for a family of three generations to live together, simply because the chances of people surviving to the age of being grandparents were slim.

What was common was that families of parents, children and their spouses often lived close to one another and had frequent contact. Households were often large, not because there were extended families living together, but because it was common practice in pre-industrial Britain for the better-off to take the children of the poor as servants, or helpers. When they grew up, they left their adopted 'home' to look for better employment.

So for most people, the nuclear family was normal, but people lived nearer to one another and had greater contact than today.

The better-off were more likely to live in extended families because they had longer life expectancies, caused by better diets and less work, and also because family members were more likely to stay at home as their parents could provide for them, with land and jobs.

The pre-industrial family

In the 1970s, two books overturned the theory that most families in Britain were of the extended type before industrialisation, as was normal throughout most of Europe.

Laslett, in *The world we have lost*, studied the parish records of births, marriages and deaths of 100 English villages from the sixteenth century to the nineteenth century. He concluded that most households throughout this period had an average size of 4.75 persons; in other words, the normal family type was the nuclear family throughout this period.

Anderson, in *Family structure in nineteenth-century Lancashire*, studied the census material for Preston, Lancashire in 1851. He concluded that there was an increase in the size of the family at about this time. He explains this by saying that the increase in jobs provided by industrialisation meant that more distant relatives were attracted to the town and these came to live with the families already living there. Some stayed at home to look after the children and some worked in factories. The result was a type of community and family structure similar to that found in East London in the early 1950s, which has now died out.

1 What was the most common family type in pre-industrial England: extended or nuclear?

2 What happened with the growth of industrialisation?

3 Why did these books change sociologists' ideas about the family before industrialisation?

4 What type of family was most common in Europe before industrialisation?

The effects of industrialisation on the form of the family in Britain

For the poor, the effects of industrialisation on the family structure were considerable. Jobs in agriculture declined and those in factories expanded rapidly, so that people were forced to move into towns. Long hours of work, in dreadful conditions, with low pay and no form of welfare state meant that the extended family became a very useful way of pooling resources in times of need or illness. Also, after the early stages of industrialisation were over, life expectancy increased. So, by the middle of the nineteenth century, the extended family had become common amongst the working class and this form of 'self-help' continued well into this century.

Gradually, better conditions of life and the activities of the Welfare State eroded the mutual need that had created the industrial extended family and there has been a move towards the nuclear family. Contact with wider kin is maintained though, through the use of telephones and cars. This means that a family does not have to live together to keep in contact.

For the middle class, the extended family was normal throughout the nineteenth century. The main reason for this was **nepotism**, that is jobs and income were obtained through the father. The younger generation stayed at home because it was in their financial interests to do so, and middle-class women were trapped at home because it was not considered right for them to work.

Early in this century there was a move towards the nuclear family, as the younger generation were able to find their own jobs, and there grew the cultural stress on the close relationship between husband, wife and children to the exclusion of the wider kin. So small nuclear families developed.

An influence on both the middle and working classes, leading to nuclear-style families, has been the increase in **geographical mobility**. In order to find work in modern societies, it is necessary to move. The smaller, nuclear family with its looser ties to kin, allows people to move more easily.

Geographical mobility and technology have altered family life

The extended family – alive and well, and living in Britain today

In the mid-1980s Peter Willmott studied family life in North London. He expected to find isolated families, but in fact he found the extended family to have altered in form, but still to be vibrant. He concluded that there were three types of extended family which encompassed most kinship arrangements in Britain.

The first type is the *local extended family*. Typically two or perhaps three nuclear families in separate households – parents and their married children, typically daughters, with their own children – live near each other. They see each other every day or nearly every day, and they provide mutual aid on a continuing basis. This kind of arrangement probably still applies to something like one in eight of the adult population of Britain. It is more common among working-class families than middle-class, in stable

communities than in those marked by residential mobility or redevelopment, and in the north of England, the Midlands, Scotland and Wales rather than in southern England.

The second type, and the one that is now becoming dominant, is the *dispersed extended family*. Like the local extended family, this is composed of two or more nuclear families, again typically made up of parents and their married children, with their children. The big difference is that it is not localised and the meetings are consequently less

frequent. Nonetheless, there is still fairly frequent contact, say once a week or once a fortnight, and support is still provided both in emergency and on a regular basis. Such an arrangement depends on cars (or a good public transport service) and on telephones. This pattern is probably more common in middle-class circles than in working-class ones. The evidence on contacts suggests that this second type probably operates for about half the adult population.

On these estimates, this leaves

under half the population for whom kinship is less important. Their type of arrangement might be called the *attenuated extended family*. The people concerned include students and other young people, both those who are single and young couples before they have any children of their own. They are at a stage when they are, as they need to be, breaking away from their family of origin – when kinship matters less, and their age peers more, than at any other phase in life.

Source: P. Willmott, 'Urban kinship past and present' in *Social Studies Review*, November 1988

1 Draw up a table to summarise the characteristics of the three types of extended family. Use the following headings: *Type of extended family, Proportion of population, Characteristics.*

2 What differences are there from the traditional extended family as described in the main text?

Two views of the contemporary extended family

Small families are only one reason for the lack of support networks. Even where exceptionally large families exist and have extensive kin-networks intact, they are often too geographically dispersed to be useful to each other on a day to day basis. And even where

relatives do still live closely together, the adults of both generations [may be working] so that the presence of a grandmother, aunt or sister just down the street is no guarantee of help, and parents may not even seek it.

1 What three reasons are there for a lack of support between people today?

2 Do you think this lack of support is true for your family? Read the next extract and see whether it reflects your experience more.

Source: Adapted from P. Hewitt and P. Leach, *Social Justice, Children and Families* (Commission on Social Justice, 1993)

But that is not the end of the story. If one looks, in the 1980s, not at the *proximity* of relatives but at *contacts* between them, a different picture comes into focus. A number of recent surveys have shown that between about two-thirds and three-quarters of people – people of all ages, not just the elderly – still see at least one relative at least once a week. I recently completed a study of married people with young children in a North London suburb, a district where as

many as a third of the couples had moved in within the previous five years. There, the proportion seeing relatives at least weekly was precisely two-thirds. Of those with parents alive, one in ten saw their mother or father or both every day, and nearly two-thirds of living parents and parents-in-law were seen at least once a month. Working-class people saw rather more of their parents and other relatives than middle-class people did, but the differences were not large.

The evidence from that and other recent studies also shows that relatives continue to be the main source of informal support and care, and that again the class differences are not marked. In my North London research, nearly two-thirds of people were helped by relatives, particularly mothers or mothers-in-law, when one of the children was ill; nearly three-quarters were helped with babysitting, again mainly by mothers or mothers-in-law. Four-fifths looked to relatives,

mainly parents or parents-in-law, when they needed to borrow money. Surveys of elderly people show that most of the informal help and care they receive comes from relatives, particularly their children or children-in-law.

So, despite a decline in the proportions of people living with or very near to relatives kinship remains an important force in the lives of most people.

Source: P. Willmott, 'Urban kinship past and present' in *Social Studies Review*, November 1988

This extract describing research in the mid-1980s tells a different story.

1 Does Willmott see the family as being actively helpful?

2 Give three examples of this help.

3 In your opinion, which extract describes life in contemporary society?

The role of the family in society

It would not be unrealistic to argue that the family forms the cornerstone of our society. A world without the family would seem strange to us. However, there is some disagreement between sociologists about whether the family is a good thing for society, or not. We can understand this better if we examine the role of the family under two headings: the beneficial view (the family is useful) and the critical view (the family is harmful).

The beneficial view

The role of the family in small-scale agricultural or hunting societies was absolutely central. Indeed, in many cases the tribe was really a few extended families joined together. Individuals were taught the skills necessary to survive, were given work and received status and authority in the wider tribe according to their position in the family.

Industrialisation, urbanisation (the growth of cities) and the sheer numbers of people in society have altered the position of the family in modern society. But it still remains an extremely important social institution which fundamentally influences the course of our lives. The family acts as the link between the individual and society and, according to the beneficial view, it benefits both.

Socialisation

The individual

In order for a person to become truly 'human', that is to act in socially acceptable ways, an individual must be socialised (see Chapter 1). This is the basic role a family performs for individuals, moulding them to the expectations of society. Only through this can a person a play a full part in social life.

Society

Society cannot exist without rules and expectations of behaviour. A society full of unpredictable individuals would simply collapse in chaos. The family socialises children into correct forms of behaviour. If children (or adults) fall out of step with society in some way, the family is usually the first place where punishment takes place, so the family not only socialises, but also acts as an agent of social control (see pages 234–7).

Emotion

The individual

Young children need to be shown care and affection to become stable adults. The family is ideally the place where this affection is freely given. Even for adults, there is a need for people to discuss their problems and to feel needed. At its best, the family can keep a person emotionally fulfilled and stable.

Society

If society is to continue, then people must be motivated to carry on and not to drop out. By giving people a reason to work, to uphold the rules of society and to conform, the family effectively ensures the continuation of society.

Economic provision

The individual

Young children need to be supported until they reach the age of self-sufficiency. The family provides for them and for adults who are not working through incapacity or unemployment. All aid from the state is channelled through the family to individuals.

Society

The modern family does not work together producing goods as in pre-industrial times, but today families do *consume* as a unit. Clothing, food and household items all make the family a major agency of spending in our society and, therefore, it is still very important economically.

Reproduction and sexual activity

The individual

Although sexual activity is common outside marriage, for most people regular sexual activity is limited to their husband/wife, or the person they intend to marry. As a result of this pattern of sexual activity, most of us are born into families.

Society

A society can only exist if there are people. Quite simply families produce the people who compose each generation. If unregulated, sexual activity causes problems of jealousy and conflict. By having a culture which stresses that the correct place for sex is within permanent relationships, much conflict is eliminated.

Social status

The individual

Being born into a family gives an individual identity – a name, background and a social class position.

Society

Families promote social order by locating people along class and status lines. Individuals know where they belong, where others are in the class structure and their own position with regard to them.

The critical view

The analysis of the role of the family which we have just examined is generally associated with the *functionalist* school of thought in sociology. This approach usually examines any social institution, such as the family, or education system by asking the question: What function does this social institution perform for society?

Asking this sort of question usually leads these sociologists to stress the beneficial aspects of the institution under question, and to underplay the harmful aspects, so the family is seen as giving such things as love and affection.

Other sociologists are critical of the functionalists' account of the family and point out the various harmful aspects of family life. These critics point out that violence against children and wives is commonplace and each year in Britain some children are actually beaten to death by their parents.

Violence

In the last ten years there has been the growth of refuges for women who are repeatedly attacked by their partners. (These are usually large houses where the women can stay to escape from their partners.)

Sexual abuse

Another disturbing aspect of family life is the sexual molesting of children, generally by their fathers. Nobody knows the full extent of this problem, as it is rarely reported. Nevertheless, according to social workers, it is far more common than generally believed.

Emotion

The intense emotional ties of the modern nuclear family can lead to forms of psychological damage and emotional hurt. Constant conflict between parents can lead to divorce, broken homes and great emotional suffering. In some cases this is associated with crime. Some psychologists have gone even further and have suggested that emotional conflict within the family can actually cause mental illness.

Women repressed

Finally, feminist writers have constantly pointed out the unfairness of family life to women. They usually give up their jobs to have children, then are isolated at home in the role of housewife, and are expected to look after everyone else in the family, unpaid.

The family, therefore, must be seen as having many drawbacks as well as benefits.

Negative views of the family

In the past, kinsfolk and neighbours gave the individual continuous moral support throughout his life. Today the domestic household is isolated. The family looks inward upon itself; there is an intensification of emotional stress between husband and wife, and parents and children. The strain is greater than most of us can bear. Far from being the basis of the good society, the family, with its narrow privacy and tawdry secrets, is the source of all our discontents.

Source: E. R. Leach, *A Runaway World?* (BBC Publications, 1967)

At the present time, at least, if not in the future, there is no better guarantee of long life, health, and happiness for men than a wife well socialised to perform the 'duties of a wife', willing to devote her life to taking care of him, providing, even enforcing, the regularity and security of a well-ordered home.

Source: J. Bernard, *The Future of Marriage* (Souvenir Press, 1973)

1 According to Leach, in the past who, apart from family members, gave aid and support to individuals throughout their lives?

2 How has this changed and with what results?

3 Does Leach see the family as a good thing?

4 According to Bernard, who benefits from marriage?

Researchers have found that wife beating is perhaps the most under-reported crime. One estimate suggests that only one of 270 incidents of wife abuse is ever reported to the authorities.

Common among women's experiences of physical assault are reports of sexual assault.

Approximately 10% of Russell's respondents who had ever been married reported being raped and beaten by their husbands.

...I have had ten stitches, three stitches, seven stitches where he has cut me. I have had a knife stuck through my stomach; I have had a poker put through my face; I have no teeth were he knocked them out; I have been burnt with red hot pokers...

Keeping the relationship together, despite the violence, is also important for practical reasons – financial support, shelter, even access to the ability to earn a living many times rests with the husband/boyfriend. ...Women often feel inadequate to cope with self-sufficiency; the lack of self-confidence often acts as a trap to keep women within a violent home.

Source: E. A. Stanko, *Intimate Intrusions: Women's Experience of Male Violence*, (Routledge, 1985)

1 In your opinion, is Stanko saying that rape and violence are common or uncommon in male–female relationships?

2 Why don't women leave violent partners?

3 Do you have sympathy for women who continue to stay with violent partners? Explain your answer.

4 Using all three extracts, draw up a list of benefits and disadvantages of marriage for:
a) males
b) females.
In your opinion, who benefits?

The negative side of the family

Child sex abuse reports rise by 90%

Reported cases of child sexual abuse have risen by an estimated 90 per cent in the past year, the National Society of the Prevention of Cruelty to Children said yesterday. The charity estimates that more than 2850 children were placed on local authority registers last year compared with 1500 in 1984.

The society believes the increase, the largest recorded, shows a growing awareness of the problem rather than a great increase in the number of children being abused. The proportion of under-fours being sexually assaulted was 14 per cent last year...

Twenty-nine per cent of young boys reported assaulted were under the age of four, compared with 11 per cent of girls. The majority of reported sexual assaults are of young girls aged 10 to 14.

Most of the people who sexually assault children are fathers, close male relatives or stepfathers. However reported assaults on under-fours contain suggestions – still to be analysed in depth – that neighbours and other child carers may be to blame.

There are more reports of sexual assaults on children among those on low incomes and living in bad conditions but this may be because middle class people tend not to be monitored as closely by social workers or health visitors.

Dr Alan Gilmour, director of the NSPCC, said: 'It is far more likely that the case of sexual abuse will be reported in a tenement rather than a stately home.'...

Dr Gilmour renewed his criticism of the Government for failing to keep national figures of the incidence of child abuse or to ask local authorities to compile standard figures. ...However, there are no moves to order authorities to keep special child sexual abuse registers.

The initial analysis of the first 200 who sought refuge in Britain's first 'safe house' for runaway adolescents, run by the Church of England Children's Society, shows that one in six who have run away from their parents has been sexually abused.

One in seven of the children – nearly all under the age of 16 – has been referred to the centre by the police after being caught soliciting in London.

Each case has been confirmed by staff at the centre, who found that many complaints to teachers or social workers had been dismissed earlier as fantasy.

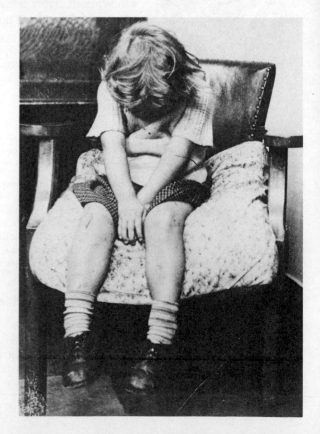

Source: *The Guardian*, 19 June 1986

1 What was the percentage rise in child sex abuse cases?

2 Which groups are most at risk?

3 Who is most likely to make the assaults?

4 Do you think the statistics reflect an accurate picture of what is happening? Explain your answer.

Lone parents

One of the most significant changes in the family in the last 20 years has been the steady growth of lone- (or single-) parent families. Today there are over 1.3 million lone-parent families with approximately 2.2 million children within them. This is double the number of the mid-1970s. Today, one in every five families with dependent children is a lone-parent family. Lone-parent families are the result of divorce or separation from a relationship, of the death of one of the original partners or the fact that the mother has never married.

In the 1990s there has been considerable debate over the effects of lone-parent families on the children involved, and also the costs to the state in social security payments. Critics argue that the growth of lone-parent families, particularly those where the mother has never been married, harms the children because they have no father both to provide financial support and to help socialise them into the values of society. They argue that the result of this is that the children are more likely to grow up with personal problems. They also point out that the state has to support the family as the mother is often unable to work because of childcare responsibilities. On the other hand, those who defend lone-parent families point out that the majority of lone mothers are there through divorce, and that generally women who are lone mothers are not in this state for a long time, as they generally will cohabit or marry within five years.

Lone-parent families

Numbers of lone-parent families

1971

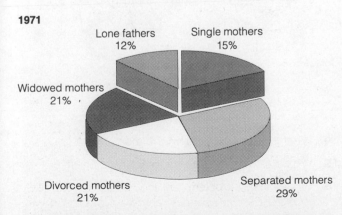

Lone fathers 12%
Single mothers 15%
Widowed mothers 21%
Divorced mothers 21%
Separated mothers 29%

Source: Office of Population Censuses and Surveys, 1979

1991

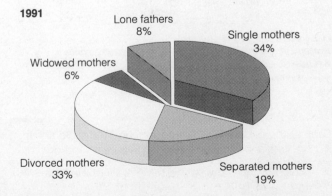

Lone fathers 8%
Single mothers 34%
Widowed mothers 6%
Divorced mothers 33%
Separated mothers 19%

Source: A. Garnham and E. Knights, *Putting the Treasury First – The Truth about Child Support* (CPAG, 1994)

Estimated numbers of lone-parent families in 1971 and 1991

Type of family with number (thousands) of dependent children			% of all families
	1971	1991*	1991
Lone mothers:			
single	90	440	6
separated	170	250	4
divorced	120	430	6
widowed	120	80	1
Lone mothers	500	1200	18
Lone fathers	70	100	1
Lone parents	570	1300	19
Married couple families (includes some cohabiting couples)	–	–	81
All families	–	6840	100

*Provisional figures (rounded) for 1991

Source: A. Garnham and E. Knights, *Putting the Treasury First – The Truth about Child Support* (CPAG, 1994)

Reasons for growth in the number of single-parent families:
- *Divorce, separation, death of partner*
- *Women not wishing to marry when pregnant.*

Look at the pie charts on page 125 and the table above.

1 Name the five categories of lone-parent families.

2 Which group is the smallest? What were the figures in 1971 and 1991?

3 What reasons could you put forward for this being the smallest category?

4 What category has grown the most?

5 What has happened to the other categories?

6 What sorts of problems are lone-parent families likely to face? Can you suggest any ways of coping with these problems?

Single-parent families – a problem?

People who choose to live as single parents were condemned yesterday by Dr Rhodes Boyson...for creating 'probably the most evil product of our time'. ...

He blamed the one-parent family for many of the problems facing Britain, and said that such families would be increased by 'the rise of artificial insemination and casual sex relations'. ...

'Low paid members of normal families are taxed at standard rate to subsidise not only those forced to be one-parent families by misfortune but also to subsidise those who have specifically chosen to be one-parent families.'

Dr Boyson said that one in seven children lived in one-parent families, with one in three in the inner cities. He blamed 'the wildness of the uncontrolled male young' on a lack of fathers.

'Boys can generally only be civilised by firm and caring fathers. The banishment of the father means that boys take their values from their aggressive and often brutal peer groups and are prepared for a life of violent crime, of football hooliganism, mugging and inner city revolt.'

The family was under attack from extreme feminists, the youth cults, and homosexual lobbies, he said.

Source: *The Guardian*, 10 October 1986

Michael Portillo last night launched a moral crusade – starting with a crackdown on teenage pregnancies.

Mr Portillo said the greatest increase in numbers receiving social security payments was among single parents.

"Over 8,000 girls under the age of 16 become pregnant every year in England and Wales, the equivalent of two in every secondary school," he said.

"Our rate of teenage pregnancies is seven times higher than Holland and not I think because the British teenager is more likely to have premarital sex than her Dutch counterpart.

"And our rate of abortions is higher, too.

"Teenage pregnancies often lead to a whole life of state dependence with few luxuries.

"The question is what action could be taken by any of us to reduce the incidence of pregnancy among those not wishing or not ready to start on family life."

Another vital question was the impact of benefits on incentives to work and the willpower to help oneself.

"Too broad a benefit system can undermine the morale of those who receive help," he said.

"Young people in particular may see no reason to work from their earliest days if they can get money for being idle."

Source: *The Daily Express*, 16 September 1993

According to the Department of Social Security statistics, nearly half the lone mothers on Income Support are aged between 20 and 29. Only 5 per cent are aged between 16 and 19.

Source: A. Garnham and E. Knights, *Putting the Treasury First – The Truth about Child Support* (CPAG, 1994)

Read the three extracts.

1 Give three criticisms made by Dr Boyson on lone parents.

2 Which group of lone parents is Mr Portillo attacking?

3 As a politician, what is he particularly concerned about?

4 Do you agree with the points made by Dr Boyson and Mr Portillo?

5 Does the final extract support Mr Portillo or not, do you think?

Varieties of family in Britain

Immigration has brought a number of family forms to Britain that are clearly different from traditional patterns. Such families put a much greater emphasis on the demands and duties of kinship.

Asian families are a clear example of this. Ballard argues that the basic pattern of a south Asian family consists of a man, his son and grandsons, together with their wives and unmarried daughters. This family has been transferred into a British setting. The man is clearly the head of the household, controlling the family finances and negotiating the major family decisions.

The male dominated nature of family life creates a very different experience for women within the ethnic minorities. In the early years of immigration, many women found themselves cut off from outside society. Social and language barriers kept them trapped in the home. Some Asian families created a state of Purdah [the woman must keep herself covered and is allowed no contact with men outside the family].

The reason for the attempt by ethnic minorities to control the lives of women is the need to maintain family honour. Every member should be seen to behave properly.

Serious problems have been created with the second generation, the immigrants' children who were born and have been brought up in the United Kingdom. School teaches these children to want more independence, as opposed to the family stress on loyalty and obedience. It must also be remembered that many of the first generation immigrants grew up in societies where there

Source: A. Wilson, *The Family* (Tavistock, 1985)

was no such thing as adolescence or youth culture, so conflict is inevitable when their children act like British teenagers.

West Indian families in Britain present a further distinct family pattern, that reflects their culture of origin. The colonial system based on slavery weakened the bonds between men and women. The lack of stable employment later left the man unable to support a family by his own efforts. The mother-child relationship became the central structure of the family.

Driver suggests that there are two types of black family structure in Britain. There is the nuclear family, where both partners share the full range of domestic tasks. But there is also the mother-centred family. The black mother is left to bring up the children, run the home and provide income. She must do this in England without the range of support that she could have obtained from female relatives in the West Indies. This is caused by the lack of stable employment for men.

1 From the description of the South Asian family, would you call it 'nuclear' or 'extended'?

2 Who is the clear head of the South Asian family? Give two reasons for your answer.

3 Describe the situation of women in the more traditional South Asian family.

4 Why should there be 'serious problems' for the Asian family 'created with the second generation'?

5 There are two patterns of West Indian family in Britain. What are they?

6 What reasons can you suggest for the growth of the two different types of West Indian family?

Alternatives to the family

Critics of the family have long sought an alternative that would provide the beneficial aspects of economic and emotional security, without the restrictions on freedom that the family normally imposes.

Abolition of the family

The first, and obvious solution is to abolish the family completely. The two best known attempts to abolish family life were in the USSR after the communist revolution, and the activities of the revolutionary Khmer Rouge which took over in Cambodia in the 1970s.

In both cases the family was seen as the link that perpetuated the values of the old society. If the new communist society was to succeed the younger generation had to be brought up with a new set of values. Family life and marriage were weakened and children encouraged to see the state as their 'family' rather than their own kin.

In the USSR (and, as far as we know, in Cambodia) the result was chaos with an increase in crime, in deserted children and social problems in general. The state simply could not cope with people as individuals, it needed the organisational unit of the family. Soon, in the USSR the family was re-introduced and even promoted as the ideal way to live. The Khmer Rouge regime collapsed and has been replaced by a society which stresses family life.

Communes

The second alternative to the family is the commune, that is a group of people living together who generally share their possessions and treat children as 'belonging' to the whole commune, not just to their parents. A number of communes exist in Britain today usually based on religious ideals. However, probably the most famous form of commune is the *kibbutz* of Israel, although only 2 per cent of the population actually live in these communes. *Kibbutzim* are generally agricultural-based, with some element of industry. Jobs are allocated on a rota (so everybody does 'good' and 'bad' work), and rather than wages, each *kibbutz* provides for all the wants of its members. Marriage is not regarded as important; couples can simply share rooms if they desire. Children themselves do not usually live with their parents but with others of their own age group in dormitories, simply sharing the evening meal with their parents if they so desire. According to the *kibbutz* philosophy, children should not see themselves as possessions of their parents but as independent members of the *kibbutz*.

1 What do you think about the idea of a commune?

2 Would you live in one with your friends?

3 What would your attitudes be to sexual relationships?

4 Who would look after the children?

5 What would happen if you had a difference of opinion? How would you sort it out?

6 How would you organise the finances?

7 Do you see any problems?

Love and marriage

A comparison of marriage types

In Britain, we regard marriage as the 'union of a man and a woman'. However, this is not the only type of marriage in the world. Below are some of the varieties of marriage that exist.

General types	Name	Description	Where?	Why?
Monogamy	Monogamy	One man married to one woman	Europe today Japan	A balance between males and females, with a cultural stress on the relative equality of male and female; Christian culture
	Serial monogamy	Couples marry, divorce, then re-marry different partners	USA Britain Europe	Decline in the sanctity of marriage; not seen as lasting a lifetime; associated with increase in divorce; secular culture
Polygamy	Polyandry	One woman married to a number of men	Parts of Tibet	Restricts numbers of children so keeps population low; useful in agricultural societies with limited amount of land
	Polygyny	One man married to a number of women	Acceptable amongst Mormons of Utah, USA, some Muslim local societies	Maximises possible number of children; important in societies with a high death-rate; possibly linked to imbalance of sexes (too many females); Muslim and Mormon cultures

Polygyny

It is widely believed that polygyny (having more than one wife) originated in response to the social and economic needs of rural African societies. It provided as many hands as possible to cultivate the land, and fight against high infant mortality. Children in Africa are believed to increase the prestige, wealth and social status of the family, and are thus always welcome. Yet polygyny was transferred almost intact to the cities among rich and poor, workers and intellectuals alike. ...In Senegal 32 per cent of men had two or more wives. However, urban polygyny is difficult to justify in terms of salaries and costs. Salaries are low, families are large and few individuals within families are breadwinners (because of unemployment).

Marianne Diop is 56; she works as a secretary in a hospital. Her husband is a retired postman. Mr Diop has married four wives in all, sired 22 children and divorced twice. He now shares his life with second and third wives, Marianne and Animata. They live in different houses but within walking distance.

Mr Diop only involves himself in crises, like the birth of an illegitimate child to his daugher. The everyday needs of the children are the mother's concern.

It would be unfair to portray Mr Diop as a selfish indifferent man. But with two wives, two households and 22 children, it is not difficult to understand why he does not find enough time for all. Some children are neglected while others are favoured; some receive enough support and guidance, others very little. It is the institution of polygyny which creates these conditions.

One evening when I was there, Marianne's husband – who always took turns in spending two nights with every wife – failed to show up when he was expected. That night Marianne said to me, 'How can one man love four wives equally?' She also confessed her husband's companionship had become less and less important to her, and she lived mainly for her children.

Source: Adapted from D. Topouzis, 'The men with many wives' in *New Society*, 4 October 1985

1 What does polygyny mean?

2 What reasons does the author suggest for its origins?

3 Have people in cities abandoned polygyny?

4 Who appears to benefit most from polygynous marriage?

5 What is the relationship between Mr Diop and his children?

6 What is the relationship between Mr Diop and his second wife Marianne?

7 Can you explain why the relationships are like this?

8 Briefly, what comparisons can you make between the typical British family and the polygynous one of Senegal?

9 How does the extract tell us that culture does not change as quickly as technology and economic situations?

The importance of marriage and the family in pre-industrial societies

Isaac Shapera studied the life of the Kgatla tribe in South Africa in the early 1930s.

The household usually consists of a man with his wife, or wives, and dependent children, but often includes other people as well. ...They live, eat, work and play together, consult and help one another in all personal difficulties and share in one another's good fortune. They produce most of their own food and material needs; ...they are the group within which children are born, reared and trained in conduct and methods of work and they perform the ceremonies connected with birth, marriage, death and other ritual occasions. ...

The family gets its food by growing corn, breeding animals and collecting wild plants which can be eaten...[and] it builds its own huts. In all these activities everybody except the infants take part, men, women and children having special jobs according to sex and age. The women and girls till the fields, build and repair the walls of the huts, prepare food and beer, look after the chickens and fetch water, wood (for fires) and collect wild plants. The men and boys herd the cattle, hunt and do all the building.

Source: Adapted from I. Shapera, *Married Life in an African Tribe* (Penguin, 1971)

1 Who lives in the household?

2 Name four examples of things that the family does together.

3 Amongst the Kgatla, being invited to certain ceremonies indicates who is regarded as most important to the person involved in the ceremony. What does this tell us about the family?

4 Some people have described the pre-industrial family as an 'economic unit'. What do you think they mean by this? Use the extract to illustrate your answer.

5 Write a brief description, or draw a diagram, to indicate the tasks of the family in Britain today. Would you say it is as important today, as in the past?

The anthropologist, Levi-Strauss, met, among the Bororo of Central Brazil,

...a man about thirty years old: unclean, ill-fed, sad and lonesome. When asked if the man was seriously ill the natives' answer came as a shock: What was wrong with him? – nothing at all, he was just a bachelor, and true enough, in a society where labour is...shared between men and women and where only the married status permits the man to benefit from the fruits of woman's work, including delousing, body painting, and hair plucking as well as vegetable food and cooked food (since the Bororo woman tills the soil and makes pots), a bachelor is really only half a human being.

Source: G. Hurd *et al.*, *Human Societies: An Introduction to Sociology* (Routledge and Kegan Paul, 1986)

1 Describe the man Levi-Strauss met amongst the Bororo.

2 What was 'wrong' with him?

3 What is the advantage of 'married status'?

4 What are our attitudes to unmarried middle-aged men? Could you give reasons for your reply?

5 What does your reply to question 4 tell you about the importance of marriage and attitudes to sexuality in our society today?

The meaning of marriage in Britain today

A 'cad' who was married to three women at the same time was jailed for eight months yesterday after being convicted of bigamy.

Passing sentence on Michael Thomas, aged 44 at Reading crown court, Assistant Recorder Humphrey Malins told him: "A civilised society must not permit men to treat women in this way. This is an affront to the institution of marriage.

"To use an old fashioned and perhaps underused phrase, you were a cad."

The crime came to light when Mr Thomas's latest wife found a set of incomplete divorce papers. She approached the police, who found he was already married – not once, but twice.

Source: *The Guardian*, 10 September 1994

MARRIED?

AT LEAST **1/3 OFF CAR INSURANCE** if driving is restricted to you and your spouse

Call CHURCHILL now
0800 200 300

Open Mon - Fri 8am - 9pm, Sat 8am - 3pm
Not available in Northern Ireland nor if insured or spouse under 25

Look at the advertisement.

1 What image does it conjure up of marriage?

2 Is this your image?

Now read the article. Bigamy, which means 'marrying' more than one person at the same time, is a criminal offence.

3 What values does the article reveal?

4 Could this happen if a man was cohabiting with two women?

5 Why is there a difference?

6 Do you think that the time has come to abandon marriage as an institution?

Pushpa Pabla had what she calls a rather progressive Hindu marriage compared with most of her teenage contemporaries in India in 1954.

Aged 19 and at a college in Jullundur, in the northern state of Punjab, she was approached by her eldest brother and told that a prospective suitor was coming. "The next thing I knew he arrived at our house with his brother, sister, father, and two sisters-in-law," said Mrs Pabla, aged 60.

"I was in another group while they sat down and discussed matters with my family. Then I was called in and saw him for about five minutes; we weren't allowed to talk, but in those days that was quite a revolutionary thing to do – most of my friends only got to see their husbands on their wedding days."

Two months later she was married. She admits she had no say in the matter.

"I had confidence in my family's choice. They knew what sort of man would be good for me, and I trusted them. I'm not angry that I didn't have a choice; that was the way we were brought up. It was part of our tradition and culture."

Source: *The Guardian*, 25 June 1994

But perhaps attitudes are changing, as the following extract suggests.

Attitudes towards arranged marriages are changing very rapidly in Britain, according to a new study.

A survey of 107 Hindus and Sikhs aged between 16 and 25 born in Britain found that 60 per cent reject an arranged marriage and want to marry the person they fall in love with. Twelve per cent of their parents had a love marriage.

The 40 per cent who accept an arranged marriage say they now have the chance to meet their prospective partners and have the final decision on whether the marriage will go ahead. Traditionally, the future couple met the day of the wedding.

Source: *The Guardian*, June 1994

If Sikhs and Hindus are increasingly marrying for love, what might we predict for the levels of divorce among those ethnic groups?

Marriage and partnerships

The collapse of marriage

There is a common belief that the institution of marriage is crumbling in Britain. People who support this argument point to the numbers of lone-parent families, usually headed by a woman, which we have seen compose almost 20 per cent of all families with dependent children. Others indicate the increasing numbers of people preferring to live together (known as **cohabitation**). Then there is the decline in the numbers of people marrying. The final and most damning piece of evidence is the large increase in divorce which took place in the early 1970s, and which continues today.

However, marriage remains one of the most important institutions of society, with over 85 per cent of people marrying at some time, and with the majority of children being brought up in a household with married parents. But it is changing rapidly. Marriage no longer lasts for a lifetime, and a third of all new marriages end in divorce. People then expect to remarry and form new households – so divorce is not seen as an end to family life. One marriage in every three is now a remarriage.

Marriage is increasingly being challenged by cohabitation as a normal setting for adults to live together and to raise children. The evidence is pointing to a shift here in the future, with the possibility for many couples of not just cohabiting before marriage, but replacing marriage with cohabitation on a permanent basis. At present more than half of all couples marrying for the first time have previously cohabited, and more than three-quarters of all couples marrying for the second time have previously cohabited. In 1961, only 3 per cent admitted to having done so.

Closely linked to this, couples are increasingly choosing to marry later in life, with cohabitation as a normal stage preceding marriage. In 1970, men typically married at the age of about 24 and women at about 21, whereas today men marry at a typical age of about 27 and women at about 25.

Marriage, remarriage and cohabitation

Marriage and remarriage, by sex, Great Britain

A

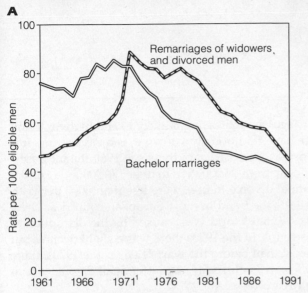

B

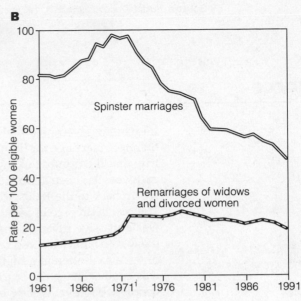

1 The Divorce Reform Act 1969 came into effect in England and Wales on 1 January 1971.

People cohabiting as a percentage of the unmarried population, by sex and age, Great Britain, 1992

C

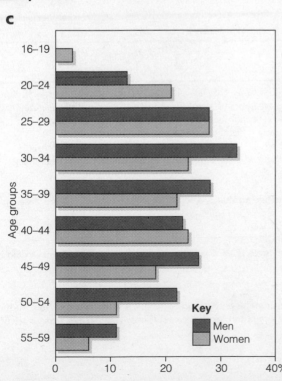

Source: *Social Trends 24* (HMSO, 1994), Office of Population Censuses and Surveys, and General Household Survey

Look at **A** and **B**. **A** tells us the numbers of men marrying, for every 1000 men of marriagable age, and **B** shows the rate for women.

1 What year had the highest number of women marrying?

2 How many married per thousand eligible women?

3 What was the highest year for men?

4 Are the figures for men and women the same each year? If there are differences, can you offer any explanations?

5 Which sex is more likely to remarry? Can you offer any reaons why this should be?

6 Overall, can you summarise what the statistics tell us?

Look at **C**.

7 Which age groups are most likely to cohabit:
   a) for men?
   b) for women?

8 Approximately what proportion of unmarried people aged 25–40 cohabit?

9 Does this tell us anything about marriage and the family?

Three-quarters of births outside marriage are registered by both parents (joint registration) and a half are registered by parents living at the same address.

What does this tell us about cohabitation?

Source: *Social Trends 23* (HMSO, 1993)

Divorce

It is commonly argued that marriages are increasingly likely to end in divorce and therefore marriage for life, as we have traditionally known it, is disappearing. It is true that the number of divorces has increased rapidly: since 1960 the increase each year has been about 10 per cent, from 26 000 then to over 170 000 today and if we go back to the 1930s, the annual divorce figures were less than 5000 per year. The rise in divorce in Britain reflects the trend in most European countries. There was a massive upsurge after the Second World War, caused by the disruption of the war to family life and relationships. In the 1950s there was a slight decline, but divorce continued at a higher level than before the war. Then, in the 1970s, there was another sharp rise to today's high level. Today, a quarter of all divorces are to people who have already been divorced once.

Patterns of marriage and divorce

Changes in the law and the divorce rate

Year	Number of divorces	Major changes in the law
1857		Divorce available through the court for the first time. This law allowed men to obtain divorces if their wives were unfaithful. However, this reason was not sufficient for women to obtain divorces; they had to prove cruelty against them, as well. The law reflected the Victorian attitudes towards women. No divorce available for the working class, only a 'legal separation'.
1921	3000	
1923		Women received equality with men under the law, regarding grounds for divorce. They began to get custody of the children.
1931	4200	
1937		The law extended grounds for divorce to include adultery, cruelty (mental and physical) and desertion. Divorce became easier to obtain.
1941	7500	
1945		End of the Second World War – great social disruption.
1949		People could apply for legal aid to obtain divorces. This was particularly helpful for housewives who had no income of their own.
1951	39 000	
1961	32 000	
1969		The irretrievable breakdown of marriage became the only grounds for divorce, no proof of 'misconduct' was necessary. Two years' mutually agreed separation, or five years' if only one partner wanted divorce, was all that was necessary.
1971	80 000	
1981	157 000	
1991	169 000	
1996		Divorce possible after one-year separation – 'no fault' basis

Source for divorce figures: *Social Trends* (HMSO, 1986 and 1994)

Using the table on page 134, draw a graph to show the changes in the divorce rate.

Today, one in three new marriages end in divorce, yet families and marriage are not dead. Seventy-five per cent of the population of Britain live in married couple families, only a slightly smaller proportion than 1961, when 82 per cent lived in this form of family. Furthermore, eight out of ten children still live in a married couple family.

1 What is the clear trend in divorce statistics?

2 What do the changes in the law tell you about attitudes to marriage?

3 Do the legal changes tell us anything about the position of women in society?

4 Give one legal reason why there has been an increase in the divorce rate since 1971.

5 If a person marries today, what chance is there of them remaining married, according to the information above?

6 What proportion of people live in households headed by a married couple?

7 The information given above seems contradictory, if you compare the likelihood of divorce with the percentage of married people.
Can you offer any explanation to resolve this apparent contradiction? (Diagrams A and B on page 133 might help.)

Reasons for the rise in divorce rates

Legal changes

Quite simply, it is much easier to obtain a divorce today than ever before. Since 1969 the only reason needed to obtain a divorce has been the 'irretrievable breakdown of the marriage'. So, if two people feel they cannot stay together any longer, they can divorce. This contrasts very strongly with the previous situation where one partner had to prove that the other partner had done something wrong, such as being unfaithful or using violence against them.

It would be wrong however to see changes in the law as causes of increases in the divorce rate. The law changed as a response to changes in the attitudes of people towards marriage and the family.

Decline of religion

The importance and influence of the churches have been in decline throughout this century. Marriage has traditionally been viewed as a holy institution and the 'bonds of matrimony' as sacred. The decline of the churches' influence has meant that people do not regard their marriage vows as tying them for life to their partners. In line with this, the stigma (disgrace) attached to divorce which prevented many people from divorcing has been considerably weakened.

The attitude of women

There is general agreement that it is women who are the 'losers' in many marriages. They give up their work, their financial independence, in return for the role of housewife and mother. The rising status of women in society and their increasing refusal to accept the traditional 'inferior' roles of housewife and mother, with the man in charge of the household, has meant that 70 per cent of divorces are now started by wives.

Divorcees talking

The views of a woman

I think a lot of women now, they all want to work because they all feel like me, feel they are chained in and life's passing them by, without going out and doing something and talking. I find this, talking I sort of want to talk and when Nick [her husband] comes home and is tired, he'll come in and he just switches off mentally and he just laughs at me and says, 'Well, I'm just neutral, coasting'. He sits back and I'm saying, 'Talk, talk to me, for God's sake talk to me.' I've got nobody to talk to all day and I do think now women need to get out, because staying in the house in the company of just little ones does drive you mad, especially when the husband comes home and can't be bothered to talk to you because he is tired out. I know when someone comes in I usually talk them to death.

Source: S. Sharpe, *Double Identity* (Pelican, 1984)

1 Why do many women want to work, according to the speaker?

2 What is the main problem in her life? How could her husband help her to overcome this problem?

3 In your opinion, who benefits more from marriage, men or women? What reasons can you give for your answer?

In Department of Social Security (DSS) research published in 1991, Bradshaw and Millar were given the following reasons for separating from, or not living with, an absent parent:

- 31 per cent of total responses gave infidelity or one person finding a new partner as the main reason;

- 33 per cent gave not getting on;

- 26 per cent of respondents gave lack of communication;

- 20 per cent of respondents gave violence as a reason (violence was the main reason in 13 per cent of cases and a supplementary reason in a further 7 per cent of cases);

- 16 per cent gave financial reasons;

- 16 per cent said their partner did not give enough time to the family;

- 15 per cent cited alcohol or drugs; *and*

- 7 per cent that a partner was lesbian or gay.

(These percentages do not add up to 100 as more than one response was possible.)

Given that the majority of divorces are initiated by women (73 per cent in 1989), it is not surprising that many lone mothers interviewed by Bradshaw and Millar said they felt better off alone because of their increased independence and control over their own lives and resources.

Source: A. Garnham and E. Knights, *Putting the Treasury First – The Truth about Child Support* (CPAG, 1994)

1 What are the three most common reason for getting divorced?

2 Do you agree that all of these reasons are of sufficient importance for divorce? Rank them in your order of importance.

3 Who is more likely to initiate divorce? Can you suggest any reasons for this?

The clash of backgrounds

The sheer size and complexity of modern urban society (large towns and cities) means that it is likely that couples from very different social and ethnic backgrounds will meet and marry. Clearly the potential for trouble between the couple will be increased by their different expectations and attitudes. Alongside this problem of 'cultural diversity' is the fact that the community in most cities has been weakened with the growth of suburbs, where everyone minds their own business. The traditional pressures imposed on a couple with a faltering marriage, by the local community and by the extended family, no longer exist.

The romantic marriage

Traditionally, and even in Asian arranged marriages in Britain today, love was not the most important element of marriage. It was more important that there was a stable union between two well-matched people, linking two families. By contrast, the cultural stress in contemporary Britain is on 'falling in love'. Indeed, a recent survey of people under 25 found that romance was regarded as the most important quality in a good marriage. But if the couple 'fall out of love', there is little to hold them together. By contrast, where love is not so important but the maintenance of the family is, the bonds holding the family together are far tougher.

Four views of marriage

Divorce is one kind of mechanism for dealing with the pressures and problems caused by marriage. However, there have traditionally been other ways of reducing marital conflict.

A

In pre-1948 China, the roles of husband and wife were clearly defined. Respect and not romantic love was demanded between husband and wife. There was an extended family system, so that intimate emotional contact between husband and wife was less intense than in our own system. Incorrect marital behaviour was prevented in part by supervision by older relatives. If the wife built up a reservoir of hatred and fear, it was more likely to be aimed at the mother-in-law, rather than the husband.

Source: Adapted from W. J. Goode, *World Revolution and Family Patterns* (Free Press, 1970)

B

For many girls, in particular working-class girls, marriage and motherhood are attractive and seemingly realistic goals. Marriage stands out against the starkness and drabness of work, it provides acceptable evidence of maturity and adulthood, and it is an important investment for the future.

It is only after marriage that women realise its isolation and emptiness.

Source: M. Brake, *The Sociology of Youth Cultures and Youth Subcultures* (Routledge and Kegan Paul, 1980)

C

Bruce Liddington, from Families Need Fathers, said: "Marriage seems to be increasingly devalued and irrelevant.

"Now it seems to be just a nice family event and has no meaning whatsoever, no contractual value."

Source: *The Daily Express*, 23 June 1994

D

Hardnev Jassar has been looking for a husband for her daughter, who is 19 for two years now. 'He must be a decent working man, but he need not be rich or educated,' she says.

Source: P. Harrison, 'The Patience of Southall' in *New Society*, 4 April 1974

1 Extracts **A** and **B** compare traditional attitudes to love with girls' attitudes in the 1980s. Write a paragraph comparing the two views on marriage. Do you think **B** is still true today?

2 Which in your opinion would lead to a lower divorce rate? Explain the reasons for your answer.

3 Look at extract **D**. Would you like your mother to find a husband/wife for you? Suggest two advantages of arranged marriages.

4 Look at extract **C**. Do you agree? How do you view marriage?

5 Rank the qualities listed below in order of importance to you in choosing a partner. Then ask your parents to rank them if they were choosing a partner for you. How different are they, if at all? Why are they different?

attractive   well-educated
good job   fun-loving
pleasant personality   sexy
honest and truthful

If you are a mature student, rank them as you would have done at 17.

The continuing strength of marriage: Conclusions

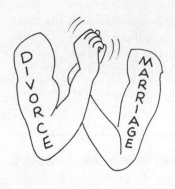

The points made so far on the increase in divorce do seem to support the argument that marriage is less firmly rooted in our society than in the past. This assertion is supported by the fact that on present trends one in three of contemporary marriages will end in divorce.

However, it is important to remember that the liberalisation of divorce (which has made divorcing easier), the weakening of pressures in the outside community, and the freedom from fear of stigma, have all encouraged people who were unhappily married to take the option of divorce instead of being trapped. More unhappiness would have been caused by two people continuing to live together when they did not really want to.

A second important point is that divorcees are very likely to marry again; indeed about 70 per cent find another partner, the majority within five years. So divorcees are not rejecting marriage, but their particular relationships. This is clearly linked to the high expectations mentioned earlier. This pattern of divorce and remarriage has been called **serial monogamy**.

Finally, surveys indicate that the majority of people firmly believe in the family and marriage, and almost 90 per cent of adults do still marry.

Children and divorce

Each year about 160 000 children are caught up in divorces, almost a third of these under the age of five. The first result of this is that many of these children will live, for some time at least, in lone-parent families. At the moment, 1.5 million children live in these circumstances.

The effects of divorce on children

It is generally agreed that unhappy marriages with all the bitterness and tension involved may be more harmful for children than a straightforward separation.

Younger children seem to adapt less well than older children. This is particularly serious when one sees the rise in the number of children under five years old who become involved in divorces. A major problem is the use of children by parents as weapons to get at each other. This, and battles over custody, may cause greater emotional disturbances than the actual divorce. Re-marriage creates step-families which do have special problems coping with the arrival of 'new' mothers and fathers. Friction is common in these situations.

Family relationships

In essence, the family is no more than a special relationship between a group of people. These relationships are never static; they are changing over time. The relationships between husbands and wives, and between parents and children are vastly different today from a hundred years ago. In order to understand the changes fully, we need to divide them into three categories – relationships between: husbands and wives; children and parents; the older generation and the family.

Husbands and wives

Sociologists have divided the changing relationships between husbands and wives into three phases.

Phase 1 Pre-industrial societies

Before Britain became a society almost totally based on industry, about 150 years ago, most people lived in the country and worked in agriculture. At this time, husband and wife were generally equal in their dealings with one another. Both of them worked to earn income and they relied heavily upon each other. However, most sociologists agree that the relationship between them was not very close.

Phase 2 Industrial family

In the second phase of the development of the modern family, during the last century, women lost their independence and equality. The result of laws restricting the working hours for women, and the Victorian beliefs concerning the purity and fragility of women meant that they withdrew from the workplace and increasingly the role of housewife and mother became the norm. Men became the breadwinners and, as they were the ones with the money, they also took charge inside the family.

It is important here to distinguish between the working class and the middle class, as there were considerable differences between them. The wife in the middle-class family was not expected to work either in or out of the home. Instead, she supervised the work of the cleaning lady and the nanny. The husband's role was to go out to business and to provide for the family.

Life in the working-class family was different in that the household chores and childrearing were seen as exclusively the wife's tasks. Husbands spent long hours at work and they preferred to pass their leisure in the pub, in the company of male companions. In these circumstances, women turned to each other for assistance, in particular to mothers and daughters. Help was freely given and very powerful bonds developed, which were much stronger than those between husband and wife. The father, although the head of the household, was also a bit of an outsider because of his long absences. Violence against wives and children was quite common.

Phase 3 The contemporary family

Between the 1930s and the 1950s, a change took place in the relationships between husbands and wives in middle class families. A warmer, closer relationship began to be accepted as normal. A slow move towards equality began too, with joint decision making and an increase in shared leisure activities. The wife remained responsible for the home and the children (now with no nanny to help her), but increasingly the husband would see it as his duty to help her. Because of this move towards equality in husband/wife roles, the sociologists Young and Willmott used the term **symmetrical family** to describe the new form of family relationship.

Gradually, these ideas spread to the working class, so that by the 1960s many younger working-class couples shared their household chores and their leisure activities, with the husband replacing the mother as the main helper to the wife.

When a husband and wife share housework and their leisure, sociologists call this a **joint conjugal role relationship**. However, when they perform separate tasks and have different leisure pursuits, sociologists describe their relationship as a **segregated role relationship**.

Using these terms, how would you describe the relationship in:
a) the phase 2 family?
b) the phase 3 family?

Reasons for the move towards the symmetrical family

Women began to reject the housewife role. They demanded a greater say in decision-making in the home and to be considered equal to their husbands. Further, they insisted that men ought to become involved in tasks about the home. Contraception allowed them to limit the number of children and gave them the freedom to obtain paid employment. Financial independence from husbands in turn strengthened their position of equality in the family.

The resettlement of many working-class people from the inner cities in the 1950s into overspill estates and the increasing affluence of others who bought their own homes led to a much greater interest in home improvements and home life generally. Men preferred to stay in, improving their homes, watching television or playing with the children than going to the pub. This new form of leisure pattern amongst working-class men led to the term **privatised worker** being used (indicating that the worker was interested in his private family life).

Changing relationships between husbands and wives

Traditional relationships

This extract comes from a 1950 study of a working-class mining community in north-east England.

The comedian who defined home as the place where you fill the pools in on a Wednesday night was something of a sociologist. With the exception of a small minority of men...the husbands of Ashton for preference come home for a meal after finishing work and, as soon as they can feel clean and rested, they look for the companionship of their mates.

The wife's position is very different. In a very consciously accepted division of labour, she must keep in good order the household provided for by the money handed to her each Friday by her husband. While he is at work, she should complete her day's work – washing, ironing, cleaning or whatever it may be – and she must have ready for him a good meal.

The wife's confinement to the household, together with the acceptance of the idea that the house and the children are primarily her responsibility, emphasise the absence of any joint activities and interests for husband and wife.

Source: N. Dennis, F. Henriques and C. Slaugher, *Coal is our Life* (Eyre & Spottiswoode, 1956).

Symmetrical family

In a study of middle-class households in the late 1950s it appeared that a change was taking place in relationships between husbands and wives. Young and Willmott later decided on this evidence and further research that the family in Britain today is best described as 'symmetrical', meaning that husbands and wives regarded each other as equal and shared domestic tasks.

Most Woodford men are emphatically not absentee husbands. It is their work, especially if rather tedious which takes second place in their thoughts...'In the old days,' as one wife said, 'the husband was the husband and the wife was the wife and they each had their own way of going on. Her job was to look after him. The wife wouldn't stand for it nowadays. Husbands help with the children now. They stay more in the home and have more interest in the home.'

The couple share the work, worry and pleasure of the children. 'We have the same routine every night,' said Mrs. Foster, 'I'd put one child to bed and my husband puts the other. We take it in turns to tell them stories too'.

Husbands usually have their own specific tasks within the family economy, particularly in decorating and repairing the home.

Source: P. Willmott and M. Young, *Family and Class in a London Suburb* (Routledge & Kegan Paul, 1960)

1 How would you describe the husband/wife relationship in Ashton: segregated or conjugal? Why?

2 Do you think the husbands and wives in Ashton spent much leisure time in each other's company?

3 In what way had the middle-class relationship changed between husband and wife?

4 By the 1970s Young and Willmott described most families in Britain as 'symmetrical'. What did they mean by this?

Symmetry or patriarchy?

Feminists have bitterly criticised this symmetrical family/privatised worker description of modern family life. They argue that husbands benefit far more from marriage than wives. It is still regarded as the woman's task to look after the children, to cook and to do the housework. Husbands 'help' their wives and are regarded as being good husbands if they occasionally relieve their wives from childminding, or wash the dishes. Women, too, give up their careers far more often than men in order to look after the children. Staying at home with young children is often lonely and frustrating, as well as being exhausting. The term **patriarchy** has been used by sociologists to describe this situation of continuing male dominance of the family.

The changing relationships within the family

1900   **Traditional middle-class family relationship**   Segregated roles   **Traditional working-class family relationship**   1900

Husband Head of family; leisure outside family; generally performs no housework; strict discipline of children	**Wife** In charge of the house; if possible, servants to help; no real role; empty life	**Husband** Sees himself as 'provider' for family; expects wife to do all household chores for him; spends leisure outside home; no close relationship with children	**Wife** Looks after children and house; close relationship with children and own mother who helps her; centre of family
Boys Educated at grammar/public schools	**Girls** Trained to be good wives	**Boys** Go to work as early as possible; not close to father; strict discipline	**Girls** Help in home; close to mother; marry early

Reached this form of relationship by 1950

Reached this form of relationship by mid-1960s

1970   **The symmetrical family**   Joint conjugal roles   **OR**   **The patriarchal family**   1970

Husband Spends leisure time at home with family; helps wife with housework and childcare; close emotional bond with wife and children	**Wife** Often has part-time work; close relationship with husband/children; main responsibility still home and children; equal head of household	**Husband** Sees his wife as having main responsibility for housework, so 'helps' her. Takes no responsibility for organisation of child care. Works full-time, his contribution to household is his wage – all else is a bonus	**Wife** Works full- or part-time. Has responsibility for housework and 'requests' husband to help. Has to organise child care if works. Makes household decisions; but major ones, plus financial issues, are largely made by the husband
Boys Close to parents; stays at school longer; treated with relaxed discipline	**Girls** Help mother; close to parents; school progress and career regarded as important; stricter control of leisure activities	**Boys** Close to parents, and expected to do some housework, but less than their sisters. Large amount of freedom	**Girls** Close to parents and expected to do more household chores than brothers. Significant amount of freedom, but less than brothers.

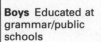

Source: Adapted from M. Young and P. Willmott, *The Symmetrical Family* (Penguin, 1975)

The view that there has been a move towards greater equality in marriage between husband and wife has been challenged by feminists.

Draw a simple chart to show which activities/tasks are done in your household in one week by:

a) the husband

b) the wife.

Which of the two descriptions on page 141 do you agree with – the symmetrical or the patriarchal family? If you disagree with both, draw your own.

The other side of the picture: Inequality at home

In the early 1970s, Ann Oakley studied a small number of housewives in London.

Wives were asked: 'Do you agree with men doing housework and looking after children?'

They replied: 'I don't agree with men doing housework'; 'I

don't think it's a man's job...I certainly wouldn't like to see my husband cleaning a room up'; 'I don't think it's mannish for a man to stay at home. I like a man to be a man.'

'Unmanly', 'unnatural', 'unmasculine' and 'henpecked' were words which constantly appeared in these replies.

Husbands' help with housework and childcare by social class

	Number of respondents	Housework			Childcare		
		High	Medium	Low	High	Medium	Low
Working class	20	2	1	17	2	8	10
Middle class	20	4	9	7	8	4	8

Source: Adapted from A. Oakley, *The Sociology of Housework* (Martin Robertson, 1974)

1 Examine the table. Overall, do husbands help with:
a) housework?
b) childcare?

2 Are there any differences between the working and middle class?

3 Looking at the comments of the wives, do you think that they expected their husbands to take equal responsibility for housework and childcare?

4 Bearing in mind this information and your own experience in your home, would you definitely argue that the typical relationship is symmetrical?

Eight out of 10 women say they prepare every meal in their household, according to a government survey yesterday that casts doubt on the reality of "new man" culture.

Just over half of men believe boys should be taught how to cook whether or not they want to learn, says the survey of more than 2,000 adults commissioned by the Department of Health's nutrition task force.

It found that while views on

cooking were generally positive, there was a contrast between attitudes and behaviour. Eighty per cent of women said they cooked every meal, 12 per cent cooked once or twice a week, 5 per cent less than twice and 3 per cent never.

Only 22 per cent of men said they cooked every meal, 39 per cent cooked once or twice, 20 per cent less than this and 18 per cent never. The Office of Population Censuses and

Surveys, which carried out the survey, acknowledges that the figures do not add up but says they should not be taken literally. Women who prepared most meals would have chosen the "every" category rather than "once or twice". However, it concludes: "The traditional model still predominates."

The survey found little class or regional difference: 16 per cent of men in non-manual jobs said they never cooked,

compared with 17 per cent of manual workers; 81 per cent of women in the South-east and North said they prepared every meal.

Thirty-eight per cent of men and 23 per cent of women said boys should be taught cooking only if they wished to learn; 55 per cent of men and 74 per cent of women thought boys should be taught regardless.

Source: *The Guardian*, 25 January 1995

This extract appeared in 1995. Have attitudes changed?

Children and parents

This century, and particularly the last 40 years, has seen a revolution in the way that children have been treated by parents. Before this the father was the undisputed head of the family, with children expected to accept his orders without question. There were no benefits from the state, little protection against the violence in the home, and it was generally agreed that children were inferior creatures whose opinions were not worth listening to.

There were, however, social class differences. The sons of the *middle class* were likely to attend a grammar or public school and be groomed for a career in the professions. The girls were not educated for a career, but to be good wives. Because the children were often sent away from home for their schooling, the relationship between parents and children would often be rather cool.

Parents and children in a simple society

But the pygmies have learned from the animals around them to doze with one eye open and a sleepy midday camp can become filled in a minute with shouts and yells and tearful protestations as some baby, crawling around this warm friendly world, crawls into a bed of hot ashes or over a column of army ants. In a moment he will be surrounded by angry adults and given a sound slapping, then carried unceremoniously back to the safety of a hut. It does not matter much which hut because as far as the child is concerned all adults are his parents or grandparents, they are all equally likely to slap him for doing wrong, or fondle and feed him with delicacies if he is quiet and gives them no trouble. He knows his real father and mother of course and has a special affection for them and they for him, but from an early age he learns he is the child of them all. ...

The pygmies have no special words to indicate their own parents, like 'mum' and 'dad'. For them all adults in the group are given the same name.

Source: C. Turnbull, *The Forest People* (Picador, 1976)

In Britain, children are extremely close to their parents, rather than any other people. Parents' love is focused almost exclusively on their own children, not on other people's.

1 Who has the 'right' to discipline children in pygmy society?

2 From your own experience, who has this right in Britain today?

3 What does the passage mean when it says 'he learns he is the child of them all'?

4 Why do you think the pygmies have no special word for 'mum' and 'dad'?

5 What does the extract show us about the belief in our society that the only 'proper' way to bring up a child is to have an extremely close relationship between parents and children to the exclusion of everybody else? (In your answer you might find it helpful to think about the idea of 'culture'.)

Among the *working class*, children were expected to contribute financially to the family at the earliest possible opportunity, leaving school and assuming adult responsibilities at a very early age. Although the relationship between father and children was cool, that between mother and daughter was usually strong.

In the last 40 years, attitudes towards children in first the middle, and later the working class have shifted towards a stress on emotional warmth, greater freedom, a decline in the father's authority and an increasing acceptance of the need to listen to the views of children.

The reasons for the changes in child/parent relationships are connected with the smaller size of families, so that children are treated more as individuals; with higher educational standards and maturity of children, and with a change in views on the correct way to bring up children. Psychologists and other experts now tell us to bring up children with love and affection in order to create an emotionally stable adult.

However, it would be wrong to say that *all* parents now bring up children with love and affection. Cruelty to children is still widespread, and the National Society for the Prevention of Cruelty to Children (NSPCC) estimate that about 600 children are deliberately injured by their parents each year.

A negative view of family life

At least 750,000 children in Britain may suffer long-term trauma because they are exposed to domestic violence, a survey published yesterday suggests.

Many develop sleeping problems, become anxious, aggressive or withdrawn, and find it difficult to form close relationships as a result, the researchers say.

The survey, by NCH Action for Children, is based on a poll of 108 mothers with 246 children, who had suffered domestic violence. It is the first to examine the effects of domestic violence on youngsters. It found that:
□ Three out of four women questioned said their children had seen violent incidents, and almost two thirds of the children had seen their mothers beaten
□ One in 10 women reported having been raped in front of her children
□ All claimed their children were aware of violence
□ Almost three in 10 mothers said their violent partner had also beaten their children
□ One in three said their children had developed bed-wetting problems, while nearly one in three said the youngsters had become violent and aggressive. Three in 10 had problems at school.

The survey also shows that children witness violence over long periods. On average, the relationships the study described as violent lasted seven years.

Tom White, director of NCH Action for Children, said domestic violence was the second most common violent crime reported to police in Britain, and made up more than 25 per cent of all reported violent crime.

The researchers estimate one in 100 marriages is characterised by severe and repeated violence, affecting at least 750,000 children each year.

Source: *The Guardian*, 6 December 1994

1 Domestic violence is usually viewed only as a feminist issue, how does this extract broaden the problem?

2 How many marriages are estimated to be characterised by severe violence?

3 Look closely at the various statistics given in the article, particularly the size of the poll. Could you make any comments?

An "outsider's" view of parent-child relationships

In 1985 Stopes-Roe and Cochrane studied 120 Sikh, Hindu and Muslim families living in Britain about their views of the British.

Our Asian respondents gave us their views of English family life. Their opinions on family life pursued a similar theme; the apparent separateness and independence of family members. The Asian parents in particular seized upon the differences in family ties in Asian and English families.

Some saw the English emphasis on the marriage relationship and the weaker ties with parents, brothers or sisters and children as a difference. But it could also be seen as destroying family life altogether. 'Their family life – what is it?' asked a Muslim father. 'They live separately and they split up soon. There is little cooperation and unity.' A Hindu mother put it down to selfishness. 'They are not willing to invest their whole lives in family and children.'

Both parents and young children commented on the expectation of early independence for children of English families – at 18 or even 16 years old. But the parents had stronger things to say about it. As two Sikh fathers put it 'Children are neglected – and their children pay rent – it's not right'. 'They're very individual – they kick their children out at 18.'

Source: Adapted from M. Stopes-Roe and R. Cochrane, 'As others see us...' in *New Society*, 1 November 1985

1 From the comments the Asian respondents made, find *four* differences between Asian family life and (their view of) English family life.

2 Which style of family life do you prefer? Give reasons for your answers.

3 Imagine a situation in which you find that you need help. Which family do you think would be more likely to give it, the British or the Asian?

4 What is your view on the comments about being 'kicked out' at 18?

5 The Asian family stresses obedience, especially by girls, to the wishes of the parents. If parents disapprove of an activity then the children cannot do it. What are your views?

Describe in your own words what has happened here

Now describe what has happened here.
Are there any differences?
What do you think the two stories can tell us concerning our expectations of male and female roles?

Gender differences emerge too in the way children are socialised (see pages 3–4). Girls are expected to help their mothers with housework, such as cleaning and washing up; while only a very small proportion of boys help their mothers. The children are given different toys, with girls receiving dolls, which they wash and dress, and boys receiving racing cars which they pull apart. We expect different behaviour too. Girls are supposed to be gentle, and boys tough and boisterous. If they do not conform to this, comments are made. Even our language is different, if boys are handsome, then girls are pretty. Clearly the family is passing on the appropriate patterns of behaviour expected of boys and girls in our society; ultimately for the girl the stress is on motherhood, for the boy on a successful career.

The older generation and the family

For the first time in history, a person can now reasonably expect to live into his or her seventies. This means that there has been a huge growth in the number of three generation familes (grandparents, parents, children).

It is often claimed that old people were held in high esteem in pre-industrial societies, though it is difficult to prove this. It is likely that, since so few people lived to any great age, there was a degree of status in simply having survived. As the oldest male in each family usually owned the land (in agricultural societies land equals wealth), he clearly remained powerful until his death.

In modern society old age is normal and, as the older generation have little economic power over the young, the status of old people generally is low. This affects relationships within the family. Some writers have gone so far as to claim that old people are often abandoned in our society and are not wanted by their children when they become a burden. To support this argument they point to the growth of 'nursing homes' for the elderly. However, the evidence does not seem to support this extreme argument. It is true that over half of those aged 75+ live alone, but this seems to be because they *choose* to do so.

Children or, more accurately, daughters still look after their parents, and maintain close contact by telephone and visits. One useful way of understanding the importance of older people in the family, is to look at the **family life cycle**. By this, sociologists mean that as people move through the various stages of life from young married couple with dependent children through to old age, help, both physical (baby-sitting) and financial (loans), flows from one age group to the other. Where grandparents are healthy and possibly financially sound, they give help to their children who are in the phase of setting up home and family and therefore in need of help. As the older generation become infirm, it is their turn to be helped.

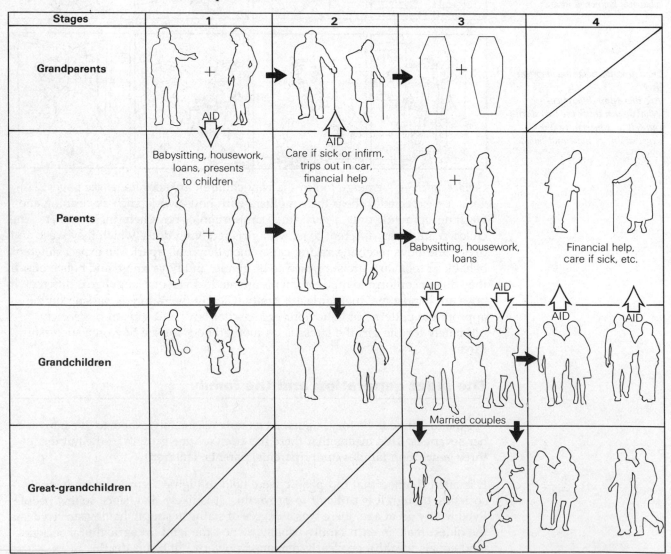

The family life cycle

The family and industrialisation: A summary

	The pre-industrial family	Industrialisation and the family	The family today
Structure	Mainly nuclear families, but the better-off had larger households, as people came to stay with them; late marriage; small families because of the high death-rate of children	Working-class families – became extended as numbers of children increased because of higher child survival rates (results of medical improvements) and people crowded into limited housing available in towns Middle-class families – became extended, as younger generation remained at home until they were economically free to leave and set up own house	Nuclear families, with connections by telephone/car to wider kin (although Asian families are extended)
Relationships	Not very close or warm; marriage and child-rearing mainly for economic reasons; idea of 'love' is unusual	Working-class – children close to mother; father and mother not close at all; women oppressed by men Middle-class – children not close to parent; father-mother, cold relationship; women oppressed by men	Close family relationships, the 'privatised' family; husband and wife fairly equal, 'symmetrical'; but women still expected to be responsible for domestic matters; children are seen as extremely important
Functions	Family very important as all worked together in the home or on the farm; family looked after its members if they survived to old age	Working-class – family very important for survival; pooling of economic resources; helped each other where possible in all matters; older generation looked after by younger generation	Mainly emotional, but still practical and financial help (loans etc.) when needed; State and voluntary services assist or replace the family in many of its functions
Wider setting	Agricultural society, people living in the countryside in small villages 	Industrialised society, people living in large towns 	A mobile family moving for promotion and to take job opportunities; people living in suburbs; light industry and offices are places of work

POPULATION

This chapter covers:
- Demography
- Births
- Family size
- Deaths
- Life expectancy
- Migration.

Demography

The study of population concentrates on the changing *size* of the population; the changes in the *age* structure of the population; the changing patterns of *where* in the country people live; and finally the proportions of one *sex* compared to the other. The correct term for the study of the population is **demography**.

The government does most of the fact finding. Every birth, marriage, divorce and death has to be notified to the local government registrar. The information is then sent on to the government statistical office. A second crucial source of information is the **census**, which is the national survey of every household in Britain taken every ten years by the government.

If a government wants to plan ahead sensibly for the welfare of the population then it needs to know how many people there are, where they live and how old they are. They can then make decisions on such things as:

- the health services – if there are going to be more elderly people then more geriatric wards have to be built, nurses trained in handling old people, etc. If more babies are going to be born, then greater investment must take place in maternity services. Also, knowing where the majority of people live allows the government to put more resources in these areas

- the welfare services – if there are more old people, for example, then more money needs to be allocated to pensions and to home helps and specialist social workers

- education – knowing the numbers and ages of children allows the government to plan the numbers, types and locations of schools.

At any one time the size of the country's population is the result of:

- the number of births
- the number of deaths
- the number of people entering or leaving the country.

The surprising pace of change

The report – the annual British Household Panel Survey, published by the Economic and Social Research Council (ESRC)...a series of interviews with 9,000 people in 5,000 households. ...

The survey found that each year 14 per cent of all homes go through some kind of change of circumstances – a birth, young people leaving, separation, divorce or a new cohabitation; 30 per cent of single-parent homes experienced a change in circumstances.

There is a belief that life changes slowly. Why does this extract help us to understand the need to study demography?

Source: *The Guardian*, 6 September 1994

Births

When discussing the changes in the number of births each year, sociologists often talk about the **birth rate**, which is the number of babies born in a year for every 1000 people in the population. The higher the birth rate, the more babies are born. Sometimes the term the **fertility rate** is used. This means the number of children born for every 1000 women of child-bearing age (approximately 15–40 years of age).

Changes in the birth-rate

Generally in the twentieth century the birth rate has fallen. In 1901, for example, the birth rate was 28.6, by 1951 it had fallen to 15.7, and in 1995 it was 13.0, under half that at the beginning of the century.

The decline in the birth rate was not regular though, and in certain periods the birth rate has actually increased. The increases occurred in the period immediately after the Second World War, then again from the middle of the 1950s to 1964, and finally since 1978 there has been a slight recovery in the numbers of births from the lowest point in 1977.

There was an old woman who lived in a shoe. She had so many children 'cos she didn't know what to do

There was a young women who lived in a shoe. She had only two children, 'cos she knew exactly what to do

Falling birth rates

Improbable though it may seem, Italy, the land that has always loved children, has virtually stopped breeding. Latest figures show that Italian women bear a statistical 1.25 children each – the lowest recorded birthrate in the history of mankind. The number of Italian women with a traditional clutch of three or more children has dropped to a figure described by demographers as 'negligible'.

'If fertility continues at this level,' says Professor Antonio Golini, director of the Istituto di Recerche sulla Popolazione (Italy's state-funded demographic think tank), 'our population – which is now 57 million – will disappear completely in just 150 years.'

Italians, by and large, live for the moment. And so, although the issue of falling birthrates has prompted some debate, there are few who have actually considered the socio-economic implications of the shrinking family. Fewer Italians still have given thought to the possibility of themselves, as a nation, being wiped out in a matter of five or six generations. ...

Barring Ireland, birthrates have plummeted across the whole of Western Europe at an alarming rate. 'You need a rate of 2.1 to maintain stability of numbers,' says Golini. 'In Great Britain, where the level is 1.8, your population could disappear in 500 to 700 years. Long before that, you face a society where children will be greatly outnumbered by the old. Within a century, 42 per cent of Italians will be over 60, and only 14 per cent under 20. In Britain the patterns will be similar. It's impossible to imagine a society like that functioning. It simply would not work, either socially or economically. The outlook is frightening.'

The factors that have brought about the demographic revolution in Italy – industrialisation, prosperity and improved education, above all for women...the rapid and relatively recent emancipation of Italian women...

More immediately, Italy – and the rest of us will surely follow – faces enormous strains on the public purse as the population ages, and as fewer young workers come on to the market.

Pensions are paid out of current tax receipts, and with the ratio of contributors to beneficiaries already as low as one to 1.3, the pressure on workers is becoming intolerable. One forecast talks of a time when all workers' wages would be needed to finance government debt and state benefits. ...

One obvious solution to the population problem might be mass immigration. After all, with populations multiplying in the Third World, there are many who would welcome the opportunity of jobs in a Europe which is no longer breeding its own workers. In order to replenish its dwindling stock, Italy – under present demographic conditions – would require an influx of 300,000 immigrants a year.

Source: *The Daily Mail*, 13 September 1993

1 What is the current Italian birth rate?

2 What is the comparable British one?

3 What is happening to birth rates across Europe?

4 What four explanations does the author of the article offer for the changes in birth rate? Explain them in your own words. (You may need to refer to the main text.)

5 What possible consequences does the author claim for the continuing existence of Italian society? Do you think this seriously possible?

6 Why will there be 'enormous strains on the public purse in Italy' (and, of course, elsewhere in a similar situation)?

7 What possible solution could there be? How feasible do you think this is?

Reasons for the fall in the birth rate

The most obvious reason for the fall in the birth rate over the twentieth century is that methods of birth control have become increasingly available and more widely used. However, to know that something exists does not mean that it will be used. People choose to use birth control methods to limit their family size. The following reasons have been suggested.

The costs of children

In the past when there was no state pension, then the best investment for old age was a large family to look after you. Today, the costs of keeping children until they leave full-time education at 16 (or increasingly 18) are high and the need for them in old age has declined.

Standards of living

Closely linked to the first point is the fact that people prefer to have a higher standard of living than spend their lives and their money rearing children.

Declining influence of religion

Churches have generally looked with disapproval on the use of birth control. The decline in the influence of the churches has meant that people no longer regard birth control as wrong.

Changing attitudes of women

This is probably the most important influence on the declining birth rate. Over this century, women have changed their views on their role. Traditionally women were expected to stay at home most of their adult lives, to be housewives and mothers. Today, women want careers of their own and see being a mother as just one part of their lives. The result has been the fact that fewer children are wanted, so that women can return to work. Childbearing now occurs much later in life, commonly around 30 years of age and women return to work on average only $3\frac{1}{2}$ years after the birth of their last child.

Cultural expectations

All the explanations above combine together to lower the birth rate and, as a result, it has become regarded as *normal* to have only two children. People are now coming to expect this from marriage and to regard larger families as slightly abnormal.

Reasons for the periodic rises in the birth rate

The reasons for the rise in births in the late 1940s was that the Second World War (1939–45) had separated many couples, and on being reunited they wished to start, or complete, their families. Six years of births were compressed into only a few post-war years.

The rise in the birth rate in the late 1950s and early 1960s was due to a period of low unemployment and high wages. Young couples were particularly well-off and married young. Early marriages plus affluence led to large families.

The latest rise in the birth rate, in the 1980s (although it is still very low compared to the 1950s) was caused by two things. First, those women who had delayed having children, as we saw earlier, now began to have them. Secondly, those people born in the 1950s expansion were now old enough to have their own children.

Family size

Family size and social class

The result of the decline in the birth rate has been smaller families. In 1900, for example, an average family had 3.4 children. Today, the size of family is almost halved, with the average number of children down to less than two per family.

However, the decline in family size has not proceeded at the same pace across the social classes. The middle class has always been ahead of the working class by about 20 years in reducing average family size. This seems to be because they first saw the advantages of smaller families and were more likely to know about, and want to use, contraceptives. Today, the differences in family size is very small; the most popular number of children in all social classes is two.

Family size and ethnic groups

The average family size for the ethnic groups in Britain varies considerably. There are two main factors which influence the size of families to Asians and Blacks. The first is the culture of the country from which they come, and the second is the age and sex distribution.

Culture

The culture of most ethnic minorities stresses the importance of having many children, in much the same way as the British culture did before the Welfare State was introduced. The reasons are the same: children look after their parents in old age. Secondly, the religion of most of the immigrant groups frowns upon forms of birth control, particularly amongst the Muslims from Pakistan and Bangladesh. However, it does appear that over time the influence of British culture and the stress upon family limitation has an effect and the children of immigrants gradually drop their birth rates nearer to those of the white population.

Age and sex distribution

This is also important. There are more people in the ethnic minorities of child-bearing age and the result is a relatively high number of births. Amongst Pakistani and Bangladeshi groups, in particular, the wives were left in the country of origin while the husbands tried to build up a new life in Britain. Only relatively recently have the wives rejoined their husbands, so that the birth rate is affected by this rather like the situation in Britain after the Second World War.

The present situation is that there has been a large drop in the number of children born to those of Caribbean and Indian origins, and a large increase in the numbers of children born to those of Pakistani and Bangladeshi origins.

The age and sex of the population

Below are three 'population pyramids'; pyramid **A** represents the typical sort of distribution of age and sex. The bottom of the pyramid is wide, because the numbers of people being born each year is gradually increasing. The pyramid gradually narrows as people die and so the numbers of older people gradually diminishes until there is hardly anybody over the age of 90.

The two sides of the pyramids represent the numbers of males and females in the population. They ought to be roughly equal.

The pyramid **B** represents Britain in 1991. The pyramid **C** is an estimate of the situation in 2021.

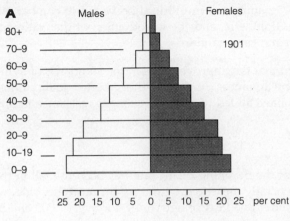

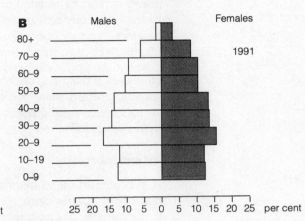

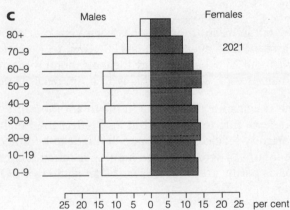

Source: *Social Trends* (HMSO, 1986 and 1993)

1 What is happening to the numbers of people over the age of 60 in the three pyramids?

2 Describe the changes in the 0–9-years-old group.

3 Can you suggest any reasons for these changes?

4 In the pyramid for 1991 what is noticeable for the group in the mid–late twenties? Can you suggest any explanation for this?

5 Comparing males with females, is there any age group in which the number of women is noticeably greater than the number of men?

6 It has been suggested that Britain has an 'ageing' population. Using the information given above, can you explain what this means?

Deaths

The usual measure of changes in the numbers of deaths is the **death** or **mortality rate**, which is the number of deaths each year for every 1000 people in the population.

The death rate declined very rapidly in the nineteenth century and in the very early part of the twentieth century. But since the 1920s there has only been a very slight fall. At present, the death rate is 11.2 for males and 11.3 for females.

Reasons for the decline in the death rate

In the nineteenth century there was a massive programme of public health improvements – decent drainage and guaranteed supplies of pure water, for example. This eliminated many of the killer diseases, such as cholera and typhoid. In the twentieth century, programmes of immunisation began to combat other diseases, such as polio and diphtheria, and the introduction of the National Health Service improved health care standards.

However, it has been argued that the improvements in the standards of living are more important than medical advances. Improved diets, better quality housing and shorter working hours have all led to a much stronger resistance to illness than ever before.

Infant mortality

A very important element of the declining death rate has been the fall in the number of infants dying, generally measured by the **infant mortality rate**, which is the number of children under one year of age dying for every 1000 children born.

The fall in infant mortality has been very marked in the twentieth century, with big reductions even in the last 30 years. In 1961, for example, the death rate was still about 22, whereas today the male infant mortality rate has fallen to 8.3 and for females to 6.3. Compare this with a figure of 72 per thousand in 1921!

The reasons for the decline in the infant mortality rate are much the same as for the death rate in general, but also reflect the much improved midwife and maternity services of the state. It ought to be noted however, that the death rate for infants of working-class families is much higher than that of the middle class. This is partly a reflection of the better standards of housing and diet of the middle class.

Births and deaths in the UK

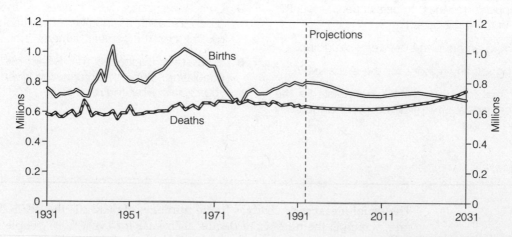

Source: *Social Trends 24* (HMSO, 1994)

Look at the graph on page 154. You may give approximate dates in your answers to the following questions.

1 In which two years were the numbers of births at their highest after 1931?

2 Can you suggest reasons for these peaks in the numbers of births?

3 What change occurred in the numbers of births after 1964?

4 What reasons can you suggest for this change?

5 What happened to the numbers of births between 1948 and 1955?

6 Can you explain these changes?

7 There appear to be two rather different relationships between birth and death rates before and after the early 1970s. Explain what these differences are. In general, what different implications may this have for the population of a country?

8 Is there any point at which deaths may be higher than births? Does this necessarily mean that the population will decrease in size? Explain your answer.

The population of the UK – the future?

Age and sex structure of the population, UK

| | Age groups (percentages) | | | | | All ages (= 100%) (millions) |
	Under 16	16–39	40–64	65–79	80 and over	
1961	24.9	31.4	32.0	9.8	1.9	52.8
1971	25.5	31.3	29.9	10.9	2.3	55.9
1981	22.3	34.9	27.8	12.2	2.8	56.4
1991	20.3	35.3	28.6	12.0	3.7	57.8
Males	21.4	36.7	29.0	10.6	2.3	28.2
Females	19.3	34.0	28.2	13.3	5.2	29.6
Projections:						
2001	21.0	32.8	30.5	11.4	4.2	59.7
2011	19.5	30.3	33.7	11.9	4.7	61.1
2021	18.5	30.0	32.3	14.0	5.2	62.0
2031	18.4	28.7	30.3	15.6	6.9	62.1
Males	19.0	29.7	30.9	14.9	5.5	30.7
Females	17.7	27.6	29.8	16.4	8.3	31.4

Source: *Social Trends 24* (HMSO, 1994)

1 Between 1961 and 2031, which age group will grow:
a) the greatest?
b) proportionately the greatest?

2 What happens to the under 16 and 16–39 age groups?

3 Can you offer any explanations for these changes?

4 Are there noticeable differences in the sex balance for any age groups? If there are, suggest a reason.

5 Is there any trend in the period shown in the overall growth in the population? Can you suggest a reason for this?

Life expectancy

The number of people aged over 65 is nearly five times greater now than in 1901. Today, 15 per cent of the population are in this age group. At the age of 20 a young man can expect to live to his early seventies and a young women to her late

seventies. In short, people live longer lives than they have ever done before, and an increasingly large number of people can *expect* to have longer lives.

Long life is caused by the very reasons that lowered the death rate; that is, higher standards of living, better housing conditions, better diets, better working conditions and shorter hours, and medical advances.

Sex differences in life expectancy

Women are more likely than men to survive into old age. Apart from biological factors, the reasons are that they are less likely to smoke or drink as heavily as men. They are less likely to be killed in motor vehicle accidents; and they are less likely to work in dangerous occupations. Of course, in the past the two World Wars led to many more men dying than women. By age of 75 women outnumber men by two to one.

Problems associated with an ageing population

For society as a whole, the **burden of dependency** increases. By this we mean that the costs of supporting the elderly, for example in pensions and extra hospital places, must be paid for by extra taxation. For families, the problem will be the need to care for an increasing number of elderly people at home. This burden falls

Would a sight like this have been likely in 1890? Explain your answer. Go to a local graveyard, check the dates and ages of the deceased. What does this information tell you?

mainly on the wife or daughter. For the old people themselves, there will be some cases of loneliness, of poverty and of a long period of physical decline before death.

Consequences of the growing numbers of elderly people

**FOR
INDIVIDUALS**
Positive consequences:
Escape from the drudgery of work; more time for leisure interests, education, learning new skills, involvement with family
Negative consequences: Loss of income, status and sense of purpose with loss of jobs (especially if it is professional/managerial); loss of social contacts and deterioration in health

**FOR
THE FAMILY**
Positive consequences:
The elderly can provide help and companionship for the younger generations, babysitting, childcare, etc. (depends on their stage in the 'family life cycle').
Negative consequences:
Infirm, elderly people place a great burden in terms of care on the younger generation. It is usually women who have to look after them, some having to give up their jobs and social lives.

FOR SOCIETY
Health and social services demands are very heavy and costly, with over 35 per cent of welfare costs for older people and pensions for the retired, involve heavy insurance burden on those working – known as the 'burden of dependency'.

The rapidly changing nature of society means that the experience of the old is no longer valued by the young. This leads to a loss of status of the elderly in society.

But
much of the so-called burden of dependency is really a reflection of *political* decisions to make people retire at 60/65, causing poverty and loss of status. Retirement creates jobs for the young.

To find out more about elderly people, take a tape recorder and ask them about their lives and their family. Compare your information with what is here.

You might want to question your own grandparents (if over 60) and some people in special homes for the elderly.

More information can be obtained from the charity 'Help the Aged'.

The burden of dependency

The dependent population of the UK, by age

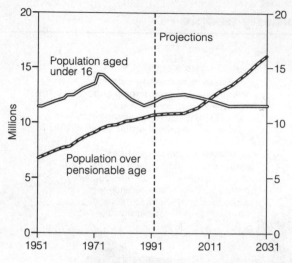

Source: *Social Trends 24* (HMSO, 1994)

1 How many people over pensionable age were there in 1951?

2 How many will there be in 2031?

3 What are the comparable figures for the under 16s?

4 People live longer. Why?

5 Do you think this is a good or bad thing for society?

Explain your answers.

Migration

International migration

In the first half of the 1990s, about 240 000 people came to live in Britain and about 220 000 went to live elsewhere. When people come into a country to live, it is termed **immigration**. When people leave the country to live abroad, it is called **emigration**.

Since the 1950s the numbers emigrating from Britain have been slightly higher than those coming here to live, although unusually in 1983 and 1984 more people came into Britain than left. The difference between immigration totals and emigration totals is known as **net migration**.

Britain attracts people from the Indian subcontinent (Indians, Pakistanis and Bangladeshis), from Australia, the EU and the United States. The majority of people who settle in Britain today are from other EU countries. British people generally emigrate to Australia and Canada.

In the 1950s immigrants began to arrive first from the West Indies and then from the Indian sub-continent. They came because of poverty at home and because there were not enough workers in Britain to fill all the job vacancies. From 1962 onward there was a series of laws restricting the numbers of new immigrants. Since then, those arriving have been the *dependent* relatives (such as children and wives) of those already here. (There is a full discussion on immigration on pages 83–4).

Internal migration

The move to the south-east

The distribution of Britain's population is increasingly becoming unbalanced. More people are emigrating to the south-east (excluding London, which is actually losing population) from other parts of Britain. The greatest decline in population has been in Scotland, Wales, the West Midlands and the north of England. In these areas, in particular, the birth rate cannot match the numbers leaving. Some of the greatest areas of growth have been Suffolk, Norfolk, Essex and Cambridgeshire.

Why? The main force driving people to move is the lack of jobs in the north, Scotland and Wales. As most of the jobs are now in the south-east, that is where people have to go.

Internal migration in the UK

Ten districts forecast to grow

	1991	2001	Growth (%)
Chiltern	89 687	102 076	13.8
South Cambs	122 493	139 170	13.6
South Bucks	62 409	70 836	13.5
East Cambs	61 176	69 403	13.4
Huntingdonshire	146 538	165 415	12.8
Fenland	75 510	85 039	12.6
Wycombe	159 829	179 087	12.0
Peterborough	155 029	173 563	11.9
Aylesbury Vale	147 972	163 355	11.7
Milton Keynes	179 232	198 971	11.0

Ten districts forecast to shrink

	1991	2001	Growth (%)
Liverpool	480 749	413 616	−13.9
Knowsley	156 853	141 632	−9.7
Inverclyde	91 580	83 940	−8.3
Glasgow city	688 600	633 762	−7.9
Wandsworth	265 258	247 427	−6.7
Salford	230 936	215 474	−6.6
Dundee city	172 420	160 884	−6.6
Haringey	211 755	199 895	−5.6
Monklands	104 010	98 309	−5.4
Motherwell	144 740	136 969	−5.3

Source: *The Guardian*, 31 May 1994

Population change, by area, mid-1981–91, UK

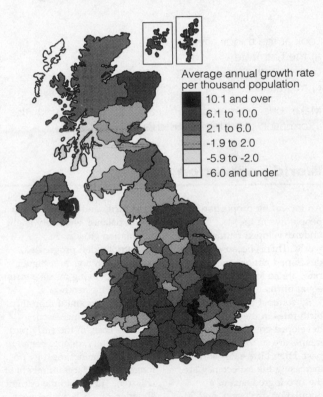

Average annual growth rate per thousand population
- 10.1 and over
- 6.1 to 10.0
- 2.1 to 6.0
- -1.9 to 2.0
- -5.9 to -2.0
- -6.0 and under

Source: *Social Trends 24* (HMSO, 1994)

1 Look at the map. Using an atlas, name the places which have grown the fastest between 1981 and 1991.

2 Which places have declined in population?

3 Overall, can you find any pattern emerging for decline and growth?

4 What reasons can you suggest for:
a) areas declining in population?
b) areas increasing in population?

5 Using an atlas (and probably the gazeteer in the back of it), find out where the ten districts of growth and decline are. Can you spot any pattern?

Factors influencing population size

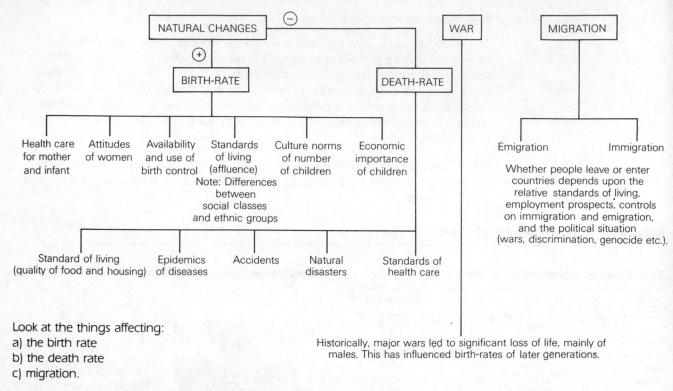

Look at the things affecting:
a) the birth rate
b) the death rate
c) migration.

Make brief comments on each of these, using the information provided in this chapter.

World population

An increasing proportion of people live in the underdeveloped nations of the world. This is because in most developed nations the birth-rates are so low that deaths equal births.

By contrast there are high birth-rates in the under-developed countries and more infants are surviving than in the past. High birth-rates and increasing life expectancy are the two ingredients of a population explosion, and 90 per cent of the increase in population of the world in the next 25 years will be in the under-developed nations.

The now affluent industrialised countries experienced population explosions themselves in the nineteenth century. Before that time, births and deaths were in a rough balance, with very slight population growth. As industrialisation progressed, medical advances and higher standard of living meant a steep decline in the death-rate, particularly in infant mortality. The population increased rapidly. Then, in the early part of this century, people began to limit their families, as they no longer needed large numbers of children. This led to the current situation of a balance between births and deaths. This process from pre-industrial slight growth of population to the present ageing population is known as 'demographic transition'.

The continuing large families in under-developed nations make perfect sense. In societies with virtually no welfare system or pensions, and high risk of unemployment and sickness, large families are a hedge against disaster. The larger the family, the more likely it is that some member will be making an income.

In such countries it is the elderly with fewest children whose poverty is most acute. The World Fertility Survey, conducted in 60 countries in 1980 showed that for Third World countries one of the main reasons for wanting a large family was to provide for the parents in their old age.

When it was thought that the demographic transition would occur automatically, when the industrial development of a country reached a certain state, it now seems that the distribution of income and welfare within a country is crucial. Poorer countries with fairer distribution of income and with social security systems show more rapidly falling birth-rates than richer countries where industrialisation has mainly enriched the better-off.

When the European countries experienced their population explosions they coped by importing large quantities of food and materials from abroad and by exporting population (to the empire). This solution is not possible for Third World countries today, too poor to import food (indeed having to export it) and with the richer countries imposing strict immigration control.

Source: Adapted from 'World Population' in *New Society*, 31 January 1986

1 Where is the bulk of world population growth taking place?

2 What three stages of population change are there in the 'demographic transition'?

3 If all the poor people in the Third World (under-developed nations) were given free contraceptives and advice, would this limit population growth?

4 Why does the theory of demographic transition not apply to the Third World?

5 What does the article suggest is the best method to ensure a decline in population growth?

6 Look at the diagram on page 160 and make brief comments on each of the factors influencing population as they apply to the Third World.

7 What differences emerge between the Third World and Britain?

Chapter **9**

URBAN AND RURAL LIVES

This chapter covers:
- Urbanisation
- De-urbanisation
- Community
- Inner-city problems
- The changing countryside.

Urbanisation

- **Urbanisation:** the process whereby the majority of the population gradually move from the countryside to live in towns and cities

The growth of cities in Britain really begins with industrialisation, around the end of the eighteenth century. Before 1800 only about 15 per cent of the population lived in towns and cities; 100 years later 75 per cent of the population lived in them.

The original growth of the cities was because people moved there from the countryside. As these were generally young people they then caused a rapid increase in the population by having children of their own – the process that is happening in Third World cities today.

The reasons for the move to the cities were of two types.

Pull reasons

There was work in the cities in the new factories and although the wages and conditions of employment were dreadful, they were better than those in agriculture.

The nineteenth century saw the rapid expansion of the cities in Britain

Push reasons

The enclosure of land by large farmers meant that small tenant farmers were evicted (made homeless) and that their land was combined into larger units by the owners. The introduction of machinery and modern mass farming techniques meant that there were fewer jobs available in the countryside. At that time there were no welfare provisions and it was a case of starve or move.

A breathing space

The Environment Secretary is to announce guidelines today, urging planning authorities to be stricter in refusing development in green-belt areas on the edge of towns. ...

Mr Gummer believes that the green belt is critical not only to the protection of the countryside, but also to reviving town and city centres. He dismisses the idea that scrubland on the edges of towns can be used without damage. He reasons that this would simply result in a bite-by-bite consumption of the green belt, leaving nothing, and is instead urging planning authorities to concentrate on rebuilding town and city centres. He sees his green-belt policy as part of a wider strategy which includes discouraging out-of-town shopping development.

Source: *The Times*, 24 January 1995

1 What do we mean by the 'green belt'?

2 According to the extract, what is happening to the green belt?

3 What is the Environment Secretary doing to change this?

4 What effects will this have for cities and towns, do you think?

De-urbanisation

The large towns and cities have come to be places where the bulk of the population live. At present 90 per cent of the population live in urban areas. However, certain important changes have been taking place.

The move out of the cities

There has been a move away from the cities, towards the outer suburbs, New Towns and the countryside over the last 20 years. At the extreme, London has lost 10 per cent of its population and actually declined by two million people from its peak. On the other hand, New Towns such as Milton Keynes and Basildon have increased their populations by 20 per cent.

Why? People prefer the better standard of housing available and the cleaner, less polluted environment of the suburbs and countryside. Cars and trains make travel into the big cities for work fairly quick and easy. However, firms are also moving out of the big cities, preferring the low costs of the New Towns to the advantages of being in the city centres.

Since the 1960s there has been considerable movement out of the cities to the New Towns and the countryside

Flight from the cities

East Anglia, predominantly a rural area, has been the region with the fastest population growth since 1961, due mainly to (internal) immigration.

Source: Census of Population

The current prosperity of the east is largely:

a) an accident of geography, with the discovery of North Sea oil and gas;

b) due to the fact that the east of Britain is now facing the right way for trade. The rise of the east coast ports reflects the growing importance of links with Europe and Scandinavia. For example, Felixstowe was almost derelict after the last war, today it is Britain's largest container port;

c) East Anglia in general has a good standard of industrial behaviour. It has the lowest rate of industrial stoppages of any region in Britain. The eastward trend in the move of British industry does seem to be a move away from old premises and old working practices;

d) Communication networks are starting to benefit the east and the rural areas with the creation of new motorways, such as the M11 and the M25 orbital around outer London. The new roads network means new patterns of employment, the new technologies can choose pleasant greenfield sites to settle in. They are not bound to go to old industrial areas like Liverpool and Manchester.

Source: Adapted from D. White, 'Tilting Britain onto its side' in *New Society*, 14 June 1985

East Anglia – the promised land!

It is the great exodus from the cities. Millions fed up with the crowds, noise, grime and traffic are being seduced by the rural idyll of green fields, fresh air and a gentler, more neighbourly way of life.

Even if they must work in the concrete jungle, more and more Britons are determined they should not live there, choosing to commute instead.

The past ten years has seen a tidal change, with families deserting London and the great cities of the North and Scotland.

This drift from town to country is confirmed in the results of the 1991 census...

East Anglia is seen as the promised land for harassed suburbanites. The region's population has soared by more than 154,000 – a jump of 7.3 per cent – to two million in ten years. Over 200 years the increase has been 350,000 as families chase the rural dream.

Better schools and a lower crime rate, together with what is perceived to be a less hectic pace of life are thought to be key factors.

Much of the increase in the region's population can be traced to Londoners deciding to move further out of the city, but still within commuting distance of work.

Greater London's population fell 300,000 between 1981 and 1991, bringing it down to 6.4 million.

Only 20 years ago it stood at 7.4 million. The North to South drift mirrors the economic climate of 1980s where the South had the most jobs and the biggest share of national wealth.

As the older, unionised industries of the North, such as steel and coal, declined, so young people headed South in search of their fortunes.

The North West of England, including Greater Manchester and Merseyside, saw the greatest population fall between 1981 and 1991.

In ten years the number fell 260,000 to 6.1 million, while over 20 years some 600,000 left the region.

Scotland, too, has lost many hundreds of thousands of residents.

The figure has fallen steadily since 1971 when it was 5.3 million to 5.1 million in 1981. Last year it stood at 4.9 million – down 400,000.

The census was the first to look at ethnic minorities and found people from this group made up 5.5 per cent of the country's 54 million population.

Source: *The Daily Mail*, 19 December 1992

1 Find the meaning of the term 'conurbation'.

2 What reasons could you suggest for people moving to the New Towns and rural (country) areas (see pages 162–3)

3 What sorts of town are considered as 'retirement areas'?

4 According to the extracts, which area in Britain has the fastest growth rate, overall?

5 Why should Europe influence the growth rate of an area in England?

6 Your local authority ought to have a 'development plan' for your area. Obtain a copy from your civic centre or central library and find out what is happening to business and population in your area.

7 Which areas had the greatest fall in population? Why?

8 Where would you prefer to live? Why?

9 Is the image of life described in the third extract accurate, do you think? Explain your answer.

Community

The loss of community

As societies moved from being predominantly rural and agricultural, to being urban and industrial, the changes that took place were not just physical, such as the growth of roads, houses and factories, they were also changes in the way people behaved and thought.

Tönnies, a sociologist writing at the end of the nineteenth century, said that it was possible to distinguish quite clearly between the social life of the traditional rural society, which he called **Gemeinschaft**, and the social life of the fast moving cities, which he called **Gesellschaft**.

Gemeinschaft

This type of society is one where people have close contact with others, forming a tight social network, and where there is a sense of 'belonging'. People hold very similar values, and in general are very similar to one another. Individuals know each other not just in one role but in many, for instance as brother-in-law/employer/next-door neighbour/regular at the pub. This form of society has also been called **community**.

Was life so idyllic then? Wages were low and healthcare was non-existent. Houses were owned by farmers who were also the only employers. People chose to move to the cities.

Interview your history teacher – ask her or him what a typical farmworker's week was like in the last century.

Gesellschaft

This is the type of society where people have only a superficial relationship with other people, seeing them only at work for instance, but never outside (having a **single-role** relationship). There is little sense of belonging to any community and people are prepared to move away with little regret.

Emile Durkheim, writing at about the same time as Tönnies, suggested that the only thing holding modern industrial (he called it **organic**) society together was the fact that people needed each other in order to survive. In the traditional, rural society (he called it **mechanical**), people were so close because they were so alike.

These sociologists supported the general belief that life is far more anonymous in the cities, with people having few close friends and what contacts they have are short-lived and very narrow.

Tönnies' community and association

	Gemeinschaft 'Community'	Gesellschaft 'Association' or 'Society'
1 Relationships	Face-to-face; personal; 'primary'	Impersonal; structured; indirect; 'secondary'
2 Values	Shared and agreed; same attitudes and goals	Lack of agreement; many competing ideas
3 Actions	Not calculated; natural, not reflexive	Rationally evaluated and planned; individual self-interest
4 Main structural institutions	The family and kinship group; village activities	City life; fragmented and formal-work; law; citizenship
5 Status	Given by membership of community ('ascribed'); the whole person as a person; little differentiation	Obtained through individual effort, mainly in work ('achieved'); highly differentiated
6 Social control	Informal, through the family and neighbours; visibility of deviants	Formal legal systems; agencies; public opinion
7 Locality	Valued as people; gives sense of identity; belonging	Indifference; population migrates; no identity with everybody else

In your own words, write a paragraph explaining the differences in social relationship between community and association.

Source: G. Payne, 'Community and community studies' in *Sociology Review*, September 1994

Community in the city

However, the research by Willmott and Young in the 1950s in Bethnal Green, London, and of Rosser and Harris in Swansea, showed that at that time there were very close-knit working-class communities within the inner cities. Although these areas have now been demolished, there is still evidence that cities may be just as much communities as are small villages. This is mainly because people break up the large towns into neighbourhoods with which they associate. Furthermore, groups of people join together into clubs based on interests and sport. All this pulls people together.

Increasingly there has been a move into city centres by affluent young people who restore dilapidated houses and create 'new' expensive upper middle-class neighbourhoods. This is known as 'gentrification'.

The community and urban life

The common view is that urbanisation has broken up traditional social bonds, replacing them with anomie (a breakdown in law and order) and alienation (people feel they do not belong); the past represents human warmth and solidarity, the present anonymity and isolation. But a recent study challenges this view. Most people do still have social relationships with people who live nearby. A sizeable minority have relatives living close at hand, have friends within ten minutes' walk and the overwhelming majority have friendly dealings with their neighbours.

It is therefore wrong to suggest that urban communities no longer exist. But there are pressures on it. The growth in mobility is one. More people own and move house, thus dispersing family and friends. One clear finding from research to date is that the sense of community is not more common in small towns than in cities. The scale of the place or the density of the population has nothing to do with it. What does count is people's length of residence. The longer they live in a place, the stronger and more extensive their links.

So newer places are likely to have weaker social networks. But physical layout is important too. The post-war programme of clearance not only broke up local networks but also redeveloped the old districts in forms that made it more difficult for people to get to know their neighbours – people in high rise flats, for instance, are more likely to say there is 'no community' in their area. ...

The upshot is that whereas in the past community attachment was particularly strong amongst the working-class residents, it may now be stronger amongst the middle class. The traditional community, a densely-woven world of kin, neighbours and friends, is being replaced by the new neighbourhoodism in which people set out to join local organisations and make new friends. Middle-class people are more enthusiastic joiners, everything from the local tennis club to the 'Stop the Bypass' campaign. In this sense they are more involved and active in the community than the working class.

Source: Adapted from J. Lawrence, 'The unknown neighbourhood' in *New Society*, 6 June 1986

1 What is the traditional view of city life?

2 Does recent research bear this out?

3 Name three factors which influence the creation of a sense of community.

4 In the past it has been the working class who have had the stronger community life. What is happening now?

5 Ask your family/neighbours if they feel there is a 'sense of community' in your area. Do they know the names of most of the people in your street? Does it fit the evidence in the extract above?

The community and rural life

Most commonly the conflict is over housing, particularly where a village is within commuting range of a large city. Local people working in a low-wage economy cannot afford to buy houses once more affluent incomers bid brices up. The younger generation is forced either to take substandard living conditions (sharing, caravans, 'seasonal lets') or move out. In areas of natural beauty, retirees move in and 'white settlers' buy holiday homes that are empty most of the year. The age-profile of the settlement becomes distorted, the local school gets closed, the shop cannot pay its way, services and collective activities decline.

Even in less extreme situations there is tension, because incomers are different. Typically they are wealthier, more educated, and not in agriculture. They take over the running of clubs and local councils. Their way of life is distinctive, usually embracing an image of the village as a community that should not change. They want peace and quiet in preference to new jobs in rural development industries or even smelly farming.

Source: G. Payne, 'Community and community studies' in *Sociology Review*, September 1994

The extract describes village life.

1 What is the most common reason for conflict?

2 What are the effects of affluent newcomers arriving?

3 Do newcomers fit easily into village life? Explain your answer.

4 List the advantages and disadvantages for the local community of people moving into villages from towns. (The extract is rather biased and only gives part of the story. Think what would happen without affluent outsiders coming with money to spend, and also think about whether agriculture as a provider of employment is expanding or declining.)

Inner-city problems

Since the early 1980s there has been a number of instances of serious inner-city disorder sometimes actually turning into 'riots'. The causes are described in the diagram opposite. The riots drew attention to the severe problems of youth in the inner cities, but we should be aware that other groups suffer tremendous deprivation too, in particular parents with young children and the elderly.

The modern housing estates of tower blocks developed in the 1960s have no play facilities for children, and women who are at home all day feel imprisoned in their apartments. Depression is common. The elderly are often trapped in areas where they no longer want to be, with neighbourhoods having changed character

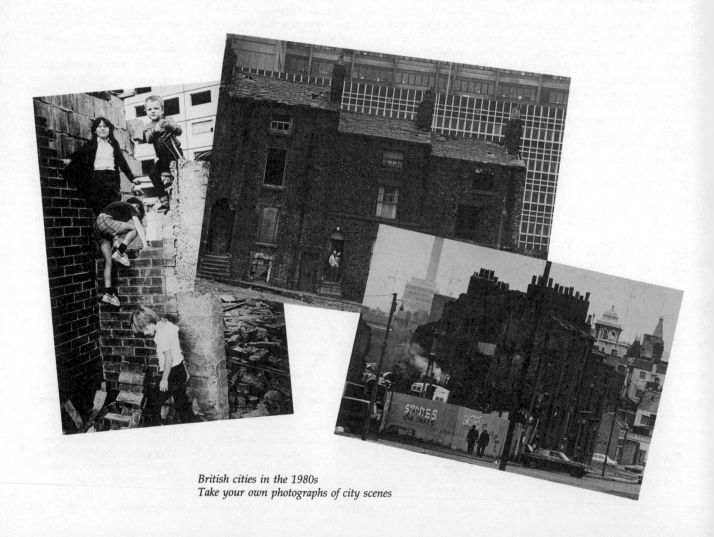

British cities in the 1980s
Take your own photographs of city scenes

drastically in the period since they went to live there. They are particularly frightened of crime.

All residents of the inner cities face similar problems of noise and pollution from traffic, and a decay in the environment as local authority spending programmes have been cut back. There are fewer doctors than in the suburbs and welfare facilities are poor. Increasingly as firms move out of the cities, employment prospects decline and when this is coupled with the very high costs of housing, this means that poverty is on the increase.

Inner-city disorder

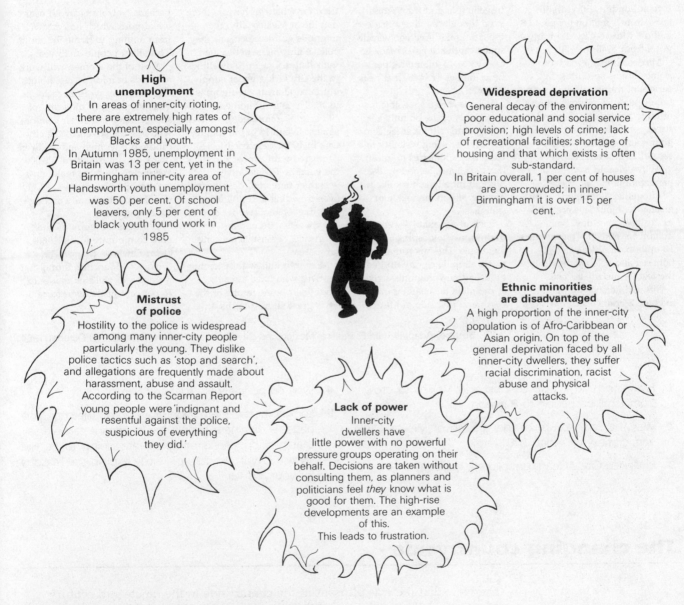

High unemployment
In areas of inner-city rioting, there are extremely high rates of unemployment, especially amongst Blacks and youth.
In Autumn 1985, unemployment in Britain was 13 per cent, yet in the Birmingham inner-city area of Handsworth youth unemployment was 50 per cent. Of school leavers, only 5 per cent of black youth found work in 1985

Widespread deprivation
General decay of the environment; poor educational and social service provision; high levels of crime; lack of recreational facilities; shortage of housing and that which exists is often sub-standard.
In Britain overall, 1 per cent of houses are overcrowded; in inner-Birmingham it is over 15 per cent.

Mistrust of police
Hostility to the police is widespread among many inner-city people particularly the young. They dislike police tactics such as 'stop and search', and allegations are frequently made about harassment, abuse and assault. According to the Scarman Report young people were 'indignant and resentful against the police, suspicious of everything they did.'

Ethnic minorities are disadvantaged
A high proportion of the inner-city population is of Afro-Caribbean or Asian origin. On top of the general deprivation faced by all inner-city dwellers, they suffer racial discrimination, racist abuse and physical attacks.

Lack of power
Inner-city dwellers have little power with no powerful pressure groups operating on their behalf. Decisions are taken without consulting them, as planners and politicians feel *they* know what is good for them. The high-rise developments are an example of this.
This leads to frustration.

In your local library ask to see the newspapers for October 1985, particularly the Sunday papers. Find out all you can about the inner city riots.

Third World cities

The fastest growing cities are in the Third World. Migration from the countryside to the towns has more to do with social changes in the countryside than with population growth as such; changes such as the growing of crops for sale rather than for use, and the introduction of agricultural machinery which replaces workers. This leads to poverty and unemployment, forcing people to seek work in the cities.

The problem with urbanisation in the Third World is that urban populations are growing faster than employment prospects and this leads to poverty and crime.

Mexico city: The city of the future

It took London 130 years to grow from 1 million people to 8 million. Mexico City did it in 30 years from 1940 to 1970.

Mexico City is a place of shanty towns sprouting TV aerials, of traffic jams and shops full of parts from wrecked cars, of huge armies of police and street vendors, of graft, political godfathers and the world's second largest national debt.

Above ground is pandemonium.

Altogether 20 million mechanised journeys are made in the city every day. Four million are taken by private car, 10 million on a fleet of 7000 battered and belching buses and the rest by metro and taxi.

City workers spend on average 2 hours every day travelling to and from work, even though few live outside the city limits. Average vehicle speed on the clogged roads is said to be 12 kilometres per hour, falling to 4 km/h at peak periods.

Vehicles are responsible for two-thirds of the pollution, which sends a thick smog across the city, reducing visibility to a couple of kilometres on most days. (It is not helped by the high altitude which results in greater carbon monoxide in exhausts.)

Lack of adequate sewers and drains make widespread disease inevitable. The rats run and the rivers stink. Each day up to a thousand new migrants arrive at the main bus stations on the north and east side of Mexico City, for whatever horrors there may be in Mexico City, the migrants go there because they believe life will be better than in the villages. One in 10 dwellings in the city lack a water supply, but in rural areas the figure is 5 in 10. Three in 10 homes in the city are not connected to a sewer against five in 10 in the country. One in 10 lack electricity compared with almost 7 in 10 in the villages. People are wealthier here and, despite the over-crowding and pollution, they live longer. Ten per cent of city dwellers are under-nourished, against 90 per cent in rural areas.

Most migrants will be joining relatives who have already made their home in one of the city's great slum suburbs – perhaps Netzahualcoyotl, near the airport, which has grown from nothing to home for about 2.5 million people in 25 years.

Most of the women will work as maids in middle-class homes. The men may work in factories, or as members of the army of shoe-shiners and street vendors who line the streets of the city centre. But women and children (there are an estimated 100 000 children in the city) make up a large proportion of the workforce – especially among the lowest paid.

In a detailed study of one poor community in the 1960s, Oscar Lewis, author of The Children of Sanchez, found that women and children made up 76 per cent of the workforce.

Source: Adapted from F. Pearce 'Mexico, the City Unlimited' in *New Scientist*, 18 October 1984

1 How long did it take London and Mexico to grow from 1 million people to 8 million?

2 Was the main cause of the growth of Mexico City immigration, or a high birth rate?

3 Is Mexico City a clean, unpolluted, quiet city?

4 Why do people want to live in Mexico City?

5 Looking at the information provided on the changing patterns of where people live in Britain, can we say that London and Birmingham are going to be like Mexico City in the future? Briefly explain the reasons for your answer.

The changing countryside

The view that life was pleasant in the countryside in the nineteenth century compared to the squalid life of the cities is a myth. Life was just as hard and poverty was just as common. Unemployment, homelessness and disease were facts of life.

In the twentieth century, there are still large amounts of poverty in the countryside; one of the lowest paid occupations is that of farm labourer, and there is a lack of hospitals, local public transport and social services. Nevertheless for those people who are able to commute to relatively well-paid jobs in the towns and cities, there are considerable attractions to life in the countryside. Since the 1950s, there has been a move away from the city, to life in the small towns and villages in the countryside. The main reasons for the move have been the development of transport links (railways and motorways) to the large conurbations, which have attracted both companies and workers out of the city centres.

The effects on the countryside have been quite dramatic. There has been a decline in agricultural land as more housing developments are created. House prices in general in the countryside have risen to the point where local people cannot afford to buy, leaving the way clear for the commuters to buy up the properties. The small, local communities have been altered by an influx of new people, bringing new attitudes and ideas. Some small communities have been completely swamped by huge new developments and New Towns, such as Milton Keynes.

Chapter 10

EDUCATION

This chapter covers:
* An outline of the British education system
* The history of schooling in Britain
* The purposes of education
* Educational attainment.

An outline of the British education system

Getting through the British education system is a bit like climbing a rockface. As you work up through it, there are a number of choices. So although most people climb up the 'rockface', some people have easier routes and therefore get further than others. Some people may be lucky and stumble across the best route, but many other people labour slowly up, and then find that they can go no further.

The education system (our rockface) has the following clear stages:
* primary education
* secondary education
* tertiary education.

Primary education

This consists of infant and junior schools. Usually these schools take any child from a particular area and are co-educational, that is they take both sexes.

Secondary education

This consists of all schools taking pupils between the ages of 11 and 16 (minimum school leaving age), plus sixth-formers up to the age of 18. Up to the late 1970s, there was a wide range of secondary schools, including grammar and secondary modern schools, but today the majority of schools are comprehensive.

Ninety per cent of all secondary pupils attend comprehensive schools, which are supposed to take the entire range of academic ability. Attendance at a particular school is through a mixture of parental choice and geographical closeness. However, since 1988 there has been a gradual move to introduce selection of students by a minority of schools which have been given greater freedom of action by the government. The other 10 per cent of secondary students attend private or 'special' schools.

Tertiary education

Education beyond the compulsory age of 16 takes a variety of forms. From 16 to 18, students can attend sixth forms of schools, sixth form colleges, further education colleges, or undertake a skills training scheme. From 18 onwards, those with appropriate qualifications can enter a university.

Independent education

- **Private schools:** all schools which charge fees
- **Public schools:** those higher status schools which belong to an organisation called The Headmasters' Conference.

The independent sector includes all schools, colleges, and the University of Buckingham, that charge fees. Public schools are the best-known and controversial part of the independent sector. About 7 per cent of school children attend private schools. Since 1980, the Conservative Government has run an 'assisted places scheme' through which the fees of 'gifted children' are paid at public schools, if the parents could not otherwise afford to send them there. (Gifted children are supposedly those of high intelligence.) Opponents of private education claim that these schools allow the children of the rich to receive a separate and special education.

The shared experiences of attending the most exclusive schools creates a sense of superiority and comradeship among the children of the rich. This sense of 'being special' is maintained throughout life, and as adults the ex-public school boys tend to help each other into positions of power, thus 'reproducing' another generation of rich and powerful people. Naturally they send their children to public schools and so the cycle is repeated.

When they leave school, they are more likely than students from state schools to go to Oxford and Cambridge and from there into the top positions of our society, where they wield great power.

One rule for the rich...

The table shows the schools that the children of members of the Conservative government went to in 1992.

The Cabinet's choice of schools

Minister	Children	Schools attended	Minister	Children	Schools attended
John Major	2	State primary, private secondary	Michael Heseltine	3	Private
Kenneth Clarke	2	State primary, private secondary	Lord Mackay	1	Private
Norman Lamont	2	Private	Peter Brooke	3	Private
Douglas Hurd	3*	Private	David Hunt	4	Private
Tom King	2	Private	Ian Lang	2	Private
Kenneth Baker	2	Private	Peter Lilley	0	
John Gummer	4	Two state primary, one private secondary, one fee-paying choir school	David Mellor	2	Private
			Chris Patten	3	State primary/ one private
			Malcolm Rifkind	2	Private
Tony Newton	2	State	John Wakeham	3	Two at private
Michael Howard	2	Private	William Waldegrave	4	Private
John MacGregor	3	Private	David Waddington	5	Private

*From first marriage; two young children from second marriage not included

Source: C. Chitty, 'The educational system transformed' in *Sociology Review*, February 1993 and *The Guardian*, 19 February 1992

1 Which type of primary school did the majority of the children attend?

2 Which type of secondary school did the majority of children attend?

3 The government is responsible for the state education sector, which 90 per cent of UK children attend. Does this suggest to you any consequences for the state schools?

The history of schooling in Britain

Before 1870

There was no organised education system. Children could possibly attend charity schools run by the various churches. The rich paid for private tutors or sent their sons to private schools.

1870 The Forster Education Act

This Act introduced a basic network of state-supported primary schools. Attendance was voluntary.

Why? Britain was falling behind its competitors (principally Germany) in industrial development. One problem was a lack of educated workers needed for the new technology of the time. This is similar to the situation today regarding computer literacy and Britain's need to compete with Japan and the USA.

The situation before 1944

The education system was clearly based on class divisions. All children received a basic elementary education up to 14, but education beyond that age was restricted to the middle and upper classes. Middle-class children went to fee-charging grammar schools, with a few scholarships available to working-class boys. The upper class sent their children to expensive public schools.

1944 The Butler Act

This introduced the concept of **meritocracy**, that is each child was to receive an education based upon his or her ability rather than his or her parents' ability to pay, as had occurred up to 1944.

Three types of schools were introduced: grammar, secondary technical, secondary modern. Children were to be sent to the type of school most appropriate to their educational needs, based upon assessment in an examination at 11 (the '11+'). Because there were three types of schools, the system was known as the 'tripartite system', though in practice only grammar and secondary modern schools were built in the main. The minimum leaving age was raised to 15.

Why? Introduced in the last year of the Second World War, the Act was partly a response to the obvious unfairness of the pre-war period to which people were not prepared to return. Educational reform was part of a wider package of reforms including the National Health Service and the Social Security system. A second reason was that industry needed an increasingly high standard of education amongst the workforce.

1944–64

In practice, the tripartite system became a means by which the middle class passed the 11+ and went to grammar schools, while the majority of the working class failed and went to secondary modern schools. The upper class continued to attend public schools. The 11+ examination was not a reliable or accurate test of a child's ability. Many bright children, who failed the 11+, were sent to secondary modern schools where they were not *expected* to achieve much. They were not encouraged, therefore, to take examinations, such as GCEs (General Certificate of Education).

1965 onward: The comprehensive school reforms

Since 1965, against considerable opposition, there has been a shift towards comprehensive schools, which take all children of a given locality regardless of their ability.

Why? Those in favour of comprehensives argued that there were three broad areas of advantage: economic, social and educational.

Economic

One large school, it was argued, would be cheaper than a number of smaller ones and better facilities, such as swimming pools or craft workshops, could be provided.

Social

There would be a breakdown of the class divisions which had been strengthened by the tripartite system where middle-class children attended grammar schools and working-class children, on the whole, attended secondary moderns. By mixing the social classes in one school it was hoped to weaken the class barriers.

Educational

Children would no longer be divided into different type schools at 11, which many believed had resulted in children at secondary moderns failing to achieve their full potential, regarding themselves as less intelligent than grammar school pupils.

Social class and comprehensive schools

There is, in short, *no evidence* that comprehensive education contributes to the breakdown of the barriers of social class which still divide adults and children alike. ...For schools reflect the structure and culture of the society as a whole. As long as we live in a class society then the influence of social class will be felt in the schools, determining the kinds of education children receive and the results they obtain from them.

Source: J. Ford, *Social Class and the Comprehensive School* (Routledge and Kegan Paul, 1969)

1 Do comprehensive schools break down social class differences?

2 According to the writer, what do schools reflect?

3 Can we therefore change society in general by changing schools?

4 Can you think of the implications of this social policy in general (the writer is a Marxist)?

1987 Some conclusions on comprehensive schools

Studies of comprehensives have not fully borne out the early hopes of the system. Much the same differences in class educational attainment appear today as in the old tripartite system.

Overall, it seems that the comprehensives offer a wider range of subjects and better facilities than the tripartite system. Late developers are not held back.

Although the majority of children attend comprehensive schools, it would be wrong to view them all as equal in the ability range they contain. There has been no demolition of class barriers, probably because of the fact that comprehensives draw their intake from the local neighbourhood. Middle-class neighbourhoods have middle-class dominated comprehensives and working-class areas have working-class dominated comprehensives. Also, some comprehensives are situated in areas that still have grammar schools. So higher ability students are often sent to the grammar school. This process, known as 'creaming', makes many comprehensive schools secondary moderns in all but name. One undisputed benefit, however, has been the increase in pupils staying on beyond the minimum leaving age of 16.

1988 and the move to schools in competition

Major changes in the education system in England and Wales were introduced with the 1988 Act. There were three key changes:

- First, there was to be a **National Curriculum**. This meant that for the first time in Britain, all school students were to study the same subjects and were to be tested against targets set by the Department for Education.
- The second new idea was the weakening of the power of local government which had traditionally controlled education. All schools were given direct control over their own budgets. This was called the **local management of schools** (LMS).
- The third element was that any school could choose to have almost total control over every aspect of its own management and educational priorities, and receive its funding directly from central government. These **grant-maintained schools** had the right to reintroduce selection if they wanted. In other words, the debate between selection (grammar) and comprehensive schools was opened up again. By 1994, a total of 75 primary and 266 secondary schools had 'opted out' and become self-governing.

City technology colleges

The government also introduced a new type of school altogether which was part privately-funded and part state-funded. These were **city technology colleges** (CTCs), which were designed to give a technical and scientific education to the cleverest children who could not afford to pay for private education.

League tables

In 1991 the government began to publish the examination results of all state secondary schools. The idea behind this was, it was claimed, to give parents and students an idea of how well their school was performing compared to other schools. This would show up poor schools.

Critics claimed that the 'league tables' just confirmed the fact that some schools which drew their pupils from middle class areas did better than others which had a mainly working-class intake. They also pointed out that measuring a school solely on its examination success meant that other elements of schooling, which were not measured by results (such as the ability of a school to produce confident, happy young people), were not measured.

CTCs and phoney sociologists!

City technology colleges, set up by the Government in inner cities as "beacons of excellence" at an initial cost of £180 million, did not figure among the top 200 schools on GCSE performance despite having more teaching hours than most schools.

[Commenting on this and on the publication of exam results in general, Sir Cyril Taylor, chairman of the CTC Trust said that] exam results had to be published, but it was also important to show the value added by schools: "A school getting 40 per cent A to C grades might be doing better than a grammar school with 60 per cent. But what we are opposed to is a phoney sociological approach based on pupils' backgrounds."

Schools should set targets in other areas, he said. As a measure of local popularity, for example, they should aim to attract at least two applications for each pupil place.

Parents' involvement should be measured by their attendance at school functions. "We think that is a sign of healthy interest," Sir Cyril said.

CTCs were created to achieve excellence. Have they?

1 What else, according to Sir Cyril Taylor, was as important as simple exam results?

2 Find out the meaning of 'value-added'. Explain how it could change our view of results.

3 What did he mean when he made the comments about 'phoney sociological approach based on pupils' backgrounds'?

Source: *The Guardian*, 22 November 1994

School exam results – the 'Premier League'

State school results

Worst GCSE
5 or more A–Cs, %

Benjamin Gott, Leeds	0
Parkside, Devon	0
St Bede's Catholic, Lincolnshire	0
Woodlands, Devon	0
Breckfield Comm., Liverpool	1
Campion Boys', Liverpool	1
Conyngham, Kent	1
Cross Green, Leeds	2
Nolmfield, Calderdale	2

Top GCSE
All 100%, 5 or more A–Cs

Altrincham Grammar School for Girls, Altrincham
Aylesbury High School, Aylesbury
Bishop Wordsworth's Grammar School, Salisbury
Clitheroe Royal Grammar School, Clitheroe
Kendrick Girls' Grammar School, Reading
King Edward VI Camp Hill School (Boys), Birmingham
King Edward VI Grammar School, Stratford-upon-Avon
King Edward VI Handsworth School, Birmingham
Newport Girls' High School, Newport
Newstead Wood School for Girls (GM), Orpington
Pate's Grammar School, Cheltenham
Queen Mary's Grammar School, Walsall
Skegness Grammar School, Skegness

The Grammar School for Girls Wilmington, Dartford
The Rochester Girls' Grammar School, Rochester
Wolverhampton Girls' High School, Wolverhampton
Woodford County High School, Woodford Green

Top A/AS level	Point score
King Edward VI Grammar School (GM), Chelmsford	31.1
Chelmsford County High School for Girls, Chelmsford	30.8
King Edward VI Camp Hill School (Boys), Birmingham	27.5
RNIB New College, Worcester	26.9
King Edward VI Camp Hill Girls' School, Birmingham	26.8
Queen Mary's High School, Walsall	26.4
Colchester County High School for Girls, Colchester	26.4
Lancaster Royal Grammar School, Lancaster	26.3
Westcliff High School for Boys, Westcliff-on-Sea	26.1
Royal Grammar School, High Wycombe	26.1

High risers (not including Independent Schools)
Based on % point improvement 93–94 for 5 GCSE passes grade A–C

Stour Valley Community School, Shipston-on-Stour	27
Midhurst Grammar School, Midhurst	25
St Clement Danes School (GM), Rickmansworth	25
Wrotham School (GM), Sevenoaks	24
Marlborough School (GM), St Albans	23
St James' CofE School (GM), Farnworth	23
Latham High School, Skelmersdale	23
Wishmore Cross School (Boys), Woking	23

GM = grant-maintained

David Blunkett, Labour's education spokesman, who has signalled a shift in party policy by recognising the information value of league tables, said: "Once again, the Government is giving only part of the picture."

He promised Labour would publish "added value" tables which would reflect the way schools had improved pupils' performance between starting secondary education and sitting GCSEs, A levels and their vocational equivalents.

Thirty-one of the top 50 schools at GCSE last summer were girls-only independents, while 14 of the top 50 comprehensives were girls only.

The boys-only King Edward's School, Birmingham, and the girls-only King Edward VI High School in the city topped the independent school table for A level points scored with 35.1. Two opt-out single-sex grammar schools in Chelmsford, Essex – King Edward VI Grammar School, with 31.1 points, and Chelmsford County High School for Girls, with 30.8 – led the state schools.

1 Produce a breakdown of types of school in the list. Which type gets the best results?

2 Carry out an analysis of the schools by single-sex (divided into male and female) or co-educational. Which perform better? (There is corroborating information in the extract.)

3 Does this mean that these schools are better?

Source: *The Guardian*, 22 November 1994

The new vocationalism

Since the late 1970s, the education system in Britain has changed considerably regarding what is considered to be important to learn. The government believed that the system was failing to deliver an adequate *vocational* education to the majority of British school pupils, as there was not enough training of young people with the technical skills needed for an advanced economy. The education system appeared to value academic, abstract teaching and to give relevant work-oriented training and education a low priority.

As a result, the government began to introduce a range of changes to education. The first of these was the National Curriculum mentioned earlier. Secondly, there has been a shift away from A-levels towards specific vocational courses with an emphasis on work-oriented skills, which provide qualifications known as **GNVQs** (General National Vocational Qualifications. To ensure that the skill training was

concentrated on those people most needing it, the government insists that those leaving school with no qualifications and no employment at the age of 16 must undertake recognised training programmes in vocational skills and work experience. If a young person refuses to take up the offer, then he or she cannot claim state benefits.

Supporters argue that as Britain has fallen behind other nations because of an unskilled workforce, the new courses will help remedy this problem, by creating new attitudes to work and new skills of working amongst young people. Critics point out that unemployment in Britain is not caused by lack of skills at all, and that increasingly it is skilled workers who are becoming unemployed. They see the new vocationalism as more of a way of creating cheap labour for employers and of keeping young people off the streets and off the unemployment statistics.

Vocational training – useful or just 'a con'?

In 1976 Mr Callaghan, then Prime Minister, argued that comprehensive schools were failing to prepare their pupils for working life: that their curricula [subjects they taught] and their teaching methods were undermining the pupils' abilities to get jobs. As the scale of youth unemployment escalated, the employment problem of young people, their inability to get jobs was to be increasingly interpreted as an educational problem. In his view young people were educationally deficient and displayed a lack of willingness and poor attitudes to work.

With well over three million unemployed, the mistakes in this argument are obvious; even with appropriate skills, there are not enough jobs for the young. I would suggest that YTS has more to do with providing employers with a pool of free labour, from which they can pick and choose their recruits...than it has to do with meeting the training and educational needs of the unemployed.

Source: Adapted from D. Finn, 'A new deal for British youth' in *The Social Science Teacher*, Vol. 13, No. 2

Shilling too has criticised the structure of vocational education, claiming that the covert and 'true' aim of the new system was to prepare students for employment in capitalist organisations. Vocational skills just teach young people to accept and adapt to the hierarchy of work, to accept the routines and to cope with the repetitive nature of work and the boredom. Shilling found that work placements were experienced as exploitive, boring and demeaning.

Source: S. Moore with S. P. Sinclair, *Teach Yourself Sociology* (Hodder & Stoughton, 1995)

1   What criticisms were made of the education system?

2   Do you think, in your own experience, that these problems still exist today?

3   What criticisms does the first author make of employment training?

4   What does Shilling suggest is the 'true' reason for vocational training?

5   Contact your local TEC which is responsible for educational training. It will be in *The Phone Book*. Ask for information about educational training in your area, and ask if you could talk to some young people who have been through (or are going through) the programme to get their views.

The purposes of education

The discussion we have just had on the move to vocational education leads us to ask questions about the point of educational systems. Why do they exist and what are they intended to achieve?

In simple tribal societies, there was no formal education system. Knowledge and the basic values of society were passed on from one generation to another quite naturally in the rhythm of everyday life.

Education in a tribal society 50 years ago

Children learn the tasks required of adults simply by doing them. They are anxious to imitate their elders, and there is never any compulsory element in the teaching of these skills. Moreover, in their education they have this advantage, that it is not carried on in an institution divorced from everyday adult activities. The child feels that he is an essential part of society; all he does is a direct contribution to the domestic economy.

General behaviour, attitudes, and values are not taught by any formal training. These are inextricably bound up with life in the society and become unconsciously adopted by anyone fully partaking in social life. ...

One night, while sitting in a hut, we watched a girl of seven learning to cook. Fermented porridge was needed for the baby and this the girl set out to make in a small pot in the presence of her mother and several other girls somewhat older than herself who happened to be there. When the water boiled, she put in some grain, twirling the porridge twirler between the palms as she had seen her mother do. She took the comments and criticisms of the company with good grace, even when they smiled at her awkwardness. Meanwhile, her mother mentioned to us how useful it would be to have someone who could cook the evening meal on days when she came home late or tired from fetching wood.

Source: J. and J. D. Krige, *The Realm of the Rain Queen* (Oxford University Press, 1943)

1   How do children learn to perform the economically necessary tasks?

2   Is it the same in our society? What do you think accounts for the differences?

3   Is the child an essential part of the economy? At what age does this happen in our society?

4   Who are the teachers in this tribal society? Is it the same today in our society?

Modern, industrial societies, however, are just too complex, with a wide variety of economic skills and a diversity of values and beliefs. Formal education (what is taught in schools) is used to teach people skills, to grade them by ability and to transmit certain values from one generation to the next.

Teaching skills

In tribal societies basic survival skills, such as knowledge of hunting or the gathering of edible roots and berries, are passed on from generation to generation.

In modern, industrial societies, the pace of technological change make one generations's skills irrelevant to the next. Computerisation for example is fundamentally altering office work. In ten years clerical work has changed from paperwork to information processing. Factory workers, too, are being replaced by computer robots and so they must learn new skills or face long-term unemployment.

The range and pace of skills means that it is impossible for parents to teach their children the necessary skills and knowledge. Schools perform this task.

Grading by ability

Schools should act as sieves to grade students, allowing the better ones to go forward to take the more skilful and demanding jobs. Examinations are devised to grade students and provide every level of pupil with an appropriate form and level of teaching. However, many sociologists dispute this description of the schools' grading activities. Although schools may have been created to give children the maximum learning opportunities, it is doubtful in practice that they actually do so. It seems that factors outside the control of the school, especially the social class background of pupils, crucially influence educational success.

The transmission of values: A form of social control

In simple societies, basic values, such as economic skills, were transmitted (passed on) from parents to children. It would be true to say that this partly occurs in modern British society as well. However, the complexity of industrial society makes it difficult for parents to perform this task alone.

In order for our society to continue there must be some common cultural background: a common language, common beliefs, common expectations. The school system knits children from a wide range of different backgrounds into one flexible whole. Children not only learn a common culture, but just as importantly they learn the rules of society. They are taught to obey the laws and customs and to avoid any form of behaviour regarded as anti-social. Schools, therefore, impose a form of social control upon pupils through the formal lessons of the curriculum, the discipline imposed by the teachers and through the general social life of the school. This prepares them to conform later in life as adults.

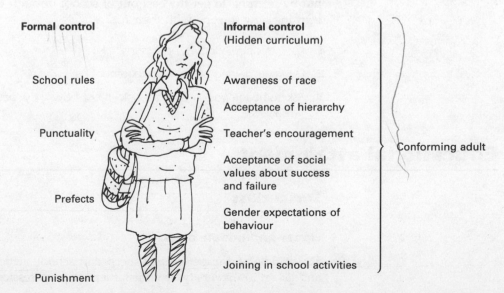

Formal control		Informal control
		(Hidden curriculum)
School rules		Awareness of race
		Acceptance of hierarchy
Punctuality		Teacher's encouragement
		Acceptance of social values about success and failure
Prefects		Gender expectations of behaviour
		Joining in school activities
Punishment		

Conforming adult

How schools teach social control

The main problem concerning the transmission of values and the imposition of social control lies in *whose values are being passed on* and *who benefits* from the social control. Radical sociologists, such as Marxists, argue that schools merely prepare the majority of pupils to be uncomplaining workers.

The relationship between school and work: A critical view

Two radical, Marxist sociologists, Bowles and Gintis, argue that the education system does not grade children according to their ability, but reproduces the class system from one generation to the next; that is, those in the top positions manage to place their children into similar top jobs. How is this done? Children of the better off attend public schools, where they are taught to believe they are superior, to think independently and to strive for the highest positions in society.

Bowles and Gintis compare this with State schools which teach conformity and obedience both in the official and hidden curriculum. The pupils learn to arrive on time, to cope with boring lessons, and most important of all, to accept society as it is, rather than to criticise it. As a result of this working class people continue to accept boring low-paid jobs without too much complaint.

1 What does the passage mean when it states that education helps to 'reproduce' the class system?

2 Which sort of schools do the children of the better-off attend?
What do they learn that helps them to be successful?

3 How do state schools, according to Bowles and Gintis, prepare working class pupils for their future jobs?

4 In your experience, do you feel there is any truth in Bowles and Gintis' argument?

5 Draw a diagram, or a cartoon, to illustrate the function of schools according to Bowles and Gintis.

The troublemakers

We have seen that the education system prepares pupils for life after school, but what about those pupils who reject the system? Will they be rebels after school? The answer in many cases is, of course, yes. But research by one sociologist, Paul Willis, has found that even troublemakers are, paradoxically, preparing themselves through their 'messing about' at school to withstand the boredom of the unskilled labouring jobs which they are bound to get. Willis argues that most working-class jobs are boring. Workers have to 'get by' as best they can, and they do this by messing about at work, 'having a laugh'. Schoolchildren who mess around in the classroom certainly confirm their condemnation to dead-end jobs, but by learning to get the best out of school through their antics, they are also learning how to cope with their future.

1 List ways pupils 'get by' in lessons.

2 Describe 'getting by' in a typical school day.

3 Ask someone you know in employment how they 'get by' at work. Are there any similarities?

Educational attainment

Social class

Upper and middle class

The middle and upper classes succeed at school, achieve the best A-level results and go on to university. If your father has a profession or works in high-level management, you stand an eleven times greater chance of getting a university degree than if he is a semi-skilled or unskilled worker.

Working class

The working class do less well from the education system. Examination results are consistently poorer for them compared with the middle class.

Race

Certain black ethnic groups do particularly badly, such as some children of Afro-Caribbean and Bangladeshi parents.

In all CSE and GCE O-level exams 6 per cent of West Indians obtained five or more higher grades compared with 17 per cent of Asians and 19 per cent of all other leavers...Asians...do about as well as white children except in English language. Bangladeshis do markedly less well than all groups majority or minority.

Source: *The Times Educational Supplement*, 15 March 1985

Gender

Females perform better than males at school, and the gap is growing. Only 20 years ago, it was the other way around with males outperforming females. Another difference is that males and females choose different subjects to study, with females more likely to study the humanities.

Social class and educational success

The table, **A**, tells you the educational level attained by people categorised by their father's occupation, while **B** compares the success at GCSE by subject and sex.

A

Highest qualification held[1]: by socio-economic group of father, 1990–1, Great Britain, percentages

	Professional	Employers and managers	Intermediate and junior non-manual	Skilled manual and own account non-professional	Semi-skilled manual and personal service	Unskilled manual	All Persons
Degree	32	17	17	6	4	3	10
Higher Education	19	15	18	10	7	5	11
GCE A level[2]	15	13	12	8	6	4	9
GCSE, grades A–C[2]	19	24	25	21	19	15	21
GCSE, grades D–G[2,3]	4	9	7	12	12	10	10
Foreign	4	4	4	3	2	2	3
No qualifications	7	19	18	40	50	60	35

[1]Persons aged 25–59 not in full-time education. [2]Or equivalent. [3]Includes commercial qualifications and apprenticeships.

Source: *Social Trends 24* (HMSO, 1994) and the General Househould Survey

B
School leavers with grades A–C at GCSE, by subject and sex, 1990–1, Great Britain

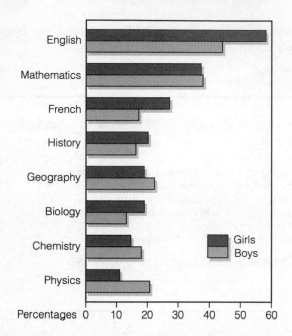

Percentages

Source: *Social Trends 24* (HMSO, 1994), Department for Education, Welsh Office and Scottish Office Education Department

Look at **A**.

1 Which group is least likely to gain a degree?

2 There is one fairly clear dividing line between the social classes I can make out which seems to mark different chances in getting a degree. Where is this line? Can you suggest any reasons for this division?

3 What is the overall pattern you can make out between educational qualification and social class?

4 What proportion of the children of unskilled manual workers got no qualifications? What does this imply for their future prospects? What does it say about the persistence of social class in Britain?

Look at **B**.

5 Go through each subject and note which sex has more passes?

6 What pattern can you see?

7 Can you give any explanations for this from your own experience?

Working-class failure in the education system

Reasons for the relative lack of success of working-class pupils fall into two broad areas: home background and community, and school.

The home background and community

Material deprivation

The lack of amenities at home can make it difficult for the child to study or attend school. Lack of money can mean a cold and damp house, inadequate levels of nutrition, overcrowding and general deprivation. These can lead to poor school attendance through illness and inability to study at home.

Studies as long ago as 1958 have consistently shown that if families are poor, then the children are less likely to do well at school.

Parents' attitudes

The degree of interest and encouragement parents show in their children's education can be a very significant element in educational success. Indeed, according to some sociologists it can overcome poverty and deprivation.

J. W. B. Douglas led a study of schoolchildren throughout their primary and secondary schooling. He found that educational success was closely related to parental encouragement in all classes, but that middle-class parents were more likely to give help and show interest in their children's progress at school.

The effects of the home on a child's education

When housing conditions are unsatisfactory, children make relatively low scores in the tests. This is so in each social class but whereas the middle-class children, as they get older, reduce this handicap, the manual working-class children from unsatisfactory homes fall even further behind; for them overcrowding and other deficiencies at home have a progressive and depressive influence on their test performance. ...

The conclusions are that the attitudes of children to their school work is deeply affected by the degree of encouragement their parents give them and by their own level of emotional stability. The children who show few symptoms of emotional instability and whose parents are ambitious for their academic success, have an increasing advantage during the years they are at primary school, largely because they pursue their studies with greater vigour and concentration than the less-favoured children are prepared or able to do.

Source: J. W. B. Douglas, *The Home and the School* (Panther, 1969)

1 Do children overcome the effects of poor housing as they get older?

2 What influences does parental encouragement have on a child's school work?

3 Are your parents interested in your education? How did their attitude influence you, do you think?

Speech patterns

The ability to express oneself clearly in speaking and writing is a crucial component of success in our education system. Middle-class children are more likely to have their writing and speaking skills developed to a higher standard and at an earlier age than working-class children.

Bernstein compared groups of youths and found considerable differences in their powers of expression. Those parents who explain their actions and discuss them with their children help to develop language skills and reasoning ability which gives them success later at school. He argued that this situation was more likely to occur in middle-class homes.

Cultural deprivation

It has been suggested that children from particularly poor backgrounds, deprived inner-city areas and certain immigrant groups suffer at school because they lack an awareness of our culture and language.

The Plowden Report (1967), an official government enquiry, concluded that children deprived of culture in their home environment and community were more likely to fail at school and be labelled as 'educationally sub-normal'. To combat this 'educational priority areas' were set up. Basically these provided extra funds for schools in particularly poor inner-city areas. This idea of giving pupils from deprived backgrounds extra resources has been called 'compensatory education'.

The school

Relationships between teachers and pupils

Pupils on average spend 15 000 hours in school. Their attitudes towards school are strongly influenced by the teachers' attitudes and treatment of them. These attitudes can assist a child to educational success or condemn him or her to a low stream and an early exit from the system.

Colin Lacey studied a Manchester Grammar School. He found that although all the boys were generally in favour of school in the first year, by the fourth year the lower-stream pupils hated school and the upper-stream ones liked school. The reason, according to Lacey was the attitudes of the teachers. Most of them disliked teaching the lower streams and demonstrated it in their attitudes to the pupils. The pupils noticed this and so they rejected the school. The opposite happened for the high-stream pupils.

Streaming

The discussion on relationships throws some light on the debate over streaming. Many educationalists oppose streaming for limiting the potential of children. Defenders argue that it allows pupils to receive the correct level of teaching, at the pace best suited to the pupil's ability. According to this approach, streaming is bad as long as teachers show the attitudes discussed above. Mixed ability teaching is only successful, however, where the teacher *believes* in this form of teaching organisation.

Attitudes and streaming

When a child was kept in the wrong stream he tended to take on the characteristics of his stream, and his academic performance deteriorated if he were in too low a stream and improved if he were in too high a stream.

Source: National Foundation for Educational Research (NFER) Report

1 What happens if a child is placed in a stream too high or low for him or her?

2 Why do you think this happens?

3 Do you feel that the class you are in influences the amount of work you do and your attitude to studying?

4 If you are in a streamed class, what do you think of the idea of mixing all the classes together, and being taught in a mixed ability class?

The importance of labelling

Teachers categorise pupils into broad groups and then treat them according to this categorisation. For example, a pupil may be 'labelled' as lazy by a teacher. Whatever the pupil does, the teacher will interpret it in this light. This labelling can have very important consequences for the pupil, especially if he or she has been labelled incorrectly or is trying to change.

Once categorised, the bad pupil can be caught in a heads-I-win-tails-you-lose-situation. The consistently rude boy who is now being polite is regarded with suspicion by the teachers; his intentions and motives come under scrutiny. His politeness may be interpreted as 'taking the mick' out of the teacher or as evidence that a crime is being concealed. The boy who turns in a first-class piece of work when normally his work is appallingly poor is suspected of copying. When such pupils behave 'out of character' and thus 'out of category' the teacher's reaction may well be preventing the process of change which the teacher is supposedly anxious to promote. What could be more devastating for a lazy pupil to find that, when he does respond to the teacher's appeal for change, his efforts are greeted with suspicion and disbelief? Would it not be reasonable for the pupil to conclude that the effort is not worth making since this is a game he can never win.

Source: Adapted from C. Lacey, *Hightown Grammar* (Manchester University Press, 1970)

1 What happens to the 'bad' child once labelled as such by the teachers?

2 Why do you think the teacher reacts this way?

3 How do you think teachers build up these definitions, or 'labels', of pupils?

4 What effect will the teacher's response have on the bad pupil who is trying to reform?

5 Do you think this is a very common experience of pupils at school?
Has it happened to you at school or college and how was the situation resolved?

Ethnic minorities at school

All the factors which produce poor school progress from working-class children also hit children from Afro-Caribbean and many Asian homes. This is hardly surprising as the vast majority of these children are from working-class homes. But there are some problems which only black or immigrant children face. For children from immigrant homes the main language of the home is generally the country of origin. So their studies are carried out, to some extent, in a 'foreign' language. Although Afro-Caribbean children speak English at home, it may be in a dialect that differs from standard English and this can cause confusion.

It is rare for teachers to be openly racist but cultural differences and poor performance in some IQ tests by black children have created the belief in some teachers' minds that black children are more likely to be slow learners. This can influence the way in which teachers 'label' black pupils and so retard their progress.

Differences in educational attainment between ethnic minorities

It is wrong to say that all black children do badly at school. Children of Afro-Caribbean and Bangladeshi origins perform particularly poorly, while most other Asian children do at least as well as Whites.

Two explanations have been suggested by the Swann Report (an official government study). First, that Asians simply 'keep their heads down' and get on with their studies without attracting attention, accepting racism. Pupils of Afro-Caribbean origin, in contrast, are more likely to protest about their problems and may receive more of a negative response from teachers. Second, the tight knit, strict Asian family and culture places great emphasis on educational success and disciplines its children to achieve this.

Race and school achievement

A Bradford study of CSE and O-level performance in 24 secondary schools between 1983 and 1987 confirmed some of the ILEA findings, but noted a marked improvement in black (Afro-Caribbean and Asian, but mainly Asian) pupil performance compared with white. The survey found that in 1987 only 7 per cent of black pupils left school without qualifications compared with 19 per cent of white pupils. Pass grades achieved by black school-leavers were also better than those of white pupils. In 1987, 47 per cent of black pupils gained grades A to C at O-level or grade 1 at CSE compared to 39 per cent of white pupils. The Bradford researchers controlled for social class, basing their analysis on how many pupils in each studied school qualified for free meals. Using this measure they found that there was little difference among Bradford's schools in terms of black and white pupil performance. ...

In February 1991, *The Times Educational Supplement* reported that, according to a University of London study, the introduction of the GCSE examination had failed to narrow the gap between different ethnic groups' examination results. The study analysed the results of 16,700 pupils who took their GCSEs in inner-London schools in 1988. ...Nuttall and Goldstein's analysis of the 1988 results showed that Indian and Pakistani pupils, who attained better results than their white classmates under the GCE system, did even better under GCSE which then gave more weight to course work in the assessment. Bangladeshi and

Afro-Caribbean pupils, whose marks were below average, achieved less than ever compared to their peers. The gender gap also widened, girls gaining higher marks than boys.

In the autumn of 1991 Nuttall and Goldstein released further analysis of GCSE results. [They looked] at the examination performance of 5,500 pupils in relation to gender, ethnic origin and eligibility for free school meals (as a rough measure of deprivation). Pupils from Indian and Pakistani families fared better than those of Afro-Caribbean, English, Scottish, Welsh or Irish origin. Indian and Pakistani pupils did better in English, while those of Afro-Caribbean origin performed half a grade behind white children in mathematics.

Source: R. Skellington and P. Morris, *Race in Britain Today* (Sage, 1992)

1 How did the various ethnic groups perform in the examination results, according to the studies described in the extract?

2 I found it a little confusing drawing up my own summary, when I first read it. Do the studies use the same way of categorising people by 'race'? What are the implications for the information given, do you think?

3 Which group(s) had improved according to the London study? Why?

4 In the Bradford study, the conclusion was that 'there was little difference among Bradford schools in terms of black and white pupil performance'. On first reading this appears to clash with the London study. What explanation can you offer?

Schooling and self-image

The West Indian child is told on first entering the school that his language is second-rate, to say the least. Namely, the only way he knows how to speak...is 'the wrong way to speak'. ...

When the pictures, illustrations, music, heroes, great historical and contemporary figures in the classroom are all white, it is difficult for a child to identify with anyone who is not white. ...

They become resentful and bitter at being told their language is second-rate and their history and culture is non-existent. ...The black child under these influences develops a deep inferiority complex. He soon loses motivation to succeed academically since, at best, the learning experience is an elaborate irrelevance to his personal life situation, and at worst it is a racially humiliating experience.

Source: B. Coard, *How West Indian children are made educationally subnormal by the British education system* (New Beacon Books, 1971)

1 What is the West Indian (Afro-Caribbean) child told at school about 'his language'?

2 Surely, West Indian children speak English at home, so why should there be any problems about language?

3 What does the black child discover about history?

4 What are the final results of the black child's discoveries?

5 How are black people portrayed in history, old films and novels?

The following are comments from teachers.

'I have noticed very few people from ethnic minorities who are in positions of responsibility. Amongst students there is a lot of evidence of racial discrimination – for example, verbal abuse, graffiti. It is difficult to pin down and to deal with.'

'I knew a coloured teacher on a temporary one year contract. She was told at her interview (initially) that senior staff were not sure that the school was ready for a black teacher – mainly because there were very few ethnic minority children in the school.'

'The very first day I came to the school a teacher remarked that coloured people should be lined up and shot. After that I have kept with staff who I know are not racially biased.'

'Ethnic minority teachers are only given jobs when they find no better teachers – all promotions go to others while we do all the donkey work and are nowhere today.'

'I think there is much more awareness of the needs and cultures of ethnic minorities than before. Teaching staff are aware of ethnic minorities' cultures and needs, and it is becoming a multi-cultural society.'

Source: Commission for Racial Equality, *Ethnic Minority Schoolteachers* (CRE, 1988)

1 Name five 'disadvantages' suffered by ethnic minority teachers.

2 Do teachers feel they are being racially discriminated against?

3 Do you think the teachers' experiences could help us in any way to understand ethnic minority students' feelings and situation?

Gender differences in education

It is not true to say that females perform less well than males at school, but they do have *different* educational careers. They choose different subjects and girls are less likely to stay on at school, to train for a technical subject or go on to university.

The reasons for differences in education between males and females can be traced to differences in socialisation in the home (see page 64) and different treatment at school, both of which reflect the different expectations we have of males and females in life in general.

Childhood socialisation

It is generally believed that girls are more emotional, more gentle and less technically-minded than boys. They are valued for their attractiveness and domestic ability (how well they can cook and keep house, for instance). In childhood, therefore, girls are brought up along these lines. If girls do not show the traits mentioned above, then people believe there is something 'wrong' with them.

Parents care more about the looks of daughters. They buy them different toys from boys; so that boys get soldiers and guns, while girls get dolls and prams. They use different language to describe them; girls are sweet and pretty, while boys are handsome and little rascals! Finally, girls are expected to help with the housework to a far greater extent than boys.

Changing times, changing girls

Below are two extracts from studies carried out by the same researcher, Sue Sharpe, with a 20-year gap between them. Sharpe's original study In 1972 of secondary school female students in their final years at school was extremely influential in sociology. In 1991 she repeated the piece of research, with some interesting results.

For girls, the pursuit of 'femininity' leads to a multitude of distractions, such as attending to physical appearance, fashion, boyfriends and the sentimentalisation of love-stories and romance. This leads to apathy and lack of interest in anything to do with study and school and influences the subsequent nature of their life and work. ...

In conclusion many working-class girls find school life boring and irrelevant. They look forward to leaving as soon as they can obtain a job that will provide money, some interest and the freedom for which they yearn. The education and class systems have always discriminated against them for being female and working-class. They absorb a self-image that is academically low and their own performance may confirm this. ...

They have grown up with feminine role models that show love and marriage and a husband and children as more important and immediate goals for a girl.

Source: S. Sharpe, *Just Like a Girl: How Girls Learn to be Women* (Penguin, 1976)

In the Seventies and Eighties ideas and beliefs about equality of opportunities became more commonplace. It might reasonably be assumed that by the early 1990s, girls' job choices would show some change. In my early research, girls from four Ealing schools described job expectations covering about thirty occupations, most of which fell into the general realm of 'women's work'. Significantly, forty per cent of these were in some sort of officework. The next most popular jobs were teacher, nurse, shop assistant or bank clerk: these accounted for a quarter of their choices. When receptionist, telephonist, air hostess, hairdresser and children's nurse or nanny were added to these, this range of jobs accounted for three-quarters of their job expectations. Almost twenty years later, girls from the same Ealing schools similarly cited about thirty jobs they expected to go into, and like the generation before them, these were predominantly in 'women's work'. Increased awareness of gender issues and rights, and equality of opportunities, did not seem to be reflected in expanding job expectations. There were, however, some significant differences. For example, the expectation or desire to do officework had shrunk to a fraction of its previous size. Hardly anyone specified wanting to be a secretary or to work in an office, and jobs like receptionist and telephonist were also missing. ...

Many young girls declare their intention of avoiding 'a boring office job'. ...

While work horizons had slightly changed but not significantly broadened growth was more apparent in girls' personal horizons. They placed a great stress on equality with men, and on their own needs. I constantly detected an increased expression of assertiveness and confidence, and an emphasis on women's ability to stand on their own feet. They almost unanimously endorsed the importance of having a job or career, and in this respect emphasised being able to support themselves if their marriage or relationship broke down, and not having to depend on, nor be dominated by men. ...Only a minority of them wanted to leave school at sixteen. The rest looked forward to moving up into the sixth form, or going to a sixth form college or further education college to take GCSEs or A levels. ...

Girls in the early Nineties recognised various social changes that had already made an impact on the lives of many of the relatives and friends.

They assumed that nothing can be taken for granted, especially in employment or marriage. Whether they wished to or not, they were aware that they should stay on at school for as long as they could, because if they left without some qualifications, there might be nothing for them in the world of work. Many rightly assumed that doing A levels would help them in a career, but it was no longer a guarantee of work where there were few or no jobs. On the personal side, their less positive attitudes to marriage acknowledged the current high trend in family breakdown.

'I don't want to get married. I don't see the point in getting married. You could live with someone, then if it broke up then it's easier than going through divorce, half this and half that. Some people think it's traditional and you should do it, but I don't see any point in it. You can make a commitment without marriage.'
Lisa

Source: S. Sharpe, *Just Like a Girl* (Penguin, 1994)

1 Explain the meaning of 'femininity' in the first extract.

2 In your opinion, is this still true today?

3 What changing attitudes to staying on at school are there? Can you give reasons for this?

4 How have female self-images changed?

5 What sorts of employment do female students want to enter today? How different is this from the 1970s?

6 How have attitudes to marriage changed?

7 Sharpe points out in her later work that it was quite possible that the original school students she studied would have daughters of the same age as the students she studied in 1991. Find women who were at school in the early 1970s and ask them about their experiences. How different are they from yours? Male students can compare with men who were at school in the 1970s. What differences are there in attitudes to females and to school?

In school

The attitudes created by the wider society about the correct behaviour for females, plus their home socialisation, is strengthened at school through the **hidden curriculum** (the underlying values of the school). Girls are often encouraged to study subjects which are more appropriate for them, such as biology and English literature, while boys are encouraged into the sciences and technical subjects. Teachers also have different expectations concerning typical patterns of behaviour for girls and boys; so girls are expected to be neater, quieter and more studious than boys who are expected to be lively and rather a handful, but to grasp technical knowledge more easily than girls.

Race and image in school

The following is an extract from a study of various anti-school groups. The speakers are members of 'The Warriors', composed of male Asians. They are discussing a rival male, Afro-Caribbean-origin gang.

The Warriors suggested that the teachers' racist stereotypes were not based upon any real differences in the behaviour of Asians and Afro-Caribbeans. Rather, it was the teachers' classification and labelling processes, to which both groups reacted, which determined teachers' perceptions of students.

MM: Do you think that West Indians cause more trouble than Asians?

Ashwin: No, don't be stupid, that's what teachers think. The Indians cause just as much trouble.

Raj: The West Indians are more obvious some'ow. They're seen more easily.

Iqbal: It's not, it's not that they cause more trouble. It's teachers, they pick on them more.

Raj: They treat them differently. I think they think the West Indians are dumber than us.

They challanged the teacher stereotype of the 'ignorant Afro-Caribbean' by pointing out that it was 'high-ability' Afro-Caribbean students who were involved in the anti-school groups:

MM: Do you think they are more dumber?

Raj: No I don't.

Iqbal: No, because they can do as well as Indian kids, better than a lot of them. The ones who have been in most trouble were the brainy ones, like Kevin and Michael, in the first year they were the brainy ones, really brainy.

These racially-based stereotypes acted as powerful social images and were of central significance to the teachers' perception of their interaction with students. They served to highlight the perceived 'rebelliousness' of Afro-Caribbean students and the perceived 'passivity' of Asians.

Source: M. Mac An Ghaill, *Young, Gifted and Black* (Open University Press, 1988)

1 Do 'West Indians' cause more trouble?

2 Are they perceived as doing so?

3 Why do you think the teachers do this?

4 Which particular type of Afro-Caribbean youth misbehaves?

5 Do you think this is an accurate description of the situation?

Chapter 11

EMPLOYMENT AND WORKING LIVES

This chapter covers:
- The changing occupational structure
- Industrialisation
- Changing technology
- Post-Fordism and de-industrialisation
- The experience of work
- Making work more fulfilling
- Problems faced by women at work
- Industrial relations
- Trade unions
- Professions.

The changing occupational structure

There are 26 million people employed in Britain today, and approximately four million people who are not employed, but would like to be.

There are three types of industry in which people are employed:

- primary (or extractive), which exploit our natural resources and include agriculture and fishing
- secondary (or manufacturing), which involve making objects for our use, such as cars or electrical items
- tertiary (or service industries), which provide services for us, such as banking, shops or restaurants.

Throughout the twentieth century there has been a move away from primary and manufacturing industries to service industries.

Fifty years ago, shortly after the end of the Second World War, 70 per cent of the workforce had jobs in the manufacturing and construction industries. The vast bulk of employees were manual workers. Today, by contrast, over 70 per cent of the workforce is in service industries, with about 20 per cent in manufacturing. The agricultural sector is now so small that it only employs about 1 per cent of the workforce. In the last 20 years, Britain has undergone a period of rapid de-industrialisation, which is reflected in the changing patterns of employment.

Automation and increasing competition from more recently industrialised countries, such as Japan, mean that fewer workers are needed for industry. There has also been a growth in the industries such as insurance and banking that employ white-collar workers.

The effects on society

The result of these changes has been the decline of the manual workers and of the traditional working-class communities based on heavy industry such as steel, coal and the docks, with their emphasis on the extended family and trade union solidarity. As an increasing proportion of the workforce moves into white-collar jobs, they are less likely to view themselves as working-class, even if their wages are no higher than those of the remaining manual workers.

Increasingly, the new jobs in the service industries are being filled by women, for although women have only a quarter of jobs in manufacturing, they have two-thirds of service industry jobs, usually the lowest paid, it should be added. Nevertheless, it does mean more women are working than ever before. This will affect family relationships as increasingly women become the breadwinners.

Unemployment has increased since the early 1980s, partially as a result of these changes in industry. Those most likely to become unemployed are those who can be replaced by automated machinery and those in the declining manufacturing and primary industries. Those most likely to be unemployed are the young who find it difficult to get work in the first place, and the older unemployed who are regarded by employers as not worth retraining.

Where have all the jobs gone?

Workers in industry

Industry	1961	1971	1981	1993
Agriculture/Fishing	710 000	430 000	363 000	283 000
Manufacturing	8 500 000	8 000 000	6 222 000	4 589 000
Services	10 300 000	11 600 000	13 468 000	15 644 000

Source: *Social Trends 24* (HMSO, 1994)

1 What has happened to the numbers of people employed in:
a) agriculture and fishing?
b) manufacturing?
c) services?

2 Which period has seen the fastest decline in manufacturing industry?

3 Have the numbers of jobs available in service industries risen to compensate for the decline in manufacturing?

The distribution of jobs

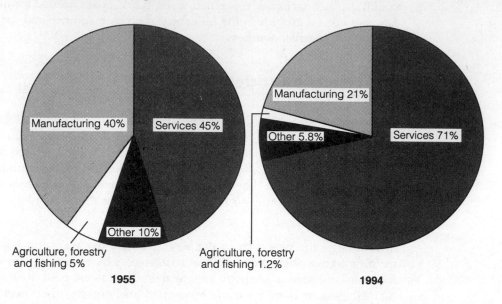

1955   **1994**

1 In 1994, what percentage of jobs were in:
   a) services compared to 1955?
   b) manufacturing compared to 1955?

2 Can you suggest where most jobs will be in the future? Give examples of these types of jobs.

3 Can you suggest any possible consequences for society from these changes?

Population of working age in the UK, by sex and economic status, 1993

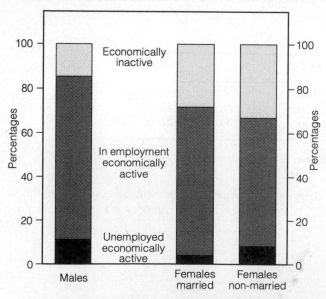

Source: *Social Trends 24* (HMSO, 1994) and Employment Department

1 In 1993, what proportion of men were employed?

2 What proportion of married women were employed?

3 What proportion of non-married women were employed?

4 Suggest reasons for these differences.

Working hours

British workers put in by far the longest hours in the European Union and Britain is the only member state where the length of the working week has increased over the past decade, according to latest statistics of the European Commission.

The average British working week, including overtime, is 43.4 hours, more than an hour longer than in 1983 and more than two hours longer than the average weekly hours worked in Portugal, second in the European Union's long hours league. ...

The contrast with the rest of western Europe is even more striking when differences between men and women are taken into account.

British men clock up an average 45.1 hours compared with 38.7 hours in Belgium. And British women have now ousted their Dutch counterparts at the top of the EU's female working week stakes with an average of 40.2 hours compared with 38.8 hours in 1983. Italian women average 35.6 hours.

Throughout the EU the pattern is mostly of a trend towards a shorter working week. In a couple of cases there has been little change. Only in Britain are employees having to put in longer hours. ...

The shift towards longer hours in Britain is partly the result of the exceptionally high level of overtime worked. But it also reflects the trend towards longer hours – often unpaid – being worked by managerial and professional employees to ensure successful career development. ...

One academic study has estimated that if the long-run trend towards to a shorter working week in Britain had continued throughout the 1980s an extra million jobs would have been created.

Working late: Changes in the usual working week, hours (EU average: 40.3)

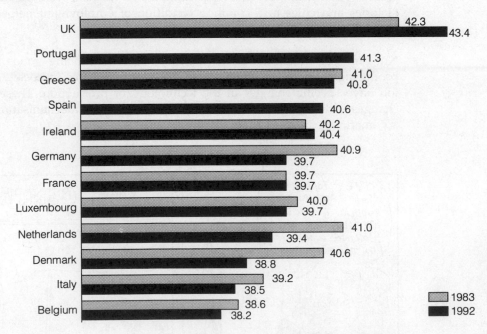

Source: *The Guardian*, 24 January 1995

1 Who work the longest hours in Europe?

2 What are the average hours worked by this group?

3 What trend is occurring in Europe regarding working hours?

4 Are long hours only worked by manual workers?

5 If Britain had continued the trend to shorter working hours like the rest of Europe, what would this have done to unemployment?

Industrialisation

Britain was the first country in the world to industrialise. During the eighteenth and nineteenth centuries, it was transformed from an agricultural society, with the majority of the population living in the countryside and farming for their living, to an industrial society where almost all the people work in offices, shops and factories, while living in towns and cities.

But the shift from agriculture to industry was not simply an economic change, it was a profound social change too. The growth of cities as we know them now, of newspapers and later television and radio, the ability to read and write for the ordinary person, social class differences and the widespread ownership of consumer goods, even democracy as it is now, were caused, or at least influenced, by the process of industrialisation.

Factories needed a large workforce near at hand which led to the growth of towns. In turn, these attracted traders and so the towns grew into cities, and eventually into 'conurbations'. In order to work the machines and perform the clerical tasks workers needed to read and write (just as now we need to know how to use computers). Consumer goods were invented and produced at a price that eventually was within the reach of most of the employed. The overwhelming power of the employers led to the counterforce of the trade unions. Finally, the fact that huge numbers of workers were pushed together in factories and cities in a common condition of employment helped to form social classes.

Not only has industrialisation (the move from producing goods by hand to producing them by machine) produced major changes in society, but so too have specific changes in the technology of production. These changes include the move from craft production to mechanisation on to automation.

The social consequences of industrialisation in Britain

Leisure
Initially, the long hours of work in factories prevented leisure. Eventually the workers obtained shorter working hours, which led to the development of modern leisure activities.

Colonies
There was exploitation of the colonies for cheap raw materials for the factories in Britain. This led to the poverty of the Third World. It created a sense of racial superiority and eventually in the 1950s, influenced the patterns of immigration to Britain.

Production
This moved from agriculture to factories and machines. Working conditions were appalling – long hours for little pay. The relationship of employer and employee was one of conflict.
Now automation – consequences?

Mass consumption
Factories and machinery led to the production of cheap articles on a large scale. Eventually this caused a decline in prices and, by the 1950s, the growth of mass consumption. The majority of the population could own articles previously thought of as luxuries.

Politics
Large numbers of workers drawn together, in factories and towns in poor conditions, led to growth of political activity, notably the development of the Labour Party. The factory owners replaced landowners and the leaders of the Conservative Party.

Transport
Modern, fast means of transport, first the railways and much later cars, led to travel, holidays, suburbs, commuting and eventually the development of factories away from the towns.

Health
The growth of the cities with large numbers of people living close together forced improvements in public hygiene – sewers, water supplies, etc. Advances in medicine occurred These, plus the rise in the standard of living, improved health standards and lowered death-rates. People lived longer.

Urbanisation
The growth of cities, with their slums and social problems of poverty and crime, and later the need to improve conditions, led to redevelopment and New Towns. Decline in the inner cities later linked to riots of the 1980s.

Industrialisation in the Third World

Production
The move has been from agriculture only to providing raw materials for developed countries. Increasingly multi-national companies are setting up business here because of cheap labour, land and lack of labour laws.

Multi-nationals
Much of the production is controlled by huge companies which are based in USA or Europe. (See **Production** and **Colonialism**.)

GOOD
CHEAP & FAST

Colonialism
During the last 50 years most colonies have gained their independence. However, the economy of these countries remains controlled by the developed 'rich' countries.

Politics
The extremes of poverty and wealth lead to totalitarian governments and violent protest. Often the army takes over and kills and tortures opponents. Governments are politically unstable.

Consumption
Prices are low and the range of goods is narrow. Life is excellent for the wealthy, but there is nothing available for the large numbers of the poor.

Health
It is rare to find hospitals and medical services of an adequate standard provided by the State. Conditions in the towns and countryside are very bad indeed. There are no supplies of clean water and no sewage systems.

Urbanisation
Extremely fast growth of cities, which are unable to cope with the large numbers of young people coming in from the countryside, leads to social problems, such as shanty towns, crime, drugs and prostitution, all the result of dreadful poverty.

Changing technology

Craft production

This is the normal form of production in an agricultural society, and in an industrial society the way in which complex tasks requiring great skill and judgement are carried out. Increasingly, this sort of job is being taken over by automated machines controlled by microchips. Craft work is satisfying to the worker who will make the complete product (for example, a hand-made chair) from start to finish. However, this form of production is slow and so the finished products are expensive.

Mechanisation

Production by machines is the most common form of manufacture today, basically because it allows large numbers of items to be made at a low price, which means that people can afford to buy them and achieve a high standard of living.

There are, however, tremendous social costs involved for those who work with machines or on assembly lines. Probably the worst of these is the fact that workers constantly repeat the same task, which leads to dreadful boredom and lack of work satisfaction. Not only this, but the worker loses any control over the pace at which he works, as this is set by the management. Furthermore, as the machine produces an identical product each time, regardless of the interest or ability of the worker, then all sense of pride and craftmanship is lost. The resulting boredom and frustration can lead to industrial action, such as strikes, as the workers try to obtain higher wages in order to compensate for the boredom of their work.

Automation and information technology

Automation is the process where machines produce items with only a minimum of supervision by workers. Generally the machines have been programmed to repeat the same task to a high standard of accuracy, and can even reject items which are not of the required standard. An example of automation is the simple welding machine, which is used in car production to perform a number of welds in set spots to car bodies as they pass along the production line.

The construction of complete products by machines without the need for workers has already had a considerable effect on society. However, the use of micro-chip technology, the tiny 'brains' inside home computers and calculators, is beginning to cause even more profound changes.

Technologically, the micro-chip allows machines to be controlled by computer to undertake highly skilled, as well as routine, tasks and to reach a standard of output of high quality. It is possible to manufacture virtually the whole of the car with automated machinery which needs only a few workers.

The use of micro-chip technology extends far beyond manufacturing though, for it allows many services to be performed by machine alone. Examples of this are the cash dispensers found outside banks and building societies, in effect replacing bank counter staff. In offices, too, tasks like typing have been made easier by word processing, and skilled work such as that performed by draughtsmen is being taken over by computers. The use of computers to generate and store information for a wide variety of uses is known as **information technology** or **IT**. It is not an exaggeration to call this micro-chip-controlled automation the 'second industrial revolution'.

Just like the first industrial revolution, there are bound to be many social consequences. We can only guess what these may be, but it certainly seems as if unemployment will increase as machines replace people. The question then is how will society support all the unemployed, if their numbers remain permanently high?

Large numbers of people living on social security payments might lead to increasing social tension. The differences between those who are in employment and those who are not might lead to a society of 'haves' and 'have-nots'. On the other hand, if the working week is cut and the jobs are shared, without a lowering of wages, then the social consequences could be very good for society.

The social effects of automation

In itself, automation is neither good nor bad, it just depends on how it is used. We know that it could be used to eliminate boring and dangerous tasks, and to cut down the numbers of employees in offices and factories. This could be excellent for society, if workers are moved to more interesting work, or if they are given greater leisure, with the income to enjoy it.

But will this be the case? It seems more likely that rather than eliminating repetitive tasks and creating more leisure time, automation is simply replacing both skilled and routine workers, making them unemployed. There is a world of difference between unemployment and increased leisure. Leisure requires enough money to maintain an adequate standard of living. Unemployment means poverty through reliance on supplementary benefit and the loss of social prestige, even a loss of a person's identity in a society where *what* you are often determines *who* you are.

Those people who do remain employed are likely to fall into two categories: those engineers, managers and scientists who are absolutely essential, and secondly those workers needed to keep an eye on the automated machinery, perhaps simply feeding information in to the controlling computer. The majority of those remaining in work then are likely to find their work deskilled, as the computers can take over the skilled element of their work and they are left only with routine supervision. It is precisely the full use of their talents and skills that makes a job interesting and satisfying to most people. The advantages to employers in needing less skilled workers is that they can be paid lower wages.

It can be seen therefore that automation is a two-edged sword, which could free workers from the drudgery of boring work and produce a wide range of high quality articles at low prices, as well as offering new services such as armchair shopping. But it could also lead to mass unemployment, deskilling, and lower wages.

1 Can we say for certain that automation will benefit or harm society

2 What is the difference between leisure and unemployment?

3 The extract states that 'what you are often determines who you are'. What is meant by this?

4 What group of workers are most likely to remain in employment? Why?

5 What are the advantages of deskilling to an employer?

The consequences of automation

The problems	The advantages
• Loss of skills	• Elimination of boring work
• Increase in boring supervisory work, looking after machines	• New, interesting jobs in service industries created
• Divisions between the few employed and the large numbers of the unemployed	• Better quality products produced
• Lowering of wages	
• Increasing unemployment	
• Poverty for the unemployed	
• Political tensions caused by the increase in poverty and the widening of social differences	

Write a brief account of a person's typical working day in the year 2010 if:
a) the very worst consequences of automation come true
b) the very best consequences come true.

Post-Fordism and de-industrialisation

Employment patterns in Britain have been changing very rapidly over the last 15 years. The most obvious change has been the decline in the number of people working in industry and the growth in those working in offices which provide us with services.

Employment in British industry has shrunk through the effects of competition from other countries, and the effects of the introduction of IT-controlled production processes, which need few workers. What happened in industry seems to be happening now in office work, with increasing use of IT.

Alongside this shift from industry to office work is another change – the way we organise how people work. When industrialisation came, the 'social organisation of work' took the form of large factories where people went to work. They were all graded, from managers down to production-line workers, and there was a clear distinction made between office workers and factory workers. This reached its peak with the 'efficient' methods used by the Ford factories for car production.

However, this form of production has now become old-fashioned. In particular, as Britain declined as a major industrial nation and the government went abroad to try to persuade foreign companies to invest here, the companies that came, particularly from South Korea and Japan, had different views on how production should be carried out, and the role of workers:

- They introduced the idea that every worker was responsible for more than just her or his 'bit', so that the overall quality was the responsibility of everyone, not just management.

- They believed that, although people had specific jobs, if someone else was ill or away, or having difficulties, then others should stand in.

- The divisions between office workers and factory workers were far less rigid and less hierarchical (that is like a pyramid with bosses at the top and workers at the bottom).

Two other important changes were relevant too:

- The first was that the new factories did not store raw materials in huge quantities, like British factories had traditionally done, but used IT to monitor the needs of the factory, so raw materials were now delivered at the very moment they were needed. This saved enormous amounts of money.

- The second change was that as much work as possible is 'farmed out' to small supplier companies or even to people working at home who were expected to deliver the right quantity and quality of material to the central plant 'just-in-time'.

In the original Japanese version of organising work, the employees were guaranteed work for life. However, as the Japanese methods of production gained ground in Britain, they were altered, with great effects for British workers. In Britain (and the USA) the new flexible production approaches meant that workers (like the raw materials) were not needed at the factory, office or supermarket all the time – only at certain busy periods. Why pay workers if they are not working flat-out? the argument goes, instead bring them in when necessary and send them home otherwise.

A new attitude to work and workers has therefore developed amongst employers. They want relatively few permanent, full-time workers and much greater numbers of part-time and temporary or 'contract' workers. As a result the majority of new jobs in Britain are now of this type. Instead of employment being seen as a job for life, it is now a series of short-term and part-time jobs, with the likelihood of unemployment or under-employment (not having as much work as you would like). This new approach to work has been called **post-Fordism**.

The social implications of the changes in employment as a result of post-Fordism are quite noticeable. The Welfare State will become more important as a means of supporting people through the periods of under-employment and unemployment. The class structure is fragmenting as traditional industries decline. Families and households need to adapt to the fact that women increasingly need to go out to work to take part-time employment.

Post-Fordism

Industrial production

Increase in work at home or in small plants. Use of IT to communicate. Large factories are now places where components are assembled. Automation allows small 'runs' of very different products at low prices. Industry no longer employs the majority of people, services have taken over.

Work relationships

Less hierarchy, with all workers dressed similarly and using the same facilities. Everyone is able to express opinions. However, wages are still very different. Many more women employed. Full-time, permanent work is rarer than temporary, and part-time work is much more common.

Social class

The old divisions are weakened as traditional industries decline, and newer work opportunities require people to move and to change jobs often. A sense of 'belonging' declines as the old divisions at work appear to have changed.

Politics

As with social class, the people are less aware of clear divisions in society and the traditional parties can no longer automatically count on the support of one class or another. But more important is the emergence of 'new social movements' which are very loose coalitions of people who will come together on some issues and not others – the feminist movement, the gay rights movement, the animal rights movement, and so on. They are rarely organised.

Welfare State

A great debate on the role of the Welfare State. It had been based on the idea of full employment and reasonable levels of taxation. Unemployment and under-employment and the desire for low taxes help to weaken the Welfare State, and there is a move to private provision.

Working lives

The assembly line

Robert Linhart worked for a year on the Citröen production line. This is his description of assembly line work.

Each man has a well defined area for the operations he has to make...as soon as a car enters a man's territory, he gets to work. A few knocks, a few sparks, then the welding's done and the car's already on its way out of the three or four yards of his position. And the next car's already coming into the work area. And the worker starts again. Sometimes, if he has been working fast, he has a few seconds' rest before a new car arrives: or he intensifies his effort and 'goes up the line' so that he can gain a little time. And after an hour or two he's amassed the incredible amount of two or three minutes in hand, that he'll use to smoke a cigarette, looking on like some comfortable man-of-means as his car moves past already welded. If, on the other hand, the worker is too slow, he 'slips back', carried progressively beyond his position, going on with his work when the next labourer has already begun his. The first car followed too far and the next one already appearing at the usual starting point of the work area, coming forward with its mindless regularity. It's already halfway along before you're able to touch it, you're going to start on it when its nearly passed through and reached the next station: all this loss of time mounts up. It's what they call 'slipping' and sometimes it's as ghastly as drowning.

Source: Adapted from R. Linhart (translated by M. Crossland), *The Assembly Line* (John Calder, 1981)

A craftsman

I won't say I exactly enjoy it. No, not enjoyment exactly but the time passes really quickly. ...what with so much to do, I just have to concentrate on the work. And it is satisfying – I have to say that...just to see, say, a chair, looking lovely, and knowing what it came in like. Yes, the money is important, stands to reason but I wouldn't change to some factory job to just earn more. No.

A furniture restorer

1 In the first extract, how complex is the task that the worker has to do?

2 Do you think that his work is satisfying?

3 What does the extract tell you about the pace of the work?

4 Does this job encourage a sociable atmosphere amongst the workers?

5 Some sociologists have suggested a link between this sort of work and high rates of strikes. Could you suggest some reasons why this might be so?

6 Do you think the worker in the second extract has a better or worse job than the one in the first extract?

7 What are the major differences between the two sorts of jobs described?

IT – changing the place of work

A tele-cottage is not, as the name might suggest, a rustic retreat buzzing with high technology – or not always, anyway. More likely it is a drop-in centre with sophisticated equipment that people can come in to use or learn on. There are now 129 of them in the UK, about 75 in England, and they boost the rural economy by encouraging town-based work to move to the country. ...

The tele-centre has become an integral part of life in the small town and its large rural hinterland. Dominic Bourton, the manager, says it has brought jobs, while commercial activity is picking up in an increasingly computer-literature population. "We have had 350 inquiries into our data base. People offer secretarial services, and we have technical abstracters, antique businesses who do book searches and link up with clients, architects who can compete with people in the middle of London, accountants, teachers. It's for everybody now, not just the computer teccies."

Source: *The Guardian*

1 Explain what a tele-cottage is.

2 How is it different from traditional types of work?

3 Supporters of IT say that it will fundamentally alter the way we all work in future. Looking at the information in the extract, do you think it is true? Give reasons for your conclusion.

The future of work?

A

People have now become a dispensable commodity...By the year 2000 it is likely only half those in paid work will be in what we think of as full-time jobs.

Source: *The Guardian*, 14 January 1995

B

Although men were finding new work opportunities, the decline in job security badly affected women with children, who were likely to hold only temporary jobs. Twenty per cent of women aged around 30 showed a pattern of "discontinuous" employment. ...

"More and more firms are demanding a flexible workforce, which means temporary contracts, laying off and taking up employment again as new markets open. Under these conditions it is likely women will fill such openings. Women will lose out in terms of pension benefits and the rights and protection associated with full-time employment and, to some extent, part-time employment."

One consequence of recent employment changes has been a growth in the number of self-employed men. In the last 25 years men's self-employment has doubled, with 15 per cent self-employed.

Source: *The Guardian*, 6 September 1994

C

Source: *The Independent*, 31 August 1993

Look at **A**.

1 Explain the meaning of the sentence, 'People have become a dispensable commodity.'

2 What implications for society by the year 2000 can you think of, judging by what the extract says?

Look at **B**.

3 What is meant by 'discontinuous employment'?

4 Explain why this is happening?

5 The extract is incorrect in that legislation by the European Union means that part-time workers will in future receive the same benefits as full-time workers. Why did British employers object to this? Why do you think the legislators of the EU impose it?

6 What has been the growth in self-employment?

7 Explain, in your opinion, why this is so.

8 Outline the benefits and disadvantages of the growth in self-employment.

Look at **C**.

9 What does the cartoon indicate that the future of work will be?

10 Do you agree?

The experience of work

As most of our waking time is spent in work, or work-related activities (such as commuting), our experience of work is fundamental to our personal happiness. Sociologists have, therefore, studied workers' attitudes to, and enjoyment of, their jobs. The results of the studies show that attitudes to work fall broadly into two categories: **intrinsic satisfaction**, meaning that workers gain pleasure from their jobs; and **extrinsic satisfaction** which means that workers find little satisfaction in their work and have to seek their pleasure outside their jobs.

Intrinsic satisfaction

This is usually found in skilled or intellectually demanding jobs, ranging from craftsmen to professional people, such as doctors. Their jobs are fulfilling and creative, with a great deal of variety. Satisfaction is therefore found *inside* their employment.

Extrinsic satisfaction

This is usually found in boring, repetitive jobs, such as car assembly lines. Jobs fail to stimulate or interest workers, stunting rather than stimulating their personalities. Workers therefore turn to the wage packet for their satisfaction. They try to earn as much as possible and gain their pleasure through spending their earnings on leisure pursuits and buying consumer goods such as cars and videos. Satisfaction is therefore found *outside* their employment.

Alienation

Karl Marx, the nineteenth-century writer, suggested the term **alienation** to describe the situation where workers experience work as something to be hated. Marx argued that in an ideal world our work ought to be an extension of our personality, yet for the majority of the population this is simply not true. As two sociologists writing about work once commented '87 per cent of workers...expend more mental effort and resourcefulness in getting to work than in doing their jobs'.

The alienated workers

Alienation at work affects a person's life outside work.

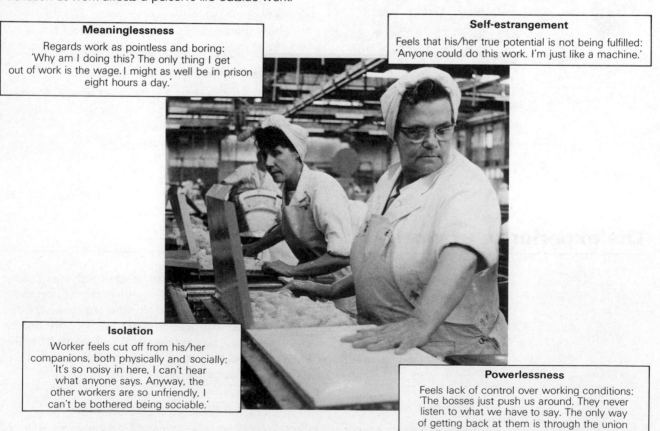

Meaninglessness
Regards work as pointless and boring:
'Why am I doing this? The only thing I get out of work is the wage. I might as well be in prison eight hours a day.'

Self-estrangement
Feels that his/her true potential is not being fulfilled: 'Anyone could do this work. I'm just like a machine.'

Isolation
Worker feels cut off from his/her companions, both physically and socially: 'It's so noisy in here, I can't hear what anyone says. Anyway, the other workers are so unfriendly, I can't be bothered being sociable.'

Powerlessness
Feels lack of control over working conditions: 'The bosses just push us around. They never listen to what we have to say. The only way of getting back at them is through the union or by "accidentally" breaking the assembly line.'

If a person is unhappy at work, how do you think it will
affect his or her:
a) family life
b) leisure choices?
c) general mood and attitudes to others?

Homeworkers 'desperate and exploited'?

A

Up to a million homeworkers, mostly women, are working long hours with no sickness or pension entitlements for an average of £1.28 an hour, according to a study published yesterday.

Home Truths, a rare piece of research on the unregulated world of homeworking, found that some were earning as little as 30p an hour. The vast majority were desperate for money and could not afford childcare. ...

There are no official statistics on the numbers involved or their working conditions and pay, because the Government regards them as self-employed and because they are afraid to talk about their jobs. ...

The survey looked at 175 homeworkers in 10 areas of the country and offers at least a snapshot of general conditions. It found that 94 per cent were women and more than three-quarters had school age children. Fifty-three per cent were white, but a large proportion – 39 per cent – were Asian women.

Only 15 per cent of those surveyed said they would suffer no financial hardship if they lost the extra income. Most were squeezed between the need for money and the need to be at home with the children.

B

Denise Burrow grew to hate snowbound robins and pouting angels during her two years of boxing Christmas cards in her sitting room overlooking Leeds' ring road.

She struggled in vain to reach the "easy" earnings of £2 an hour forecast by the neighbour who introduced her to homeworking. "£2? Nothing like," she said yesterday. She and her friends were getting between 12p and 25p an hour, "and it was taking us forever."

Mrs Burrow, aged 45 and determined to escape homeworking by starting a seamstress service, joined the rock-bottom tier of part-time workers because the school comings and goings of her daughter, Louise, and son, John, were impossible to dovetail with weaving work at Yates's mill.

Source (A and B): *The Guardian*, 13 September 1994

Look at **A**.

1 We normally associate work with factories and offices. How does this extract change our opinion?

2 What sort of people do the work described?

Look at **B**.

3 How much did Mrs Burrow and her friends earn?

4 Would you do it? Why did they do it?

Making work more fulfilling

Attempts to make work more fulfilling fall into two broad categories: on the one hand, the formal methods of researchers and management; and on the other, the informal methods practised by workers of all kinds in their daily work.

Why people work

Formal methods

The first method of overcoming alienation at work is simply to compensate workers for the boredom of their jobs with high wages. The usual method is for 'time and motion' experts to work out the most efficient way of doing the job and then, with the savings gained, to pay higher wages. However this may compensate, it does not actually make work itself any more fulfilling.

An alternative approach, which derives from a famous study by Elton Mayo in the 1930s, is to create a sense of community amongst a firm's workers and the belief that they are valued by the employer. This can involve working in small groups, in pleasant conditions and the firm may provide various welfare provisions such as a subsidised canteen and a social club.

Both approaches mentioned above have left the methods of work the same, but have offered some form of compensation in wages or pleasant working conditions. A third approach is to actually change the way in which the product is made. A famous example of this is the Volvo car assembly plant where the traditional assemly line has been scrapped and teams of workers build virtually the whole car. This gives the workers a feeling that they are members of a team actually creating a product with which they can identify. In the traditional 'division of labour' approach on an assembly line, each individual works alone adding only a small piece to a vehicle.

Informal methods

In their daily work situation, workers are continually trying to make their work more interesting in unofficial, sometimes illegal, ways. These include daydreaming, playing tricks on workmates, taking unofficial breaks and lengthening official ones.

Strategies for fulfilment at work

Those who find work satisfying are typically found in *professional* and *managerial* occupations

Those who are alienated from work are typically found in *routine office/factory work*

Formal methods of combat alienation:

- Increase extrinsic satisfaction through higher pay to purchase a better standard of living
- Make working conditions more pleasant create sense of belonging
- Worker's participation through elected representatives in management
- Forms of employee ownership

Worker's own techniques:

- Daydreaming about life outside work and leisure activities
- Humour at work – practical jokes, humorous stories, chatting
- Work avoidance – 'skiving' at work, absenteeism, extended breaks, restrictive work practice
- Pilfering
- Getting back at management

Schools and colleges, in some ways, are similar to offices and factories in that students need to be motivated to study and accept the discipline of the school.

1 How does the school/college *formally* motivate students?

2 How do students *informally* cope with the school day?

3 Use the ideas given in the text as a basis for your answers plus your own experience.

Enriching work

A The formal approach

Mayo, the researcher discussed in this extract, felt that he had found the clue to a new kind of industrial management approach that would be more humane and efficient. His work led to the development of the 'human relations' approach in American management which stressed the creation of close ties at work and loyalty to the firm.

In 1927 at the Hawthorne plant of the Western Electrical Company in Chicago, a series of experiments were made to see how changes in the physical work environment would affect the output of the workers: in particular changes were made in the lighting arrangements for a particular small group of workers. Very curious results emerged. It was found that the productivity of the group kept climbing irrespective of the various changes. Mayo (the chief researcher) came to the conclusion that as a result of the experiment, enormous amounts of attention had been bestowed upon the group and members of the group had come to feel much closer ties with each other. Mayo decided this was the crucial factor and his work led to an appeciation of the importance of the informal group in industry.

Source: Adapted from P. Berger and B. Berger, *Sociology: A Biographical Approach* (Penguin Education, 1976)

B Informal methods

This is an extract from a study of women working in a tobacco factory. How do women deal with their boredom?

Val: I goes to sleep. I day-dream. But when we don't talk for two hours, I starts tormenting the others, pulling the rag about, muck about sort of thing. With the Irish, you know, I picks on them. About Ireland – take the soldiers back, the bombings, all that – only mucking about like, I don't mean it. But then we have a little row, but we don't mean what we says. But I get so bored, I got to do some-thing, or I start going out the back and have a fag. (Music comes on.) It's the best part of the day when the records come on.

Source: A. Pollert, 'Girls, wives, factory lives' in *New Society*, 22 October 1981

C All workers from managers to unskilled shop floor operatives share this desire to control their pace of work. For professionals and managers it is easy, but for assembly line workers the only method apart from trade union bargaining is the drastic one of deliberately breaking the production machinery.

Piece work employees (those paid by the number of products they make), contrary to what you would expect, restrict output and in doing so keep the price paid for each 'piece' higher. Workers who go too fast are brought back into line by sarcastic comments, practical jokes and, if all else fails, they are 'sent to Coventry'.

1 In **A**, why were the experiments originally held?

2 What happened when they changed the working environment?

3 What conclusions did Mayo reach?

4 What is the meaning of the term 'human relations approach'?

5 In the approach to management, who would be likely to benefit most, do you think?

6 In **B**, describe two ways in which Val keeps herself amused.

7 Could you link the fact that management play records to the 'human relations approach' described earlier?

8 According to **C**, why do workers on piece work restrict output?

9 What happens to those who work too hard?

10 Do you think that management agree with this practice?

11 Some sociologists have talked about the 'culture of the workplace'. Using the information given in the extracts, can you explain what this term might mean?

Problems faced by women at work

Women suffer from three major disadvantages compared to men in their working lives:

- They are paid less than men. On average women receive only two-thirds of the wages received by men. Remember, since 1975 it has been illegal to pay women less than men for doing the same level of job (as a result of the 1970 Equal Pay

Act). The difference in earnings can be explained by the fact that women are concentrated in low-paid jobs and have less opportunity for overtime.

- They are more likely to be in part-time employment. Ninety per cent of part-time workers are women. This is because generally women regard the role of mother and housewife as the most important. Women are expected to be first and foremost wives and mothers, and secondly to go out to work. Part-time working reflects the need to be at home to look after children when they are out of school. Women tend to have higher absenteeism than men because they need to stay away from work to care for any member of family who is ill. Women, therefore, face **role conflict** at work.

- Women are concentrated in low-paid, less-skilled jobs with few holding positions of authority. Over half of all women are in clerical work or the personal services, which are usually low paid. When women do have professional jobs, it is usually in the lower-paid 'marginal' professions such as nursing (92 per cent of nurses are women). However, less than a third of doctors are women and less than 10 per cent of women were in the higher professions or senior management.

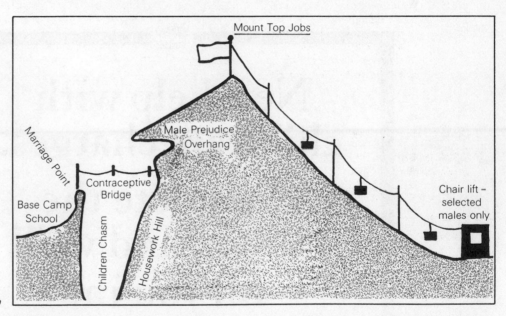

Women: the climb to the top

The pattern of women's working lives

The *typical* pattern of a woman's working life is to work from leaving school until the birth of the first child, then to give up work for the time it takes to raise her children (usually to secondary school age) and then to return to work. Of course this interrupted pattern of work means that employers are less likely to promote them or train them for a career. The employer will generally believe that the woman is less likely to remain with the company than a male worker.

Part-time workers

Reasons for taking a part-time[1] job: by sex and marital status, Spring 1993, UK (percentages and thousands)

	Males	Females		
		Married	Non-married	All females
Student/still at school	29.4	0.6	33.4	6.9
Ill or disabled	3.3	1.0	1.3	1.1
Could not find a full-time job	29.0	8.4	18.3	10.3
Did not want a full-time job	36.2	88.0	45.4	79.9
Part-time workers[2] (=100%) (thousands)	886	4078	967	5045

[1]Part-time is based on respondent's self assessment.
[2]Includes those who did not state the reason for taking a part-time job.

Source: *Social Trends 24* (HMSO, 1994) and Employment Department

New help with childcare charges. Complete the coupon and we'll fill you in.

From October, these charges will be taken into account for some working parents claiming Family Credit, Housing Benefit, Council Tax Benefit or Disability Working Allowance. To qualify, they must use a registered or approved childcare provider, and their child has to be under 11. They must work for at least 16 hours a week. If they have a partner they must both be working for 16 hours, unless one of them is disabled.

So parents who thought they couldn't afford to work, or to work extra hours, because of the cost of childcare may want to think again.

To find out more, use the coupon. Or ring us free on **0800 88 44 11.**

WORKING WITH BENEFITS, FREEPOST (BS4335) BRISTOL BS1 3YX.

1   Which group is most likely to work part-time?

2   What explanation is given in the table?

3   Can you explain the real reasons behind this? (The advert gives a clue.)

Domestic labour

When we talk about 'work' it is usually taken to mean paid employment. However, women who do not have paid employment are usually 'housewives', cooking, cleaning the house and caring for the family. This too is full-time work, which is often boring and seemingly never-ending. It can also be exhausting and, if there is no family nearby, the housewife can feel isolated.

(For further discussion on women at work see pages 67–72.)

Who says housewives don't work?

A friend who recently celebrated her 60th birthday was told she was ineligible for her old age pension because her husband is still employed and the woman has not "worked" for 10 years.

But if raising a family, looking after a husband and managing a home isn't considered "work", then God didn't make little green apples.

How different from France, where women who stay at home and raise their children are paid a "wage" by the State.

1 Do you agree with the extract? Is 'housework' really work?

2 Should women get a wage? Who will pay it? (If you say the government, explain where the money will come from.)

Source: *The Sunday Express*, 16 October 1994

One view of part-time work

This is part of a letter written to *The Guardian*.

1. Virtually all the part-time jobs created in the past 5–10 years have been the low-wage service sector. The growth of these jobs primarily reflects the flexible exploitation of employees by enterprises faced with fluctuating markets. Because demand for luxury goods and personal services is fickle, workers in high-street retail, fast-food chains, hotels and catering are increasingly employed only for the specific hours, days or months that they are most needed, and they must often be available at short notice. In this context flexibility is a euphemism for insecurity.

2. 80–90 per cent of part-time workers are women. Paul Gregg has shown that the majority of these women belong to households in which there is already a wage earner. This means that a considerable proportion of female part-timers can "afford" to work part-time.

Their wages may contribute to the household's disposable income, and they may be free to value what is often servile labour because it gives them a sense of liberation from the private sphere.

3. Meeting women's preference for part-time jobs and a favourable balance between work and home may obscure a more fundamental imbalance. Many women do not look for full-time work because their exclusive responsibility for housework and childcare precludes it. The selective reduction in working hours thus strengthens the male monopoly on secure, permanent, full-time work.

It retards the demand for a redistribution of reduced working hours across the whole of society.

Source: *The Guardian*, 25 January 1994

1 The writer of the letter makes three rather complicated points. Explain in your own words what the writer is saying.

2 Look at point 1. How does this relate to the concept of post-Fordism we looked at earlier?

3 Look at point 2. Do you agree this is why women work?

4 Look at point 3. Do you agree that part-time work helps men to keep the secure, full-time employment? What can be done about it?

Industrial relations

British society is based on the economic system of capitalism. This means that industry and commerce are owned by groups of individuals, as opposed to the state in communist societies. The owners wish to make as much profit as reasonably possible and therefore wish to keep their costs, which include wages, as low as they can. Employees wish to obtain the highest possible wage for themselves and to work in the best conditions possible. The resulting conflict between the two groups as a result of their different wishes is known as **industrial conflict**.

Forms of conflict

- **Strike:** backed by trade union, usually with strike pay
- **Work-to-rule:** workers stick rigidly to conditions and regulations of employment; effective where workers routinely break regulations to achieve output
- **Overtime ban:** refuse to work longer than the official hours
- **Sit-in/work-in:** as response to redundancy, workers continue working and lock management out
- **Sabotage:** if striking is impossible/illegal, workers may express anger through wrecking machinery or the film's products

The business of manufacture

Industry is organised to make profit. Most people accept this as fact and recognise that the more profit their company makes the better chance it has of providing a good standard of living and security for its employees and their families. This is not only because everybody's future earnings depend on the Company continuing to make a profit, but because a good profit encourages more investment – a good safeguard for the future.

Human resources, however, are scarce and expensive and therefore it makes sense to see that they are fully used and not misused. Just as it does not make sense to build more plants before we fully use the ones we have, neither does it make sense to keep on hiring men when some of those we have cannot make a full contribution because of bad organisation or working habits.

A Ford official publication

'It's just the situation they (management) are in. They've got to make a profit or they're finished. It's as easy as that. They've got to screw the blokes or they get screwed. That's the way it is. ...'

A shop steward

Source: H. Benyon, *Working for Ford* (Pelican, 1984)

1 What do the Ford management wish to do, according to the first extract?

2 How do they wish to do it?

3 Using the information in the quote from the shop steward, do you think that the Ford workers view the situation this way?

4 Given the different views, what sort of outcome is almost inevitable?

The decline in strike action

In the 1980s and 1990s, the number of strikes, and the number of working days lost because of strikes, fell considerably from the 1979 peak (although the miners' strike in 1984–5 did break the pattern). By 1985, the number of days lost was a tenth of the 1979 figure. There are two main reasons for this.

Firstly unemployment: the fear of losing one's job frightened most workers. Secondly, government action: new, stricter laws were introduced by the Conservative Government in the early 1980s effectively limiting the power of unions to strike.

Trade unions

Trade unions represent the workforce, negotiating working conditions and wage levels with the management.

Since the 1950s considerable changes have taken place in the trade unions. The number of trade unions has declined. There are now fewer, but bigger, unions.

The total membership of the trade unions has fallen. In the 1980s alone, the trade unions lost over 2 million members. The membership of trade unions has changed. The traditional view of trade unionists as male manual workers is now out of date. The growth area in trade union membership is in white-collar workers, reflecting the change in the whole employment structure.

White-collar workers are joining trade unions because they see themselves falling behind professional workers and some manual workers in wage levels. This has made them more militant and so more likely to join trade unions. Secondly, the old idea that clerical workers are part of the management is no longer true (if it ever was!). Working in huge numbers in open plan offices has given them a sense of 'solidarity' (a feeling of sharing a similar situation).

The declining unions

Specialised craft-workers employed to carry out specific jobs have been replaced by multi-skilled workers, required to carry out any task and undergo retraining when necessary. Permanent full-time employees are being replaced, where possible, by temporary or part-time workers. Indeed, companies increasingly contract out work to smaller firms, to specialised providers of services, such as head-hunting agencies, or to self-employed workers, using them as they need them and avoiding the costs and regulations involved in employing people directly. Such practices challenge and undermine trade unions, which

have sought to build up their power and protect their members through agreements or laws which regulate employer actions, restrict their members' work-tasks and, in some cases, control entry to occupations, ...and give workers security of employment. ...

[There has been a] steady decline of [union] membership since its peak in 1979. At first the decline seemed to result from the sharply rising unemployment of the early 1980s but it continued after employment began to increase in 1983.

The problem was not unemployment but the changing character of work and

related changes in the composition of the labour force. The membership and power of the unions were [highly] concentrated in those industries, such as shipbuilding, steel, mining, and engineering, that suffered most from the industrial crisis of the 1970s, or in occupations, such as printing and dockwork, transformed by technical change. When employment started to rise again in 1983, it did so in occupations concerned with consumption and services rather than production, in areas such as distribution, marketing and finance, which are much harder for the unions to organise. Furthermore, these occupations

tended to recruit part-time workers, women, the young, groups that are less likely to join unions than the full-time, adult, male workers typical of the traditional industries. There has also been a dispersal of employment to small units, and to small towns and rural areas, which has reversed the process of concentration [in factories] that had earlier facilitated union organisation. Finding it difficult to recruit new members to replace those they have lost, the unions have resorted to mergers instead [so there are fewer unions with few members in total].

Table 1: Union membership

	Union Membership (000s)	Annual % change
1968	10,200	
1969	10,479	+2.7
1970	11,187	+6.8
1971	11,135	−0.5
1972	11,359	+2.0
1973	11,456	+0.9
1974	11,764	+2.7
1975	12,026	+2.2
1976	12,386	+3.0
1977	12,846	+2.1
1978	13,112	+2.1
1979	13,447	+2.6
1980	12,947	−3.7
1981	12,182	−5.9
1982	11,593	−4.2
1983	11,236	−3.1
1984	10,994	−3.2
1985	10,821	−1.6
1986	10,539	−2.6
1987	10,475	−0.6
1988	10,376	−0.9
1989	10,158	−2.1

Table 2: Union density in Great Britain

	Men %	Women %
1970	56.4	31.5
1979	63.4	39.5
1989	44.0	33.0

Union density is a measure of the proportion of employees who are members of unions.

Sources for tables: G. S. Bain and R. Price 'Union growth: Dimensions, determinants, and destiny', in G. S. Bain (ed.) *Industrial Relations in Great Britain*, Basil Blackwell, 1983, pp. 5 and 9.

Employment Gazette, June and July 1991.

Source: J. Fulcher, 'A new stage in the development of capitalist society' in *Sociology Review*, November 1991

1 Look at Table 1. Describe the changing trends in union membership.

2 Look at Table 2. Explain the meaning of union density in your own words.

3 What does Table 2 tell us about:
a) males?
b) females?

Look at the extract.
4 What new employers' practices 'challenge and undermine trades unions'?

5 Earlier we talked about post-Fordism. Explain the links between these practices and post-Fordism.

6 What industries and types of worker did unions traditionally gain their membership from?

7 What is happening to threaten this?

8 As a result, what is happening to unions?

Professions

The professions are organisations that represent the interests of the jobs which are traditionally considered as the most skilful and which carry the highest status, such as medicine and the law.

There are two views concerning professions. One group of sociologists argues that the professions are organisations which are just middle-class trade unions, protecting the interests of their members by restricting the number of new entrants. As there are few professionals about, they can demand high fees. A second group of sociologists take a slightly kinder view of the professions and argue that they exist to protect the public by placing very high standards on behaviour in these jobs.

Chapter 12

UNEMPLOYMENT, CONSUMPTION AND LEISURE

This chapter covers:
- Unemployment
- The extent of unemployment
- The causes of unemployment
- The unemployed
- The different experiences of unemployment
- Leisure
- The influences on leisure patterns
- Leisure: The future
- The influence of work on our lives.

Unemployment

The difference between unemployment and leisure

There is a simple distinction between unemployment and leisure. Leisure means free time you have chosen to spend doing something you want, and having the finances to do it. Unemployment means free time not of your own choosing and with little money to spend. So the difference lies in choice and finance.

The importance of employment

Employment is important to people for three main reasons: finance, status and self-respect.

Finance

Without money it is impossible to buy all the objects and the style of life that is regarded as normal. Unemployed people are usually poor.

Status

This is bought with consumer goods in our society. The latest registration car and the latest fashion in clothes indicate the position of a person, and in many people's eyes give that person status.

Self-respect

In British society the job you have is what you are (hence the opening question, 'What do you do?' in many conversations). Not to have a job is, therefore, to be nobody, not to have an identity. Clearly this is very closely linked to status, mentioned earlier.

The extent of unemployment

There is considerable dispute over the exact figures of the unemployed. The 'official' figure given by the Department of Employment in Spring 1994 was approximately 3 000 000. However, this probably under-estimated the true extent of unemployment.

Only those receiving state benefits and registered to work are counted. This omits most married women. If their husbands are working they cannot receive benefit, and if their husbands are unemployed, then the benefit (and the unemployment statistic) is in his name. Secondly, people on the various training schemes are not included. Thirdly, men over 60 who are long-term unemployed are omitted.

Adding all these together, it has been estimated that there are really about 4 million people who would like to work, but cannot.

The changing face of employment

Economic insecurities are well described. Even though household income has risen, the experience of unemployment has affected many millions, and the long-term unemployed now account for 45 per cent of all unemployed people, compared with 28 per cent in 1991. The number of males working part time has almost doubled in the past decade, the most common reason cited being the inability to find a full-time job. The numbers of those working on fixed-term contracts has risen dramatically, as careers become less a "job for life". And if these insecure jobs are forced options – as the figures suggest – there is little reason to believe that others are immune to those changes. In other words, "It could happen to me".

Source: 'A nation both richer and insecure' by B. Tyrrell, T. Rubenstein and R. Waterhouse in *The Independent*, 26 January 1995

1 Long-term unemployment (when people remain out of work for six months or more) usually has a much greater effect on peoples' lives, in that over time their savings decline and their self-confidence declines. What type of unemployment is growing?

2 Why has there been an increase in part-time employment?

3 What does 'fixed-contract' employment mean? What are the benefits and drawbacks for:
a) employers?
b) employees?

4 What effect on the general society have these changes in employment had?

5 Ask a sample of ten people in employment if they feel worried that they might be made redundant or could lose their employment. If you receive varying answers, pool all the replies in class and compare the patterns of jobs. What types of job are more secure, and which are insecure?

The causes of unemployment

The first point is that, in the mid-1980s, there was a worldwide decline in employment, although some countries were affected more than others. Japan, for example, peaked at 3 per cent unemployment, while it was over 10 per cent in countries such as Canada, Holland, Spain and Britain.

In Britain there are three main causes of high unemployment. Firstly, the increasing competition from abroad for manufacturing goods: a quick glance will show that the bulk of clothes, electrical goods and a large proportion of the cars are manufactured abroad. Secondly, automation: the increasing use of automation has led to the loss of traditional jobs. Initially this occurred in the unskilled labouring area, but this has now spread to skilled work. The third reason is that British government policy from the 1980s onwards was to lower the costs of British workers and to increase competition between them for work. Unemployment means that those in work are frightened to ask for high wage increases in case they lose their jobs to unemployed people who might accept lower wages.

Check a) the electrical goods in your home (stereo, washing machine, TV, etc.)
       b) your clothes.
How many of these were made in Britain?

Tackling unemployment

A
Some European governments want to share the available work more evenly among those after a job. ...Cutting working hours is one method...like the Irish who cut the working week from 48 to 40 hours and banned workers from holding two jobs. In Belgium, the government has passed laws making cuts in workers' pay in return for cuts in working time and more recruitment...working time cuts

of 5 per cent were compensated by 3 per cent less pay and 3 per cent more jobs.

Can you persuade older people to retire early and replace them with younger workers? That's one way to redistribute work. West Germany has encouraged men aged between 60 and 65 to retire early and by 1980, only one third were working. In the Italian steel industry retirement at 50 was adopted last year.

The young come at or near the top of everyone's list for special attention. The stress throughout Europe...on training for the young turns on two considerations. Training seems as good a way as any of keeping youngsters off the streets, even if there are no jobs at the end of it all. More positive is the awareness that technological change has outmoded old patterns of education and training.

With its plan to roll back dismissal rights and to water down the Wages Councils (official organisations which set wages for certain industries), Britain is quite an enthusiastic backer of a different approach, freeing the market by making it easier for employers to sack workers and pay them lower wages.

Source: Adapted from D. Thomas 'Learning about job creation' in *New Society*, 23 May 1985

B Two quite different approaches are emerging in debates amongst the members of the European Union. The majority of countries wish to increase protection for their workers and to raise the general standards of living for their workers through a wide range of measures including letting employees have some say in the running of

companies by means of work councils, by giving them security of employment, by implementing minimum wages and by generally limiting the ability of companies to exploit workers.

The second route, favoured by Britain, is to decrease the security of workers so that they are prepared to work harder, to decrease wages so that workers

are competitive with low wage economies in less-developed countries, and to limit the intervention of government.

Both sides claim victory. Britain has achieved lower levels of unemployment than some countries – but has done so by having a cheap, insecure and low-paid workforce.

1 Extract **A** mentions four methods of combating unemployment. What are they?

2 Rank these methods in order of usefulness, in your opinion, in combating unemployment. Give reasons for your ranking.

3 Are there any alternative proposals you could suggest?

4 Read extract **B**. What is your view? Is it better to have more employment with lower wages, or less employment with better conditions for those in work?

Claimant unemployment and job centre vacancies, UK

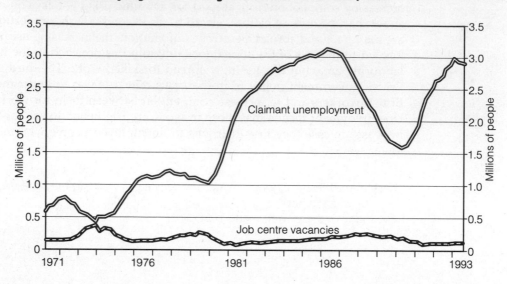

Source: *Social Trends 24* (HMSO, 1994) and Employment Department

1 What was the level of unemployment in 1993?

2 If all the vacancies at job centres were filled, how many unemployed people would have remained in 1993?

3 When did unemployment begin its rise?

4 Go to your local job centre. What sorts of job are on offer?

The unemployed

Unemployment hits those at each end of the labour market: the young and the old. The unemployment rate for the under 25s is about 23 per cent and for the over 55s it is about 17 per cent. In the country as a whole it is about 12 per cent. The ethnic minorities, too, have higher than average unemployment rates. The rate for adult men of Asian and Afro-Caribbean origin is twice that of Whites.

There is disagreement over the extent to which women are affected by unemployment. As they are generally employed in the lower-paid jobs and are more often likely to have part-time work, it seems that they are not as likely to be laid off as men. But as we saw before, the official statistics do not include any married women who would like to work but are not eligible for benefits, so they seriously underestimate the extent of female unemployment. Finally, the less-skilled worker is far more likely to be made unemployed than the skilled worker.

One major change that has taken place has been the growth of **under-employment**, by which we mean that people who work part-time (90 per cent of whom are women) may, in fact, really want full-time work, but are unable to get it. They are not unemployed, but can be said to be under-employed.

The facts and impact of unemployment

A

Unemployment in the UK, by region, 1992

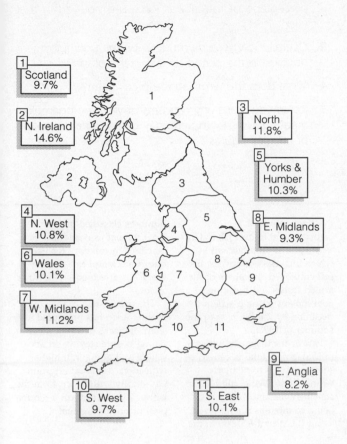

1	Scotland 9.7%
2	N. Ireland 14.6%
3	North 11.8%
5	Yorks & Humber 10.3%
4	N. West 10.8%
8	E. Midlands 9.3%
6	Wales 10.1%
7	W. Midlands 11.2%
9	E. Anglia 8.2%
10	S. West 9.7%
11	S. East 10.1%

B

Men on 'the scrap heap'?

Men with little or no job prospects (percentages)
Top five local authority districts:
1 Tower Hamlets 34.5%
2 Middlesbrough 31.0%
3 Easington 29.9%
4 Sunderland 28.5%
4 Liverpool 28.5%

Bottom five:
362 Hart 5.6%
362 South Bucks 5.6%
364 S. Cambridgeshire 5.5%
365 Chiltern 5.2%
366 S. Lakeland 5.1%

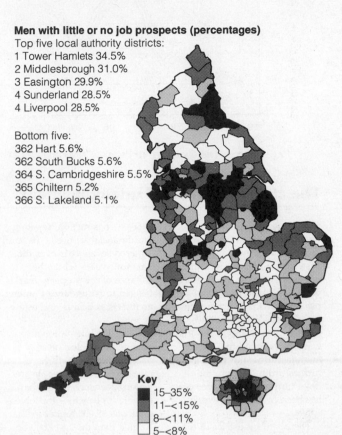

Key
- 15–35%
- 11–<15%
- 8–<11%
- 5–<8%

C

The jobless male

The study found that most of those men over 55 and unemployed or on government schemes were concentrated in the older industrial districts that have suffered most from manufacturing decline – such as the Midlands, Tyneside and Merseyside. In Sunderland and Easington, about one third in that category were "on the scrapheap".

Tower Hamlets, one of the most deprived areas of London, came top with 34.5 per cent. The lowest-ranked 50 districts that had more than 80 per cent of people aged 55 or over in employment are concentrated in the commuter belt around London. None is in the North.

Source (B and C): 'Shift in wealth divides, rich south and poor north' by H. Mills in *The Independent*, 1 February 1995

Look at map **A**.

1 Which two regions have the highest unemployment rates?

2 Which region has the lowest rate?

Look at map **B**.

3 According to this map is there the clear north–south divide in overall unemployment that most people talk about?

4 Is the same answer true for the unemployment statistics for older men, according to the text?

5 What explanations can you suggest for the variations in unemployment in Britain?

Unemployment in the UK, 1970–94

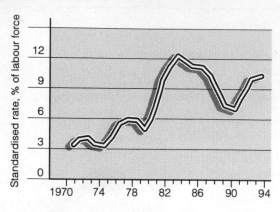

Source: *The Guardian*, 13 February 1995 and OECD

1 What percentage of the labour force was unemployed in 1970?

2 In which year did unemployment peak? What was the percentage of the labour force unemployed in that year?

3 Overall, how would you describe the unemployment situation in the period shown in the graph?

4 What does the term 'labour force' mean?

5 Could you make any criticisms of why the unemployment figures shown here may be an underestimation of the 'real figures'?

The changing face of unemployment

The changing face of unemployment in the current recession was underlined yesterday with the news that unemployment in the Southeast of England has risen above 10 per cent for the first time since the depression of the 1930s. ...

Where the slump of the 1980s was concentrated in manufacturing and the regions furthest from London, the downturn of the past three years has been much more evenly spread.

The boom industries of the 1980s – construction, retailing and financial services – have all suffered severe cuts over the past four years, while the collapse of the property market has led to redundancies among architects, solicitors and estate agents. ...

Using the internationally accepted definition of unemployment – which measures whether people are looking for work rather than eligible for benefit – the jobless total was 95,000 higher in August than the 2,811,000 on the claimant count. ...government figures [show] the workforce in employment – which includes employees, the self-employed, members of the armed forces and those on government training schemes – declining by 2 million since the summer of 1990. ...

Part of the disparity with the official jobless total is caused by some people – particularly women – not being eligible for state benefits, and hence not being counted as unemployed.

But the rise of 600,000 in the numbers classified by the Government as economically inactive – a category for people not in work and not seeking work – is affected by two other factors.

The diminished chance of finding a job has prompted a sharp increase in the number of young people staying on at school and going into higher education. But another group has simply withdrawn from the labour market to form a hidden pool of unemployment.

Source: *The Guardian*, 18 December 1992

1 According to the extract, unemployment is spreading to which groups?

2 Why is this different from the past?

3 What are the implications for British society, given that industrial employment is declining rapidly?

4 Are unemployment statistics accurate? If you answer no, explain why.

5 What is the effect on education of a lack of jobs?

6 In your opinion, is this a good or bad thing, in the long run?

Youth unemployment

A million under-25-year-olds are now out of work, with graduates experiencing a higher unemployment rate than those with vocational qualifications, according to an analysis published today.

Based on a study of government figures, two charities calculate that the jobless rate among young people has virtually doubled since the recession began in April 1990, outstripping the increase among the general population. Youthaid and the Unemployment Unit contend that there are 111,110 jobless 16- and 17-year-olds – and 80 per cent of them have no income. Official figures show only 15,746 out of work: those under 18 are not entitled to unemployment benefit and are not counted as jobless by the Department of Employment, which aims to guarantee them Youth Training places. ...

A spokeswoman for the Department of Employment said increases in unemployment reflected world circumstances. Youth unemployment was too high, but it was below the European Community average.

Source: 'Unemployment among under–25s reaches 1 million' by B. Clement in *The Independent*, 5 March 1993

1 How many under 25s were out of work in 1993 according to the 'analysis' by Youthaid and the Unemployment Unit?

2 How many 16- and 17-year-olds were out of work?

3 Did the government agree with these statistics?

4 If there is a difference, suggest an explanation.

The different experiences of unemployment

The experience of unemployment will not be the same for each social group. The experience of unemployment for a man of 50, for example, who has worked since leaving school can be devastating. We know that men in particular take much of their identity from their job. When asked what we are, we reply in terms of our job. Lack of work can lead to crisis of identity. For those women workers who see their primary identity as a wife and mother, loss of employment need not be so devastating a blow to identity.

Although the majority of women workers have seen employment as an *escape* from the home and their return to the role of housewife may make them feel trapped.

Experiences of unemployment

A

A man, in his fifties, reflecting on his experience of unemployment after having been made redundant, said:

'It affected me a lot when I was unemployed. I didn't think I was going to get another job. It was very depressing and got worse the longer I was unemployed. It wasn't so much the money or the way I felt. It was degrading – in the dole office or when people asked me what I was doing. People would say – 'are you still unemployed?' 'Are you not looking for work?' I was looking. It was very degrading. I have worked all my life and got angry. People who have never been unemployed don't know what it is like; they have never experienced it...When you are unemployed you are bored, frustrated, and worried, worried sick: at least I was. Of course it is worse for the man who has got a family: he has got responsibilities. So you worry for the wife and the bairns.' (Sinfield, 1981, p. 41)

Source: N. Abercrombie and A. Warde, *British Society* (Polity Press, 1994), quoting A. Sinfield, *What Unemployment Means* (Oxford University Press, 1981)

B

...the conversation between Stephen Woods, who was unemployed, and his 19 year old girlfriend, the mother of his child. He was anxious for them to set up home together.

Girlfriend: 'I says to him, "Why should I work?" when he should work. He should support wer, not me support him and the bairn, then meself. Like if he got a job, I would like get a part-time job when she's one or two.'
Stephen: 'But you've got a better chance of getting a proper job 'cos you're the lass. Lasses can be on supermarket tills and what have you. You could get a start tomorrow, but they wouldn't start me there with us having a criminal record and that.'

(ibid., p. 127)

Fourth, the work ethic was challenged. The fact that it was possible, albeit inadequately, to carve out an existence on social security, contradicted some people's sense of what was proper and legal. Furthermore, when some young people were just about able to do this whilst still living at home, some parents worried that their children might grow accustomed to an existence on social security. They would thus lose the urge to work. Mrs Robson said:

'It's easy for people to get into a rut if you start off your life not knowing what work is but you're still going to get kept. Maybe it's a minimum, but you're still getting kept aren't you? It might be easy to go that way.'

(ibid., p. 80)

Source: N. Abercrombie and A. Warde, *British Society* (Polity Press, 1994), quoting from *Youth Unemployment and The Family: Voices of Disordered Times* (Routledge, 1992)

C

Here is a 19-year-old woman speaking:
'At first, it was OK, you know, because all the girls from school were in the same boat – I mean there just weren't any jobs so we didn't have to worry. But, like, after a while – er about a year, well we began to drift apart. Michelle went to live with her boyfriend, Sharon moved away and, like some, got rotten jobs – but they were jobs. Me and Sarah stuck together, but I felt, I *feel*, ashamed and Oh, I can't explain it – but somehow not myself, I mean I feel just fed up and bored and sick.'

1 What emotions did the unemployed man in extract **A** have?

2 He comments on his wife and children. In what way is unemployment a blow to a man's view of what his role is?

3 What gender role expectations are emerging in this discussion between the two 19-year-olds with a young child in extract **B**?

4 Who do you agree with? Or do you disagree with both?

5 Do you agree with Mrs Robson's comments?

6 When the young woman in extract **C** was unable to find work, did it affect her as strongly as the males?

7 List the advantages and disadvantages of working for young people? What would you prefer?

D   Unemployment rates by age, UK, January 1993

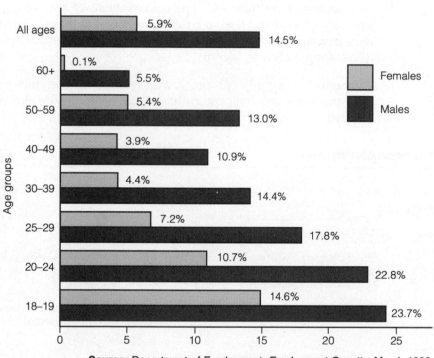

Source: Department of Employment, *Employment Gazette*, March 1993

Look at **D**.

8 Which two age groups are the most likely to be unemployed?

9 Overall, which groups, male or female are more likely to be unemployed?

10 Can you suggest any reasons for the differences?

11 Can you suggest any possible consequences for society of the levels of young people's unemployment?

Young people without a lifetime of work behind them may well find the result of unemployment very different from the middle-aged. It could be argued that living on social security, freed from the drudgery of work could be, for a short time at least, a pleasant life. However, all this is marred by a number of hidden problems that develop individually and socially the longer unemployment lasts. The first problem facing many young people is that they need to remain at home, continuing to receive financial support and are, therefore, subject to attempts at control by their parents. Friction soon develops and the traditional way out, finding a flat or getting married, is no longer available. Paul Willis in a study of youth unemployment in the Midlands has found that some girls deliberately get pregnant in order to escape from their family, relying upon the state for support.

Working-class youth, both black and white, has wholeheartedly embraced the ethics of the consumer society. Who you are is expressed through ownership of Ford Escort XR3i and the smart clothes carrying the chain store's impressive sounding Italian labels. But unemployment is increasingly robbing working-class youth of the legitimate ways of obtaining these goods. The affluent culture of the 1970s does not change just like that. It carries on into the age of unemployment, so you cannot 'pull' a girl without a flash car, money for drinks in the pub and some smart clothes. So develops the bitter inarticulate demands of youth, who see little justification in the way money and jobs are distributed at present. If they need something and the system is unfair then it is OK to get the goods for themselves in whatever way they can.

'Consumerism' and unemployment have combined to create another feature of our current high streets, the groups of youth who are just hanging around. They have nothing to do and little money to spend. So they gather in the place where they can see and be seen by others of their age. In doing so they present a 'threat' to the middle-aged and 'respectable' shoppers. The police are called in to move the youth out and so develop the origins of resentment against the police.

1 Do all people respond in the same way to the experience of unemployment?

2 Why is it possible that at first young people may not find unemployment as 'a blow to their identity'?

3 Describe the feelings that youth have towards the possession of clothes and cars, etc. What happens when they are unemployed?

4 How can unemployment lead to resentment against the police?

5 How do some girls escape from being trapped at home, according to Willis's research?

6 Do you feel this is an accurate description of the young unemployed that you know? If not, state your reasons.

The possible consequences of unemployment

Political unrest
In the gap between the living standards of the employed and the unemployed becomes too wide, there could be political problems as the poor look for ways out of their problems.

Scapegoating/racism
If there is no easy explanation for the high rates of unemployment, people often look for scapegoats to blame their problems on. This might increase racism.

Crime
Crime rates increase as the gap between rich and poor grows. The goods are in the shops to tempt the unemployed, but they simply cannot afford them. Therefore they may turn to crime (and political action?).

Family conflict
Women may be forced back into the mother/housewife role as jobs disappear. Alternatively, it is possible that as husbands lose their jobs, the only income will be that of the wife. Males may find this 'role swop' difficult to accept

Inner city
As unemployment rises, it appears to be youth in the inner cities who bear the brunt. The resentment and desperation is reflected in crime, riots, racism and drug abuse.

Drugs and alcohol
The despair of the young appears to be expressed by the increase in drug abuse. (See **Inner city** and **Crime**.)

Can you think of any more?   If so, include them in the boxes.

Leisure

In modern industrial societies there is a strict division between what we consider to be 'work' that is paid employment, and what we consider to be 'leisure'. People work for a set number of hours each day and then at 5 p.m. they finish, and start their leisure.

This has not always been so. In most societies, throughout history, there was no clear distinction between a work time and a leisure time. In order to survive, people had to work in the fields or hunt. They performed these tasks until they had obtained enough food to eat, and adequate clothes and shelter. This work was not planned to happen at special times. As far as we know, there has never been a tribal society in which all the members started to hunt at 9 in the morning, stopped for an hour for lunch and then continued until 5 p.m.!

Leisure, as we know it, is related to the development of industry. Employers wanted a workforce that arrived at a particular time, so that the work of the machinery and employees could be coordinated. Work was so brutal and unpleasant that the few hours each day when people were not in the factories and offices was spent in trying to recuperate. Work then became separated from ordinary life; it became a fixed period of unpleasant labour each day. Work was time regarded as 'lost' from people's lives.

Gradually, the trade unions won shorter working days for their members and so the hours of non-work, or leisure, increased. However, the distinction in our lives between work, which is not expected to be enjoyable (for a large portion of the workforce), and leisure, which is expected to provide us with our fulfilment, has come to be seen as normal and natural.

Defining leisure

Although it may seem a very easy idea to define, leisure is a very slippery concept to grasp. It is not just *time* spent out of work, because we often have things to do which are forms of work in this time (for example, I wrote this book in my 'leisure' time). It is certainly not just *activities*, for one person's leisure is another's job. For example, some people dance for fun, others do it for a living. In the end, we have to say that there are certain characteristics more often found in leisure than in work, though these characteristics overlap.

The characteristics of work and leisure

Characteristics	Leisure	Work
Paid	No	Yes
Freedom	Yes	No
Choice	Wide	Limited
Self-imposed	Yes	No
Relationships with others based on power	No	Yes
Pleasurable	Yes	Only for those in skilled work

1 Give three examples of activities which in some situations are 'leisure' and others 'work'.

2 Can leisure occur at work? If so, give an example.

The influences on leisure patterns

Our choice of leisure pursuits is influenced by a number of social factors. The most important ones are our social class (and within that our specific occupation, or lack of one), our age group and our sex.

Social class and income

We know that social class is related to differences in income, standards of education, amount of free time and cultural differences.

Put together, these mean that middle- and working-class people often like different leisure pursuits. They read different newspapers and books, watch different programmes and films, and join different clubs.

Consumption and leisure

The percentage of household income spent on leisure

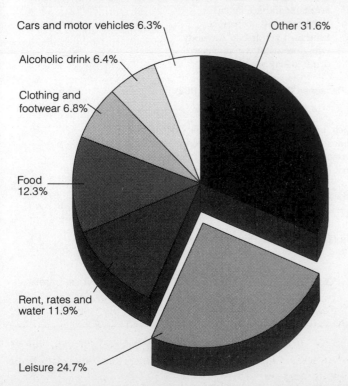

1 What is the single largest element of spending which is specifically named?

2 Does the answer surprise you? Explain why.

3 Do you think the pie chart has any weaknesses?

4 Work out what proportion of (a) your own and (b) your family's budget (if different) goes on 'leisure'. (How you define leisure may be an interesting exercise in itself!)

Source: A. Tomlinson, 'Buying time: Consumption and leisure' in *Social Studies Review*, January 1991 and *Leisure Management*, Vol. 9, No. 5, 1989

Occupation

If social class differences create broad divisions in our choices of leisure pursuits, occupation influences us in more specific ways. It has been suggested that there are three types of occupation–leisure relationships: **extension**, **neutrality** and **oppositional**.

Extension

This is when the job a person does is interesting and very fulfilling. In leisure, the person will often choose pursuits directly connected with work. This relationship is typical of people in professional occupations, such as social workers, teachers, etc.

Neutrality

This is when the job a person does is basically uninteresting and is seen as just a way of getting money to pay for an adequate style of life. In leisure, the person will emphasise the family and social enjoyment. Typical occupations are clerical workers and semi-skilled workers.

Oppositional

This is when the job a person does is exhausting and involves periods of intense physical effort. In leisure, the person looks for the complete opposite of work in order to refresh themselves. Typical occupations are miners and building workers.

The relationship between work and leisure

Why is it that fishermen drink so much? In many cases it is not even true to say that they do drink more than the average man, they are merely concentrating their drinking (while ashore). ...Is it that they are trying to forget the cold, black void of the Arctic which awaits them once again? Fishermen say: 'Of course fishermen get drunk. Anybody who does what we do has to drink to stay sane.'

Source: J. Tunstall, *The Fishermen* (McGibbon & Kee, 1962)

Mr Lane, for instance, manages his own factory. He goes to work every morning at eight and often doesn't leave for home until ten or eleven at night. Mr Milner was a similar sort. An accountant in a large company he did not have such long hours in his office but almost every night and every weekend he brought papers back to work on in his study.

Some men like these work very long hours, spend a good deal of time travelling and do not necessarily share even their leisure with families much of it being spent with business colleagues.

Source: P. Willmot and M. Young, *Family and Class in a London Suburb* (Routledge & Kegan Paul, 1960)

1 Parker has suggested three relationships between work and leisure – oppositional, extension and neutrality. Classify each of the extracts.

2 Overall, do you think there would be any link between these types of relationships and social class?

3 How would you classify your own and your parents' pattern of leisure?

The importance of leisure in people's lives

A higher proportion of people in Britain place less value on work than any other country in Western Europe, according to a survey released yesterday.

The survey, based on interviews conducted by the European Value Systems Study Group, found that 12 per cent of the British consider work of little importance, compared to an average of 4.5 per cent for Europe as a whole.

Britons also believe, along with people in Scandinavia, the Netherlands and Germany, that leisure is more important than work.

1 How important is leisure in people's lives, according to the survey?

2 How important is it in your own life?

Source: *The Independent*, 13 July 1991

Age group

As we pass through certain ages of life then our tastes, income and abilities alter:

- Childhood is usually spent in play, but with very limited income.
- In youth, people have a considerable amount of uncommitted money (no household bills to pay), which can be spent on the pursuit of style and excitement.
- Young marrieds use money to purchase/renovate houses and to spend on young children. Leisure is family based.
- In middle age children leave home and both partners often work, so this is the most affluent period of life. Luxury items and holidays are purchased.
- Over 65, income and physical abilities decline. Home-based activities such as reading, watching television, going for walks are favoured.

Consuming leisure

A

For people in advanced capitalist economies work not just to survive, but to live in particular ways and to display the evidence of their success and status.

B

...the 1980s saw changes in the market which pushed particular leisure activities more and more into a privatised sphere within the home itself. Colour television was available to 73% of homes in 1980; only 16% of households then had two or more television sets; and only 2% had video recorders. In 1989/90 'colour TV penetration' was up to 89%, 61% of households had two or more TV sets, and the figure for video recorders was up to 58%. This is some way beyond the Centre's assertion three years or so previously that the video market would reach saturation point at around the 40% mark.

Analysts throughout the last few decades have recognised that the home has been the dominant site for the use of leisure time. Eighty per cent of all leisure time is spent in or near the home, and a survey on the nature of home-based leisure – focusing on 523 households in Nottingham in the mid-1980s – reported that 86% of all 'leisure events' took place in the home. As Sue Glyptis put it, 'The home dominated the lifestyles of all social groups, and especially women, single parents, people of retirement and pre-retirement age, the professional class and the unemployed.

Young people and employed working-class adult males are revealingly absent from this list, no doubt still seeking traditional forms of excitement and escape in the public spaces of the youth market and long-established male preserves such as the pub, the club and the sports field.

Source (A and B): A. Tomlinson, 'Buying time: Consumption and leisure' in *Social Studies Review*, January 1991

C

Participation in home-based leisure activities, Great Britain, 1990

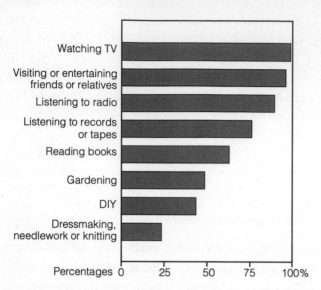

Percentages: Watching TV (~100%), Visiting or entertaining friends or relatives (~95%), Listening to radio (~90%), Listening to records or tapes (~75%), Reading books (~63%), Gardening (~48%), DIY (~43%), Dressmaking, needlework or knitting (~23%)

Percentages 0   25   50   75   100%

Source: *Social Trends 24* (HMSO, 1994) and General Household Survey

Look at extract **A** (on page 229).

1 Explain what the extract means, in your own words.

2 Would you agree with this statement?

3 Give three examples to prove your point.

Look at extract **B** and the chart **C**.

4 Increasingly, leisure has been spoken about in terms of 'consumption', that is something you need to buy. What does extract **B** tell us about this idea?

5 Where does most leisure take place, for older people?

6 Where do younger people engage in leisure?

7 Explain why, according to the extract and adding your own views.

8 In your household, keep a log of household leisure activities for members of the family. What are your results?

Sex group

As the culture of our society stresses different expectations of males and females, this influences their choices of leisure. Males are far more active than females in virtually every area, particularly sport, which is regarded as more appropriate to males. Females are more likely to go dancing, engage in keep-fit and yoga. Most importantly, women have less leisure time than men as they are expected to the bulk of the housework, even if they have a full-time job.

Women's leisure

The Henley Centre for Forecasting has estimated that in general men in this country have more leisure time available to them than women, after taking into account time devoted to paid and unpaid work, travel and essential activities like washing and eating. The least leisure time available is found amongst employed women, followed by employed men. Unemployed and retired women have less leisure time than their male counterparts. ...It is not just leisure time and quality which is differentiated by gender but also patterns of leisure. Whilst men's leisure is often out of the home and may revolve around sport (more often spectating rather than playing) and informal group activities like going for a drink, women tend to spend more leisure time at home (sometimes through necessity rather than choice), whether alone or with friends and are, once out of their teens, seldom involved in sport. ...

Women's at-home leisure often consists of things which, like TV, listening to the radio, baking, gardening and sewing, are inexpensive, can be done in short, often unpredicted and interrupted time-spells or are easily combined with household work. Significantly, they also typically do not require a special place or facilities; indeed, the only place in most homes which is seen as women's special preserve is often the kitchen, which unlike a garden shed, study or child's bedroom, is heavily used by other members of the household too and is primarily a work place rather than a leisure location.

Source: R. Deem, 'Women and leisure – All work and no play?' in *Social Studies Review*, March 1990

1 Rank the groups mentioned in order of leisure time. (Note that in a different survey, the group with the least leisure of all were women who were engaged in full-time domestic labour or 'housework'. Add this to your ranking.)

2 What sorts of leisure do men engage in?

3 What sorts of leisure do women engage in?

4 Can you suggest reasons for these differences?

Leisure: The future

In the future, the numbers of workers and the hours they will be required to work will fall as increased automation occurs. Sociologists have realised that this will make a significant impact on the role of leisure in society.

The optimists see the increase in leisure as giving us a chance to become more fulfilled. Increased time can be spent on the arts and on educating ourselves. The social class divisions caused by occupational and income differences will disappear as fewer and fewer people work.

The pessimists disagree. Where, they ask, will all the money come from for these leisure pursuits? In our society, people either receive a salary with which they can purchase leisure, or they live on state benefits which are not enough to purchase leisure. Leisure is usually provided by large profit-making companies. Unemployment will lead to boredom for the majority.

The leisure society – for the affluent

Our leisure activities have become more varied, our holidays more frequent and our tastes more diverse. In 1993, 23 million holidays abroad were taken by British residents – more than three times as many as in 1971. We are far more likely to go to the cinema, the opera, the theatre, to listen to classical music, and to visit museums, galleries and historic monuments. The home is also the venue for increasingly varied forms of leisure: from exercising to computer games.

The extract says that leisure has increased. How many of the activities mentioned are free?

Source: 'A nation both rich and more insecure' by R. Tyrrell and T. Rubenstein in *The Independent*, 26 January 1995

The changing patterns of leisure

In Victorian England leisure habits were sharply class-divided. Professional men and their families took no part in the street culture of working-class areas. There are still some socially exclusive pastimes. Hopeful show-jumpers need rich fathers. But the most popular leisure activities, such as watching television and taking holidays away from home, are now classless.

Paid vacations were still a middle-class perk in many firms throughout the inter-war years. Since then middle-class holiday entitlement has grown slowly, if at all, while manual workers have almost closed the gap. (On average today senior managers and the self-employed work longer than men on the shop-floor.) There is no longer any sense in which our economic and political elites can be labelled a 'leisure class'.

This trend towards a leisure democracy has been strengthened as class differences in leisure tastes and habits have grown smaller. The middle classes still do more, but usually more of the same things that occupy working-class leisure. Class divisions in styles of holiday-making have collapsed. The main divisions now follow age, rather than class divisions. Discos cut across class barriers and it is the public in general, rather than high society, that dictates trends in fashion.

Source: Adapted from K. Roberts, *Youth and Leisure* (Allen & Unwin, 1983)

1 Why do you think that leisure patterns were so sharply divided along class lines in Victorian England?

2 Is leisure now divided along class lines?

3 What do you think the author means when he talks about the 'leisure class'?

4 What divisions are now stronger than class? Do you agree?

The influence of work on our lives

The impact of work on our lives does not end at the office or factory door; it spills over into many aspects of our lives. In very broad ways, our occupation determines our social status and our income. Differences in income cause different standards of living, and differences in social status influence the way people treat us. In narrower ways, too, our occupation influences our daily lives. The number of hours we work determines how much time we spend with our family, or in leisure. The demands of our job influence our personality and leisure activities.

Occupations do not only influence us as individuals, but whole communities too can be affected. A good example is the way in which traditional mining communities were pulled together by the close bonds of the miners' working relationship.

The influence of work on wider social relationships

Friendships

Maureen Cain studied the lives of policemen. She found that policemen's time outside their work is strongly influenced by the demands of their job. Policemen develop a sense of identity and inter-dependence because they need to trust one another in their work, both from physical attack and from allegations against them. Policemen are also isolated by the public who are wary about coming into contact with them. Finally, the unsocial hours caused by shiftwork adds to their difficulties meeting people from outside the police force. The result is that policemen tend to have their friends from within the force and are isolated from wider contacts.

The community

Perhaps the most striking feature of the traditional East End economy is its diversity: dockland, the many distributive and service trades linked to it, the craft industries, notably tailoring and furniture making, the markets. This diversity meant that people lived and worked in the East End – there was no need for them to go outside in search of jobs. The extended family remains intrinsic to the recruitment of the labour force and even to the work process itself. Son followed father into the same trade or industry while many of the craft and service trades were organised into family concerns. As a result of this, the situation of the work place its issues and interests remained tied to the situation outside work – the issues and interests of the community.

Source (both extracts): P. Cohen, 'Subcultural Conflict and Working Class Community' (Centre for Contemporary Culture, University of Birmingham, 1972)

1 Why was there no need for the people of the East End to leave their community?

2 What result would this have for community life, do you think?

3 Were there any consequences for the family?

4 Today, the docks and the industries have closed in East London. Do you think this has had any effect upon the community, apart from increasing employment?

5 Having read the extract on the influence of work on policemen's lives, could you make any comments on the social lives of firemen and members of the armed forces?

6 Copy out the diagram opposite so that it is large enough to write on. Complete the boxes to show the relationship between work and leisure, work and community, work and family life, work and income.

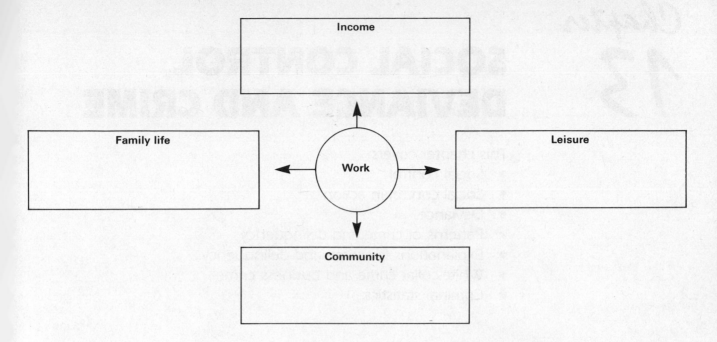

Criticism: The influence of leisure on work

Not all sociologists put all the stress on work influencing leisure: a study of Luton car workers suggests that people may choose dull and boring work in order to have a good lifestyle. In other words, the workers in the study chose boring, but better paid, work in preference to more interesting work to be able to afford to have a high standard of living.

Chapter 13

SOCIAL CONTROL, DEVIANCE AND CRIME

This chapter covers:
- Social control
- Social control in action
- Deviance
- Patterns of crime and delinquency
- Explanations for crime and delinquency
- White-collar crime and business crime
- Criminal statistics.

Introduction

In this chapter we examine the way in which the society controls people and ensures that order is maintained. We start by examining the concept of social control and how all of us are engaged in ensuring that our family, friends and colleagues conform to what we think they should do, while they meanwhile are busy ensuring that we act like everyone else.

We then move on to look at the more formal mechanisms for keeping people in line. This leads us to a discussion of the nature of deviance, who deviants are, and how their behaviour comes to be labelled as odd, bizarre or dangerous. We then examine the criminal justice system in some detail. In particular, we look at which crimes are committed, by whom and the explanations for their criminality.

We move on to look rather sceptically at the official statistics and note that they may not give us an accurate picture of the enormous amount of law-breaking that really exists. Finally, we look at the techniques which sociologists use to uncover the real extent of crime.

Social control

When we speak and write in English, we are aware that it has a grammar (a set of rules), even if we are not sure how to explain it. We work within these rules, maybe using different words in different combinations, but always working within a framework of grammar that we have learned since childhood. We make mistakes; we have different dialects in different parts of the country and amongst different social classes. In the end, however, we know that there is a clear distinction between English and French or Italian, and you do not need to be an academic to know it.

Society too has its own 'grammar', or 'culture', which guides us in our actions, even though we may not be too aware of it. No one disputes that, in language, grammar is a good thing, but the situation is different when it comes to social rules. Sociologists are divided in their opinions of who exactly benefits from the rules and values of society. Some sociologists argue that we all benefit from having a common set of values, as life is predictable. Others disagree, claiming that the rules guiding our behaviour are to the benefit of those who are more powerful and wealthy, because they persuade us to act in the ways that they want us to. **Social control** is the process whereby people are encouraged to conform to the common expectations of society.

Types of social control

There are two types of social control: **informal control** and **formal control**.

Informal control

This form of control is based on the approval or disapproval of those around us whose review of us we regard as important, for instance family, friends and peer group (a group of people usually of similar age with whom we compare our behaviour, our classmates at school, or colleagues at work, for example). If they disapprove of our behaviour we usually alter it to conform to their expectations.

How is it enforced?

People around us may tell us they do not like our behaviour, they may ridicule us, they may argue with us, they may play practical jokes on us, or they may even 'send us to Coventry'.

Informal social control is part of the 'socialisation process' by which we become a truly 'human' being, by learning the expected patterns of behaviour in society.

Formal control

Whenever we are given rules to follow, as in school or the laws which are the legal system of society, this is formal control. These rules are almost always written down.

How is it enforced?

Usually, formal control is enforced through official 'sanctions', such as a fine for speeding, or imprisonment for robbery.

Social control – every society needs ways of gently persuading people to obey rules

Social control in action

We have seen that social control operates in two ways, formally and informally. In society there are a number of 'institutions', or 'agencies', which impose social control upon us. The most important are the family, the school, the peer group, the mass media, the workplace, the legal system and, to a much lesser extent, religion.

The family

The basic socialisation takes place in the family and it is here through parents and relatives that we learn the accepted morality of society, to distinguish between 'right' and 'wrong'. Delinquency has been linked to the failure of parents to socialise their children correctly. Not only do we learn what is right and wrong in general, we also learn the expected behaviour for males and females (gender roles).

The school

The process of socialisation continues, formally in the content of the lessons we are taught and informally in the expectations of us by the teachers and fellow pupils. (See pages 181 and 190 for a discussion on 'the hidden curriculum.') Pupils are divided into the successes and the failures, and they develop appropriate attitudes to cope with these situations (see page 186).

The peer group

People of our own age to whom we look for approval are crucial in forming our attitudes to society. The peer groups develop in school and studies have shown how pupils divide themselves into those who accept the school rules and those who do not. The groups appear to develop from the different streams as a result of teachers' differing attitudes and expectations of high- and low-stream pupils.

The mass media

The term 'mass media' includes such things as newspapers, radio and television. These influence us by providing models of behaviour which we copy and by condemning other deviant forms of behaviour. Although they do not affect us directly, in the sense that seeing something on television does not immediately make us want to copy it, they do create a certain climate of opinion regarding acceptable behaviour. As the media are part of the 'establishment', they tend to reflect conservative views.

The workplace

At work, conformity is ensured by the fact that if we are troublemakers, or a bit 'weird', then we may not be promoted, or in some certain circumstances even sacked. Amongst our work colleages, if we fail to conform to their values, then they use such things as practical jokes at our expense to show us we ought to change our behaviour (see pages 208, 209–10).

The legal system

The most powerful institution dealing with social control is the legal system, by which we mean the police and the courts. People breaking the law are arrested and judged. Usually the law is reserved for what many people regard as the most serious breaches of our values.

Religion

Historically, the Church was one of the major forms of social control. Each week people used to attend church and through the sermon were advised on the way to behave. In contemporary society the influence of Christian religion has waned for the majority of the British population, although for other religious groups, such as Muslims, religious teachings have retained their importance.

A free society?

Social control is so much part of our experience of daily life that we often overlook it. Yet, all of us are constantly experiencing control by others, and helping to control others as well. Furthermore, there is a massive 'industry' of people whose job it is to control others. Although we immediately think of police officers, in fact there is a much wider range of people, keeping us 'in line'.

...social control, that is the organised ways in which society responds to behaviour and people it regards as deviant, problematic, worrying, threatening, troublesome or undesirable in some way or another. This response appears under many terms: punishment, deterrence, treatment, prevention, segregation, justice, rehabilitation, reform or social defence. It is accompanied by many ideas and emotions: hatred, revenge, retaliation, disgust, compassion, salvation, benevolence or admiration. This behaviour in question is classified under many headings: crime, delinquency, deviance, immorality, perversity, wickedness, deficiency or sickness. The people to whom the response is directed are seen variously as monsters, fools, villains, sufferers, rebels or victims.

Source: S. Cohen, *Visions of Social Control* (Polity Press, 1985)

1 Is the writer referring to formal or informal control in this extract?

2 Cohen says that behaviour is classified under many headings. For each of these types of behaviour there are 'professionals' employed by society to provide a form of social control.
Suggest one or more professionals that work with people accused of this form of behaviour. (For example, we have police officers, amongst others who attempt to control crime).

3 Cohen also mentions various 'responses' such as punishment. Try to link these with the professions.

4 The final sentence lists the people who are the objects of social control 'as monsters, fools, villains, sufferers, rebels or victims'.

Give an example of people who you regard as falling into each of these categories. What would you suggest ought to be done to them to control them?

5 Give four examples of behaviour that you encounter in your daily life (at college, at home, in places of entertainment, etc.) that you regard as 'deviant, problematic, worrying, threatening, troublesome, or undesirable'.

6 How do you control this behaviour? If you do not control it, then what do you do?

7 Do you find that your daily life is constrained by others who control you? Give at least three examples. How do you feel about this?

Deviance

Social control exists to prevent 'deviance', that is behaviour which is considered to be threatening or disruptive of order in society. Deviant behaviour encompasses an enormous range of actions which appear to have little in common. It can include, for example, crime, mental illness, unusual sexual activities, strange religious rites, and strange ways of dressing. What they all share is the fact that they challenge normal behaviour.

Deviance: In the eyes of the beholder

Most behaviour is not deviant in itself, it is how people define and respond to the behaviour which makes it deviant. It is rather likely beauty, in that it exists in the eye of the beholder! What is considered deviant in one situation is not in another. Take, for example, a man with a large amount of make-up on, who is dressed in strange clothes, and keeps pretending to throw water over people who look at him. Strange behaviour perhaps in the streets of Manchester, but quite amusing in a circus tent!

Sociologists have spent a great deal of time trying to explain the circumstances in which certain acts are tolerated and others are regarded as deviant, or even criminal. The following factors have been suggested as being very important:

- **Place** Lovemaking, for instance, is regarded as deviant if it takes place in public, but 'normal' in private

- **Society or culture** Curing illnesses through traditional medicine or even 'magic' is considered odd in Britain, yet perfectly acceptable in many African and Asian societies.

- **Time** Only 20 years ago if a woman went to a pub on her own she was considered to be out of her place, yet today it is commonplace.

- **Who commits the act** It is considered wrong for children to be out late in the evening, yet normal for adults.

- **Power** The more powerful a group are in society, then the less likely it is for their activities to be seen as deviant. Gangs of working-class youths chasing stray cats or dogs across towns in order to beat them to death would cause an outcry. Fox-hunting is defended as a British tradition and a cruelty-free way of limiting the number of pests.

- **Accepted values** The further away from accepted values an act is, the greater the chance of it being labelled as deviant, even if it may do no harm.

The relationship between crime and deviance

Most forms of deviant behaviour are merely disapproved of and dealt with by informal means of social control. However, in certain circumstances deviant behaviour can become illegal.

The most obvious example of this is where an action is most strongly disapproved of by the majority of the population, it is made illegal. Therefore murder or rape are against the law, and there are severe forms of punishment.

Secondly, a group of people may have particularly strong views on certain forms of behaviour, and may form a **pressure group** (see page 267), especially to have laws passed making these acts illegal. Of course, pressure groups are also formed to change the law to make some criminal acts legal! Pressure groups use many different means to persuade governments to make acts illegal, including street demonstrations, advertising and trying to enlist the help of individual MPs. Sociologists call these attempts to change the law **moral crusades**.

Thirdly, very powerful groups in society will use their influence to have the laws altered to their benefit.

Radical sociologists argue that the laws in Britain seem to be designed to protect the property of the rich from the poorer sections of society. They also argue that laws are enforced differently. In Britain, it is the least powerful groups in society, such as the working, the young, the homeless and the poor who seem to be the target of police activity. On the other hand, enforcement of the law against illegal stock exchange trading is almost completely absent.

Labelling and criminal careers

Labelling

Howard Becker, for example, believes that there is no such thing as a deviant act – it is merely behaviour that people so label. ...

The essence of labelling theory is, therefore, not so much what the individual does, but the reaction of others. Often the same act of deviance is treated differently – a car theft by a middle-class youth is played down as high spirits, while a working-class youth, especially if black, might be likely to go to Borstal. ...

Certain *master* labels, such as being declared homosexual, criminal or lunatic, tend to override all others, and, once applied, are very difficult to live down. An ex-prisoner, though he has served his sentence will find it difficult to get a job and settle back into normal life. Employers, families and friends often no longer trust him and fear being tarred with the same brush. Stigmatised and rejected by society, many such people turn back to crime, thus fulfilling suspicions about there being the criminal type – a 'born villain' – a sort of 'self-fulfilling prophecy'.

In this sense, the labellists are saying the cause of deviancy is often not the action itself, but the reaction of others to it. It is possible, they say, that social control, far from preventing crime, can help cause it.

But critics argue that it fails to explain people's actions before they are labelled. Why do some people commit crime while others do not? Marxists add the criticism that this theory fails to explain who has the *power* to label and why. In their view the power to label is an important part of the bourgeoisie's control. By labelling those who threaten its power and privilege as deviants, it can neutralise them. So left wingers are labelled 'militants', or 'loonies'.

Source: Adapted from M. Slattery, *The ABC of Sociology* (Macmillan, 1985)

The story of Student Anne

Steals lots of textbooks and takes loads of drugs

Has lots of fun

Gets good results

And is now a famous lecturer in Sociology – lucky Lecturer Anne

The story of Student Brenda

Had just one puff, stole just one book

Sent to prison

Never got a degree, and no one wants to give an untrustworthy drug-taking thief a job

Now cleans Lecturer Anne's house – unlucky cleaner Brenda!

1 Using the two stories on page 239, explain the meaning of the term 'labelling'.

2 According to Becker, is there such a thing as 'a deviant act'?

3 Can the same act be treated as deviant by one person and not deviant by another? Explain your answer.

4 What is a 'master label'?

5 What is a deviant career?

6 Give two criticisms of the labelling theory.

7 Can you make up a deviant career of your own to illustrate the idea of labelling?

Scapegoating and moral panic

In the mid-1960s, Stan Cohen studied the way in which the image of mods and rockers (in both the senses, of style of dress and of forms of behaviour) was created in the media as a result of some minor disturbances in Brighton and Clacton. This influenced how young people saw themselves and it encouraged them to behave in the (false) way portrayed by the media. The police and the politicians were equally alarmed by the media coverage. They insisted on very strict action against all young people who fitted the stereotype of being a mod or a rocker. The end result was a series of disturbances and large-scale arrests. There was a public outcry against the mods and for a while they were seen as a dreadful threat to law and order in Britain.

Cohen explained this 'moral panic' by saying that whenever the tensions of society start to become too great, then certain groups, usually powerless and young, are used as scapegoats on which many of society's problems are blamed. The effect of the scapegoating is to draw the bulk of people in society together in response to the supposedly dreadful behaviour of the scapegoated groups. Clearly this approach is closely linked to labelling.

Since Cohen's original study of mods and rockers (in *Folk Devils and Moral Panics*), there have been moral panics over single mothers, joy-riding, travellers, drugs in schools, and begging in city centres.

1 Who created the images of mods and rockers?

2 How did the youth of that period respond to the 'labelling'?

3 How did the police respond?

4 What did Cohen call this?

5 What do sociologists mean when they use the term 'scapegoats'?

6 Why do moral panics occur?

7 Can you give an example of a moral panic not mentioned in the extract?

8 Turn to page 318 for a 'map' of a moral panic. Using this, devise some typical newspaper headlines for an imaginary moral panic. What responses will there be from:
a) the public?
b) the police?
c) the politicians?
d) the labelled groups?

Patterns of crime and delinquency

- **Delinquency:** acts of crime by those under 17; dealt with by special courts, known as Juvenile Courts

Offences and offenders

A
Notifiable offences recorded by the police, by type of offence (England and Wales)

Type of offence	No. of offences (thousands)		
	1981	1991	1992
Violence against the person	100.2	190.3	201.8
Sexual offences	19.4	29.4	29.5
of which: rape	1.1	4.0	4.1
Burglary	718.4	1219.5	1355.3
Robbery	20.3	45.3	52.9
Drug trafficking	..	11.4	13.8
Theft and handling stolen goods	1603.2	2761.1	2851.6
of which: theft of vehicles	332.6	581.9	585.5
theft from vehicles	379.6	913.3	961.3
Fraud and forgery	106.7	174.7	168.6
Criminal damage	386.7	821.1	892.6
Other notifiable offences	8.9	23.2	25.6
Total notifiable offences	**2963.8**	**5276.2**	**5591.7**

B
Notifiable offences recorded by the police, by type of offence, 1992 (England, Wales and Northern Ireland)

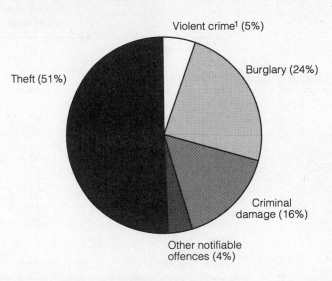

1 Violence against the person, sexual offences and robbery.

C
Known offenders[1] as a percentage of the population, by age and sex, 1992 (England and Wales)

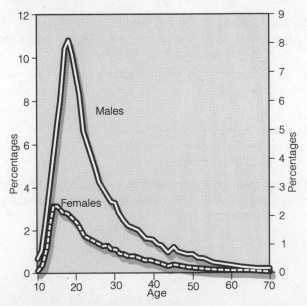

1 Persons found guilty or cautioned for indictable offences.

Source: All figures from *Social Trends 24* (HMSO, 1994) and the Home Office

Look at **A**.

1 What are the two most common offences? How many of each were committed?

2 Overall, what comment can you make on the change in the number of offences between 1981 and 1992?

Look at **A** and **B**.

3 Many people would argue that the worst types of crime are violent or sexually-motivated. Looking at **A** and **B**, to what extent have these crimes changed compared to the general pattern? (Is it higher/ average/lower?) Do the statistics suggest that they form a large proportion of all crimes? So, when people say that 'Britain is a violent society today', what comments could you make, based on these statistics?

Look at **C**.

4 According to the official statistics, is it males or females who commit most crime?

5 Between what ages are:
a) females most likely to commit crime?
b) males most likely to commit crime?

6 Is the peak age of crime committal the same for males and females?

7 If, therefore, you had to make one statement to describe a 'typical' criminal, what would it be?

Victims of crime

A

Predictors of fear (British Crime Survey, 1992)

	% feeling unsafe out at night	% feeling unsafe at home	% v. worried about burglary
All BCS respondents	32	11	19
Gender:			
Women	49	17	22
Men	14	4	15
Age:			
16–59	29	10	19
60+	42	12	18
Household income:			
Less than £10,000	43	15	24
More than £10,000	26	8	15
Ethnic group:			
White	32	11	18
Afro-Caribbeans	29	15	35
Asians	38	18	37
Area:			
Inner city	43	15	27
Non-inner city	30	10	17

Source: *Research Findings No. 8* (HMSO, 1994)

B

Burglary rate, by age of head of household, 1991 (Great Britain)

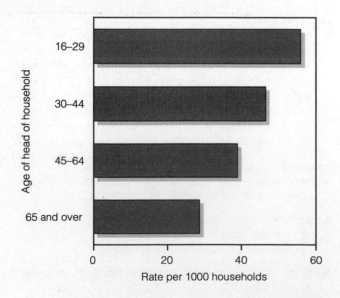

Source: *Social Trends 24* (HMSO, 1994) and General Household Survey

Look at **A**.

1 Describe the characteristics of those who feel most unsafe to go out at night.

2 Which group of income earners are more afraid of burglaries? Does this surprise you? Explain why they might be more afraid than the other group.

3 Which ethnic group is most afraid to go out at night? Why should this be, do you think?

Look at **B**.

4 Which age group of people are:
a) most likely to be burgled?
b) least likely to be burgled?

5 Does this agree with table **A** on individuals' fear of burglary? Can you offer any possible explanations, for this contradiction?

Explanations for crime and delinquency

Four key elements emerge from looking at the official statistics on crime. These are that criminality and delinquency are related to:

- **age** – The period in a person's life when they are most likely to commit a criminal offence is 14–20.
- **gender** – There is a marked difference between the crime rates of males and females, with the male rate being about five times higher than the female rate.
- **class** – Crime and delinquency are directly related to social class, with working-class youth, for instance, having a crime rate eight times higher than upper middle-class youth.
- **place** – Crime rates are significantly higher in inner cities than in the suburbs or the country areas.

Age

...The Centre (Henley Centre for Forecasting) estimates that the cost of households and businesses of burglaries, car thefts and arson committed by 18–21-year-olds will be around £3.8 billion in 1998...

Source: *The Guardian*, 31 May 1994

Youth is a period when there is a great stress on excitement and 'having a laugh'. This search for a 'good time' can often lead to clashes with the law. It is also true to say that youth is a period when social control is weak. It has been suggested that the weakness of social control, coupled with the search for excitement, can lead to a drift into delinquency. People move away from delinquency as they get older because of the stability provided by marriage, family and employment. (Of course, this suggests that if rates of unemployment stay high for young people, then they may not move out of crime.)

Gender

The different expectations we have of boys and girls leave their mark on us as we grow up. Typically masculine values, such as toughness, can lead directly to fighting, for instance. On the other hand, feminine values stress conformity, domesticity and 'getting a boy' – hardly values that will lead to delinquency!

Well we girls commit less crime because we are gentle, soft and naturally better behaved than those horrible tough boys!..

... And of course we're not so stupid as to get caught!

Women and crime

The criminal statistics suggest that women are less likely to commit most crimes than men, for example women constitute only 12 per cent of all offenders and in the more serious crimes such as robbery, wounding and murder, women represent only 5 per cent of offenders. In the past, this has been explained by the physical differences between men and women. However, feminists dispute this. In *Women and Crime*, Frances Heidensohn argues that much of the explanation for the conformity of women is that they are far more constrained than men, particularly by the roles they are expected to play in society: 'It's hard to bring off a burglary if you're pushing a twin baby-buggy and its contents; caring for a demented elderly relative hardly gives a woman time to plan a bank robbery. In fact women are burdened with duties which act as a constraint. ...In public, appropriate behaviour for females is different than it is for men. For example males virtually have a monopoly over the use of force and violence in society. ...It is unacceptable for women to be violent, yet relatively normal for men to be so.'

There is evidence to suggest that police treat female criminals differently. They tend to think that females are 'naturally' more law abiding than males and therefore have been 'led astray' into crime. This is particularly true for female delinquency. Girls caught for delinquent acts are much more likely to be put in custody for 'care and protection' then male delinquents. Police are sometimes more lenient on females than males. For example, two girls fighting is less likely to result in arrest than two males fighting, as it is not regarded as so serious. Once again this is related to policemen's views on male and females as different.

1 What proportion of crimes are committed by women?

2 In the past, what explanations have been offered for the differences in crime levels between men and women?

3 Explain how the social role of women is supposed to explain the low proportion of crimes committed by women.

4 Given the importance of gender roles what sort of crimes do you think women are most likely to commit?

5 Why do police treat female offenders differently?

6 What results is this different treatment likely to have?

7 Do you think that the official statistics on crime could be affected by the attitudes of police towards female crime? If so, how?

8 In your experience, have you ever been in a situation in which males and females have been involved with the police? Describe the experience and compare it with the points made in the extract.

Women as victims of crime

If women do not figure highly as people who commit delinquent acts, they certainly figure as the main victims of crime. The main areas of sociological research have been in women as victims of sexual assault, and as victims of domestic violence.

Sexual assault

- *The place:* It is a commonly-held view that rape occurs in dark alleys and is committed by disturbed men who choose their victims at random to act out their fantasies. Yet the fact is that the majority of rapes are committed by someone known to the victim. Furthermore, about one-third of reported rapes occur in the victim's home, exactly the same percentage as occurs in the street.

- *The cause:* Traditionally it was believed that rape was the result of certain men's 'uncontrollable' sex drive and that rapists were 'monsters' who were very different from normal males. But increasingly it is argued that rape is another aspect of male domination in society and that rapists are little different from other men. Sexual assaults and rape are merely *extensions* of the normal sexually aggressive behaviour of men.

Rape as normal behaviour

In *Women, Crime and Criminology*, Carol Smart argues that rape is to some extent 'normal' in a society in which the women are expected to engage in sexual bargaining. According to her view, the very basis of marriage has traditionally been the exchange of regular sexual favours by women for the security of the relationship. Smart points out that the images of women portrayed in the media and the attitudes socialised into both sexes from an early age stress the importance of sexuality and attractiveness of females.

Furthermore, men are encouraged to seek sex, and women to put up an initial resistance before 'giving in'. Indeed, a woman who appears to encourage sex is regarded as 'loose' by many men. The men are, therefore, encouraged to be active (possibly even aggressive) and the women to appear reluctant.

The significance of Smart's argument is that rape is not some distinctive, deviant act which is opposed to the normal sexual relations in our society, rather it is an extension of normal sexual values and gender relationships.

Source: S. Moore, *Investigating Deviance* (Harper Collins, 1988)

1 According to the main text, what is the traditional explanation for rape?

2 Are rapists therefore 'normal'?

3 Explain in your own words how Smart explains rape.

4 Do you agree that this is an accurate descriptionof the relationship of males and females in our society?

Class

Most delinquents and criminals arrested by the police are drawn from the working class. There are various explanations for this.

Subculture of the working class

The values of the working class, such as toughness and immediate enjoyment, can easily lead working-class people into criminal activities.

Poor socialisation

This is most often found amongst the working class. Parents fail to bring up their children to uphold the values of society.

Anomie

If a society fails to provide enough ways for people to be successful, then they will feel frustrated and possibly turn to crime. This happens particularly in periods of high unemployment. The term 'anomie' refers to a situation where large numbers of people fail to follow generally accepted values, instead adopting various deviant forms of behaviour, such as theft or drugtaking.

Status frustration

Working-class youths are more likely to fail at school and be in bottom streams. They feel that everybody looks down upon them and so they express their frustration in delinquent behaviour, which helps them to 'get their own back' on society.

Criticism

One law for the rich and one for the poor: Marxist writers suggest the explanations given so far miss out the obvious and centrally important point that the wealthy and powerful pass the laws which benefit themselves, but harm the working class. If this is so, then it is bound to be the working class who commit most crime. For instance, the theft of money from a bank is quickly pursued by the police, but stock exchange swindles and tax avoidance are rarely punished or even investigated.

Place

Crime rates are higher in inner-city areas and some 'problem' housing estates, because the people concentrated in these areas are often poorer and have more social problems than the bulk of the population. Consequently, the explanations which we have just looked at regarding the working class are especially true here.

An alternative explanation put forward by many sociologists is that policing in inner-city areas, particularly in areas where there are many Blacks, is particularly strict. Indeed, it is suggested that Blacks are 'harassed' by the police. The result is higher arrest rates and greater social tension, which can lead to rioting in certain circumstances.

From street crime to serious crime

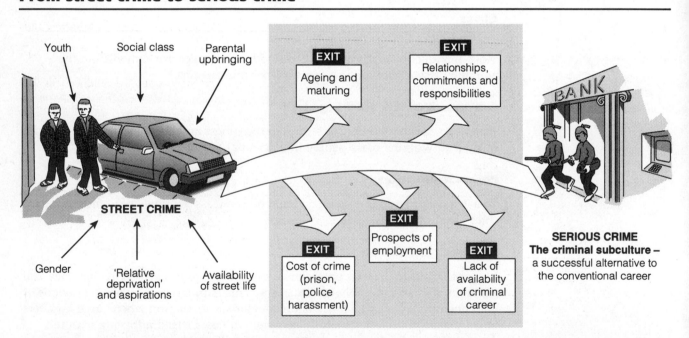

Chapeltown subculture

The lure of the frontline is made more attractive by the sight of older drug dealers pulling up in the Hayfield car park in their BMWs, decked out in gold bracelets and chains and with state-of-the-art mobile phones in their back pockets.

"There's no jobs around in Leeds and if you're from Chapeltown nobody will even give you a chance. They just think, 'Oh, the place is full of black muggers and drug dealers'. What other options have we got?" asks Luke. ...

"The police can't really explain the high crime, a sociologist would probably be able to give a better answer. There's unemployment, lack of benefits, lack of opportunity.

There are other factors that you have to recognise but the police don't have any control over them." ...

While the likes of Luke hit the streets every night, Ricky Barker is busy hitting the telephone as one of the workers of the Leeds Media Project. Located in a modern building on the edge of Chapeltown, it was set up last

July, and aims to give local youths experience of the media and music industry and put them in touch with people from the professions. Ricky, aged 23, grew up in Chapeltown and admits that some of his friends work the frontline. Smart and eloquent, he studied music technology at Manchester University before returning home to plough some of his newly acquired skills back into the community: "I can't blame the guys on the frontline, because there are very few options available if you come from Chapeltown. There's a lot of talented people out there but they are not getting the chances and we need to help ourselves." ...

The former affluence of the area can be seen in the handsome Victorian houses, neat parks and rows of trees and grass verges lining the streets. The wealthy residents began moving out during the 1950s, abandoning Chapeltown to the wave of immigrants from the Caribbean and Asia, who were joined by immigrants from eastern Europe and Vietnam. But once Yorkshire's mills and factories began closing down

deprivation set in and Chapeltown became just another blighted inner-city area left to rot during the free market anarchy of the 1980s. ...

"Hash, you want good hash? Want some weed?" visitors are asked by the groups of young men huddled around their cars or lurking in the Hayfield's elegant doorways. Others plant themselves on the wall, mobile phones in hand, busy arranging another deal or waiting for the drive-bys, people pulling up in cars and looking to score and cruise out of the area as quickly as possible. ...

By late afternoon Luke, aged 15, and a dozen friends have gathered, chatting in huddled groups, smoking joints and planning the evening's work. The bookmakers and post office provide fruitful pickings for the

mob – one of several that patrol the frontline looking for fresh victims or re-acquainting themselves with old ones.

Like most of his friends Luke has not attended school for 18 months. He admits that favourite victims are elderly Asian women or white men in suits. Dressed in expensive Nike trainers, hooded top, baggy jeans and with intricate patterns carved on his cropped head. Luke says he works the frontline because "it's better than school and you get more money than working."

He shows me the tools of his trade – a chair leg or lump of wood, which can easily be ditched on to the street or in a garden if the police approach, and can be explained away as everyday inner-city rubbish.

Find a safe viewing area

overlooking the frontline as night sets in and you can see urban warriors like Luke, faces covered with bandanas, looking for fresh scalps. Luke will not say if he was part of the pack I saw on Saturday evening lurking by a bus stop on Chapeltown Road, kicking their heels and surveying passers-by. And he won't say if he was part of the same pack that followed an elderly man who got off the bus carrying three bags of shopping, who saw the hungry mob and instinctively started running. He didn't get far, soon he fell under a hail of punches and kicks, his shopping scattered, his jacket ripped, wallet and watch snatched from him: another sad chapter in Chapeltown's recent troubled history.

Source: *The Guardian*, 1 November 1994

1 The description of a subculture 'in action' gives a vivid account of life on the streets and how this may eventually lead to permanent criminal lifestyle. From the extract, find as many points as you can to illustrate the diagram.

2 Do you have any sympathy for Luke?

3 If you were asked to propose a solution for the problems described here, what would you suggest?

Why do people commit crime? Non-sociological explanations

Psychologists have suggested there are particular types of people who are more prone to be anti-social. Some have gone so far as to argue that certain people are actually born with anti-social tendencies. Hans Eysenck, a famous psychologist, argues there are basically two personality types, the result of socialisation in childhood and natural instincts. These are the introvert and extrovert. The introvert is quiet and reserved, he 'keeps his feelings under control, seldom behaves in an aggressive manner and does not lose his temper easily'. The extrovert is fun-loving and outward-going, but 'tends to be aggressive and loses his temper quickly; his feelings are not kept under tight control, and he is not always a reliable person'.

According to Eysenck, the extrovert person is more likely to turn to crime, unless his/her parents train him to control his impulses and instil a strong conscience in him.

Bowlby, another well-known psychologist, has suggested that people who are deprived of motherly affection in their infancy later are likely to become criminal.

Sociologists are doubtful that this is the full explanation for crime. They suggest instead that cultural factors are important in two ways, firstly in helping to decide which acts are illegal, and secondly in motivating a person to commit crime. They point to such factors as feelings of frustration at being unsuccessful at school [status frustration], or being unable to

purchase all the consumer goods advertised in the media when they have a low-paid job or are unemployed [anomie], or the values of neighbourhoods where crime is regarded as an acceptable way of life [subculture].

They question who makes laws for whose benefit. Whereas some sociologists suggest the law is the reflection of the values of the majority of the population, others argue that law is the reflection of the will of the more powerful in society. In either case, law is not something natural that people can be born to break. It is a social creation and varies from society to society.

1 Give two explanations psychologists have suggested for people committing crime.

2 Is it true or false to say that some psychologists believe that certain people are born with anti-social tendencies (and are, therefore, likely to become criminal)?

3 Do sociologists agree with these explanations?

4 Explain the meaning of the following sociological terms: status frustration, anomie, subculture. (You may find it helpful to turn to the main text.)

5 'Law is a social creation.' Why is this important in understanding why people cannot be 'born rule breakers'?

White-collar and business crime

When we talk about crime, most people think of things such as burglary or theft of a motor car. However, there are other types of more subtle crime which probably cost more to society than the value of all the burglaries and bank robberies put together. This hidden crime consists of two types of overlapping crime:

- white-collar – where the employee uses his or her position in a company to steal
- business crime – the routine abuse of the law by companies in order to make greater profits.

It was estimated in the late 1980s that the total cost of fraud amounted to about £2500 *million* pounds each year. One fraud perpetrated by the bank BCCI may have amounted to about £15 billion in total, while it is estimated that fraud involving agricultural subsidies in the EU costs about £100 million each year.

White-collar crime

This usually consists of such things as:

- Fiddling – This is routine in most organisations, and usually consists of such things as claiming false expenses, or claiming things are broken or lost when they have been sold privately.
- Small-scale theft – Again this is most common. For most shopping chains, more is stolen by staff than by shoplifters. This is known as 'shrinkage' and can add up to 10 per cent to the cost of articles to the shopper.

Computer crime

This is increasing as more financial transactions are conducted via computers. Because of the complexity involved in tracking this down, no estimate is possible of the extent of computer crime.

Tax fraud

This is common for self-employed people, but is not even regarded as particularly bad by the majority of the population. An entire industry of financial advisers help to guide the better-off to pay the minimum amount of taxation possible.

Corporate crime

The consumer as victum

This may consist of direct crimes or 'borderline' practices against consumers, such as the adulteration of foodstuffs.

The employee as victim

This may be the routine ignoring of health and safety regulations. Each year in Britain over 500 people die from work-related accidents, and it is estimated that two-thirds of these are the result of failure to adhere to the Health and Safety regulations by businesses.

Society

Deliberate discharges of dangerous material and general pollution make all members of society victims.

White-collar crime

Security guard shot in raid on High Street bank! Old lady beaten and robbed of her life savings by two thugs!

These are the sorts of typical newspaper headline which help to create our images of crime. Yet few people realise that these *street crimes* actually cost the nation less, in terms of injury and loss of money, than those crimes which sociologists call *white-collar crimes*.

White-collar crime often involves swindling money from companies, or even from private individuals. Sometimes it is committed by a manager who fiddles the accounts in order to steal money for himself. In cases like this, when the employers find out, they will prefer to simply sack the offender and avoid publicity, which might harm the image of their company.

But this sort of white-collar crime, although important, is dwarfed by a far more serious version, which is the deliberate breaking of the law by companies or top directors in order to swell their profits. One of the major problems of studying this sort of crime in Britain is that it is rarely uncovered and even less rarely brought to court. After all, the directors of these companies may be very important people, with a considerable number of powerful contacts in the world of finance and politics.

But one more important point that needs to be made is that our very definition of crime is influenced by powerful groups in society. These groups can have certain behaviour branded as crime and enforced by the police, while other activities, which *you* would consider harmful to people, are not covered by criminal law – or even if they are, they are rarely enforced.

Take the example of cigarette smoking: virtually everyone (except the cigarette companies) accepts that smoking tobacco greatly increases the risk of a person contracting cancer. Yet cigarettes are still allowed to be sold. What about the difference in attitude of most people to tax avoidance and fiddling social security? If you are self-employed and can get away without paying taxes, then well done! If you are 'scrounging' off the DSS, then the full weight of the law falls on you.

One last example – health and safety laws at work are there to protect workers. Unfortunately for employers, the costs of conforming with the laws can be quite high. The result? Some employers prefer to ignore them. This is a trade unionist at a toy factory talking: 'When the inspector comes to the factory we always point out the dangerous wiring, defective machines, unsafe stacking of heavy boxes, and so on. He goes in to see the management and after 20 minutes is out again. It's always the same old story – if we wish to press ahead with complaints, the factory owners will shut the place down and move production to the Far East [where the parent company is located]. If we keep quiet, production will continue here. Well, what can you do when there are hundreds of jobs at stake? We always shut up.'

1 On reading this, one student remarked: 'Law and crime – it's all about power, isn't it?' Why do you think the student said this? Give two examples to illustrate your answer.

2 Cigarette smoking is given as one example of a group that is able to avoid having its activities labelled as criminal. What do you think about this? Is it a good example? Should the manufacture and sale of cigarettes be prohibited like other drugs? Give reason for your answer.

3 What reasons can you suggest for the fact that street crime is heavily under-reported to the police compared to white-collar crime?

Criminal statistics

All the discussion on crime and delinquency so far has made the assumption that the official statistics of crime accurately reflect the amount and type of crime committed and the people responsible. This may not be true. Sociologists studying the accuracy of official crime statistics have come to a surprising conclusion – only a small proportion of crimes are reported to the police. For example, less than a quarter of acts of vandalism are reported. The difference between official statistics of crime and what actually occurs is known as the 'dark figure'.

Three elements influence the official crime statistics: reporting of crime to the police, recording of crime, activities of the police.

The real crime rate

The diagram below shows the number of crimes which have taken place compared to the number of offences which have been reported to the police and then recorded by the police.

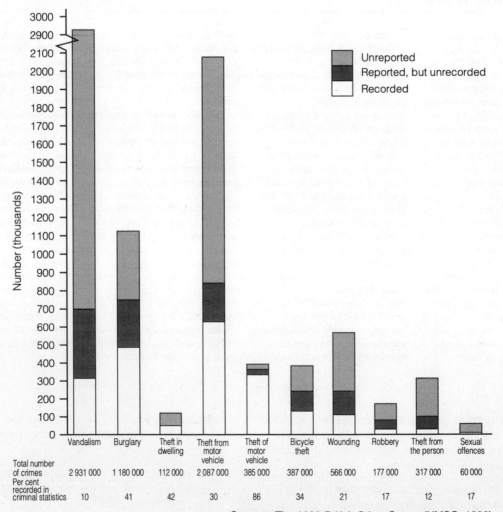

Levels of recorded and unrecorded crime, 1987

	Vandalism	Burglary	Theft in dwelling	Theft from motor vehicle	Theft of motor vehicle	Bicycle theft	Wounding	Robbery	Theft from the person	Sexual offences
Total number of crimes	2 931 000	1 180 000	112 000	2 087 000	385 000	387 000	566 000	177 000	317 000	60 000
Per cent recorded in criminal statistics	10	41	42	30	86	34	21	17	12	17

Source: *The 1988 British Crime Survey* (HMSO, 1990)

1 Explain what the diagram is intended to show?

2 According to the diagram, are the majority of crimes reported to the police?

3 Are all 'crimes' reported to the police actually recorded by them?

4 a) How many burglaries were there according to the diagram? Give appropriate figures.
   b) How many were reported to the police?
   c) How many were recorded by the police?

5 Which categories of crime are least likely to be reported to the police? Suggest reasons why this might be so.

6 What crime is most likely to be reported to the police? Suggest why this might be.

7 What is the most commonly occurring crime? How many acts are committed in total according to the diagram?

8 Are the answers to questions 6 and 7 the same? Could you give any reasons for your answer?

9 Look at the text below. Give four reasons, each with an example of your own, why people fail to report crimes to the police.

10 Even if a crime is reported, it may not be recorded by the police as an offence. Why should this happen?

11 Explain the meaning of the term 'moral panic', and give one example you know of (see page 318).

12 Explain how a moral panic might influence the official statistics on crime.

13 Can you think of a 'moral panic' that has happened recently?

Reporting of crime to the police

People often fail to report crimes because:

- they regard them as too trivial (a scratch along the side of a car)
- they do not believe the police can do anything (a wallet stolen in a busy market place)
- they regard it as a private matter (theft by a member of the family from another family member)
- they feel humiliated (rape).

But people do report crime when it is insured (car theft) and there is some evidence to suggest people make false claims in cases of burglary in order to claim larger amounts on the insurance.

Recording a crime

Police use their discretion in deciding whether an act is worth defining and recording as criminal. Sometimes they feel that they do not want to be involved, for instance, in a dispute between husband and wife. On other occasions, they regard the offence as too trivial, meriting only a warning to the person involved (riding a bicycle on the pavement).

As the law is changed, or the police interpretation of the law changes, an 'increase' or 'decrease' in a particular offence may take place. During the 1984–5 miners' strike, for instance, the police started to use the law on 'riot', unused for half a century.

Finally, the police forces in different parts of the country, record and enforce laws differently. The Metropolitan Police, for example, are reputed to be much laxer on prostitution than the Manchester police force. This leads to different levels of official statistics on prostitution.

Fiddling the crime figures

Crime experts say at least 220,000 crimes, including burglary, assault, theft and car crimes, vanished from official statistics last year as a result of police manipulation of the figures. ...

This weekend chief constables revealed a range of "Spanish practices" which allowed them to conceal the full extent of crime. These included cases where:

- Victims of violent attacks, previously classed as actual bodily harm, are having the crimes described by police as common assault, a civil offence which does not feature in official crime statistics.
- Attempted burglaries are logged as criminal damage to windows and doors and not put down as crimes.
- Thieves caught breaking into cars are being charged with tampering – which is not a recordable offence – rather than theft.
- A whole category of offences such as malicious telephone calls, assaults, deception and minor criminal damage are not classified as crimes because police say they are too trivial to record.

Home Office figures released last month reveal that only 57% of the nearly 10m reported crimes in England and Wales were recorded in official statistics. A spokesman said the government could not explain why the proportion of recorded crime was falling. Police chiefs and experts, however, said the practice is the inevitable result of recent Whitehall [government] pressure on police to improve crime statistics.

Source: *The Times*, 16 October 1994

1 What percentage of 'reported' crime is not being recorded by the police?

2 How many other 'crimes' are claimed to have 'vanished' from official statistics?

3 According to the article who does this?

4 Give three examples of how the official statistics are manipulated.

5 Why, do you think, does this occur?

6 What warning can we draw from this article about relying upon official statistics of crime?

Activities of the police

More police are used to patrol inner-city districts. This leads some to argue that they therefore discover more crime, simply by being there! Police officers work with certain assumptions about 'criminal types'. This leads them more often to stop working-class youths, for instance, and so this might account for the high proportion of these youths in the official statistics. Similarly, racist attitudes on the part of some police have led them to 'pick on' black youths.

A final point is that the police are often influenced by the media and may become 'sensitised' to certain types of crime (or suspect). This leads to a 'blitz', or 'moral panic' on these crimes or those suspected of committing them, and so the figures for this form of offence grow alarmingly. A famous example of this is the rapid increase in mugging which took place from the mid-1970s, as the police responded to a number of lurid newspaper articles.

How sociologists find out the real crime rate

The diagrams we looked at earlier, and the discussion we have just had on the reporting and recording of crime, all demonstrate that the 'real' crime rate is much higher than the official statistics. So sociologists need ways to uncover the true extent of crime. Two main techniques have been used: **self-report tests** and **victim surveys**.

Self-report tests

These are lists of criminal or deviant acts which are given to people and they are asked to tick off the activities which they have committed. It is always given anonymously so that people can feel free to admit to crimes. It is very helpful in that it avoids the embarrassment of an interview, so that people are more likely to admit to crimes, and it also allows researchers to measure the proportion of crimes committed by people who have never been arrested or charged by the police.

Victim surveys

These are usually large-scale surveys of the population in which people are interviewed and asked what crimes had been committed against them in the previous year. These are likely to be accurate for most crimes, because this form of survey 'cuts out' the problems associated with official statistics, such as the failure of people to report crime to the police and the failure of the police to record crime.

Although victim surveys are generally very accurate, it is often claimed that they under-estimate certain categories of crimes where the victim is embarrassed to tell the interviewer, such as sexual offences, or where the victim is not interviewed such as in cases of child abuse.

The most well-known examples of a victim survey is the British Crime Survey, a national survey undertaken every five years. The diagram on page 250, 'The real crime rate' is taken from the British Crime Survey.

How delinquent are you?

This is an example of a self-report test.

1 I have ridden a bicycle without lights after dark.
2 I have driven a car or motor bike/scooter under 16.
3 I have been with a group who go round together making a row and sometimes getting into fights and causing disturbance.
4 I have played truant from school.
5 I have travelled on a train or bus without a ticket or deliberately paid the wrong fare.
6 I have let off fireworks in the street.
7 I have taken money from home without returning it.
8 I have taken someone else's car or motor bike for a joy ride then taken it back afterwards.
9 I have broken or smashed things in public places like on the streets, cinemas, dance halls, trains or buses.
10 I have insulted people on the street or got them angry and fought with them.
11 I have broken into a big store or garage or warehouse.
12 I have broken into a little shop even though I may not have taken anything.
13 I have taken something out of a car.
14 I have taken a weapon (like a knife) out with me in case I needed it in a fight.
15 I have fought with someone in a public place like in the street or a dance.
16 I have broken the window of an empty house.
17 I have used a weapon in a fight, like a knife or a razor or a broken bottle.
18 I have drunk alcoholic drinks in a pub under 16.
19 I have been in a pub when I was under 16.
20 I have taken things from big stores or supermarkets when the shop was open.
21 I have taken things from little shops when the shop was open.
22 I have dropped things in the street like litter or broken bottles.
23 I have bought something cheap or accepted as a present something I knew was stolen.
24 I have planned well in advance to get into a house to take things.
25 I have got into a house and taken things even though I didn't plan it in advance.
26 I have taken a bicycle belonging to someone else and kept it.
27 I have struggled or fought to get away from a policeman.
28 I have struggled or fought with a policeman who was trying to arrest someone.
29 I have stolen school property worth more than about 5p.
30 I have stolen goods from someone I worked for worth more than about 5p.
31 I have had sex with a boy when I was under 16.
32 I have trespassed somewhere I was not supposed to go, like empty houses, railway lines or private gardens.
33 I have been to an 'X' film under age.
34 I have spent money on gambling under 16.
35 I have smoked cigarettes under 15.
36 I have had sex with someone for money.
37 I have taken money from slot machines or telephones.
38 I have taken money from someone's clothes hanging up somewhere.
39 I have got money from someone by pretending to be someone else or lying about why I needed it.
40 I have taken someone's clothes hanging up somewhere.
41 I have smoked dope or taken pills (LSD, mandies, sleepers).
42 I have got money/drink/cigarettes by saying I would have sex with someone even though I didn't.
43 I have run away from home.

Source: A. Campbell, *Girl Delinquents* (Blackwell, 1981), which was based on H. B. Gibson, 'Self-reported delinquency among schoolboys and their attitudes to the police', *British Journal of Social and Clinical Psychology*, 6, 168–73

1 Tick the activities you have done. How many have you ticked?

2 As a class exercise, compare the results of the males versus the females. Are there any differences?

3 Do you have any criticisms of the questions, or do you think they are representative selection of deviant acts that might be performed by young people?

Chapter 14

POWER AND POLITICS

This chapter covers:

- The nature of power
- Political systems
- Political parties and philosophies
- Political socialisation
- Voting behaviour
- Democracy in action: The activities of pressure groups
- New social movements
- Opinion polls
- The state.

The nature of power

When we talk about 'power', we generally think only of politics. However, power is something that is used and experienced every day by all of us. If we obey someone else, we do so because they have power over us. So parents, teachers, police officers, bullies at school and referees in hockey games all make us obey them.

Sociologists are interested in power in all its senses, not just as something related to politics and government. At the beginning of this century, Max Weber suggested that to understand how some people get others to obey we ought to distinguish between *power*, which is when we obey people because they can threaten us if we ignore their wishes, and *authority*, which is when we willingly obey people because we believe it is right for them to boss us around. Examples of power include the power of prison officers over the inmates (from the prisoners' viewpoint), and the power of kidnappers over their victims. Examples of authority include the authority of parents over their children, and the authority of managers over their employees.

Power and authority

The whole idea of social relationships involves the notion of power. Whenever two or more people are engaged in some activity, potential conflicts will arise and will have to be resolved.

Questions of obedience and disobedience arise in families, in the classroom, between couples and at work, as well as in dealings with the law.

In our own system of government, which we regard as democratic, power is usually invisible. But, as with personal relationships, this does not mean that it is not there. If a person breaks the law or challenges the state in some way (as in Northern Ireland), then the whole weight of the law can be used to ensure that the person does what he/she is told.

Source: Adapted from 'Power and Authority' in *New Society*, 21 February 1985

Look at the photographs.

Indicate which illustrates power, charismatic authority, traditional authority, or legal rational authority.

Power can be divided into two broad categories. First people do what others tell them because they have to, otherwise they may be punished or face penalties of some kind. This is known as *coercion*. Secondly, people do what they are told because they believe the person giving them an order has the right to do so. This is known as *authority*.

The nature of the power in totalitarian societies is usually coercion, as people have not freely chosen the government. In democracies the nature of power is generally accepted to be based upon authority.

However, Marxists argue that western democracies are really based on coercion, but the ruling class have managed to trick the population into accepting that the political and economic system is really to the benefit of everybody. Consequently they rarely have to resort to open threats and violence. The task of persuading people to believe in the system is usually dealt with by the education system and the media. If these fail then the police or the army are used, as happens in Northern Ireland or in the serious industrial disputes such as the 1985–6 miners' strike.

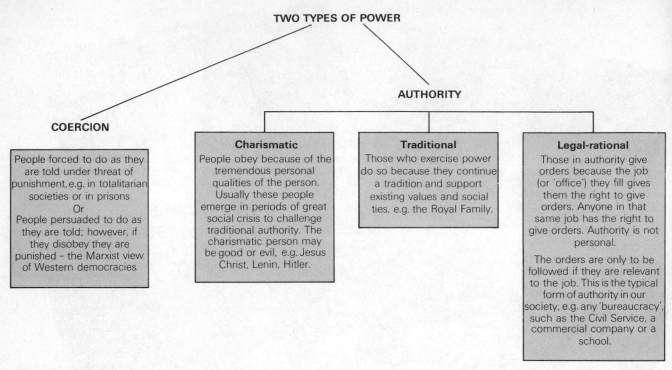

The nature of power

1 Give two examples of power in everyday life.

2 What does coercion mean?

3 Give an example of a country/area where coercive power is used.

4 What is the major difference between coercion and authority?

5 What are the three types of authority?

6 What is the difference between the reason for obeying a figure like Hitler and obeying your boss in the office?

7 Why do people listen to what Prince Philip or Prince Charles have to say?

8 Why do Marxists disagree with the argument that the form of power in democracies is 'authority'?

Political systems

Societies vary in the amount of power ordinary people have to influence the decisions of the government. In some societies the people have very little say indeed and these are generally described as **totalitarian**, On the other hand, societies which try to give ordinary people a strong influence in what decisions are made, are known as **democracies**.

Totalitarian societies

Totalitarian societies are those controlled by a very few people who usually arrange the society for their benefit. The rulers refuse to allow the population any say in the important decisions that affect them and they may well ensure their view holds by controlling the police, courts and the mass media. Criticism is forbidden.

Types of totalitarian society include:

- monarchy, where a king or queen has absolute power, as in Britain in the Middle Ages
- dictatorship, where one person (the dictator) holds absolute power, for example in Germany in the 1930s and early 1940s under Hitler
- oligarchy, where a few people rule, as in the case of the People's Republic of China.

Democratic societies

A true democracy would be a society in which every decision made by the government was voted on by the members of society, but this is not practical as it would be too complicated. Instead, most democratic socities have a system called 'representative democracy', in which certain people (MPs in Britain) are elected to represent the interests of communities (known as 'constituencies' in Britain). This is the model used in Britain, the USA and in Europe for example. We elect Members of Parliament to represent constituencies of about 60 000 people.

But a democracy is more than just voting once every five years for an MP. It also involves freedom to express opinions critical of the government, to have an uncensored media, free from government control, and an independent legal system. If all these things exist then it is likely that the laws passed by the government and the decisions made by it will reflect the will of the people.

When democracy collapses...

The extract below describes the situation in Algeria when a democratic election was cancelled, because the army refused to recognise the fact that a fundamentalist Muslim organisation was going to win power. The army took power and you can read the result yourself.

The dead lie side by side: the local policeman, the musician, the feminist, the schoolmistress, the head of the fine arts academy, the film director, the student and the unknown prisoner.

In life, they were symbols of social and economic injustice, cultural diversity and frustrated political aims, who became targets in the three-year-old power struggle between Islamic militants and Algeria's army-backed government.

Back in the graveyards of Alia, Qattar and Garide, they are equals; civilians trapped in an escalating bloodbath.

In January 1992, Algeria's militant Muslims were on the verge of winning control of the legislature. Then the government cancelled the elections. The military asserted control, and a struggle began that has killed about 30,000 people, many of them civilians and foreigners.

The government said at the weekend that 6,388 civilians were killed by militants last year, and scores more have died since. At least 42 people died when a suicide bomber blew himself up in a crowd outside the Algiers police headquarters on January 31.

Last month, the victims gunned down included intellectuals and artists, school heads who refused to wear veils, and female architects.

On Feburary 17, Djamel Ziater was shot as he stood over his mother's grave, the 36th journalist to be killed since the revolt began.

Source: *The Guardian*, 7 March 1995

A checklist of the elements of a democracy

	Yes	No
Is there more than one political party competing to gain power?		
Are there regular elections?		
Do the majority of people have the right to vote?		
Is it possible to express criticism of the government openly?		
Is there a range of opinions expressed in the newspapers, on radio and television?		
Are the mass media free of government control?		
Is there any way in which ordinary people can communicate with the decision makers (such as MPs) between elections?		
Are the police and the courts free of direct government control?		

For a society to qualify as democratic all the answers ought to be Yes.

1 According to the checklist above is Britain a democracy?

2 Give two other examples of democracies.

3 Find two other nations where the majority of the answers to the checklist are No. (The *New Internationalist* magazine has a useful section on political rights. Your school/college library should have copies.)

Political parties and philosophies

A political philosophy, or ideology, is an explanation of how society works and a prescription on how to act based upon this explanation. Political parties are organised groups who share a common philosophy and who try to win political power, usually aiming ultimately to form the government of a country.

The main political philosophies are **communism**, **socialism**, **conservatism**, **social democracy** and **facism**.

Communism

This is the belief that those who control the economy control society. It argues for ownership of all the economy by 'the people'. In practice this has meant ownership by the government, which is usually not representative of the people, nor democratic.

The political party associated with this philosophy is the Communist Party.

In 1989 and 1990, all the Eastern European 'communist' regimes which had existed since the end of the Second World War collapsed and were replaced by democracies. The Communist Parties in these countries which had ruled unchallenged for 50 years had to submit themselves to elections.

Socialism

This is also the belief that ownership of the economy leads to political control. Socialists argue for an elimination of the extremes of poverty and wealth through the government keeping some degree of control of the economic life of a country.

Social democracy

This philosophy accepts the inequality of capitalist society and the fact that the ownership of economic enterprises should not be taken by the state. However, they see the government as having some role to play in caring for the worse-off.

The Labour Party has its roots in socialism, but has increasingly become social democratic.

Conservatism

This is the belief that the government should not interfere in the economic life of a country and that it is not the job of government to iron out the extremes of wealth and poverty. Private individuals, rather than the government, ought to own industry. (This is known as capitalism.)

The political party associated with this philosophy is the Conservative Party.

Fascism

This is the belief that some groups are racially superior to others and the superior group ought to have preferences in social and economic affairs. Where fascist parties have come to power they have always eliminated democracy.

The political parties associated with this approach are the British Movement and the National Front. They have been associated with organised violent attacks on those of Afro-Caribbean, African and Asian origins.

Political socialisation

Just as individuals learn about the general beliefs and values of society and the correct forms of behaviour, they also learn about political values. We talk about **political socialisation** as the term for this process of learning political values and preferences. In Britain, most people are socialised into an acceptance that the democratic process which we have is the best political system. Within this, however, they are socialised differently in their preferences for political parties.

People learn their political preferences through the media, the family, the school and the peer group/social class, in just the same way that they learn ordinary social values (see Chapter 1).

Media

Newspapers in Britain generally support the Conservative Party. This is hardly surprising as the newspapers are usually part of large companies, precisely the sorts of institutions that would lose out under a Labour government and would benefit from a Conservative government. The radio and television are not allowed to support any particular political party and they could best be described as supporting the 'establishment' view of the world, which is basically to keep things as they are.

There is little evidence to show that people's voting choices are determined by the media. However, it is clear that general opinions about political events are formed by the way in which they are portrayed by the media. Support of the British capitalist, democratic system is constantly expressed in the way world events are described. So people learn to interpret the world around them through the framework provided by the media.

The family

The most important agency of socialisation is the family (see pages 4–5). It is where we first learn the expectations society has of us and these lessons stay with us throughout our lives. It is hardly surprising therefore that political attitudes are also learnt in the family.

The school

At first it may seem surprising that the school has any political influence on us. Yet here we learn a particular version of history, one in which Britain plays the part of the 'goodie', a belief in the value of British society as it is, the habit of obeying rules, the need to compete against each other, and the acceptance that the more successful ought to take higher rewards. These may not appear to be political at first sight, but they are all values on which our political system is based.

The peer group/social class

The people we mix with in our daily lives are very influential in reinforcing or weakening our own opinions. Usually the people with whom we mix (peer group) are drawn from the same social class and as the experiences of social classes are so different, people in each class develop very different views on political events.

Voting behaviour

In a representative democracy, such as Britain, the government is chosen by the electorate and people vote for the party which they prefer. Sociologists have tried to uncover the reasons for people's choices. They suggest that the most important factor is social class. Other less important factors are party images, the influence of the mass media, the role of the family, and geographical location.

Voting and class loyalty

Britain has traditionally been regarded as a country which voted mainly on the basis of people's social class. From the 1950s to the early 1970s, working-class people generally voted for the Labour Party, while middle- and upper-class people, broadly speaking, voted Conservative. Only the Liberal Democrat Party drew its limited support from across the main social classes. During this time, the class structure was stable and there was a relatively little switching from one party to another.

Partisan de-alignment

From the mid-1970s a great change took place in the voting patterns. What happened for the next 20 years was that, although the majority of the people actually voting for the Labour Party were working class, the majority of the working class as a whole voted for the Conservative Party. Also, an increasing number of middle-class people began to vote Labour, although this was still a minority of all middle-class people. The term **partisan de-alignment** was used to describe this situation.

These changes benefited the Conservative Party, which won four elections in immediate succession after 1979.

Explanations for the changes in social class and voting behaviour

Changes in voting behaviour reflected changes in traditional values associated with social class and changes in the actual class structure itself.

Changing social class

Traditionally the British working class had a fairly distinctive set of values and beliefs about society, compared to the middle and upper classes. The working class supported trades unions, and saw the middle and upper classes as being against them. Working-class people generally lived in large council estates, or in poorer sections of the inner cities. They earned lower wages than middle-class people. They worked in industries, doing manual work. Perhaps most important of all, they saw themselves as being a social class and were proud of it.

The decline in traditional industries, the increase in people buying their own homes, the increase in standards of living for large sections of the working class and the rise of office work began to blur the divisions between the middle and the working classes. After all, where did the working class end and the middle class begin?

> Eeny, meeny, miny, mo!...

LABOUR
LIB. DEM
CONSERVATIVE

Sociology does not attempt to explain every voter's choice

The result was that increasing numbers of the working class began to drift away from their automatic support for the Labour Party. So, within the working class there emerged a more affluent, home-owning and 'materially acquisitive' section, more likely to be found in the south of England, who increasingly chose to vote Conservative.

On the other hand, within the middle class a split developed between those graduates, often of working-class origins who were employed in the public sector, and the businessmen and managers working in commerce and industry. Each group saw its interests as being very different, with the Labour Party associated with a better public sector, and the Conservative Party with a more dynamic commercial sector.

Perceptions of party competence

A second explanation has been that the *perceptions* of the public concerning the competence of the political parties are extremely important. As people have become more concerned about their economic well-being, the main question for voters has been which party can provide them with a better standard of living. For 20 years since 1979, the public's perception of the Labour Party was that it was less able to provide the economic conditions for growth, so the more affluent working class voted Conservative.

The debate suggests that voting is a complex mixture of consumer choice based upon perceptions of what is most beneficial to the individual voter and her or his family. This is related in turn to changes taking place in the British social structure.

Party images

One recent survey showed that over 20 per cent of Labour voters actually agreed more with Conservative policies than with Labour ones, while 7 per cent of Conservative voters preferred Labour policies. Ask anyone (including teachers of sociology) exactly what the *specific* policies of the Labour and Conservative Parties are in a forthcoming election and they are unlikely to know!

It seems that people have a general image of the main political parties: Labour is for the working class, the trade unions and the Welfare State; Conservatives stand for business, law and order and the better-off; the Liberal Democrats stands for a restricted degree of reform, but no radical changes.

These party images may not be accurate, but they are the main guides people have to help them decide which party they are going to vote for.

The influence of the media

The media, or mass media, are the newspapers, radio and television. The media do not appear to have any direct influence on voting behaviour. It appears that people *select* information which *reinforces* the views they already hold and ignore other information. What the media does, though, is to *set the agenda*, by which we mean that they decide which issues are regarded as important and newsworthy.

One study found that 33 per cent of Labour voters read a newspaper that supported the Conservative Party, yet they continued to support Labour. They ignored the information in the newspapers that did not fit their views. The researchers also found that television coverage of general elections neither made the public better informed on key issues, nor influenced people's minds on which party to support. (There is further discussion on the media and politics in Chapter 16.) What the media do is to create a general 'climate of opinion' about issues which fits in better with the political stance of one party rather than another.

The impact of the media

The Tory tabloids' assault on Labour

Where, then, did this primal sense of trust come from? One answer was offered by the former Treasurer of the Conservative party, Lord McAlpine: 'The heroes of this campaign', he wrote in the *Sunday Telegraph* (12 April 1992), 'were Sir David English [editor of the *Daily Mail*], Sir Nicholas Lloyd [editor of the *Daily Express*], Kelvin MacKenzie [editor of the *Sun*] and the other editors of the grander Tory press'. In his resignation speech as Labour leader the next day, Neil Kinnock drew attention to these words and went on: 'Never in the past nine elections have they [the Conservative press] come out so strongly in favour of the Conservatives. Never has their attack on the Labour party been so comprehensive...This was how the election was won'.

Certainly the Tory tabloids launched a sustained onslaught on the Labour party. The day before the election, under the front-page headline 'A QUESTION OF TRUST', the *Sun* asked 'When you're in trouble, who do you go to for help: the big mouth or the bank manager?' The next day its election-day front page had a picture of Neil Kinnock's head inside a light bulb and the headline 'IF KINNOCK WINS TODAY WILL THE LAST PERSON TO LEAVE BRITAIN PLEASE TURN OUT THE LIGHTS'. Two days later the *Sun* crowed 'It's THE SUN WOT WON IT'.

But did it? As shown in the table, according to one estimate *Sun* readers swung by a massive 7.5% to the Conservatives in the last days of the campaign. Moreover, the *Sun* is particularly popular among the working class in the South – a large and key group of relatively non-partisan voters. But one should avoid hasty conclusions. By the same estimate there were above average swings to the Conservatives among readers of the non-partisan *Independent* (7%) and of the stridently Labour *Daily Mirror* (5.5%) whereas the swing was below average among readers of the *Daily Express* (2.5%), *Daily Mail* (4%) and the *Times* (0%) – all solidly Conservative newspapers. The most one can infer is that some Tory tabloids, like the *Sun* and *Today*, gave an extra push to a Conservative bandwagon that was already rolling.

The impact of the press on voting intentions

Newspaper	Vote intention	
	Con	Lab
Daily Telegraph	76	9
Times	62	13
Independent	18	44
Guardian	10	57
Daily Express	64	16
Daily Mail	61	18
Today	33	33
Sun	36	42
Daily Star	32	58
Daily Mirror	14	68
None	34	34
All voters	37	39

1 Which party received the majority of the support from the newspapers, according to the extract?

2 What was the view of the defeated leader of the Labour Party after the 1992 election, and of the Treasurer of the Conservative Party, regarding the effect of the media?

3 What did *The Sun* claim?

4 Does the evidence support this?

5 What conclusion does the extract reach regarding the influence of the media?

Source: I. Crewe, 'Why did Labour lose (yet again)' in *Politics Review*, September 1992

The family

This most important agency of socialisation teaches us to be a social being, accepting the rules and values of society. Amongst the values we learn are political values both general, in the sense that we learn to support democracy, and specific, so that we learn to support one particular party. This sympathy for one particular party often stays throughout the whole of a person's life, especially if reinforced by social class.

A study of the influence of the family on voting behaviour found that over 80 per cent of people's original political preference is the same as their parents. This gradually fades over time, but, later in life, a majority of the electorate still vote as their parents did. Fading of party loyalty only takes place when the voting loyalty learned from the parents is contrary to the normal political support of the children's class. So if the children are middle class and they have learned to support the Labour Party, they may change their voting habits to Liberal Democrat or Conservative.

Geographical location

People in the north of England, Scotland and Wales are more likely to support the Labour Party. In the south, the Conservatives and Liberal Democrats receive more support. Also, Labour voters are more likely to live in the inner cities.

The reason is partially that there are more working-class people in the north and inner cities, and these face greater problems than those in the south and in the suburbs or New Towns.

Voting choices

At the time of writing (May 1995), there is likely to be a general election in the next 18 months. The last election in 1992 was won by the Conservative Party under Mr John Major. The tables and chart below provide information about voting preferences in the 1992 election.

A

Voting choices by age and sex, 1992

Age/sex	Con	Lab	Lib Dem	Con lead over Lab
Men	41	40	19	+1
Women	45	36	19	+9
First-time voters	35	40	25	−5
People aged 22–29	43	41	16	+2
People aged 30–44	40	39	21	0

B

Voting choices by occupation, 1992

Occupation	Con	Lab	Lib Dem	Con lead over Lab
Professional/ Managerial (AB)	55	23	22	+32
Office/Clerical workers (C1)	50	29	21	+21
Skilled manual (C2)	41	40	19	+1
Semi-skilled/ unskilled manual (DE)	31	55	14	−24
Unemployed	27	56	17	−2

C

The voting preferences of manual workers, 1987 and 1992

Voting preference	The new working class				The traditional working class			
	Lives in south	Owner occupier	Non-union member	Works in private sector	Lives in Scotland or north	Council tenant	Union member	Works in public sector
Conservative	40	40	37	32	26	22	29	36
Labour	38	41	46	50	59	64	55	48
Liberal Democrat	23	19	17	18	15	13	16	16

Voters were asked the following questions and the bar chart **D** shows the results:

1 Leaving aside this particular election, would you say you generally think of yourself as Conservative, Labour, Liberal Democrat (in Scotland/Wales: Nationalist), or what?

2 Taking everything into account, which party has the best policies?

3 Think of all the urgent problems facing the country at the present time. When you decided which way to vote, which two issues did you personally consider most important? Which party did you think could best handle these problems?

4 And which party has the best leaders?

D

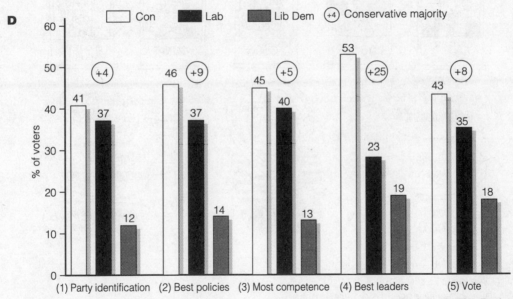

Source: *Politics Review*, September 1992

Look at **A**.

1 What percentage of males voted Conservative?

2 What percentage of females voted Conservative?

3 Overall, can you state what the differences are between males and females in their choice of votes?

4 The table refers to 'first-time voters'. Approximately what age are these likely to be?

5 Are there any differences between the voting preferences of people of different ages?

Look at **B**.

6 Which occupational group was most likely to vote Labour?

7 Which occupational group was most likely to vote Conservative?

8 Which occupational group was most likely to vote Liberal Democrat?

9 Is there any relationship between voting and social class that you can see?

Look at **C**.

There has been considerable debate about the growth of the 'new working class'. **C** shows the differences between the voting preferences of the new and the old working class.

10 What are the main characteristics of the new working class according to the table?

11 Which group, the old or the new, was more likely to vote Conservative?

12 Were council tenants more likely to vote Conservative or Labour?

13 Who is more likely to vote Labour, people living in the north or the south of Britain?

14 Can you identify any particular category or categories which vote Liberal Democrat?

Look at **D**.

The main text describes how voters are increasingly moving away from social class loyalties, towards voting for the parties which seem to look after their interests best, and which are more competent.

15 Does the chart give any support for this idea of self-interest?

16 Does it support the idea that voters are more likely to choose the party which is perceived to be more competent?

17 Conduct a small survey of your own. Ask the questions given in **D** to a small sample of people over 18. Construct a series of bar charts to illustrate your results.

The influences on voting and political attitudes

The diagram above shows the main factors influencing voter's choices of political parties in elections. Write a very short explanation of each influence, using information given in the main text.

Women and political power

Politics remains, by and large, a male preserve, with only slow changes taking place – in 1987 there were only 26 women MPs, yet even with all the talk of equality between the sexes, in 1996 there were still only 63 female MPs out of a total of 651 Members of Parliament.

1 How many female MPs are in parliament today?

2 What is the breakdown by political party?

3 Does it matter anyway, in your opinion, that there are so few female MPs?

Democracy in action: The activities of pressure groups

As we saw earlier, democracy involves more than just the right to vote in elections every five years. Most important of all, it involves a constant flow of communication from the people to their representatives in Parliament. In many cases this simply involves MPs meeting their constituents (the people who elected them) and listening to their views.

However, far more important are the activities of organised groups who agitate in order to persuade Parliament to pass laws which benefit them or they believe would improve society. These groups are known as **interest groups** or **pressure groups**.

Types of pressure group

There are two types of pressure group:
- those which defend their own interests, such as trade unions or the Confederation of British Industry (representing the owners of industry), these are known as **protective** or **defensive pressure groups**
- those which promote new initiatives which they argue will benefit society, known as **promotional groups**, examples of which include the Child Poverty Action Group, which campaigns for better benefits for low-income families, and the Royal Society for the Protection of Birds.

In reality, the division between the two groups is not completely clearcut. Some pressure groups might wish to promote change in order to benefit themselves. For instance, those groups who campaigned for Sunday shop opening were mainly linked to the major chain stores who saw great financial benefits from Sunday opening.

Pressure groups and political parties

There are two main differences between pressure groups and political parties. Firstly, pressure groups generally do not try to win electoral power, they just wish to influence MPs or those in authority. Secondly, they generally concentrate on one issue rather than the wide range of issues supported by political parties.

Pressure groups and the decision makers

Lobbying

This involves sending representatives to see MPs, or whoever is in authority. The representatives try to persuade those in authority of the sense of their campaign. This is usually supported by leaflets, letters and documents. In recent years, there has been the growth of professional lobbying firms, who will lobby for any pressure group if paid to do so.

Retaining the services of those in authority

A number of Labour MPs are 'sponsored' by trade unions to look after their interests. On the Conservative side, a considerable number are paid 'retainers' (a yearly salary) to represent the interests of groups of companies or commercial interests. In the 1985–6 scramble to obtain the contracts to build the Channel tunnel, a number of companies took on MPs as 'advisers'. However, MPs are required to register any such payments to ensure there is no corruption.

Publicity

For many groups who have contacts with those in authority, the best way of gaining attention is to attract publicity. Pressure groups may give stories to the press or engage in newsworthy exploits. Greenpeace, the environmental group, is particularly good at this. The aim is not just to attract attention, but also to win public sympathy.

Protest

Demonstrations and public meetings within the law, as well as direct action outside the law, may attract publicity and bring pressure to bear on the authorities to change their attitudes. Protest is usually the method of the weakest, as the powerful generally have direct access to the politicians and civil servants. One group which has moved towards illegality in recent years is the Animal Liberation Front, which protests against the use of animals in experiments. Its members break into laboratories and free the animals. There are also hunt sabateurs and opponents of larger road schemes.

Criticism

The idea that the activities of pressure groups guarantee democracy has been most strongly criticised for the fact that it overlooks the real differences in *resources* that various pressure groups have at their disposal. The Confederation of British Industry, which represents the owners of British industry, employs over 400 people and is very rich. Yet other groups such as Help the Aged, a pressure group to look after the needs of pensioners, has only a tiny staff and little money.

New social movements

Pressure groups are usually concerned with only one particular issue. Pressure groups form and then disband after a time. But in the 1980s it became clear that a new form of political 'organisation' was emerging. Groups of (usually) young people began to develop alternative ways of thinking and acting, which included challenging the traditional political structures of parties and pressure groups. The 'organisations' consisted of like-minded people who began to think and act in alternative ways from normal. There was no formal membership, nor was there any particular central organisation. Generally people followed their own ideas, but there were enough of these people 'sharing their own ideas', that they found they were a political force in their own right. These new ways of thinking and acting have been described as 'movements', and more specifically **new social movements**. The best known examples of these are the feminist movement, the green movement and the 'new age' travellers.

The movements promote alternative *lifestyles*, as opposed to clear political programmes, and they do not set out to put together political parties, or to win power. Within movements there are many different strands with individuals sharing some beliefs and not others.

One recent example of a new social movement has been the increasing opposition to cruelty to animals in any form, including hunting, animal experiments, the mistreatment of animals before slaughter, even opposition to killing animals for food. The mid-1990s saw a burst of **direct protest** against all these activities.

The influence of new social movements on voting preferences

The decline of the unions in the 1980s is but one aspect of a more general decline of class organisation. There is much evidence of a decline in class voting since the 1960s, as new social movements centred on gender, ethnicity and the environment, together with the rise of issue politics and the increasing influence of the mass media, have combined with occupational changes to diminish traditional party loyalties and loosen the links between class and party. This has presented a particular problem to the British Labour party, which has had to adapt to decline in the size of the working class and a decline in the proportion of workers voting for it, and has done so by distancing itself from the unions, moving away from traditional socialist policies, and improving its media image. Class membership linked to one's position in production was once the central determinant of beliefs, identity, and behaviour, but in today's world this is no longer the case.

Source: J. Fulcher, 'A new stage in the development of capitalist society' in *Sociology Review*, November 1991

1 Explain what is meant when the text refers to 'new social movements centred on gender, ethnicity and the environment'.

2 What is the importance of the new social movements in affecting voting choices?

3 What problems have the Labour Party faced in keeping its support?

4 How has it resolved this problem?

5 Overall, is class still the most important factor in determining voting?

Direct protest

Animal welfare protesters are winning the battle of Shoreham, police and Whitehall sources admitted yesterday.

The protesters have succeeded in halving the number of calf and sheep lorries loaded in the last three days. Their pressure is causing delays which mean that calves and sheep from most parts of Britain cannot be shipped to France and the Netherlands because journey times are exceeding the maximum 15 hour "rest, water and food" laws set by the Ministry of Agriculture. Exporters are now threatening to sue officials for upholding the law.

More than 1,000 police have been deployed since last Wednesday – at a cost exceeding £500,000 – to hold back protesters trying to block shipment of the animals brought to Shoreham following the big ferry operators' decision to abandon the trade.

The police and local authorities are desperate to scale back the operation, but this may prove impossible with the return today of more than 13,000 students to the nearby universities, many of whom may join the demonstration to support local people who have formed the bulk of protesters.

Source: *The Guardian*, 9 January 1995

1 What are the protesters angry about?

2 Is there any particular pressure group or organisation controlling the protests?

3 What sorts of people have joined the protest?

4 In what other ways do you think that people who object to the poor treatment of animals could change the laws?

The reality of decision-making

This extract refers to the argument about the future of roads in Britain. One group wishes to build more roads and motorways, while the other opposes new motorways.

On the road-building side of the argument are ranged the Department of Transport; the big construction companies such as Tarmac, Balfour Beattie and Trafalgar House; the Retail Motor Industry Federation, reputedly as tough and aggressive as its car-dealer members themselves; the oil companies; road hauliers; the AA and RAC; and a host of other companies, ranging from the people who dig up gravel to those who make Weetabix. It has been a successful lobby: as recently as 1989 the roads programme was doubled.

On the anti-road-building side, there is now the DoE, which began to become more aggressively green under Chris Patten, and is fighting hard against its sister department, transport. The Transport 2000 organisation, which mirrors the British Road Federation, includes most of the well-known green groups, such as the Council for the Protection of Rural England, Friends of the Earth and Greenpeace; the National Trust; and others. ...

The road builders...rely on heavyweight support from captains of industry with excellent access to Conservative ministers. This is not a simple case of donors pulling strings: the economic argument is their main weapon, and they have relied on powerful support from the Treasury. Though Kenneth Clarke is personally sympathetic, this support is under review.

The anti-road-builders have a range of tactics. There are, of course, the direct-action protesters and a huge network of protest groups which has formed across the country, ranging from deep-green hippies to white-haired ladies. Meanwhile "establishment" greens have burrowed deep into Whitehall, exploit the sympathy of public figures such as the Prince of Wales and are in close alliance with the DoE.

Source: *The Independent*, 27 September 1994

1 Which groups want to build more roads?

2 Which groups are opposed to road-building?

3 Which group has the ability to talk directly to Conservative ministers?

4 What tactics do the anti-road-building groups use?

5 Which group do you think is more powerful?

Some groups advertise in the media to make their views on current issues more widely known

Pressure groups and new social movements in action

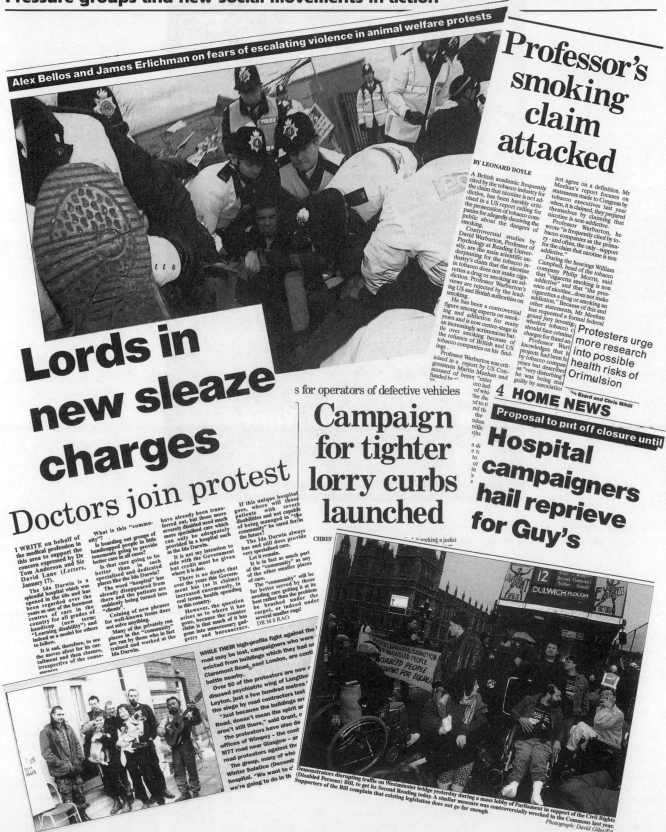

Alex Bellos and James Erlichman on fears of escalating violence in animal welfare protests

Professor's smoking claim attacked

BY LEONARD DOYLE

A British academic frequently cited by the tobacco industry for the claim that nicotine is not addictive, has been harshly criticised in a US report calling for the prosecution of tobacco companies for allegedly deceiving the public about the dangers of smoking.

Controversial studies by David Warburton, Professor of Psychology at Reading University, are the main scientific underpinning for the tobacco industry's claim that the nicotine in tobacco does not make cigarettes a drug or smoking an addiction. Professor Warburton's views are rejected by the leading US and British authorities on smoking.

He has been a controversial figure among experts on smoking and addiction for many years and is now centre-stage in an increasingly acrimonious battle over smoking because of the reliance of British and US tobacco companies on his findings.

Professor Warburton was criticised in a report by US Congressman Martin Meehan and accused of being "external funded by..."

not agree on a definition. Mr Meehan's report focuses on statements made to Congress by tobacco executives last year when, it is claimed, they perjured themselves by claiming that nicotine is non-addictive.

Professor Warburton, he wrote "is frequently cited by tobacco companies as the primary – and often, the only – support for the claim that nicotine is non addictive".

During the hearings William Campbell, head of the tobacco company Philip Morris, said that "cigarette smoking is not addictive" and that "the presence of nicotine...does not make cigarettes a drug or smoking an addiction." Because of this and other statements, Mr Meehan has requested a formal federal grand jury investigation to whether tobacco company should face criminal charges for fraud and...

Professor Warb knowledges that h projects had been ful by tobacco compan years but described as "very disturbing" he was being ma guilty by associatio

Protesters urge more research into possible health risks of Orimulsion

... Ezard and Chris Mihill

4 HOME NEWS

Lords in new sleaze charges

s for operators of defective vehicles

Campaign for tighter lorry curbs launched

CHRIST

Proposal to put off closure until

Hospital campaigners hail reprieve for Guy's

Doctors join protest

I WRITE on behalf of the medical profession in this area to support the concern expressed by Dr Tom Andeoe and Sir David Lane (*Letters*, January 17).

The Ida Darwin is a splendid hospital which was opened in the 60s and has been regarded over the years as one of the foremost centres of care in the country for all grades of handicap (new term: "Learning disability") and indeed as a model for others to follow.

It is sad, therefore, to see the moves afoot for its curtailment and then closure, irrespective of the conse...

What is this "community"?

Is boarding out groups of handicapped people in little tenements going to provide better care in all cases?

Is that care going to be better than in such specialised and dedicated places like the Ida Darwin?

The word "hospital" has already disappeared from there and the patients are suddenly being turned into "clients".

Coining of new phrases for well-known items does not solve anything.

Many of the privately run places in the "community" are run by those who in fact are trained and worked at the Ida Darwin.

have already been transferred out, but those more severely disabled need much more specialised care which can only be adequately provided in a hospital such as the Ida Darwin.

It is my intention to side with the Government where credit must be given where it is due.

There is no doubt that over the years this Government has (as it claims) increased enormously, in real terms, health spending in this country.

However, the question arises as to where it has gone, because the counter claim is that much of it has gone into unnecessary gadgetry and bureaucracy.

If this unique hospital goes, where will those patients with severe disabilities and not capable of being managed in "the community" be cared for in the future?

The Ida Darwin always has and still does provide very specialised care.

Let it remain.

It is in fact as much part of the "community" as any of the other smaller places of care.

The "community" will be far better served by those needing care getting it at its best rather than the problem be brushed under the carpet, or indeed under several smaller rugs!

DR M S RAO

WHILE THEIR high-profile fight against the road may be lost, campaigners which they had or evicted from buildings Claremont Road, east London, are conti battle nearby.

Over 50 of the protestors are now c disused psychiatric wing of Langthor Leyton, just a few hundred metres from the siege by road contractors last

"Just because the buildings are Road, doesn't mean the spirit ar aren't still there," said Grant, c

The protestors have also de offices of Wimpey – the cont M77 road near Glasgow – ar road protestors against the

The group, many of who Winter Solstice (Decemb hospital. "We want to c we're going to do in th

Demonstrators disrupting traffic on Westminster bridge yesterday during a mass lobby of Parliament in support of the Civil Rights (Disabled Persons) Bill, to get its Second Reading today. A similar measure was controversially wrecked in the Commons last year. Supporters of the Bill complain that existing legislation does not go far enough

Photograph: David Giles/PA

Collect as many newspapers as you can for one week. How many reports of pressure group activities can you find?

DECEMBER 19 1994 – JANUARY 1 1995 N° 110   60p

THE BIG

ISSUE

WEEKLY

THE BIG CHRISTMAS ISSUE

Coming up from the streets

Merry Christmas

A Happy New Year

35p OF COVER PRICE GOES TO VENDOR

People who were trying to help the homeless decided that the best way to do so was to publish their own magazine and then sell it. The magazine is The Big Issue *and it makes money and acts as a way of drawing attention to homelessness.*

Power, politics and big business – the circle

The links between government and business are very close indeed. In the mid 1990s the Conservative Party in government had a large number of MPs holding various directorates and advisory positions.

Angela Rumbold's sudden resignation from the lobbying company Decision Makers Ltd has highlighted the lucrative relationship between the top jobs in the Conservative Party hierarchy and the multi-million pound business of influencing government.

All but one of the senior appointees to the Conservative Party hold paid posts with companies which are keen to influence government policy. Unlike ministers they do not have to give up their business contacts when they take an unpaid vice-chairmanship of the party. All they have to do if they are an MP is to declare their consultancies, but not salaries, in the Register of Members' Interests.

John Maples, the deputy chairman who lost his seat in the last election, holds the chairmanship of Saatchi and Saatchi, at a six figure salary. His job is to mastermind its worldwide list of clients.

Altogether the deputy chairman and six vice-chairmen represent some 37 clients or firms either directly through paid directorships or indirectly through lobbying companies.

Declaring an interest

The seven Conservative vice chairmen and women in 1995 declared the following interests.

Sir Geoffrey Pattie
Vice chairman (international)

- Non excutive Chairman GEC Marconi; electronics group subsidiary of GEC
- Non executive member of supervisory board of Leica C.V. microscope manufacturers
- Partner in Terrington Management, management consultants. Clients include Knight Piesold; consulting engineers and T.I.Plc, engineering group of companies.

Sir Graham Bright
Vice chairman

- Public affairs consultant, Safeways
- Director, unpaid International Sweetners Association (which is a client of Ian Greer Associates)
- Director of Dietary Foods Ltd
- Director of Cumberland Foods Ltd
- Director, Mother Nature

Eric Pickles
Vice chairman
(local government)

- Parliamentary Adviser to Coopers and Lybrand

John Maples
Deputy chairman

- Chairman, Saatchi and Saatchi

Angela Rumbold
Deputy chairman, vice chairman (candidates)

- Executive Director of Decision Makers Ltd (resigned) Clients: Hunting Engineering Ltd. Blue Circle Properties, Dartford Borough Council, Citibank, Richard Ellis Local Government Consortium, Barclays, Mercantile, John Brown UK, European Food Service and Packaging Association, McDonalds

Patrick Nicholls
Vice chairman
(campaigning)

- Parliamentary Consultant to Hill & Smith Holdings plc
- Parliamentary Adviser to the Federation of Associates of Specialists and Subcontractors
- Consultant to Port Enterprises Ltd, conference organisers
- Parliamentary Consultant to the MinOtels Europe Group, hotel group
- Parliamentary Consultant to Howard de Walden Estates Ltd., property company
- Consultant to the Waterfront Partnership public affairs consultancy
- Parliamentary Consultant to the National Sub-Contractors Council
- Parliamentary Adviser to the British Shops and Stores Association
- Partner in Mssrs Dunn & Baker, Solicitors.

Baroness Seccombe
Baroness Seccombe vice chairman (women). Not an MP so need not declare outside interests.

Source: *The Guardian*, 29 October 1994

From pensioner to prince – the hunting controversy

Hunt ban clears the first hurdle

A total ban on hunting was backed by MPs yesterday.

They voted by a stunning 253-to-nil to support Labour MP John McFall's Bill to outlaw foxhunting, hare coursing and stag hunting.

Pro-hunting MPs declined to vote – fearing that if they had and still been defeated, the damage and humiliation would have been far greater.

They will now almost certainly break cover, however, to use procedural devices to sabotage the Wild Mammals (Protection) Bill's further progress through Parliament and prevent it becoming law. ...

Opponents of the Bill claimed it had been hijacked by powerful lobby groups backed by a massive advertising campaign.

Former Cabinet Minister Tom King claimed the Bill had been written by the League Against Cruel Sports and told Mr McFall: 'Some of its supporters have a different agenda to you.'

Tory Michael Colvin, MP for Romsey and Waterside, intervened to ask: 'Was it just pure coincidence that the day the poll tax rioters were burning down Trafalgar Square, not one single hunt in this country was sabotaged? Opponents also accused Mr McFall who represents a constituency where there is no hunting – Dumbarton – of failing to vote for a similar anti-hunt measure just before the last election.

That attempt, by shadow Cabinet member Kevin McNamara, went down by 12 votes.

Before the debate began, a Tory MP claimed private interest groups could 'bid for' backbechers piloting a Bill through the Commons.

Alan Duncan, MP for Rutland and Melton, said: 'I am concerned that the rise of new lobbying practices requires the House to reconsider the rules which govern the improper influence of MPs.'

Referring to the anti-hunt campaign, he went on: 'In the last fortnight, MPs have received hundreds of computer-printed cards. There has appeared in the press nearly £1million worth of full-page newspaper advertising, mentioning Mr McFall and his Bill.'

Source: *The Daily Mail*, 4 March 1985

STOP THE BLOODY

HARE COURSING!

MPs support move to ban fox hunting

LLS AND HARRY JOIN THE CHASE

of foxhunting   PHOTOGRAPH: ALEX MACNAUGHTON

PRINCELY PACK: Charles leads his party, with Wills and Harry in the rear, at the Beaufort Hunt yesterday   Picture: CHARLIE VARLEY

A demonstrator m **Landmark anti-hunting vote unlikely to bring ban**

Young Royals ride into hunting storm

Look at the extract from *The Daily Mail*.
1 What organisation was behind the attempts to outlaw hunting foxes?

2 What methods were used by the opponents of fox hunting to gain MP's sympathy?

3 There is also mention of another activity: what is it?

Opinion polls

Opinion polls are generally used to find out people's opinions on topical subjects, or to carry out market research on consumers' preferences. They involve asking questions of a typical cross-section of the population, and the results are then assumed to be generally true for everybody. Opinion polls are widely used by political parties and newspapers to find out voters' intentions at elections. However, they have been criticised for possibly having an effect on the outcomes of elections.

Why? Voters, who realise that the party of their first choice has absolutely no chance of winning according to the opinion polls, may decide to switch votes to another party in order to defeat the third party that the opinion polls put in the lead. For example, there is some evidence that in seats where the Labour Party is clearly in the lead, Conservative voters may switch to the Liberal Democrats in order to defeat Labour. Opinion polls are then actually influencing the outcome of the elections, not just informing people of the situation.

Clever use of opinion polls by political parties becomes an important weapon in the electoral battle. The result is that people vote into power not the party of first choice, but the one *least disliked*, a rather different matter. Of course, this all assumes that the opinion polls have actually predicted correctly the voting intentions of the electors. As we discussed on pages 14–25, it is possible that opinion polls (which are a type of survey) may be inaccurate.

Opinion polls – an unfair political weapon?

Opinion polls have become a political institution. They influence four aspects of the political process:
- party morale
- the election date
- election campaigns
- policy formation.

Party morale
The steady publication of opinion polls forms a permanent background to the party political stage. When they are favourable, the party leader is confident and the MPs and media are respectful. When they are unfavourable, opponents in the government who wish to get power for themselves, flex their muscles and the media criticise.

This inevitably affects the morale of the party.

Election date
The Prime Minister decides the election date and always seek a time most favourable to his or her party. Opinion polls guide the choice of date, as they give an indication of how the electorate feel.

Election campaigns
The political parties pay for private polls which tell them how the campaign is going and what issues they should concentrate on. Parties tailor their propaganda according to the information and feedback they receive through the polls.

All parties now leak selected information to the media about how the various candidates are doing, in the hope of making electors switch their votes tactically. For example, if it seems likely that Labour will win an election because voters who normally vote Conservative are considering voting for the Liberal Democrats as a form of protest (not because they want the Liberal Democrats to actually win, but to give the Conservatives a 'scare'), they may be frightened back into voting Conservative, on seeing the results of an opinion poll showing that Labour may actually gain the seat as a result of the protest vote. The same applies to

Labour, and for slightly different reasons to the Liberal Democrats.

Policy formation
Political parties are strongly influenced by what people indicate they want in opinion polls. Indeed, the parties go so far as to change their policies to fit in with what the public wants.

One last point – opinion polls have been more often incorrect in predicting the outcomes of general elections than correct! In the 1992 elections, even when people were asked after they had voted about their voting preferences, the opinion polls still predicted the results inaccurately.

1 What is meant by opinion polls?

2 Are they always accurate?

3 In what four ways do they influence politics?

4 It has been suggested that opinion polls should be banned during elections (as they are for a certain period in the French elections). Why have people said this?

The state

The state is the decision-making agency of British society. It consists of three elements:
- a decision-making body – Parliament
- a bureaucracy that carries out the decisions – the civil service
- an organisation that enforces the law – the police and judiciary (the courts).

Parliament

The House of Commons is the elected body of representatives. The Members of Parliament (MPs) are divided along party lines. Normally the party that has the most MPs elected at a General Election forms the government. There is also the House of Lords which is not elected. Proposed laws (known as 'bills') have to be passed three times to become law and are then passed to the Queen for her assent.

Many critics have pointed out the unrepresentative nature of MPs. They are overwhelmingly male (in 1996 only 63 of 651 MPs are women), white and middle class. Is it therefore possible for them truly to reflect the will of the people?

The civil service

The civil service is the bureaucracy that runs the state on behalf of the government. In total there are over 600 000 civil servants.

Some sociologists have commented on the power of senior civil servants over ministers. They have argued that ministers, who are the politicians appointed by the Prime Minister to run civil service departments, are themselves controlled by the civil servants.

Whereas ministers rarely stay in one ministry (government department) for more than two years, civil servants spend their whole careers there. They are, therefore, able to manipulate the ministers into taking the decisions that they want them to. The result is that the country is run more by the civil service than by elected politicians.

A second point of concern is that top civil servants come largely from a very exclusive social background. In the early 1990s, for example, about a third of all recruits to the top jobs in the civil service came from public schools, which are the sorts of schools attended mainly by the British upper class.

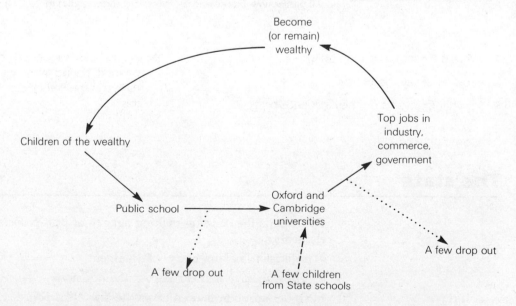

The circle of power and wealth

Are the top positions open to all, or is the diagram untrue?

The judiciary

The judiciary, composed of judges and magistrates (who judge lesser offences), have the role of interpreting and fairly applying the law passed by Parliament. It should be noted that judges too are drawn from a very restricted social class background, just like senior civil servants and have generally attended public schools.

Does the state reflect the will of the people?

There are two basic views on this, put forward by pluralists and neo-Marxists.

Pluralists

This approach suggests that power is spread right across society and that everybody, in some way, is able to influence government decisions. They can join a political party or pressure group, vote in elections and see their local MP if they have any views or problems. The term 'pluralism' simply means that there is more than one (plural) centre of power. According to this approach the government reflects the will of the people.

Neo-Marxist

This approach argues that power lies in the hands of very few people, the rich, and that the vast majority of the population really have no effective way of influencing the decisions of the government. Supporters of this view point to the great differences in resources and contacts between the pressure groups representing the interests of industry and those representing the ordinary person. They also point out how control of the media by very few people can lead to their views (generally in support of the rich) being imposed upon the majority of people.

The distribution of power in society

The dominant feature of advanced industrial societies appears to be an elitist distribution of power (that is, a small group of people who are very powerful). Specialisation has given rise to a large number of elites in every walk of life – top politicians, businessmen, and civil servants. The question sociologists have tried to answer is whether these elites form a ruling class governing in their own interests (the Marxist view). Or is it a large number of elites like a market place competing against each other, so that no one single group has overall power (the pluralist view)?

The case for the Marxist view:

On the face of it, we are a grossly unequal society, with the top 10 per cent, for instance, owning 60 per cent of all personal wealth. ...Our top institutions are dominated by people from privileged social backgrounds, educated in the main at public schools and the universities of Oxford and Cambridge. Only about 5 per cent of the population go to public schools, but 47 per cent of MPs did, over 50 per cent of senior civil servants, over 80 per cent of judges and army officers, as well as 65 per cent of the chairmen of major companies. ...

The mass media are controlled by fewer and fewer hands. One man, Murdoch, owns four Fleet street newspapers, for instance. In their studies of television news, the Glasgow University Media Group have argued that by careful selection it presents a pro-establishment point of view while appearing to be neutral and objective. Strikes, for example, are given a bad image and controversial topics carefully vetted.

The case for the pluralists:

But pluralist writers are not convinced by these arguments. This evidence might prove the existence of a British establishment, but it fails they say to prove 'that it rules'.

A study by Christopher Hewitt of 24 major policy issues faced by successive British governments over a 20-year period found that no one significant group managed to get its way on most issues. Indeed on only one issue did Parliament go against public opinion and that was when it stopped capital punishment for murder.

In a detailed study of the influence of the Confederation of British Industry, the organisation which speaks for most of the large British companies, Grant and Marsh, found that 'the CBI's ability to influence events is limited by the government's need to retain the support of the electorate and by the activities of other pressure groups.'

The debate continues:

But the reply of many of those who believe in the idea of a ruling class has been to develop the idea of 'non decision making', which is the ability of the powerful to ignore or suppress all but the safest of issues, and to ensure that threats to their own most important interests (such as redistribution of private property) are never seriously debated in parliament.

Source: Adapted from *New Society*, 21 February 1985

1 What does the term 'elite' mean?

2 What is the dominant feature of industrial societies according to the extract?

3 What do sociologists mean by the term the 'ruling class'?

4 Briefly summarise the Marxist viewpoint.

5 What evidence do pluralists put foward to refute this?

6 So, what do pluralists suggest is the best way to understand the distribution of power in British society?

7 What does the non-decision-making approach argue?

8 Whose argument, the pluralists' or the Marxists', does it support?

---

1 Find out who the MPs for your town are. What party do they belong to? What is their majority of votes over their opponents? Check the local papers to see what their views are on major topical issues. Are there any clear influences of pressure groups on them?

2 Delegate a small group to arrange a visit with your local MP. Devise a questionnaire for him or her concerning such things for example as the rights of women, education, the public service, the power of the civil service, whether an establishment exists.

3 Is there a local issue of great importance currently being debated in your town? If so follow the history of it, find out which groups are influential and what the outcome of the issue is.

Chapter 15

POVERTY

This chapter covers:

- Defining poverty
- The extent of poverty
- Who is more likely to be in poverty?
- The causes of poverty
- Debates in the provision of social security to combat poverty.

Defining poverty

Britain is one of the richest nations in the world, yet one in seven of its inhabitants live in poverty. But what is poverty? Sociologists have defined it in three basic ways: **absolute poverty**, **relative poverty** and **consensual poverty**.

Absolute poverty

Towards the end of the last century, a number of concerned people began to argue that something ought to be done about the dreadful problem of poverty that existed. Most powerful people laughed at this, denying there was any serious problem (just as happens today).

To prove just how bad the situation was, Seebohm Rowntree conducted a survey to discover the extent of poverty in Britain. First, though, he had to provide a clear guide to the point at which people fell into poverty. He created a poverty line with which nobody could disagree. He decided that the line was the income needed to ensure that a person was able to live healthily and work efficiently.

To find the amount of income to reach this point, Rowntree added together: the costs of a very basic diet; the costs of purchasing a minimum of clothes; the rent for housing. The poverty line was then drawn at the income needed to cover these three costs.

Criticisms

The main problem with this sort of definition is that it fails to take into account the fact that what is regarded as poverty *changes* over time. What is a luxury today may be a necessity tomorrow. For example, a basic diet today is very different from a basic diet of 100 years ago.

1 Make a list of necessities for two adults and two children for one week. What total sum of money would they add up to?

2 Can you agree exactly what necessities are?

Relative property

The criticism of Rowntree's definition led sociologists to create a different definition of poverty. This is based on the idea that poverty is really the situation in which some people are denied what most people normally expect to have. For instance, 30 years ago central heating in homes was a luxury for the better-off. Today it is regarded as a normal convenience for the majority of households. At that time televisions, telephones, and cars were all luxuries. Are they today? Rowntree allowed a set of warm clothes, but surely a degree of fashion is important today?

The result of this was that sociologists began to search for a poverty line reflecting the fact that poverty was closely related to the general standards of living of the population.

How is the poverty line measured in relative definitions?

There are two main ways of defining the poverty line:

* the government's own level of income support, plus an allowance for housing, etc., which adds up to approximately another 40 per cent of the income support. The reasoning behind this is that income support reflects the minimum level of income the government itself believes it is reasonably possible to live on. So poverty equals 140 per cent of income support.

* having less than 50 per cent of average income. This, of course, means that there is no way that poverty can ever be eliminated. This is how the British government currently measure poverty.

A third approach, which is now being used in studies which compare poverty across different countries, is to take the percentage of the population who spend less than 50 per cent of the average expenditure of people in that society. So, if most people spend £200 each week, those who are poor are those who spend only £100.

Advantages and disadvantages of the relative approach

Relative poverty suggests that people are poor if they do not have what is normally expected in society. There are some problems with this definition.

Advantages	Disadvantages
It relates the poverty to the expectations of society. It gives a realistic picture of deprivation within a society. It broadens the idea of what poverty is, from basic necessities to a range of other needs that people have in a society, and which makes life bearable.	Taken to its extreme, this approach means that as long as there is inequality there is poverty. It could be argued that just because a person does not have the 'extras' which most people have come to expect in contemporary Britain, they are poor. As long as they are fed, housed and clothed then they have all that is needed. The relative approach can lead to people ignoring the differences *across* societies. Thus the approach seems to say that in a Third World society, as long as person is not starving they are not poor, because expectations are so much lower in that society. If government benefits are used as the measure of poverty, the absurd situation occurs that the higher the level of income support the more the numbers of people there are in 'poverty'!

Consensual definitions of poverty

We have seen that there are a number of problems with both the absolute and relative approaches to defining poverty. To overcome these problems, a **consensual** measure has been suggested. This involved asking people to rank in order of importance what they considered to be necessities. These were then put together, and as a result a list of necessities was produced which was agreed by a large majority of the people questioned. Using these agreed (hence, consensual) necessities, they were then able to work out what most people regard as an unacceptable level of deprivation.

Mack and Lansley's list of necessities

In 1985 and 1991, Mack and Lansley asked over 1000 people what they thought 'necessities' were, and then from their replies made a list of the most commonly agreed necessities. Below is the list that Mack and Lansley produced from the first phase of their research, and which they then asked people to rank in order of importance.

New, not second-hand, clothes	A holiday away from home for one week a year, not with relatives	A roast meat joint or its equivalent once a week
Heating to warm living areas of the home if it's cold	Public transport for one's needs	A 'best outfit' for special occasions
Enough bedrooms for every child over 10 of different sex to have his/her own	A garden	An outing for children once a week
	A television	Meat or fish every other day
Leisure equipment for children, e.g. sports equipment or a bicycle	A night out once a fortnight (adults)	A dressing gown
	A hobby or leisure activity	Children's friends round for tea/a snack once a fortnight
Carpets in living rooms and bedrooms	Celebrations on special occasions such as Christmas	Indoor toilet (not shared with another household)
Presents for friends or family once a year	Damp-free home	Friends/family round for a meal once a month
Three meals a day for children	A warm water-proof coat	Beds for everyone in the household
Toys for children	Two hot meals a day (for adults)	Self-contained accommodation
Refrigerator	A telephone	A washing machine
Bath (not shared with another household)	A packet of cigarettes every other day	Two pairs of all-weather shoes
A car		

Source: J. Mack and S. Lansley, *Poor Britain* (Allen & Unwin, 1985)

1 As a group, try to come to agreement over what you collectively agree are the first five necessities.

2 Check your results against those of Mack and Lansley on page 300.

3 Do you agree with the order of 'necessities' according to Mack and Lansley?

Different definitions of poverty

A

...by almost every material measure it is possible to contrive: health, longevity, real income, ownership of consumer durables, number and length of holidays, money spent on entertainment, numbers in further education...not only are those with lower incomes not getting poorer, they are substantially better off than they have ever been before...

B

[poverty] is defined by reference to the actual needs of the poor and not by reference to the expenditure of those who are not poor. A family is poor if it cannot afford to eat...A person who enjoys a standard of living equal to that of a medieval baron cannot be described as poor for the sole reason that he has chanced to be born into a society where the great majority can live like medieval kings.

C

The picture which emerges is one of constant restriction in almost every aspect of people's activities. ...The lives of these families...are marked by the unrelieved struggle to manage, with dreary diets and drab clothing. They also suffer from what amounts to cultural imprisonment in their home in our society in which getting out with money to spend on recreation and leisure is normal at every other income level.

D

It is not just money that decides how people live – it is access to resources that makes the difference between drowning in poverty and managing just to keep your head above water. To measure poverty only by income is inaccurate – what facilities do people have and what social activities are they able to engage in, are the real indicators of poverty.

Source: All extracts from R. Lister, *The Exclusive Society* (CPAG, 1990)

1 These quotes reflect different approaches to defining poverty. Indicate which of the three approaches (absolute, relative and consensual) you think underlies the quotes.

2 Which of these do you feel is the most accurate?

The importance of different definitions of poverty

Sociologists are concerned about defining poverty because the outcome of their work has very important results for poor people.

If poverty is simply the level below which people cannot live and work efficiently, as Rowntree suggests, then very low levels of financial support are needed from the government, and the number of people considered to be in poverty is very low. On the other hand, if poverty is not having what is regarded as normal and desirable, as the relative poverty group argues, then the level of financial support required from the government is high and the numbers of people defined as poor are very high too.

Poverty and region: Where do the poor live?

There is a sharp north–south divide. Over two-thirds of those in poverty live in Scotland, the north of England and the Midlands, with half of the poor coming from the large cities of the north, such as Merseyside (the area around Liverpool).

Average gross normal weekly household income by region in 1990–1

	£ per week	As a % of UK income
North	275.70	79%
Yorkshire and Humberside	295.17	85%
North West	319.65	92%
East Midlands	339.93	98%
West Midlands	319.28	92%
East Anglia	338.95	98%
South-East	432.60	125%
South-West	355.15	102%
Wales	283.25	82%
Scotland	305.53	88%
Northern Ireland	273.95	79%
UK	347.17	100%

Source. Central Statistical Office, Family Spending, A report on the 1991 Family Expenditure Survey, Government Statistical Service, HMSO, 1992.

Source: C. Oppenheim, *Poverty: The Facts* (CPAG, 1993)

1 Which two areas have the lowest gross incomes?

2 Which have the highest?

The extent of poverty

The number of people living in poverty depends upon how poverty is defined. If we take the absolute definition, there are very few poor (destitute) people in Britain. Taking the **index of deprivation**, however, as many as 12 million people can be considered poor (deprived of one or more of the most commonly agreed necessities).

The figures below are those which are increasingly being used by researchers, and reflect a relative definition:

In the early 1990s:

- about 4 500 000 people, or 8 per cent of the population, were living below the level of income support
- 11 500 000 people, or 20 per cent of the population, were living on or below income support level
- 12 million people, or 22 per cent of the population, were living with an income of less than 50 per cent (after housing costs) of the average income for the UK.

Poverty and the life cycle

Explain why, in each period, the individuals are either in poverty or out of poverty.

When we talk about the poor, it would be better to talk about those groups *at risk of poverty*. For those with little money, certain periods of their lives will be difficult ones when they will fall into poverty and then other periods when they will climb out again. For example, those with young, dependent children who have a low wage, will probably be in great financial difficulties because of the great costs of the children and they will, therefore, be likely to go into poverty. Only a few years later as the children leave home, and possibly both parents are working, they will move out of poverty (just!). As they grow old and their incomes decline again, they may fall back into poverty.

Living in poverty in Britain today

'I cannot go for a job interview even if I could get one, as after three years of unemployment my clothes are virtual rags, and I cannot buy any more, as it costs so much to keep my son decent – scruffy children have their lives made a misery at school and whatever else I do without, he will not have to go through that.

He wets the bed and has to wear nappies. His sheets and bedding must still be washed every day. When my washer broke, I asked if the DHSS [now DSS] could help and was told that the washer was not regarded as a necessity, and I should use the launderette.

He has not had either birthday or Christmas presents since he was two. He asks for Lego and cars from Santa, but Santa is dead in this house; how does one explain that to a child of five?

I have no chance of getting out to meet people; a babysitter here costs £1.50 an hour. I have no relatives to help out and since I can no longer entertain or go out, I have literally no friends. So I spend every day alone and every night.

I sat down and worked out roughly what you spend per week. And now you've got washing-up liquid, you got toilet paper, you got soap to wash with. Well, what is it, you go out and you think to yourself, now if I buy washing-up liquid I can't have a loaf of bread. Which do you do? Buy the loaf of bread or the washing-up liquid? You've got to keep yourself clean and you've got to eat. So which way do you sway?

Some days I just go into a corner and won't let anybody come near me. I just sit in a corner and bang my head against the wall. And say why me?'

Source: J. Mack and S. Lansley, *Poor Britain* (Allen & Unwin, 1985)

'It just seems to get worse, no matter how hard we try. Jack (the husband) works all the hours he can, but the bills always seem to beat us. On Thursdays we sometimes don't have a thing to eat except bread and beans in the house. It breaks my heart seeing the children eating the rubbish I give them, but what more can I do?

Shopping is the worst thing, because it's so public. In the supermarkets I feel so stupid buying only a couple of things while everyone else has those trolleys filled to the top. Anyway I can't go anymore to Tesco's as it's been moved to a bigger superstore out of town and without a car you can't get there. So I go around the corner (to the local small shops). Everything is more expensive...then there's these special offers you get for buying the really big packs of things, but I haven't got the cash so I always end up with the small jars and packets...costs a lot more.

Clothes for the kids – oh, it's always the Oxfam shop – the one place I am a regular! I've tried buying from the mail order catalogues as you can pay the clothes off weekly, but the prices were much higher than in the shops.

Holidays? You must be joking! Our kids have never been anywhere.

Oh, the house is just awful. It's damp and it never gets warm. Well, we just can't afford the heating for more than this room.

We only got the fridge because a friend of my sister was chucking it out.

Life, well it's just a struggle. I feel like giving up sometimes...but then there's always the kids.'

1 Why do the poor have to pay more for the goods they buy?

2 Can you suggest reasons why, once a family is poor, it becomes increasingly difficult to escape from poverty.

3 Apart from lack of money, what other problems does poverty cause?

The poverty trap

The poverty trap occurs when a person or a family receives a number of means-tested benefits from the state when they are unable to obtain work. If the person then finds employment, it is possible that the gains in income from that employment may well be lost, because the Department of Social Security withdraws some or all of the means-tested benefits.

Deprivation
Living in poverty means going without necessities. Those in poverty spend half the national average on food, and 75% lacked two or more necessary items of clothing 50%+ had less heating than they wanted.

Lack of leisure
There is no money for leisure or social activities. 85% of free time is spent inside the home, as 'normal' social activities are too expensive.

Stigma and lack of status
Being poor usually means having little or no status in society, and having the stigma of taking 'handouts' from the state.

Negative effects on children
Children brought up in poor homes are less likely to go out, have presents and 'treats', have holidays, and lack clothes.

Poor housing conditions
Those in poverty are likely to fall behind with rent or mortgage payments. They are likely to live in the worst housing conditions in damp, overcrowded, insanitary buildings. In the extreme they are likely to become homeless, and have to be accommodated in bed and breakfast.

Poverty

Stress
The constant struggle to make ends meet leads to disputes between family members and can affect health. Women in particular were stressed through having to cope with the budgeting.

Ill-health
There is a direct relationship between deprivation and ill-health. This is caused by inadequate nutrition, poor housing conditions and lack of warmth, plus the effects of stress.

Debt
This is an increasing problem in the UK. The government itself helps create a problem of debt through its policy of the social fund. In 1990, there were almost 400 000 people repaying social fund loans. If people are unable to cope with the ordinary budgeting on their incomes, then they are forced into debt, which then simply magnifies the problem. In 1990, over 20 000 households had their electricity disconnected. 1 in 7 single parents are in 'severe' debt.

Extra costs
Supermarkets which offer the best choice/cheapest prices are increasingly moving to out-of-town locations, which require cars to shop there. Small corner shops tend to have higher prices. Also bulk purchase is considerably cheaper, but the initial costs are too great for the poor and too great a quantity for pensioners.

Neighbourhood
The poorest groups live in the most deprived areas with fewer GPs than most areas, the worst schools, problems of crime, etc. However, we should remember that it is not just inner cities that have high levels of poverty, some of the worst poverty is in the countryside.

The poor talking

Poverty hits people in unexpected ways. Below are some quotes from people living in poverty.

A

'You end up pulling your hair out because you can't ever get away for a night out like working people...Tensions build when you get a bit of time on your own.'

B

'The children are always asking for things – they say their friends have this and this...we have to say no, so the children get upset and we feel upset.'

C

- 44% of men compared to 28% of women had personal spending money;
- 86% of men and 67% of women spent money on leisure pursuits.

D

'He liked cars and drinking and there wasn't the money for it. Me and the kids used to go short on food and clothes because he spent the money.'

(Vanessa, lone mother)

E

'He wanted extra money off me which I couldn't give him, which led to rows and then in the end I were saying there were only the £5 electricity money left and he were taking it and spending it. And then on Monday when I cashed the family allowance, he wanted money out of that as well. So that didn't help.'

(Carol, lone mother of three, expecting another)

F

'I don't see a lot of people, so I feel I'm boring in conversation sometimes. I think back on what I've done and talk about that, but nothing concrete about what I've been doing over the last few months, because it's all the same. Days become the same, unless you break it up and do something.'

(Katje, unemployed woman in Manchester)

G

'I am treated differently now. You sometimes came across people who, when you said you were living in B&B, gave you that look. It's difficult to describe but you feel it. They make you feel small and nothing. Now that you have your own place you think, I can start living normally like other people. I can start sorting out my life. You start to think ahead.'

(Lisa)

H

'I was earning roughly £35 to £40 a week. It was piece work, 13p per skirt – you had to sew hundreds to get to £35–£40...I had to work sometimes until midnight, from nine in the morning, just to pay rent, electricity and gas.'

(Sevin, mother of three)

Source: All quotes from C. Oppenheim, *Poverty: The Facts* (CPAG, 1993)

1 Explain what aspects of poverty the quotes illustrate, referring if you wish to the diagram on page 285.

2 The quotes also illustrate inequalities of poverty within families. Explain this.

Who is more likely to be in poverty?

The unemployed

The number of people who are out of work changes with the overall situation of the economy. However, there have been very significant changes in the British economy over the last 15 years, which seem likely to maintain a permanently high level of unemployment.

The main changes include increasing automation in industry and in offices so that fewer, less-skilled workers are needed, and the fact that there has been a general decline of British manufacturing because of foreign competition. The most important factor, however, was the attitude of the Conservative governments in the 1980s and 1990s who believed that relatively high levels of unemployment benefited industry by helping to keep wages down and by providing a pool of cheap leabour which was readily available at low cost for employers.

Long-term and short-term unemployment

There are two types of unemployment: **long-term** and **short-term unemployment**. Those who are unemployed for a long time face much greater problems than those out of work for a limited period. These problems include a lower level of income (because benefits go down after a certain period of unemployment), exhaustion of savings, and a gradual running down in the condition of clothing, furniture and general possessions. A government study in 1990 found that after three months of unemployment, the average disposable income of a family dropped by 59 per cent. Of course, the psychological effects of lack of confidence, stress and depression are more acute for the long-term unemployed.

Unemployment does not strike all groups in the population equally, however. Certain groups are more likely than others to be made unemployed. These include:

- the least skilled – as automated machinery has replaced them. Unemployment levels for unskilled manual workers can be as high as six times that of professional workers.
- those living away from the south/south-east of England – The south-east of England has a number of advantages for employers, including a skilled workforce, proximity to Europe, and a large, affluent population to purchase the goods or products.
- ethnic minorities – Partly as a result of racism, and partly because skill levels are lower overall amongst the younger Afro-Caribbeans and some of the Asian communities, there are significantly higher levels of unemployment amongst the ethnic minorities. It is estimated that twice as many Blacks and Asians are unemployed as Whites.

The wider effects of unemployment

Individuals

If a man becomes unemployed, it is likely that his wife will have to give up work as well, because the benefit system works in such a way that what she earns he loses from income support. By the time travel, etc. is taken into account, the family becomes worse off if the wife continues to work. As a result, the two-earner family rapidly becomes the no-earner family.

Unemployment has powerful effects on individual's mental state too, which can help trap them in poverty. When an individual is made unemployed, he or she loses self-esteem, and of course this affects his or her ability and will to seek a job. The stress resulting from lack of employment affects a person's health, so that standards of health amongst the unemployed are significantly lower than the population in general, so they are less able to take on employment. A cycle begins, preventing the person getting employment and thereby escaping from poverty.

Communities

Unemployment is more likely to occur among certain groups and in certain areas than others. When this occurs, a gradual rundown of an entire area can begin. Without adequate income people cannot afford to maintain their accommodation, they cannot afford to shop, or to purchase decent leisure services. The result is a lack of shops and leisure amenities, high crime levels and a general dowdiness of the area, which, in turn, discourages employers and new businesses. So, a cycle begins leading to yet more poverty and further decline in the area.

The risk of poverty

A

The risk of poverty, by economic status, 1987

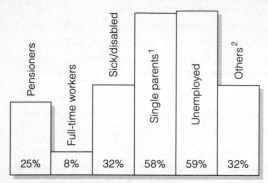

Pensioners	Full-time workers	Sick/disabled	Single parents[1]	Unemployed	Others[2]
25%	8%	32%	58%	59%	32%

Proportion living in poverty
(below 50 per cent average income after housing costs)

1 Single parents who are not in full-time work
2 Men aged 60–64, widows, students, people temporarily away from work, carers, people who are unemployed but not available for work

B

The risk of poverty, by family status, 1987

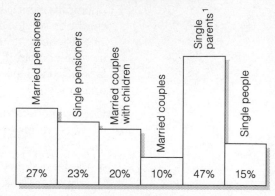

Married pensioners	Single pensioners	Married couples with children	Married couples	Single parents[1]	Single people
27%	23%	20%	10%	47%	15%

Proportion living in poverty
(below 50 per cent average income after housing costs)

1 All single parents

Source: Both diagrams redrawn from C. Oppenheim, *Poverty: The Facts* (CPAG, 1990)

Look at **A**.

1 Which two groups of people had the highest proportion of their members in poverty?

2 What percentage of pensioners were in poverty?

3 How can any full-time employees be in poverty?

4 There is a category headed 'others'. What groups do you think this includes? Suggest an explanation why each of these groups might be in poverty.

Look at **B**.

5 What does this diagram illustrate?

6 Which type of family has the highest proportion of its members in poverty?

The low paid

The extent of low pay

During the 1980s and 1990s there has been a very great growth in the number of people who are classified as 'low paid'. According to the Council of Europe's 'decency threshold' levels of pay, in 1991 5.72 million (or 36 per cent of the full-time adult workforce) and 4.3 million (or 77% per cent of the part-time workforce) were low paid.

Reasons for the increase in the numbers of the low paid

There are three reasons for the increase in the numbers of low paid workers. These are government policy, working conditions and employment patterns, and unemployment.

Government policy

There has been a significant amount of government legislation concerning employment in the 1980s and early 1990s. Most of the resulting changes have weakened workers' rights. Attempts were even made to prevent part-time employees having many effective rights at all, but this was stopped by the European Commission which said that taking away part-time workers' rights was illegal.

Nevertheless, the British government has weakened many workers' rights for example by curbing the rights of trades unions and abolishing minimum wages for young people.

Working conditions and employment patterns

A second important change has been the changing nature of employment in Britain. There has been a growth in part-time workers, so that between 1984 and 1996 the increase in the number of these is estimated to be nearly 25 per cent, while the comparative figure for full-time employees is about 8 per cent.

There has also been an increase in temporary employees, so that between the early 1980s and early 1990s, the number of temporary employees grew by 12 per cent. Women make up 90 per cent of both the temporary and the part-time workforce.

Unemployment

As we saw in the earlier section, the changes in levels of unemployment affect the low paid, in that employers are able to offer lower wages when unemployment is high. Low-paid workers are particularly often caught in the poverty trap, whereby an increase in earnings means the loss of means-tested benefits. In 1990, over 400 000 people in Britain were caught in this 'poverty trap'.

The low paid with children

Over half of all people living in poverty comprises the low paid and their children. The income earned from employment is inadequate to pay for the extra costs of having children.

Increasing inequality

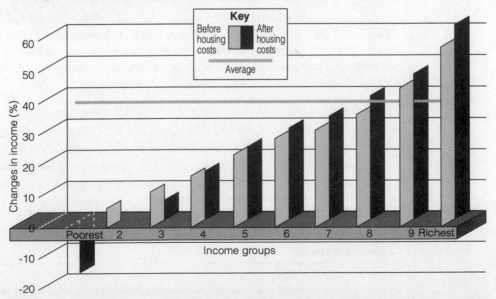

Changes in income, by income group, 1979–91

Source: 'A powerful indictment of the eighties' by N. Timmins in *The Independent*, 10 February 1995

1   What happened in terms of real increases in incomes to the majority of people during the 1980s, according to the diagram?

2   How was this change distributed amongst the various groups?

3   The chart illustrates the debate between those who believe in absolute definitions of poverty and those who believe in subjective ones. Explain the different ways that this information can be used by those who support the two viewpoints?

4   In your opinion, if most people are better off, but there is greater inequality between them, is this a good thing or a bad thing?

Lone-parent families

Poverty is not something that happens to particular individuals, but rather something that happens to *individuals in particular situations*. For example, someone who is low paid, but manages to live adequately, or perhaps who has been married and then is abandoned by her partner, can be pushed into poverty by the extra burden of children. One of the more common causes of poverty derives from the high costs of having children, and the low income that can be earned because having the responsibility of looking after children limits the chances of earning high wages.

If we look at the lowest earning 25 per cent of the population, we can see that those without children earned significantly higher amounts of money than those with children. In the early 1990s, for example, a couple in the lowest earning group without children actually earned £50 per week more than those with two children, and within this poorest 25 per cent of the population, lone parents with one child earned only half the average income of single people.

So, single parents are likely to be among the very poorest of the poor, with six out of ten single parents existing in poverty.

Sick and disabled people

According to government statistics, there are 6.2 million adults (14 per cent of all adults) and 360 000 children (3 per cent of all children) who suffer from one or more disability. Of these people with disabilities, 34 per cent were living in poverty, and the average income for an adult, under pensionable age with a disability was 72 per cent of non-disabled people.

The reasons for the poverty of people with disabilities are:

- Limited work opportunities – People with disabilities may be unable to work, or may be limited to particular kinds of low-paid employment.
- Expenses – A person with a disability has greater outgoings than a fully able person. He or she may need to have the heating on longer or may need a special diet, or special aids, for example.

Older people

About 18 per cent of the population (11 million people) are over retirement age. Women form over 65 per cent of elderly people. With the gradual raising of life expectancy, the number of elderly people in the population is likely to continue to increase until the end of the first decade of the twenty-first century.

Elderly people are usually dependent upon pensions for their income. This means living in poverty for those who only receive the state pension as this is so low. The state pension is only about 17 per cent of the average male weekly earnings.

Poverty in old age is not something that happens to all pensioners. Rather the poverty reflects the divisions in employment, income and fringe benefits that exist throughout a person's employment. Those people who are poor in old age are most likely to be those who have earned least in their working lifetime. Therefore, the groups we looked at before, the low paid, the lone-parent families, disabled and unemployed people are all poor people in their old age.

People from ethnic minorities

People of Afro-Caribbean and Asian origin have substantially higher rates of unemployment – almost twice that of Whites. This holds true even if the Black or Asian pension has the same educational qualifications as a White person.

Afro-Caribbeans and Asians are also more likely to earn lower wages than Whites, and to be employed in the lower-paying sectors of the economy, although Afro-Caribbean women earn more than White women.

Race, age and poverty

Is there a relationship between poverty and 'race'? Look at the charts.

Income, by ethnicity and age, 1990

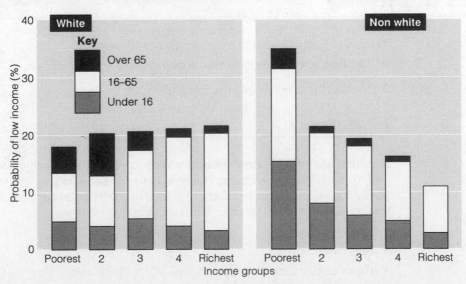

In 1990 only 18 per cent of the "white" population was in the poorest fifth of the population, agaist more than a third of the "non-white". "We are particularly concerned at what is happening to the non-white population," the inquiry states, and there are "alarming" disparities between ethnic groups. In 1988–90 only 21 per cent of all those aged 16–24 had no qualifications, but the figure rose to 48 per cent for Pakistanis and 54 per cent for Bangladeshis. Over the same period, 8 per cent of white men were unemployed, but 14 per cent of all ethnic minorities and 22 per cent of Pakistanis. Among women the gaps were even greater: 66 per cent of white women were in work, 48 per cent of all ethnic minority women, but only 16 per cent of Pakistani women.

Source: 'A powerful indictment of the eighties' by N. Timmins in *The Independent*, 10 February 1995

1 What percentage of Whites are in the richest fifth of the population? What is the proportion of non-Whites?

2 What are the percentages for these groups in the poorest and second most poor groups?

3 Can you spot any differences in affluence by age group, irrespective of 'race'?

4 What differences in unemployment are there by ethnic group and gender? What explanations could you suggest for this?

Women

The majority of the poor in Britain are women. In fact, in all the groups of poor people that we have looked at – the unemployed, the low paid, lone-parent families, the sick and disabled people, and older people – women form the majority of them. In all, there are about 4.5 million women living in poverty today.

In 1996, 95 per cent of lone parents on income support were somen, and over three times as many women over pensionable age had to ask for additional state support compared to men. This is because they are less likely to have savings.

The causes of poverty

There are two explanations for the causes of poverty:
- The first stresses the process of **dependency**.
- The second stresses the process of **exclusion**.

Dependency

Explanations which centre around the concept of dependency often stress that people who are in poverty are there because of some failing in themselves or the particular social group to which they belong. Within this approach to explaining the causes of poverty, we can distinguish:
- the individual
- the underclass
- the culture of poverty.

The individual

Quite simply poverty is a result of the failure of the individual to achieve success through his or her own efforts. People who are poor are lazy or incompetent, and should try harder.

The underclass

This is a rather more subtle development of the individual explanation, and suggests that a distinct 'underclass' exists of people who are lazy and who make no effort to work or look after themselves. These people prefer to live off the state rather than having to work.

It is important to remember that the underclass refers only to those groups of poor people who make no effort to help themselves, and the people who put forward this explanation accept that there are poor people who are in this state through no 'fault' of their own. Nevertheless, the bulk of poverty is caused by those who do not make the effort to earn a living and/or squander what they do have.

The culture of poverty

This approach stresses that the way people act is the result of how they are brought up by their family. It differs from the underclass explanation because it does not see poverty as a fault of the person. It stresses that individuals are brought up in such a way that they never have a chance to escape the poverty of their parents

Cultures develop to give people a guide as to how they should behave. In different societies people behave differently because they learn different cultures. Usually a particular culture develops because it enables people to cope with their surroundings. Cultures are always changing, but the main outlines are passed on from one generation to another mainly by parents and those who influence people when they are young.

The culture of poverty argument was first developed by Oscar Lewis when he studied very poor people in Central America. The values and behaviour (the culture) of these poor people was significantly different from the majority of the population. Lewis argued that this was because these particular values enabled the very poor to cope with circumstances which would otherwise lead to despair and hopelessness.

The cycle of poverty

A development from the culture of poverty argument is the claim that a cycle of poverty, or a cycle of transmitted deprivation, exists. This explanation concentrated on the way in which some poor people failed to help and support their children, for example by not encouraging them to work hard at school. The result was school failure and another generation condemned to poverty.

The cycle of deprivation, the culture of poverty and the underclass

'So I explained to her that the real problem was that she was suffering from the culture of poverty. She looked surprised and said that as far as she could tell she was suffering from lack of money.'

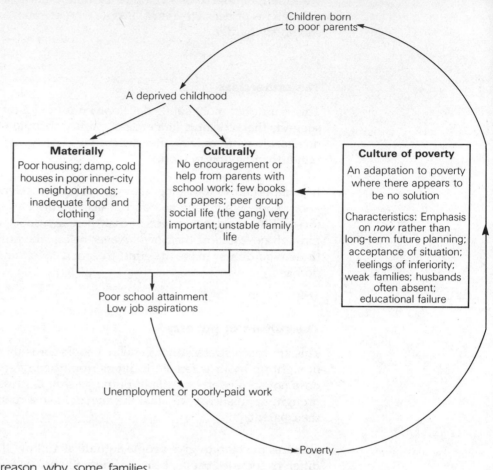

This explanation ignores the reason why some families start off poor.
Could it be that an unfair proportion of the wealth and resources of society are taken by the rich and powerful?

A

The underclass spawns illegitimate children without a care for tomorrow...Its able bodied youths see no point in working and feel no compulsion either. They reject society while feeding of it, giving the cycle of deprivation a new spin...No amount of income redistribution or social engineering can solve their problem.

Source: *The Sunday Times*, 26 November 1989

B

For increasingly, low incomes are associated with behaviour such as irresponsible sexual habits and unstable family formation, lack of commitment to work...and failure to save or spend prudently.

Source: *The Sunday Times*, 29 July 1990

C

It represents an effort to cope with feelings of hopelessness and despair which develop from the realisation that there is no possibility of achieving a comfortable standard of living.

Once it comes into existence, it tends to perpetuate its effect on the children. By the time deprived children are aged 6 or 7 they have usually absorbed the basic values and attitudes of their subculture and are not psychologically geared to take full advantage of changing conditions or opportunities which may occur in their lifetimes.

The distinguishing traits of the culture of poverty include:
- acceptance of unemployment
- low expectations of life
- lack of self-discipline
- no desire to be successful
- early sexual experiences
- violence in households
- fatalism
- lack of 'deferred gratification'...

D

'The Economic and Social Research Council commissioned a review of evidence about transmission of deprivation. *Cycles of Deprivation* – the review by Rutter and Madge – concentrates upon longitudinal studies like the National Child Development Study, which follow the progress of a cohort of individuals, gathering information about them and their circumstances at regular intervals...With respect to intelligence, educational achievement, occupational status, crime, psychiatric disorder and problem family status there are moderate continuities over two generations'...yet...Over half of all forms of disadvantage arise anew each generation. ...At least half of the children born into a disadvantaged home do not repeat the pattern of disadvantage in the next generation.

Source: M. Banton, 'The culture of poverty' in *Social Studies Review*, January 1990

1 What does the author mean in **A** when he/she refers to the underclass spawning 'illegitimate children without a care for tomorrow'?

2 Explain also the reference to 'rejecting society while feeding off it'.

3 Summarise and explain the traits of the underclass mentioned in **B** and **C**.

4 Why do you think people who support this viewpoint claim that the Welfare State plays a large part in causing the growth of the underclass?

5 What policies do you think the people who support the idea of an underclass as an explanation for poverty would suggest for getting rid of it?

6 Does **D** give much support for the continuation of an underclass over a couple of generations?

7 What is your view about the underclass and the related idea of a culture of poverty?

8 Do you think that poor people are unlucky or that they are in that state for reasons explained in the text? Give reasons for your view.

Exclusion

The second set of explanations for poverty are based on the idea of exclusion – meaning that the poor are in that situation, because they are squeezed out of a decent standard of living by the actions of others. Another term for this process is **marginalisation**. This approach stresses differences in power between the various groups in society. Those who lose out – disabled people, elderly people, women, the ethnic minorities, and of course, children – have significantly higher chances of living in poverty.

Within this approach we can distinguish the:
- dyswelfare view
- economic system approach.

The dyswelfare view

Dyswelfare describes the process in which some people lose out in complex industrial societies, through no fault of their own. They are the casualties of industrial and social change. The 'victims' of dyswelfare include physically and mentally disabled people, single parents, etc. The points to emphasise here are that their poverty is blameless and is the result of the changes in the nature of society. Secondly, society does not deliberately discriminate against any group (compare this view with the power approach below), but that it is inevitable that some people will lose out in any form of society.

It is this explanation for poverty that largely underlies the foundation of the Welfare State.

The economic system approach

The final, and most radical, explanation for the continuation of poverty comes from those who argue that society is a competition between various groups. Some groups have considerably more **power** than others and are able to impose their will on the rest of society. Power and wealth generally go together, as do poverty and powerlessness. The groups in poverty are largely formed from the powerless, in particular women, children and the ethnic minorities. Low pay and poor state benefits are the result of the fact that to pay more would be harmful to the interests of those who are more affluent.

This approach contrasts with the dyswelfare explanation, because it says that the poverty is the result of the direct and intended outcome of modern western society.

Attitudes to poverty

This is a letter written in reply to a letter published the previous week in a local newspaper. Read it carefully.

There is only one part of Mr "Paw's" letter that makes any sense and that is his statement that there is a link between illness and bad diet.

His suggestion that people on low incomes are more likely to consume a poor diet is nonsense. A good diet is a simple diet and such foods are cheap compared to expensive 'convenience' foods.

Let's look at Mr "Paw's" low income group – most people in this category are unemployed, but that is no reason to be unhealthy. In fact, the opposite should be the case because these people have the time to keep themselves fit and well.

The eight hours a day the unemployed don't work should be occupied in useful activity. Shopping for bargains in good wholesome food can be both stimulating and educational.

The basis of any sound diet is fresh fruit and vegetables and when these are bought in season they are quite cheap. New potatoes are 10p per pound at present, bananas 32p per pound.

Another important food is wholemeal bread and my local supermarket is selling a large wholemeal loaf at 38p – a penny cheaper than five years ago.

For protein, minced beef can be bought for less than £1 per pound. Fresh milk, another nourishing food, is much cheaper if bought from a supermarket than a doorstep delivery.

Mr "Paw's" glib phrase 'poverty trap' emphasises his negative thinking on this subject. Any trap is a self-imposed one created by people squandering their dole money on non-essentials like beer, baccy and junk food.

Used sensibly, the current supplementary benefit allowance can even provide the occasional luxury like a bottle of good wine.

Source: Adapted from the *Southend Standard Recorder*, 19 September 1986

1 Briefly, summarise the letter writer's viewpoint.

2 This is a reply to a previous letter. What do you think it said? Try to reconstruct the original letter by 'Mr Paw', as he wrote it to the newspaper.

3 Do you think people living on state benefits are in 'real need'? First find out the current levels of benefit by going to your local post office or benefits agency office, where you will find leaflets giving this information. In your opinion, are they adequate?

4 Conduct a small survey. Ask the following question: 'People living on income support are in real need. Do you agree or disagree?' What results do you get?

Debates in the provision of social security to combat poverty

A key theme which reappears in debates on social security provision is **targeting** (or selectivity) versus **universalism**.

Targeting and means-testing

Targeting is the term used to describe a system of welfare provision that aims benefits at particular groups in the population – those who are identified as most in need. The very concept of 'most in need' usually has a moral element in it that says these people are the most deserving, as opposed to others who, if forced to, could escape from their poverty. The best known example of targeting is the exclusion of young people under 18 from Income Support. The arguments underlying this are that it is up to the parents of the young people to support them, and that they ought to be on a work experience programme. This has led to cases of significant hardship.

What I say is – if a person can afford to smoke – well, they can't be poor!..

Targeting is closely linked to the idea of **means-testing**. By this we mean that individuals are eligible to certain benefits not just because they fall into a certain category, such as pensioners, the disabled, etc., but because they fall into this category *and* are poor. The idea of means-testing has a long history in the provision of social benefits, from outdoor to indoor 'relief' (under the Poor Law of nineteenth-century Britain), through to today's Income Support.

Means-testing is a system of awarding benefits on the basis of comparing the actual income of a person or family against what the state thinks they need in order to have an adequate standard of living. The person or family have then to prove that their income is so low that they cannot manage, and then the state makes up the difference between the actual income, and the state's level.

The advantages of means-testing

- It targets help to the most needy, and does not give money or services to those who could afford to pay and who would otherwise be subsidised by the rest of the population. Some of these people may actually be worse off than those receiving benefits. For example, free travel is given by some local authorities to pensioners, yet many of these pensioners may, in fact, be well off, while other people, paying the full fares, could be earning lower wages.
- Providing help to targeted groups should cost less to the state, as fewer people should receive benefits.
- The savings made could be spent on providing better services for the recipients, or it could be used by the government to lower taxes.

The disadvantages of means-testing

- Means testing is complex and creates a large bureaucracy to administer it. Large bureaucracies cost a large amount of money. Much of the 'savings' would not return to the government but would be used up in higher administration charges. This is precisely what happened when the community charge (now replaced by the council tax) was introduced in 1991.

- As targeting is complex, it means that quite often mistakes are made by those giving out the benefits.
- People are often confused as to what they are entitled to, as the complexity of the system acts as an obstacle to claimants.
- It is claimed that people often fail to take up the benefits because they feel embarrassed to ask (they feel 'stigmatised') or because they are ignorant of what they might claim.
- As income rises, so state benefits decline, and this can lead to what is called the poverty trap, whereby people actually lose more in state benefit than they gain from the increase in income they receive when they get a job.

Universalism

The alternative to targeting through means-testing is to give benefits to everyone who falls into a particular category. Unemployment Benefit, for example, is not means-tested. Everyone who becomes unemployed, and has paid adequate contributions to National Insurance, receives Unemployment Benefit – even though some people may not need it. Similarly, everyone who has a child receives Child Benefit.

When everyone in a particular category receives benefits, then it is known as **universalism**. Those who argue for universalism claim they are defending the Welfare State, yet very few benefits available since the Welfare State began are truly universal. The overwhelming majority of state benefits are means-tested.

Advantages of universalism

Supporters of universalism argue:
- that it eradicates the poverty trap
- that it ensures that everyone who is in need obtains the benefits, and no one is omitted through their ignorance of benefits available or through fear of stigma
- that it is cheap to operate because there is no expensive bureaucracy working out entitlement through means testing.

Disadvantages of universalism

Critics of universalism dismiss these points, claiming that it is highly expensive because so many people receive benefits unnecessarily. Money is wasted, which could go to other more needy groups. Critics also argue that giving people benefits which are not really needed encourages them to rely on the state rather than on their own resources.

An argument against universalism

Universalism has many harmful consequences. By multiplying public expenditure, it distracts finances from productive investment which would raise the general standard of living. By creating huge centralised bureaucracies, it weakens the vitality of the family, the local community and voluntary associations, which are the natural arenas of genuine mutual help. It fails to get help to those who most need it. The disadvantaged lose out to more sophisticated, better organised fellow citizens. It gradually reduces the capacity of the population for personal autonomy by schooling them to welfare dependency.

Source: D. Marsland, 'Face to Face', *Social Studies Review*, November 1989

The case for the principle of universalism

The alternative to universal provision for education, health and social security is not independence but selective provision. If these things are left to markets and families, then a substantial minority will not be able to afford them. This means a choice between leaving them to die, and providing selective 'targeted' services for those who can prove they are in serious need of state provision.

Selective 'targeted' services really do create a kind of one-way dependence,...excluding [people] from the opportunities and incentives enjoyed by their fellow citizens. For example, if a person who is unemployed can get free education, free health care and means-tested benefits, while a person in paid work must pay for schools and [medical] treatment, and food out of [their] wages, then many unskilled and partially disabled people will not be able to afford to work. If people with low wages get benefits and services which they lose as their earnings rise, they have no incentives to improve skills and increase earnings. And if savings disqualify people from getting benefits and services, poor people won't try to save.

Source: B. Jordan, 'Face to Face – The Case Against', *Social Studies Review*, November 1989

Throughout its [the social security system's] history, its primary role has been to uphold the operation of a capitalist labour market, with its social and sexual divisions of labour, and to control and contain the inequalities and poverty that result.

Source: Novak, 1988, quoted in M. Hill, *Social Security Policy in Britain* (E. Elgar Publishing, 1992)

1 Marsland rejects universalism and puts forward four objections to it. Explain what he means by 'distracting finances from productive investment which could raise the general standard of living'.

2 In what way do you think bureaucracies weaken the family, the local community, etc.?

3 Explain clearly what is meant by 'the most needy losing out to the better organised'.

4 Explain the concept of 'welfare dependency'.

5 Jordan defends the principle of universalism. What does he mean by 'selective provision'? Why is selective targeting bad?

6 What positive arguments does he make for universalism?

7 Explain the point that Jordan is making about poor people and saving.

8 Novak, in the third extract, takes a completely different viewpoint. What is this argument? Which ideological approach does this reflect? Why would he reject both universal and targeted benefits?

9 Which argument of the three do you find most persuasive?

Results of Mack and Lansley's research (page 282)

Standard-of-living items in rank order	% classing items as necessity	Standard-of-living items in rank order	% classing items as necessity
1. Heating to warm living areas of the home if it's cold	97	18. New, not second-hand clothes	64
2. Indoor toilet (not shared with another household)	96	19. A hobby or leisure activity	64
3. Damp-free home	96	20. Two hot meals a day (for adults)	64
4. Bath (not shared with another household)	94	21. Meat or fish every other day	63
5. Beds for everyone in the household	94	22. Presents for friends or family once a year	63
6. Public transport for one's needs	88	23. A holiday away from home for one week a year, not with relatives	63
7. A warm water-proof coat	87	24. Leisure equipment for children e.g. sports equipment or a bicycle[a]	57
8. Three meals a day for children[a]	82	25. A garden	55
9. Self-contained accommodation	79	26. A television	51
10. Two pairs of all-weather shoes	78	27. A 'best outfit' for special occasions	48
11. Enough bedrooms for every child over 10 of different sex to have his/her own[a]	77	28. A telephone	43
12. Refrigerator	77	29. An outing for children once a week[a]	40
13. Toys for children[a]	71	30. A dressing gown	38
14. Carpets in living rooms and bedrooms	70	31. Children's friends round for tea/a snack once a fortnight[a]	37
15. Celebrations on special occasions such as Christmas	69	32. A night out once a fortnight (adults)	36
16. A roast meat joint or its equivalent once a week	67	33. Friends/family round for a meal once a month	32
17. A washing-machine	67	34. A car	22
		35. A packet of cigarettes every other day	14

Average of all 35 items = 64.1
[a]For families with children only

Source: J. Mack and S. Lansley, *Poor Britain* (Allen & Unwin, 1985)

Chapter 16

THE MEDIA

This chapter covers:

- The media and social control
- The media and behaviour
- Democracy and the media: the debate on ownership and control
- Types of media and variety of content
- The new technology and the media
- The media and ... gender
  - ... race
  - ... politics
  - ... industrial relations
  - ... crime
- Scapegoating: The creation of folk devils and moral panics.

The media and social control

- **The media** (or the **mass media**): refers to *all* forms of written communication to the public, such as newspapers, magazines and books and to *all* forms of transmitted communication, such as radio, television and cinema

(Incidentally, the word 'media' is the plural of 'medium' and we say such things as 'the media *are...*'.)

Every society needs order and predictability: this involves persuading people to behave in certain socially acceptable ways, and punishing those who refuse to do so. This is the process known as social control. As the media are one of the main sources of information about the world for most people (virtually all of us watch television, read newspapers and magazines for instance), they play an important part in making people conform. They give us correct models of behaviour to follow, at the same time criticising anti-social behaviour.

Of course, the media are not *always* acting to promote social control. They also act as critics of current trends in society. Newspapers can promote alternative values just as much as they do traditional conservative ones.

Examine the newspapers over the last week. *Underneath* the actual stories, can you uncover a number of values?

The media and behaviour

Claims...that watching violent or pornographic videos or TV programmes can incite young people to commit crimes were supported yesterday by a psychiatrist in charge of Britain's only secure unit for severely disturbed teenagers.

Dr Susan Bailey, a consultant adolescent psychiatrist at the Gardner Unit, Prestwich Hospital, Manchester, looks after some of the most violent and disturbed children in Britain. Since 1983 she has been working with, among others, 40 child murderers aged from five to 18.

Dr Bailey told a London meeting of the Royal College of Psychiatrists that a quarter of the murderers had a history of extensive viewing of violent videos. She said she could not say that the videos made the children kill, but they certainly had an effect on the methods used and many of the murders reflected the films' contents.

"One boy was obsessed with martial arts and samurai videos. He committed his murder using a samurai sword."

She said many young sex offenders she saw had acted out fantasies provided by pornographic or violent films.

"There's no doubt that violent and pornographic videos or TV does have an effect. It influences the nature of the crime."

Source: *The Guardian*, 20 March 1993

Prosecutor Peter Skandalakis said Jason Lewis opened fire with a shotgun at their home in Coweta County, Georgia in a bid to emulate the recent Oliver Stone film Natural Born Killers in which a couple kill 52 people.

Source: *The Guardian*, 9 March 1995

1 Does Dr Bailey believe that videos made the children kill?

2 What effect does she claim videos have? Give two examples.

3 From observing which group of people has Dr Bailey formed her views?

4 Has she observed people who have not committed crimes, but watched the videos?

5 Can you see any weaknesses in Dr Bailey's evidence?

We know that the media play an important role in society by channelling social behaviour into socially acceptable patterns, but specifically *how* do the media affect individuals? Sociologists have suggested four ways of understanding the effects of the media on individuals:

* the personal (or behaviourist) approach
* the opinion leader approach
* the audience selection approach
* the cultural approach.

The personal approach

This approach stresses that the media have a very direct effect on the individual. They are said to respond to the 'stimulus' (message) of the media. For instance, a child watching a television programme containing violence is likely to be influenced into violent acts him or herself.

The opinion leader approach

This approach argues that most people have one or a number of individuals whose opinion they respect, and they are more likely to be swayed in their opinions by the views of these 'opinion leaders' than directly by the media. So, people are only influenced by the media when the opinion leaders are in agreement.

The audience selection approach

This approach starts from the fact that the audience *chooses* which films and programmes to watch and which newspapers to buy. Depending upon why they have bought it, or are watching it, the newspaper or film will influence them. Therefore, someone who likes the idea of committing violence may watch a violent film and enjoy it for that. Another person may simply enjoy the elements of suspense in the same film, and may see the violence as of no importance or even irritating. The content is therefore understood in different ways by the viewer or reader.

The cultural approach

This approach follows on from the personal approach, but goes further in exploring the culture within which the media exist and influence people. The media are not seen as having an immediate effect on individuals, but they have instead a very slow effect, building up a climate of opinion and expectations about society.

Attitudes towards women, for instance, are strongly influenced by the way they are portrayed in the media. The daily 'page 3' photograph does not directly drive men into raping women, but it does strengthen (or create?) the way in which they see women as sexual figures whose looks count more than their personalities.

What is your view of 'pin-up' photographs of women: an insult or a 'bit of fun'?

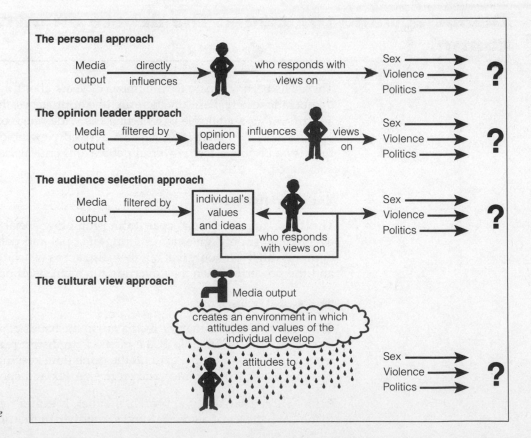

How the media influence people

The effects of the media

Early researchers supposed a sequence of events. First knowledge and opinions change, then feelings, and finally behaviour changes. We can see why such a simple model was abandoned when we note McQuail's list of six possible effects. The media might:

● produce the major change it intends
● produce a major change that was not intended
● stimulate a minor change
● bring about some change when other influences occur as well
● reinforce what already exists
● prevent some change that would otherwise have occurred.

Add the possibility that any effects may be long-term and gradually build up.

...Insofar as there is a consensus about the effect of television, it involves the following. First, television does not have a strong independent effect. It is too easily ignored, talked over or switched off. Furthermore, people perceive *selectively*. They see and hear those things which tend to confirm their present world-view; they pass over or filter out information which does not have a place in their mental cupboards. Consequently, the main impact of television is *confirmatory*. If it presents images which fit with what people already believe, it bolsters those views; if what it presents clashes with views already held, it is ignored or explained away. Second, television messages influence only the sympathetic. Only those disposed to see some issue in a particular light respond positively to attempts to influence them in that direction.

Source: Adapted from S. Bruce, 'Pray TV: Observations on Mass Media Religion' in *Sociology Review*, November 1991

1 Explain in your own words what the early researchers first thought.

2 Draw a diagram to illustrate the six possible effects of the media on people.

3 What does the extract mean when it says that people perceive *selectively*? Why is this important to our understanding of the effects of the media?

4 Explain the meaning of the term 'confirmatory'?

5 Suggest a way in which you could test this with a group of people.

Democracy and the media: The debate on ownership and control

There has been a debate for a number of years about the role of the media in a democratic society. Basically there are two approaches, the puralist sees the media as performing a vital role in reflecting the wide range of views on political and social issues. The alternative, Marxist-derived view holds that the media reflect the views of only a few powerful people and critical views of our society are smothered.

The pluralist view

This holds that the media, apart from promoting social control for the good of everyone in society, gives a free airing of social and political issues where opinions differ. Not only that but they also act as watchdogs, criticising politicians and the powerful when they override the interests of ordinary people.

The Marxist view

This approach argues that the media are in the hands of a few people who impose their views on us. The role of the media is to distort reality, justifying the deep inequalities of wealth that exist, at the same time keeping the masses happy with pictures of attractive women and stories on sex and sport.

Before we can say which approach, if either, is nearer the truth, it may be helpful to look at patterns of ownership and secondly patterns of control of media output.

Ownership of the media

The evidence clearly shows that a few companies and owners dominate the media. The newspaper industry is dominated by just five companies, the cinemas by two, radio by the BBC, and television by the BBC and the five biggest independent companies. One man alone, Rupert Murdoch, through his company, News International, owns newspapers which account for 40 per cent of newspaper sales and about 7.5% of television viewers.

The trend of ownership is one of concentration, which means that the media of all types are coming under the ownership of fewer companies. Linked to this is the trend towards internationalisation, which means that companies owning the media have international links, so there will be fewer independent sources of information in the world. The recent development of satellite television transmissions means that one company can now broadcast to whole continents.

Ownership of ITV companies

In 1993, the government relaxed controls on the ownership of TV companies. The result was for the bigger companies to buy up the smaller companies.

Television insiders suggest that the 15 ITV companies will be reduced to four large groupings.

ITV first blood: The playing field for the most likely predators

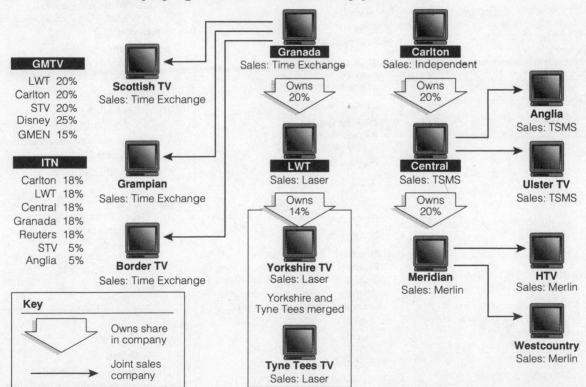

GMTV

LWT 20%
Carlton 20%
STV 20%
Disney 25%
GMEN 15%

ITN

Carlton 18%
LWT 18%
Central 18%
Granada 18%
Reuters 18%
STV 5%
Anglia 5%

Scottish TV
Sales: Time Exchange

Grampian
Sales: Time Exchange

Border TV
Sales: Time Exchange

Key

Owns share in company

Joint sales company

Granada
Sales: Time Exchange

Owns 20%

LWT
Sales: Laser

Owns 14%

Yorkshire TV
Sales: Laser

Yorkshire and Tyne Tees merged

Tyne Tees TV
Sales: Laser

Carlton
Sales: Independent

Owns 20%

Central
Sales: TSMS

Owns 20%

Meridian
Sales: Merlin

Anglia
Sales: TSMS

Ulster TV
Sales: TSMS

HTV
Sales: Merlin

Westcountry
Sales: Merlin

Source: *The Guardian*, 20 November 1993

1 What did informed people expect to happen to the ITV companies?

2 Which are likely to be the four biggest companies?

3 These are known as 'terrestrial broadcasting' channels. Why, do you think?

4 Which big competitors are not on the diagram?

Ownership of the media

MIRROR GROUP NEWSPAPERS

[N] **Mirror Group Newspapers (100%)**
Daily Mirror, Sunday Mirror, People, Sunday Mail, Daily Record, Sporting Life

[□] **Pergamon Media Trust (100%)**
Central TV (19.8%), Border TV (15%), MTV (25%), Maxwell Cable TV

Pergamon Professional & Financial Services
AGB Research

[M] **Maxwell Communication Corporation (52%)**
Pergamon Journals, British Magazine Publishing Corporation

[P] Mid Somerset Series

[□] Macmillan (US)

[□] Canal 10/Film Success (10%)

Key

[N] National Newspapers

[P] Provincial Papers

[M] Magazines

[□] Books

[□] Television

[📻] Radio

NEWS INTERNATIONAL CORPORATION

[N] **News Group**
Sun, News of the World

[N] **Times Newspaper Holdings**
Sunday Times, Times, Times Educational Supplement, Times Literary Supplement, Times Higher Education Supplement

[N] **News UK**
Today

[□] **Sky Television**

[M] **Murdoch Magazines**
New Woman, TV Guide, Sky Magazine (50%)

Times Books

[□] **William Collins**
Reuters (5.75%)
Reed (3.8%)
Pearson (approx. 18%)

UNITED NEWSPAPERS

[N] **Express Newspapers**
Daily Express, Sunday Express, Daily Star, Scottish Daily Express, Scottish Sunday Express

[P] **Regional newspapers:**
8 dailies, 95 weeklies

[M] **Magazines & Exhibitions**
● consumer 40
● business 94
● business directories 18
● exhibitions 9

Information Services
Extel Financial, Exchange Telegraph Co.

Advertising periodicals (4)

[📻] Yorkshire Radio Network (9.4%)

DAILY MAIL & GENERAL TRUST

[N] **Associated Newspapers**
Daily Mail, Mail on Sunday, Evening Standard

[P] **Northcliffe Newspapers**
13 provincial dailies, 17 provincial weeklies, 27 free newspapers

[P] Bristol Evening Post (23.8%)

[P] **Bristol United Press**
Ordinary shares (40%)

[P] **Portsmouth & Sunderland Newspapers (5%)**

[M] Burlington Publishing
5 titles

[📻] Swansea Sound (18%), GWR (8%), Crown Communications (9.3%), Essex Radio (6.9%), Gloucester Broadcasting (7.7%), North Staffordshire & South Cheshire Broadcasting (10.4%)

Reuters (7.7%)

LONHRO

[N] The Observer, 2 magazines

[P] **George Outram & Co. Ltd**
Glasgow Herald, Evening Times

[P] Scottish & Universal Newspapers (22)

[M] **Outram Magazine Division (4)**

[📻] Radio Clyde (4.5%)

GUARDIAN & MANCHESTER EVENING NEWS

[N] The Guardian, Manchester Evening News, The Rochdale Observer series, Lancashire & Cheshire County newspapers, Surrey Advertiser series, Specialist magazines

[📻] 17% of Piccadilly Radio, Red Rose, Red Dragon, Radio Aire

[□] Anglia TV (5%), Broadcast Communications (14%)

PEARSON

[N] **Financial Times Group**
Financial Times, Westminster Press (8 dailies, 69 weeklies, 3 monthlies), FT Business Information (conference/newsletter/database), Investors Chronicle, Economist (50%)

[□] **Penguin**
Viking, Michael Joseph, Hamish Hamilton, Puffin, Frederick Warne

[□] Yorkshire Television (20%), British Satellite Broadcasting (13%), Pickwick Group 21%

[□] **Longman**
Ladybird, Pitman

HOLLINGER

[N] **Daily Telegraph (83%)**
Daily Telegraph, Sunday Telegraph

[M] Spectator

[N] United Newspapers (3.36%)

Source: Adapted from *Social Studies Review*, September 1989

1 Make a list of the national newspapers shown in the table opposite. Now list those which are not in the table (these are not part of large corporations).

2 Would you describe the pattern of ownership of national newspapers as:
   a) concentrated?
   b) widespread?

3 What does this table and the chart on page 305 tell you about ownership and control of broadcasting in the UK?

4 What does the chart on page 305 suggest will happen in the future?

5 Does the information we have extracted from the table tell us anything about the possible range of views that will appear on radio, television and in the newspapers?

Content of the media

It is clear that the media are owned by very few people, but this does not mean that the owners totally control their contents. Publishers and broadcasting companies have to take into account that the medium, whether television or newspapers, must be commercial; that is, that it attracts a large (or at least affluent) audience and that the medium attracts advertising. Although the personal views of the owner are important, these can be overridden by the need to make money.

Broadcasters and publishers need to ensure a large audience with the sort of interests and income to afford the products of advertisers. On the other hand, they must be careful not to offend advertisers. An exposé on the dubious practices of a travel firm is unlikely to attract advertising from that firm! The result is that publishers and broadcasters choose between two options: to appeal to a very small audience with proven attractiveness to an advertiser – the **specialist approach** (such as specialist car magazines); or to appeal to as many people as possible – the **mass market approach**. Media which do not rely on advertising revenue, such as record companies and film companies tend to follow the mass market approach.

News values

When journalists set up a news story for television or for the newspapers, they work on the assumption that there are certain components that a good story must have. These components are known as **news values** or **journalist values**, and include the following elements:

- **frequency** The time period of the event should be short and self-contained. A good story is one where there is a clear beginning and end. A terrible famine one year in Africa is news, but the long-term malnutrition of Africans from poverty is not a good story.

- **importance** A good story must be fairly important to the person watching or reading. Often this means that the item of news must be national or local.

- **clarity** Complex events do not make good stories, so the simpler an event is the better.

- **meaningfulness** A viewer is not interested in things that are beyond his or her understanding or culture. So the broadcaster or editor must be sure that the story will strike some chord in the viewer.

- **unexpectedness** There should always be a hint of surprise, otherwise why is it noteworthy?

- **composition** For newspapers and general news programmes on television, there has to be a mix of news, such as sport, human interest stories, politics, humour, and so on. News is covered if it is needed for that 'slot'.

- **personalisation** Stories are far more interesting if they are about people, not about issues or events. The media always try to include a 'human angle' in their stories.

- **political and legal pressures** Finally, there are 'outside' pressures on journalists from such things as the laws of libel (you are not allowed to print or broadcast untrue statements about people) and in politics there are special 'briefings' given by senior politicians, or spokespersons speaking on their behalf, which allow journalists to give special 'insights' to the public. Journalists therefore often tell the public what politicians want them to say, but the public don't realise it.

Media content: The influence of the owners

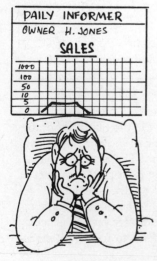

'By and large the editors will have complete freedom', promised Lord Matthews the...proprietor of Express Newspapers since 1977, 'as long as they agree with the policy I have laid down'. 'I did not come all this way (from Australia)' declared Robert Murdoch, owner of *The News of the World* and *The Sun*, 'not to interfere.' '...He (the owner) did this by persistent derision of them (opponents of Mrs Thatcher) at our meetings and on the telephone, by sending me articles marked "worth reading", which supported right-wing views, by pointing a finger at head-lines which he thought could have been more supportive of Mrs Thatcher' – Harold Evans, former editor of *The Times* (owned by Rupert Murdoch).

But normally, editors and journalists have understood the sorts of news items and ways of presenting them that would be acceptable to the owners, which has made heavy-handed interference by them unnecessary (in other words that the paper is generally conservative and supports the views of big business, the law and the police – with only slight criticism of these institutions allowed). Owners have usually had a power over the appointment of senior managers too.

Source: Adapted from M. Grant, *The British Media* (Comedia, 1984)

The power of an owner to influence people ultimately depends upon the sales

1 Do editors and journalists decide exactly what sort of stories go into newspapers? Give one quote to support your answer.

2 Give two examples of how the owner of *The Times* influenced its contents.

3 Normally 'heavy handed interference' by owners is not necessary, according to the extract. Why not?

Types of media and variety of content

There are different types of media, including television, radio, newspapers and magazines. The content of the media varies mainly according to the audience that they are aimed at. This can be illustrated by the clear differences in content between the BBC radio stations. Radio 2 for middle-of-the-road entertainment (for middle-aged people) and Radio 1 for contemporary music (aiming at the younger audience).

The newspapers, too, reflect these divisions and in some ways mirror the class differences in British society, with the 'quality' papers (such as *The Guardian* and *The Observer*) and the 'popular' papers (such as *The Mirror* or *The Sun*). The contents of these papers vary considerably with the information in the quality papers being more detailed and less sensational than that in the popular papers. The focus of the quality papers tends to be on politics and economics, while the stress on the popular papers is on sensational stories often involving some sexual or criminal element.

The new technology and the media

In the last ten years there have been great changes in broadcasting and printing, brought about mainly by the power of new technology.

Broadcasting

Two developments have affected broadcasting in recent years – cable and satellites. Both of these technologies mean that it is possible for many more television stations to broadcast. The potential exists for a massive increase in stations to cater for all tastes and interests, but two things limit this. First the increased competition for advertising means that there is a greater inclination to go for the most popular, if not necessarily the best, programmes. Secondly, the enormous costs of setting up broadcasting networks by cable or satellite mean that only the richest and biggest companies can enter the market.

Print

The developments in Information Technology allows newspapers and books to be produced with fewer staff, at lower costs, in a shorter time.

Media audiences

1 Collect a cross-section of daily newspapers. Suggest who they are aimed at, giving reasons for your conclusions.

2 Listen to BBC Radio 3 and 4, and to local radio stations. Suggest what audience they are aimed at. How does this influence their contents and presentation?

3 In one evening (starting at about 4 p.m.), check every hour which programmes are on each channel and suggest their target audience. Give your reasons.

National newspaper circulation

The circulation of national dailies and Sunday newspapers, January 1995

Dailies		Sundays	
Sun	4,106,278	News of the World	4,854,766
Daily Mirror	2,460,691	Sunday Mirror	2,519,511
Daily Record	751,999	People	2,091,780
Daily Star	746,881	Mail on Sunday	2,001,679
Daily Mail	1,807,719	Sunday Express	1,438,936
Daily Express	1,297,259	Sunday Times	1,262,772
Today	614,459	Sunday Telegraph	657,901
Daily Telegraph	1,069,818	Observer	473,331
Guardian	410,836	Independent/Sunday	313,051
Times	631,449		
Independent	290,804		
Financial Times	279,253		

(*Source* ABC)

1 Which was Britain's best selling newspaper in January 1995?

2 Which was its main rival?

3 Which sold the fewest copies of the daily newspapers?

4 Does the number of copies sold determine how profitable a newspaper is?

5 Which is the biggest selling Sunday newspaper?

6 Look at the diagram of media ownership on page 306. Which company owns the best selling daily and Sunday newspapers?

Design a newspaper

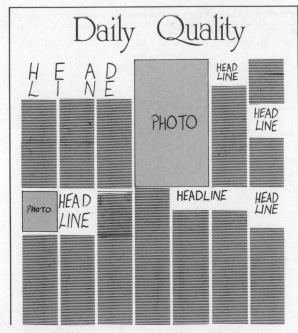

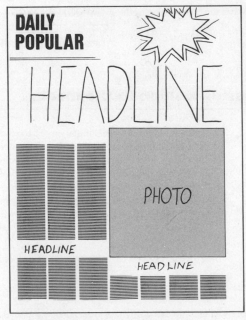

1 As a group, obtain copies of as many of the daily and weekly newspapers as you can, both national and local.

2 Do they have different sorts of story in them? Classify the differences in terms of content, style of language, layout, etc.

3 What explanations can you give for the differences?

4 Design your own front page, with imaginary headlines, layout and content.

The media and...

In this section, I want to look at the specific relationship between the media and a number of important areas of social life, in particular gender, race, politics, industrial relations and crime.

Gender

The media reflect (and help maintain) the two main roles of women: to be sexually attractive to men, and to be 'caring' mothers and housewives. The first of these two roles is to be found in the 'news' which is repeated daily on page 3 of *The Sun* that women have breasts! We are so accustomed to descriptions of women which describe them as 'attractive blond, 25...' and to comments on their clothes, that we think little of it. If similar comments were made about men, however, it *would* be noticeable.

As for the 'mothering' role, this is catered for by the large number of women's magazines on sale. These deal with recipes, household problems and romance stories. Those aimed at the younger, supposedly 'liberated' women (such as *19*) are largely concerned with attractiveness to men and, to a much lesser extent, careers (though usually in traditional areas of women's work such as secretarial and nursing work).

Ferguson in *Forever Feminine* found that there were certain themes which could be found in all women's magazines. These included the value of youth and beauty, female unpredictability and the importance of love in women's lives. She argues that these strengthen the lower-status position of women in society.

Images of women in the media

Even the most superficial glance at a selection of magazines will confirm that women are portrayed and addressed primarily in terms of their role as homemaker, wife or mother and their sexuality...magazines aimed at women fall into two broad categories – those which focus on fashion, beauty and 'getting a man' and those which deal with 'the three Cs' – cooking, cleaning and caring.

In newspapers it almost seems that whatever women do they will be treated in terms of their domesticity and/or their sexuality. Most obvious, of course, is the titillating way in which rapes and sexual assaults are reported in the popular press.

Source: R. Gill, 'Altered images of women in the media' in *Social Studies Review*, September 1991

1 According to the extract, how do women's magazines portray women?

2 According to the extract, what two categories do the magazines fall into?

3 Obtain as many women's magazines as you can. Analyse the photographs and the articles. Do you agree with the writer of the extract?

4 How are women portrayed in the daily newspapers? Obtain a cross-section of newspapers and analyse them. Do you agree, or are there differences between types of paper? If there are differences can you explain them?

This process of analysing the contents of the media is known as **content analysis**.

The media and gender

A nationwide poll has just revealed the secret behind sexual attraction. Women all over the country were asked just what attracted them most to a man. The result? Over 76 per cent put 'a good personality' which could 'make them laugh' as their first choice. As for the men, the number one choice was a women with a 'good bottom and legs'.

1 Examine a sample of recent newspapers and magazines (there will be some in the library) and make a list of the words used to describe men and women. Are there any differences? What sort of images of men and women do they present?

2 In what ways might the mass media be said to influence the different attitudes of men and women towards each other?

3 Collect pictures from newspapers and magazines showing the different images of men and women portrayed in the media.

Race

The attitude of the press towards race has been to see the whole topic in terms of a social problem. The general position of the press has been to stress the negative aspects of black Britons. Massive prominence is given in the 'tabloid' press to crime and riots, yet relatively little to the achievements of Blacks in sport for example, where the successful athlete is rarely described as 'black'. But the criminal, on the other hand, is. There are only three million Blacks and Asians living in Britain and most of these are concentrated in a few major cities, so the image of Blacks as a social problem, always causing trouble, as presented in the media has created a stereotype in the minds of the majority of Whites.

The media and race

Newspapers have been strongly criticised for offering only a negative view of race, and of always relating race with immigration. Under the guise of news stories, critics claim that racist feelings are encouraged.

Source: *The Daily Mail*, 13 March 1995

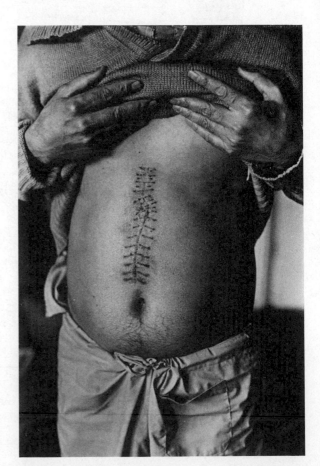

A black victim of a racial attack

The media stress the bad things done by the ethnic minorities and ignore the unpleasant aspects of their lives.

Have you read about the regular attacks on the ethnic minorities in the newspapers, or seen anything on television?

Politics

We have already discussed this in the section on the media and democracy (see page 304). The point is that the press predominantly supports the Conservative Party, while broadcasting (television and radio) is generally liberal or conservative. Neither challenge the current society and rarely present alternatives. Only two of the major daily newspapers do not support the Conservative Party. However, it has been pointed out that there is nothing stopping radical newspapers: they fail because there is no public support for them.

Political bias and the media

The following research was undertaken during the 1992 election campaign.

Research...by Loughborough University shows that the daily tabloids – with the exception of the Labour-supporting Daily Mirror – are surpassing their reputation for Tory bias, while broadcasters stick religiously to fair shares for all. ...

In broadcasting, the two main parties achieve a broadly similar profile of presentation, attack and defence. ...

In the daily tabloids, by contrast, the Conservatives present and attack, but never defend, while Labour defend far more than they present or attack, although their proportion of policy presentation (thanks, probably, to the Mirror) exceeds that of the Tories. ...

Peter Golding, co-director of the Communications Research Centre at Loughborough, [said] "In the tabloid press a very different show is on display, with outright partisanship as distinct and sharp as ever. ..."

Source: *The Guardian*, 30 March 1992

1 Which paper supported the Labour Party in the 1992 election?

2 Name the papers which supported the Conservative Party in the 1992 election, according to the analysis?

3 Is there any difference between the press and television/radio?

Industrial relations

We have seen throughout this discussion of the media and their relationship to society, just how conservative they are. This reflects patterns of ownership and the expectations of the audience. The media are just as conservative too when it comes to strikes. They portray workers on strike as 'greedy' and as 'standing in the way of technological advance and efficiency'.

The Glasgow University Media Group studied the television coverage of strikes in the late 1970s. They concluded that the news constantly over-simplified the issues, laying the blame on the workers. The views of the management were given greater support than those of the workers. The actual styles of interview for the news were different too, with managers being interviewed in their offices and workers outside on the picket line. The impression this gave to the viewer was that the manager's view was far more reliable and authoritative.

Strikes and the media

In the case of a strike...

The basic 'facts' of the case are taken from management usually in a studio interview – while 'opinions' and events themselves are sought from the workers – usually outside the factory gates, even when they are not picketing. Interviews involving both sides often contain more 'supportive' questions to management:

'What will this strike cost your company?' or

'Do you think the workers have been misled by their leaders?' and more challenging or hostile questions to workers:

'After this strike will there be a job to go back to?'

'Aren't you cutting your own throats?'

'Do you realise the public hardship you are causing?'

Hardship to the public caused by strikes is newsworthy, but the hardship of low wages and poor working conditions of that same 'public' is not. The media tend to see their audience as consumers rather than workers, and strike-breaking is explicitly approved – the one train that does run is more newsworthy than the thousands that do not.

The 'cost' to the company of industrial action is very often stressed, usually in misleading terms of the total selling price of the goods and not simply lost profits. Savings to the company in wages, materials, fuel and other production costs are seldom taken into account. Nor is the fact that, sometimes, 'lost production' could not have been sold anyway: many strikes occur during periods of high production and low demand, and managers may then even push their workers into strike action (for example by cutting break times) precisely because this can save overall costs. The cost to the workers themselves in lost wages is rarely stressed, although because of the very real hardship involved workers will usually strike only as a last resort and only over a deeply-felt grievance.

Source: Adapted from M. Grant, *The British Media* (Comedia, 1984)

1 Tape a range of interviews from the TV and the radio. As a group, compare the style of questioning.

2 Is it true what the author says in the extract?

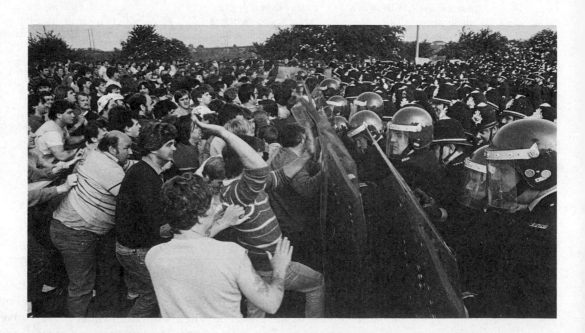

Crime

False impression of the patterns of crime

Press and broadcasting coverage of crime tends to concentrate on certain areas and gives the impression that these sorts of crime are far more common than they are in reality. In order to give exciting headlines, the press concentrates on violent crime and sex cases, which are over-reported by a minimum of 20 times their actual occurrence. This creates stereotypes of crime and criminals in people's minds, so that older people, for instance, may be too frightened to go out.

Women, crime and fear

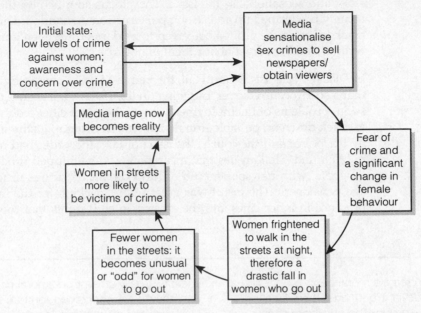

Initial state: low levels of crime against women; awareness and concern over crime

Media sensationalise sex crimes to sell newspapers/ obtain viewers

Media image now becomes reality

Fear of crime and a significant change in female behaviour

Women in streets more likely to be victims of crime

Fewer women in the streets: it becomes unusual or "odd" for women to go out

Women frightened to walk in the streets at night, therefore a drastic fall in women who go out

Source: S. Moore, *Investigating Deviance* (Collins, 1987)

Crime and the media

Just like prices, the amount of violent crime always seems to be going up.

However,...when four sociologists examined the *Leicester Mercury*'s reports of violence throughout Britain between 1900 and 1975 and compared this to the memories of retired policemen, they found that our times are not particularly violent and that people are less tolerant of street violence than they once were.

Why do people imagine that we live in a period of great violence? The authors suggest that the style of newspaper reporting of violent crime has changed and that it is now increasingly sensationalised (made to seem more exciting than it really is), as this sells more copies. So, the authors think that newspapers are more likely to over-report violent disorders than ever before thereby creating the impression of greater violence.

Source: *The Economist*, 1 March 1986

1 Do the media give a true impression of the extent of crime?

2 Why is this so?

The police viewpoint

Because the bulk of the information about crime and police activities comes from the police, reporters tend to give their viewpoint sympathetically. Although in cases where disputes arise over abuses of power by police, this often means that alternative views are not fairly treated in the press.

Scapegoating: The creation of folk devils and moral panics

Certain groups in society are often seen as posing a particular threat to the social order, for instance football hooligans. The media exploit the possibilities of a good story and sensationalise the issue. They focus so much on the area that public anxiety is whipped up and strong police action demanded. This results in a severe crackdown on the groups perceived to be dangerous, even if much of the material written and broadcast about them is not true.

In *Policing the Crisis*, Stuart Hall, through a Marxist perspective, analysed the way that a scare occurred over 'mugging' in the 1970s. Hall argues that in the 1970s the social problems of unemployment and of the inner cities led to a need by the state to crack down on possible trouble makers. In order to justify increased repression by the police and the courts, the issue of law and order had to be brought to the public mind. Hall argues that a campaign was whipped up against (black) muggers, with newspapers full of lurid details of vicious muggings against old age pensioners. The result was great public backing for the increased police presence in inner cities and the erosion in civil rights that took place.

A moral panic

The media can help to create a moral panic by labelling a group of people as deviant/bad and then creating a stereotype image of this group. The public are concerned and demand action by the police. Anyone who fits the public stereotype of this type of troublemaker is then under suspicion.

There is usually at least one moral panic each year. In the past they have concerned football supporters, inner-city black youths, drug takers (particularly glue sniffing) and the yearly 'peace convoys' to Glastonbury.

Using the model below, follow the history of any one moral panic.

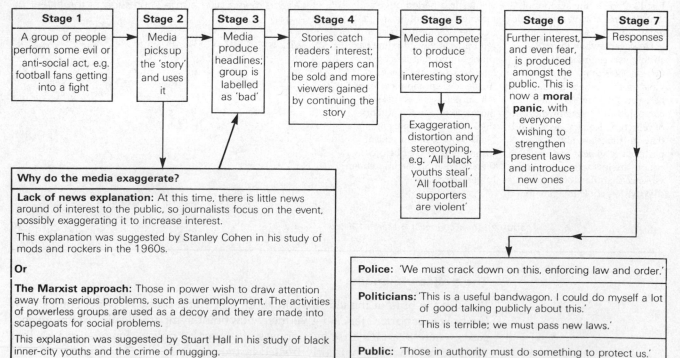

Advertising

In *The Hidden Persuaders*, Vance Packard exposed how advertisers were trying to 'ferret out' and then exploit our deepest needs – emotional security, 'reassurance of worth', status, sex and so on in attempts to sell products.

Market researchers are still using nearly all the strategies Vance Packard described, and new ones have been added. Peter Cooper, a psychologist who founded the Cooper Research and Marketing Agency, says, 'We want to attach *meanings* to brands, ones appropriate to those different groups in society, to get people to buy those brands rather than other similar objects,' for example Lux lather on the face of a beautiful, mature women – soft skin, fewer wrinkles, youth, beauty, sexual attraction, or a Renault 5 surrounded by disco dancers – youthful, fun-loving, stylish.

Is the advertising expertise of decades now doing its deadly work and manipulating us unawares? Politicians have started hiring ad agencies, which should be enough to make us re-examine the role of media persuasion.

But, research seems to show that we are not *that* gullible. A recent report 'Advertising, Brands and Markets' concluded that whether or not ads are successful depends on many other factors including, surprise, the quality of the brand. Price is also important, packaging, distribution, competition and so on.

Second, if advertising could really 'dictate how our society must think, act and dream' as some critics claim, then heavily advertised products should grab an ever increasing share of the market at the expense of less heavily promoted products – 'but such trends cannot be identified'. Third, if advertising were such a powerful manipulator, the report says, the failure rate for new products backed by heavy advertising would not be anything like the estimated nine out of ten.

Source: Adapted from M. Tysoe, 'Never give a sucker an even break' in *New Society*, 2 May 1985

1 Briefly explain how advertisers try to make us buy products.

2 What sort of 'meanings' do advertisers create concerning:
   a) perfume?
   b) beer?
   c) jeans?
   d) cars (there could be more than one meaning here depending upon the 'market')?
   e) Coca-Cola?

3 According to the extract, are advertisers wholly successful in selling things? Give two reasons for your answer.

4 What other important factors are there?

5 What are the two most effective advertisements which have influenced you? Explain why they did so.

Chapter 17

RELIGION

This chapter covers:
* The relationship between religion and society
* Christian religions: Declining or changing?
* The growth of sects and new religions
* Non-Christian religions in Britain.

The relationship between religion and society

In every society people are frightened about the certainty of their deaths; they need some explanation for their brief stay here on earth. Surely it must all have some meaning? It is precisely this question that religion answers. Life does have meaning and there is a life after this one on earth.

The relationship between religion and society has been the subject of furious debate amongst sociologists. They agree on one thing only: that religion is important to society and *does* affect the way people act. Basically, there are three views on religion:

* that it is good for society, helping to draw people together and creating a sense of community
* that it is a bad thing for the majority of people, stopping them complaining about the unfairness of society
* that it can be important in bringing about social change.

Before we go on to discuss these viewpoints we ought to note that sociologists are not concerned about the question of whether God exists or not, that is a question far beyond the powers of mere sociologists! They are only concerned with the *role* of religion in society.

Religion is good for society

This was the viewpoint of the nineteenth-century sociologist, Emile Durkheim. He pointed out that religion helps both society and individuals in different ways.

For society

Religion provides the moral backing to the rules and laws of society, placing them beyond question. The result is a generally accepted way of behaving, which pulls people together in a shared morality. Those who do not share these basic values

To work hard, to obey those above you, to accept with patience and humility the unhappiness of this life – for your reward lies beyond this life, in Heaven.

Religion: the opiate of the people?

are regarded as outsiders and deviants. The result is that religion plays a major part in keeping societies stable and preventing abrupt change.

For the individual

Religion can provide a sense of purpose and meaning in life. We are here because God put us here and after our death we will go on to an after-life. Secondly, it gives us emotional support in times of crisis. So, death is not such a tragic event if we know that the dead person has gone to Heaven. Thirdly, for many people the church provides them with a sense of community. They feel they belong to something that cares about them.

Religion is a bad thing

This approach derives from the nineteenth-century sociologist, Karl Marx, who saw religion as a means by which people are tricked out of seeing the way they are being cheated and used by the rich and powerful. Although most people spend their lives working for the rich, they are comforted with the knowledge that if they cause no trouble and do their best to live a 'good' life (that is, to do what they are told), then they will go to heaven after death. Religion then prevents them from ever questioning society the way it is. For Marxists, religion acts as a form of social control.

Religion as a cause of social change

A criticism of both the above approaches is that religion can also lead to social change, as well as maintaining stability, and can be used as a focus by the poor and underprivileged to challenge their position in society. The Iranian revolution which overthrew the Shah of Persia was led by the Islamic religious leaders.

Max Weber, writing at the beginning of the twentieth century, suggested the idea that religion always plays a major role in maintaining social stability is not true. He argued that religious ideas are just as likely to bring about change as to prevent it.

Weber described how the ideas of a Protestant sect, the Calvinists, played a crucial part in bringing about industrialisation (production by machines in factories) in Britain more than 200 years ago. Calvinists believed that working hard and not spending money on enjoying oneself was the way to win God's approval. To be successful was taken as a sign of approval by God and an indication that one was likely to go to Heaven. The result of the Calvinists' hard work (and no play) was considerable savings, which they were able to invest in factories. People with other religions which stressed giving money away to the poor, for instance, which resulted in them having only small savings would not have been able to finance the building of factories and machinery. So Weber concluded that the values of Calvinism led to savings which in turn led to industrialisation as we know it today.

It is important to remember that Weber was not saying that Marx and Durkheim were wrong, only that religion can bring about change as well as stability and that it is not always a way of manipulating people.

Religion and social control

The Ragged Trousered Philanthropists is a classic novel published in 1914 which tells of the lives of a group of workers of that period. The author uses the book for some very bitter criticisms of British society. Amongst the objects of his attacks was religion.

'Well the vicar goes about telling the Idlers that it's quite right for them to do nothing, and that God meant them to have nearly everything that is made by those who work. In fact he tells them that God made the poor for the use of the rich. Then he goes to the workers and tells them that God meant them to work very hard and to give all the good things they make to those who do nothing, and that they should be very thankful to God and to the Idlers for being allowed to have even the very worst food to eat and the rags and broken boots to wear. He also tells them that they mustn't grumble, or be discontented because they're poor in this world, but that they must wail till they're dead, and then God will reward them by letting them go to a place called heaven.'

Frankie laughed, 'Do they believe it?'

'Most of them do, because when they were little children like you, their mothers taught them to believe, without thinking, whatever the vicar said, and that God made them for the use of the Idlers. When they went to school, they were taught the same thing: and now they've grown up they really believe it, and they go to work and give nearly everything they make to the Idlers, and have next to nothing left for themselves and their children.'

Source: R. Tressall, *The Ragged Trousered Philanthropists* (Granada, 1965)

1 Who is the author referring to when he talks about 'the Idlers'?

2 What does the vicar tell the workers?

3 Why shouldn't they complain?

4 Why do they believe it?

5 Why do sociologists call religion 'an agency of social control'?

6 Today the influence of religion has declined. Are there any other agencies which have taken over the job of social control? If so, what are they?

7 Can you suggest any ways in which these modern agencies help to control people? (It may help you to look at pages 234–7.)

Christian religions: Declining or changing?

One hundred years ago about 40 per cent of the population claimed to attend church each week. Today the figure is a little over 10 per cent. The obvious conclusion drawn by some sociologists is that people are less religious today than in the past.

The argument then continues that the churches have lost much of their influence in modern society. Fewer people believe in God, and use religious values as their guidelines on how to behave. For example, 'traditional' teachings of the churches on contraception, abortion, homosexuality, the marriage of Catholic priests and the ordination of women priests in the Church of England, have all come under considerable strain over the last 20 years. Indeed, it seems that the reverse is true today and the churches follow the general change in attitudes, an example of this is the Church of England's acceptance of the right of people to divorce.

The political influence of the Church of England has declined too and is rarely listened to by those in power. The importance of religious teaching in schools has slowly eroded so that it no longer has an important place in most schools' teaching programmes.

The functions of the churches have been lost to other agencies. Social workers, for example, paid by the state take the main responsibility for care of those with problems.

The status of the church has declined, particularly amongst the young. Church membership is seen by young people almost as an embarrassing thing to admit to. The rate of church attendance is far higher amongst the elderly than it is amongst the young.

All of this is summarised in the word 'secularisation'.

Reasons for the secularisation of society

The reasons given for this decline are that people now explain the world in scientific terms. Rather than understanding such things as the creation of men and women in terms of Adam and Eve, people now understand it as a result of evolution.

In general then people look for natural explanations for events rather than supernatural ones. This has also influenced the idea of sin and morality. For example, illness was once seen as punishment by God and having done something wrong. Today, we see illness as a result of having caught some 'bug' and so we go to the doctor. Of course, this has also weakened the importance of the clergy in the community.

This is part of a general movement in societies towards what sociologists have called **modernism** – all of modern western societies' activities are now dominated by a way of thinking which is rational and logical. Scientific discoveries have created the belief that societies are based on the laws of nature not on the laws of God. In social affairs, too, the influence of the social sciences, political philosophies and economics have persuaded people that society can be controlled, and that it is not simply God-created and unchangeable in the way it is organised.

Along with the change in ways of explaining the world, there has also been a change in the values of society. Modern society stresses that success in the ownership of as many things as possible. For example, a successful married couple is one with a large house, car and all the consumer goods that their family wants. The traditional values of stress on community and mutual help, strongly associated with the churches, have declined.

Churches: The changing membership

Church membership in the UK

Church	No. of active adult members (millions)		
	1970	1980	1992
Trinitarian churches			
Anglican	2.55	2.18	1.81
Presbyterian	1.81	1.51	1.24
Methodist	0.69	0.54	0.46
Baptist	0.30	0.24	0.23
Other free churches	0.53	0.52	0.66
Roman Catholic	2.71	2.34	2.04
Orthodox	0.19	0.20	0.28
All Trinitarian churches	8.78	7.53	6.72
Non-Trinitarian churches			
Mormons	0.09	0.11	0.15
Jehovah's Witnesses	0.06	0.08	0.13
Spiritualists	0.05	0.05	0.04
Other Non-Trinitarian	0.08	0.11	0.14
All Non-Trinitarian churches	0.28	0.35	0.46
Other religions			
Muslims	0.25	0.31	0.52
Sikhs	0.08	0.15	0.27
Hindus	0.05	0.12	0.14
Jews	0.11	0.11	0.11
Others	0.05	0.05	0.08
All other religions	0.54	0.74	1.12

Source: *Social Trends 25* (HMSO, 1995) and Christian Research Association

Religious attendance[1] in Great Britain, 1993

	Percentages
Once a week or more	11.7
Less often but at least once in two weeks	2.0
Less often but at least once a month	5.6
Less often but at least twice a year	10.3
Less often but at least once a year	5.2
Never or practically never	22.7
Varies too much to say	0.6
Not answered	0.1

[1]Respondents were asked how often, apart from special occasions such as weddings, funerals and baptisms, did they attend services or meetings connected with their religion.

Source: *Social Trends 25* (HMSO, 1995) and Social & Community Planning Research

1 Which four churches have declined in numbers of their membership?

2 What do we mean by the term 'sect' (see main text page 326)?

3 What has happened to their membership?

4 What has happened to the membership of the Muslim, Hindu and Sikh religions?

5 Why has this change occurred?

6 According to the figures above, would it be entirely true to say that Britain is becoming a less religious (secular) society? Explain your answer with references to the statistics above.

7 Do you think that to be religious it is necessary to be a member of a church, or to attend church regularly?

8 Bearing in mind your answer to the last question, what problems can you see in measuring how religious a society is by church membership and attendance alone?

The continuing importance of Christian religions

It has been argued that the statistics, which so convincingly show a decline in religious belief, in reality only show a decline in attendance at church, which is a very different matter. After all, believing in God does not mean attending church. If people are asked if they believed in God, over 85 per cent reply that they do, and if asked what church they belong to, over 70 per cent of the British population claim membership of a church.

The majority of people still use the churches for the major ceremonies and **rites of passage** of life and death – baptism, marriages and funerals are still religious ceremonies. For example, although statistics show that 48 per cent of all marriages take place in registry offices, if we restrict our gaze to first marriages (as the church discourages second marriages in church), only 31 per cent of first marriages take place in registry offices, meaning that about two-thirds of first marriages take place in church still.

In the past there was great social pressure on people to attend church each Sunday, because it was a sign of social respectability. People may have attended but not really believed in God. Today, not attending church is perfectly acceptable. Those who do attend, do so for the right reason – that they truly believe.

British society is still based upon Christian values, with at least 80 per cent of people questioned regarding seven or more of the Ten Commandments as applying to them in their own lives. The importance of the church in the lives of people is still very strong. This is shown by the way that the major rites of passage (major points of change in our lives) are still marked by religious ceremonies. Baptism, marriage and the funeral service are all important church rituals for most families.

Finally, and most importantly, the decline in church attendance usually refers to the more traditional churches, such as the Church of England, or the Catholic Church. There has been a great growth in sects (as we discuss on page 326), such as the Moonies and Scientology, as well as in pentecostal churches, such as the Elim Pentecostal Church. Sects which are primarily attended by West Indians, for example, showed a growth in membership of more than 20 per cent, in the five years up to 1980. Non-Christian religions have shown remarkable growth in Britain and across the world too, as we shall see later. For example, the Muslim faith has shown an increasing growth in its membership in the UK, more than doubling its membership in the last 25 years.

Is religion on the decline, or is it simply changing?

Conclusion

The death of religions does seem to have been exaggerated. Clearly there has been an overall decline in the importance of religion in British society, but to measure that solely in terms of church attendance is mistaken. However, much of the decline in attendance appears to be in the older-established churches, such as the Methodist, Church of England, Catholic, etc. Amongst the newer religions and the non-Christian faiths, such as the Muslims, there is significant growth and the rules of their faith seem far more important to them.

The growth of sects and new religions

When discussing religion, we people commonly talk about churches, meaning religious organisations that meet regularly to worship God. However, sociologists find this a little too vague and prefer to distinguish between three different types of religious organisations: the church, the sect (or new religion) and the denomination.

Basically, the more formal, the larger, the more tolerant and the more conformist, a religious organisation is, the more likely it is to be a church. It follows then that the smaller, the more radical, and the stricter a religious organisation is, the more likely it is to be defined as a sect. In the middle lies the denomination.

- **A church:** a religious organisation with paid officials, usually fully integrated into the values of society. It has regular formal acts of worship in a special place put aside for that purpose. One of the major churches is generally linked to the state, and is known as the 'estalished church'; in England, this is the Church of England.

- **A sect** or **new religion:** a small religious organisation which is very strict in its beliefs and control of its membership. Usually they believe that only they have found the truth concerning God. There are rarely any paid officials. They are generally strongly opposed to the accepted values of society. An example is the Jehovah's Witnesses.

- **A denomination:** a religious organisation which is accepted by the wider society, although it has no connection with the state. It is smaller in size than a church and the running of the church is far more in the hands of the congregation than in a church. Often denominations are sects that have grown in size and have become less critical of other religious groups. The Methodists are an example of a denomination.

The most noticeable thing about the changing face of religion in Britain has been the decline of the older established churches, and the growth of sects and new religions. Sociologists have suggested the main reason for this is that sects are performing the functions that the older established churches are no longer providing. So the sects have taken their places. The small size of the sects, their discipline and stress on shared experience provides a home for those who are lonely, or searching for a creed full of certainty.

The membership of sects and new religions

Membership appears to be drawn from two very different groups, the rejecters and the rejected.

The rejecters

The rejecters are those who feel that the values of society are wrong and that the modern stress upon ownership of possessions as the one gauge of value ignores the need for inner harmony and contentment. These rejecters are usually younger people from well-off homes who are themselves not financially deprived, but feel they need a sense of purpose in their lives. Sects such as the Moonies and Hare Krishna draw their recruits from these sorts of people.

One of the beliefs of these new religions is that as the world is so corrupt, the only way to achieve spiritual peace is by members cutting themselves off from society. Once new members join, they are expected to give their entire lives over to the religion, including working for it, handing over their possessions and possibly often living together. The leaders of the sects are seen as carriers of messages from God. Famous examples include Rev. Sun Myung Moon and Guru Maharji.

The 'world rejecting' religions recruit members from amongst those people who are unhappy with their lives and are seeking an escape. The 'world affirming' new religions do not contradict the values of society, but claim that personal fulfilment can only occur through religion. These religions typically do not demand full-time commitment or that members live in communal accommodation, but they do demand 'contributions' or fees from members. Often a form of meditation or 'exercises in human growth potential' are practised which aim to allow people to develop their potential to the full. The best known example of this type of world affirming new religion is scientology. Members often come from middle-class backgrounds and wish to find ways of achieving western society's goals, of power, status or personal attractiveness.

The rejected

The rejected, on the other hand, are from the poorer, deprived groups in society who need comfort and explanation for their situation. In particular sects and new religious have arisen amongst those of Caribbean origin.

Sects and new religions

In the USA, as in Britain, a considerable number of sects and new religions developed from the 1960s onward. One of these was the Black Muslims. Kaplan argues that the growth of this sect amongst poor blacks was because:

It offers him a rebirth. He can shed his old despised identity. It offers him an emotional if not physical outlet for his hostility toward the white man. It offers him hope. Joining the highly moral and disciplined Black Muslims gives him the prospect of raising himself from his condition of poverty and frustration. It also provides him with the goal of building for a new glorious future in a united and powerful black society.

Source: Adapted from H. M. Kaplan, 'The Black Muslims and the Negro American's quest for communion' in *British Journal of Sociology*, 20 June 1969

1 Why was it more likely that the membership of the Black Muslims should have been amongst the poor Blacks, than amongst the better-off Blacks in the USA?

2 What sort of people generally are attracted to sects?

'How I became a teenage cult member'

In this article the writer describes how, as a teenager, she was drawn into a Glasgow sect by its charismatic leader.

I first met Hamid when I was at secondary school in Glasgow. I was 14 years old. Hamid was 28 and was just beginning to establish himself within a group of teenagers, some of whom were my school friends. He would visit us at lunchtimes and chat to us about the mental "conditioning" that we were being put through by our school and families.

Like most young people, we were rebellious towards our parents and society. We were also vulnerable, impressionable and in search of identities.

He dressed entirely in black at the time – later it was blue – and he urged us to wear photographs of him around our necks. He referred to our parents as bears because bears are frightening – and he said he could protect us from them. He said we could do anything as long we were with him.

When I met him, I was spinning in a world of teenage confusion. My best friend had cut off all communication with me six months previously after she had joined his group. I had been hurt and I was angry with him for taking her away, but I was also in awe of him. Under his influence, my friend had changed completely. Once, she had been outgoing and fun, but after joining him, the only time she spoke to me was to insult me.

I wanted my friend back. I felt like an outcast, rejected by my best friend and ostracised by members of his group. I was torn between my own family and my need for a "social" family, which he controlled. ...

Hamid's ideas were spiritual and powerful and he seemed truly to believe in them – that was what made him so charismatic. Even those who did not share his faith were intrigued by and drawn to him.

Eventually, of course, many fell for him hook, line and sinker.

His philosophy was that purity of soul and body was the way to God. This involved a staunch anti-drug stance that extended from illegal substances to aspirin. He ruthlessly adopted any broadly promoted idea to achieve purity of body. ...

The group played power games which, at the time, seemed fun. One game was called "Kings". Four or so people were picked at random out of a group of 20, and for a certain length of time everyone else became slaves and had to do exactly what they were told. If anyone did something that he saw as a "crime" (ranging from smoking dope to saying something negative about Hamid or having a relationship with another group member) they were put on "trial". The punishment was a period of slavery even harsher than the game of "Kings". ...

If you did not go along with all this, you would be forced to leave the group. That meant not only giving up your social scene but losing the feeling of elitism conferred by group membership, which Hamid had ingrained within each individual. Ordinary people were "dorks" because they were not "enlightened"; he said they were still "unconscious".

Source: *The Independent*, 18 October 1994

1 At what age did the writer become involved in the cult?

2 Would you classify the cult as world-affirming, world-rejecting or world-rejected?

3 What power did Hamid have over his followers?

4 What does the term 'charismatic' mean?

5 How did the group treat people who were regarded as having misbehaved?

6 Why didn't people just leave the group if they were unhappy?

How sects and new religions can change into denominations

Over time the original founders of sects and new religions die, and as the dominance enjoyed by them over everybody else (known as 'charisma') in the sect declines, so rules of behaviour replace the orders of the founder. New recruits may not be as fervent as those of the first generation and gradually, as the sect grows in size, the radical ideas become watered down to attract yet more members. So, over a considerable period, the sect takes on the characteristics of a denomination. Methodism is an example of this.

The rising tide of evangelism

While the more traditional churches are declining in membership, newer, more vigorous churches are rapidly expanding. The pentecostal and charismatic churches, for example, now claim a worldwide membership of 110 million people.

NEW LIFE, MIRACLE and HEALING CRUSADE

IN THE

ELIM PENTECOSTAL CHURCH
GLENDALE GARDENS
LEIGH-ON-SEA

18th MAY to 23rd MAY
SUNDAY at 6·30pm
MONDAY to FRIDAY at 7·30pm

INTERNATIONAL EVANGELIST
REV. JEFFREY BROWN has been on Christian Satellite T.V. and many radio broadcasts. He has seen many miracles of healing, deliverance from oppression, broken marriages reunited and homes transformed.

NO TICKETS NEEDED. ALL SEATS ARE FREE AND CAN BE RESERVED IF YOU WISH.
IF YOU COME FOR HEALING, YOU WILL BE ABLE TO SPEAK PERSONALLY TO THE:
EVANGELIST, JEFFREY BROWN.

GOD CARES FOR YOU. SO DO WE!

PLEASE NOTE:

THIS CRUSADE IS NOT JUST FOR BELIEVERS OR CHURCH PEOPLE ONLY, BUT FOR EVERYONE, WHATEVER THEIR FAITH, RACE, AGE, OR EVEN THEIR DOUBTS.

IN THESE MEETINGS YOU ARE ONLY A STRANGER ONCE

Non-Christian religions in Britain

As Britain has changed from a predominantly single culture to a multi-cultural society, reflecting the immigration of the 1950s and early 1960s, so there has been a large growth in non-Christian religions. The number of Muslims in Britain now totals over half a million, and there are third of a million Sikhs, 140 000 Hindus, as well as the traditional British Jewish community which numbers about 110 000. Apart from the well-established Jewish community, the growth of the other religions has been quite remarkable. For example, there were only 250 000 Muslims in 1970, so the figure has doubled, while that for Sikhs has more than trebled in the same period. It would seem that far from declining, there is a continuing growth in non-Christian religions and their views are increasingly being taken into account in the wider society – so their influence is growing.

When Asian immigrants began coming to Britain in the 1950s, they brought with them their religions. The values of these religions have provided the Asians with a sense of their cultural identities. They unite the various Asian groups from particular areas and help them to preserve their own values while living in Britain. The main religions are Islam, Hinduism and the Sikh religion. It is important to note that whereas each religion draws together those from similar backgrounds and origins, there is considerable friction between the different religions, reflecting the divisions in the Indian sub-continent, where Pakistan (Muslim) and India (Hindu) have fairly poor relations and where the Sikhs are trying to obtain an independent state from India by sometimes violent means.

The followers of Islam are Muslims and believe in the prophet Mohammed. They believe that Jesus was not the son of God (whom they call Allah), but an earlier prophet and that the preachings of Mohammed overrule those of Jesus. Their holy book is the Koran (Qur'an) and they are very strict in their interpretation of it. One of the main social differences is their stress on the role of women, who are expected to be extremely modest, covering most of their bodies and to accept the control of their husbands or fathers in most matters.

The Hindus believe in reincarnation, which means that after death they return again on earth in another form. What you return as depends upon your behaviour in your previous lifetime. They do not believe in one individual God (whom they call Brahman), but that God is part of everything, taking different forms. Socially, they too stress the importance of modesty and obedience in women. Traditionally they believe in the caste system, in which people are graded according to their holiness and 'inferior' people must accept the superiority of others. These social rules appear to be breaking down in Britain.

The Sikhs come from Northern India, they are instantly recognisable because of their turbans. They gather for worship, which consists of readings from their holy book, the Granth, and then listen and sometimes discuss sermons based upon it.

Two views on religious education in Britain

Children are being left ignorant about the basic tenets of Christianity because schools and councils are flouting the law on religious education, according to an official inquiry.

The investigation into the state of religious education in schools uncovered "disturbing" evidence that new syllabuses issued by education authorities fail to spell out what pupils should learn about God, Christ and the Bible. None of the syllabuses complied in full with legislation that makes Christianity the main religion children should study, according to the confidential report which is being studied by John Patten, the [then] education secretary.

The findings coincide with evidence from government inspectors that many primary schoolchildren have no religious education lessons at all. In some schools it amounts to little more than colouring in pictures, or is part of a general topic – in one school, Noah was studied as part of a theme on journeys.

In others, humanism, Greek mythology and even the role of witch doctors in tribal societies are included in children's religious education, which critics say has become a multi-faith mishmash that leaves pupils with only a superficial understanding.

A separate study of children by researchers in Wales showed that only one in 20 admitted to

reading the Bible once a week or more. And in a recent MORI survey of school leavers, more than half did not know it was Judas who betrayed Jesus and 44% did not know what happened on Easter Sunday.

Government advisers are so worried that they are consulting the Church of England and other faiths in order to produce guidelines on what children should know about Christianity and other world religions.

Most syllabuses were so vague it was impossible for the advisers to discover how much of the schools' teaching would be about Christianity. One in three set no limit on the number of other religions that could be studied.

The London borough of Hounslow's syllabus lists Christianity as one of seven "core areas" for study, with Buddhism, Hinduism, Islam, Judaism, Sikhism and humanism. A 40-page booklet for Oldham schools does not even mention God or the Bible. South Tyneside's guidelines for junior schoolchildren say teachers could get pupils to "explore festivals and celebrations from various faiths", listing examples ranging from Passover to the Sikh Guru Nanak's birthday.

The result is a fragmentary approach that destroys the integrity of each faith, according to Colin Hart, director of the Christian Institute.

Source: *The Sunday Times*, 21 February 1993

1 What does the British law (referred to as 'legislation') say about the religious education in schools?

2 According to this extract, is the law being upheld?

3 What do the government inspectors say?

4 What percentage of children knew what happened on Easter Sunday?

5 According to Colin Hart, what is the result of religious education in schools today?

6 Do you think Mr Hart is completely impartial in his views?

"Part of the British establishment hoodwinks itself into thinking this is a white, Anglo-Saxon, Christian country," says Moeen Yaseen, a spokesman for the Muslim Education Forum. ...

There are 250,000 Muslim school children in this country, the largest concentration of non-Anglican children after Roman Catholics. Most of them go to state schools. There are 28 private Muslim schools educating about 2,500 children. Most but not all of these want to join the state sector. About six of the schools for older children offer religious training for pupils preparing for a vocation. Two are schools for children of expatriate workers, well resourced and separate.

The Education Reform Act of 1988 says that RE syllabuses must "reflect the fact that the religious traditions in Great Britain are, in the main, Christian while taking account of the teaching and practices of other principal religions that are represented in Great Britain".

Dr Syed Pasha, secretary of the National Muslim Education Council of the UK, believes that stressing Christianity to Muslim children at best confuses and at worst undermines the spiritual teaching which the children receive at home, at the mosque and in the supplementary schools.

Like many other Muslims, he would like to see the emphasis on Christianity deleted from legislation. His organisation would like Islam taught to Muslim children in state schools by state-funded Muslim teachers.

"Our main idea is that RE should be done in such a way as to be acceptable to parents of all religious communities," he says "At the moment it is tilted toward the Christian parents."

Source: *The Guardian* (Education section), 23 March 1993

---

1 How many Muslim schoolchildren are there in Britain?

2 How many go to state schools?

3 How many go to private schools?

4 What criticisms does Dr Syed Pasha make of religious teaching in state schools?

5 What would he like to see for Muslim children?

6 What would he like to see regarding religious education for all children?

7 Do you think he is impartial?

Religions around the world

The membership of religions worldwide

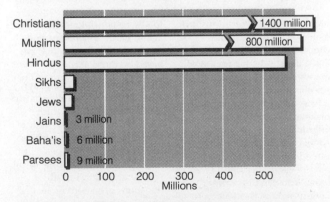

World figures: author's estimates based on various sources.
It is impossible to estimate the number of Buddhists, both in the UK and elsewhere. Like Quakers, Buddhists often refuse to be labelled. Membership includes people from ethnic groups and Westerners who have converted. Worldwide estimates vary from 200 million to 400 million.

Source: *The Guardian*, 30 April 1991

1 What are the two biggest religions in the worl?

2 How many Hindus are there?

3 Which is the fourth biggest religion?

4 We tend to forget that some religions not represented in the UK in significant numbers are actually quite large religions. Find out and briefly summarise the main beliefs of all the religions included in the chart.

Shopping around for religion – *The Big Issue's* religious supermarket

The Big Issue is a magazine sold by homeless people. It produced this light-hearted review of religion.

Hinduism

Brief history:
All Hindus worship one Supreme Being – Brahman. The origins of Hinduism are linked to several cities in the plain of the river Indus (now Pakistan). Hindus believe that, in the whole maelstrom of existence, the only constant is Brahman. Central to Hinduism is the belief that a soul inhabits many bodies before it reaches its final goal, which is to become as one with Brahman.

How do you join?
Turn up at a temple, but remember to take your shoes off before you enter. Talk to a priest, who will instruct you in the broader aspects of the faith. Western converts are warmly welcomed and, unlike many other religions, there's no initiation ceremony. "You don't get dipped in water or anything like that," says Manju Kumar, a young Hindu woman from Birmingham. "The main thing

you need is faith. Once you have that, everything else is easy."

What are you guaranteed in the afterlife?
Central to Hinduism is the belief in reincarnation. It's a pity that hippies hijacked the word *karma* and peppered their speech with it. *Karma* literally means "actions". Hindus believe that past deeds are influential in determining the nature of your future rebirth. "If you're good in this life, your next life will be

quantifiably better," says Manju. Yuppies, who have experienced life at both ends of the financial spectrum, used to call this process "trading up". Perhaps if they taught the law of *karma* at business schools then City dealing rooms would be much nicer places.

Judaism

Brief history:
For those amongst you who respect tradition and history, it should be gratifying to learn that Judaism, founded 5,755 years ago, is the oldest religion known to humankind. Unlike Christianity, the Jews are still waiting for the Messiah; they

consider Jesus to be a false prophet. So, while Christians have been waiting 2,000 years for an encore, the Jews have been patiently waiting for the show to start.

How do you join?
Judaism is not to be embraced

by the mere dilettante. In stark contrast to practically every other religion, Judaism has no missionaries and does not actively seek converts. Becoming a Jew is a difficult process. The first step is to approach the Beth Din, the faith's governing body. If you

decide that the Chosen Ones are your kind of people, then it takes seven years to fully convert to orthodox Judaism. For males, there is a catch. Or rather a snip. The good news is, it's done under a local anaesthetic.

Islam

Brief history:
The teachings of Islam were revealed by Allah (or God) to the prophet Muhammad ("Peace be upon him", which you have to recite every time you mention his name). Scholars concur that the prophet Muhammad was born in 570AD. When Muhammad hit 40, suffering a religious mid-life crisis, he wandered into a dark cave where he was visited by the Angel Jibril (or Gabriel) who told Muhammad the teachings of Allah and demanded he write them down. As Muhammad was illiterate, this proved difficult, so he had to memorise them instead. These teachings

were documented in what is now known as the *Koran*.

How do you join?
You become a Muslim through Shadada, a formal declaration made before two other Muslims that there is one God, Allah, and one Prophet, Muhammad.

What can you expect to get out of it?
Accepting reality for what it is and believing that life is a personal testing ground which simply prepares you for death (which is to be welcomed) are central to Islam. You refine your inner being by praying five times a day. Islam's seven basic beliefs and Five Pillars (specific

requirements of every Muslim) make for an intellectually challenging faith. One of the Five Pillars is fasting for a whole month during Ramadan. Another is that Muslims should, if health and wealth permit, make a once-in-a-lifetime pilgrimage to Mecca in Saudi Arabia. You have to have earned the money for the pilgrimage by the sweat of your brow. You can't blow your Lottery winnings on a trip to Mecca because that doesn't constitute pilgrimage.

What are you guaranteed in the afterlife?
That you'll be judged and sent to either heaven or hell. You're

totally responsible for how you act on Earth. The justice you receive in the afterlife will be based on those acts.

Do you have to pay to pray?
No. There is an Islamic charity called the Zakat, to which Muslims can donate 1/40th of anything they have a surplus of. Anything from a bushel of grain to a million barrels of oil will be accepted, but all donations are anonymous and boasting about your generosity is forbidden.

Scientology

Brief history:
The movement (or religious philosophy) was founded by L. Ron Hubbard (1911–86) around 1952. Hubbard had formulated Scientology, a belief system which he claimed could instill supernatural powers in anyone. The first Church of Scientology was established in Los Angeles in 1954 and there are now over 1,000 churches in 100 countries worldwide.

How do you join?
Ever walked down Tottenham Court Road and been accosted by people outside what looks like a bookshop, asking if you want to have a free personality test? If you agree, the 200 questions are designed to elicit the maximum amount of information and the results always seem to highlight the distress in your life. As with any fringe religion, it seems to attract more than its fair share of the totally gullible.

What can you expect to get out of it?
"Scientology is a path to increased awareness and spiritual freedom," says Peter Mansell, press officer at the Church of Scientology's HQ in East Grinstead. Once converted, you'll spend a lot of time trying to recruit others. It's the nearest a religion comes to pyramid selling. ...Basically, if you have a spiritual void in your life, Scientology will fit it as efficiently as cavity wall insulation. But at a price. If anything happens to you then your misfortunes are deemed to be "self-generated" and you'll be called a "victim" who has "pulled-in" their calamities. Expect no sympathy; Scientologists don't believe in it.

What are you guaranteed in the afterlife?
Scientologists don't really believe in the afterlife. Instead, they advocate a theory of "past lives": that people have lived lives prior to their current one. This, they say, is not reincarnation, but a guarantee that, having lived, you will live again. So convinced was Hubbard of this theory that he frequently put his employees on billion-year contracts.

Source: *The Big Issue*, No. 110, 19 Dec.–1 Jan. 1994–5

Chapter 18

HEALTH

This chapter covers:
- The meaning of health
- Models of health and illness
- Being ill
- Medicine and social control
- Inequalities of health
- The medical professions.

The meaning of health

When we talk about being healthy or ill, we generally think that there is some *real*, or *natural* difference. Yet many sociologists have challenged this very simple biologically-based distinction and argue that what has been considered to be normal in one society or in one period of history is abnormal or healthy in another. Just like ideas of what is good or bad, illness is related to the culture of society. In Britain, for example, what appears to have happened is that people's expectations of health have risen over time, as have their expectations of length of life, and even more extraordinary their acceptance of 'pain' has declined. What is illness now was normal bodily functioning 200 years ago.

If you think about this for a moment, all of us already accept that health is not a fixed thing. As people get older, they get more aches and pains, yet this is accepted as just a normal part of ageing, but for a younger person these aches and pains would be unacceptable. Standards of health vary across society, across time and between groups in society.

The changing definitions of 'health'

When the National Health Service was started in 1948, experts assured the politicians that there was a pool of ill people who were suffering because there had been inadequate medical treatment in the past. (The health service was based on either payment or charity before the NHS was set up.) The experts argued that if a great push was made to give these ill people drugs and surgery, then within ten years the pool would be emptied and after that there would be a much smaller demand for medical services.

On the basis of this advice, the government introduced the NHS reforms. They felt that the initial enormous costs would slowly decline with the declining numbers of 'sick people' who needed curing. In fact, by the early 1950s, it became clear to the government that what was viewed as health was socially-defined in much the same way as poverty. Health, it was found, was relative to the society in which it was defined. As people became healthier, so they became more aware of 'being ill'.

The result of this was that the demands for health care increased rather than decreased, and the 'healthier' the population, the more it demands yet higher standards of health care! In the future, the demands will continue to increase, and there will be no point at which people will be satisfied with their health.

1 Why did the government think it could afford the NHS?

2 How were their assumptions regarding the costs of the service shown to be wrong?

3 What does this mean for the future of health care?

4 Can you explain the statement that health is 'socially-defined' like poverty?

Defining health

Fierce feuding has broken out among people with Myalgic Encephalomyelitis [or ME] the chronic fatigue syndrome sometimes known as yuppie flu – in a row about the true nature of their condition that reflects the widespread public horror of psychiatric illness.

A specialist in ME has been sacked, a researcher has received hate mail and abusive phone calls, a campaign is under way to unseat the chairman of the ME Association and an ME pressure group has sought publicity to discredit the chairwoman of a rival group.

In the eyes of ME sufferers, believed to number more than 100,000 in Britain, the targets of these assaults have committed a common sin by highlighting the psychological component of the illness. Many sufferers reject the suggestion they may have emotional problems or need psychiatric treatment.

Theories about the cause of ME range from a viral infection to a disorder of the central nervous system. But the psychological aspects of the illness are increasingly being seen as essential to its treatment, a view that angers many

sufferers who believe the "reality" of their illness is being denied. ...

[One leading campaigner to show the psychological elements of ME is Caroline Richmond, chairwoman of the Campaign Against Health Fraud.]...

But Ms Richmond last week denied inaccuracy or nastiness: "I'm not saying ME patients don't have a real illness. They do and an awful lot are getting a bad deal from their GPs.

"Everyone knows psychological problems have physical symptoms. Every time

I swot really hard I get piles because I tense up my guts, but you can't say the piles are in my mind."

Many doctors despair of helping patients because of their resistance to accepting the psychological aspects of their illness. Dr Tony Pelosi, psychiatry lecturer at the Royal Edinburgh Hospital, said: 'I say to my ME patients: 'I think you might be depressed.' They say: 'How dare you say there's nothing wrong with me'.

Source: *The Sunday Correspondent*, 3 December 1989

A family doctor survey of chronic fatigue syndrome has debunked the "yuppy flu" label, finding that less than a quarter of sufferers were students or teachers and only 5 per cent were professionals.

The researchers also found a shift of attitude among doctors. While 10 years ago many GPs were highly sceptical about the syndrome, 71 per cent now accept its existence, 7 per cent do not and 22 per cent are undecided.

Several of the "undecided"

doctors also said they might be persuaded to change their minds if the illness was found in non-professionals.

While students and teachers made up 22 per cent of 293 GP patients, manual workers were the next highest category accounting for 17 per cent. Retired people accounted for 16 per cent; housewives 13 per cent; people in service industries 11 per cent; clerical staff 9 per cent and hospital workers 7 per cent.

Source: 'Fatigue syndrome in patients poses problems for GPs' by C. Hall in *The Independent*, 5 August 1991

1 What physical symptoms affect people with ME, according to the extracts?

2 Why was there a bitter dispute in the ME Association?

3 What does this tell us about the way we define illness?

4 How have doctors changed their views over the illness?

5 Who is more likely to get ME or 'chronic fatigue syndrome'?

6 The second extract refers to several 'undecided' doctors who were prepared to believe in the existence of chronic fatigue syndrome – but under what circumstances?

7 Can you explain why this information would change their opinions?

Models of health and illness

Traditional healing

Before Europe was industrialised, people understood health to mean both a healthy body and a healthy state of spiritual well-being. Health was closely linked to morality. If someone was ill, this was often supposed to be a punishment for some bad behaviour. Curing illness usually had two elements as well – the moral and the physical. So, traditionally, ill people would use a mixture of herbal remedies, prayers and special rituals or practices to ward off the devils – the **holistic model**.

This belief in the intricate mixture of mind and body is found in most other simple societies. For example, the Azande society studied by Evans Pritchard in the 1930s distinguished between two types of illness – those to be treated by natural remedies and those which resulted from witchcraft. Sick people visited a healer who gave them remedies which were usually a mixture of plants (for the biological part of the illness) and ceremonies (for the evil).

However, during the nineteenth century a change occurred in approaches to illness, and the holistic model of traditional medicine was slowly replaced by **bio-mechanical model**, which is the one that most doctors, and probably most people, believe in today. It sees the body as being like a machine, and just as a machine breaks down and needs to be repaired, so does the human body. The role of the doctor is to decide what has gone wrong and then to cure it, usually through prescribing drugs or perhaps through surgery.

The close relationship between disease and society

This article appeared after an outbreak of bubonic plague in Surat, India, in 1994.

We all understand why cholera erupts after major disasters (the contamination of drinking water by sewage spreads the disease) but why is diphtheria now so common in Russia? Why is TB now increasingly common in Britain? Why, indeed, has the plague erupted in Surat?

The answers to these questions are not medical but political. Diphtheria has returned to Russia because the social consequences of the collapse of communism have destroyed the network of clinics that once immunised the population.

TB has returned to Britain because we no longer round up the vagrants. Fifty years ago, the police would pick up the homeless, to place them compulsorily in hostels. There they received medical care. But many of the anti-vagrancy laws

have now been repealed and alcoholics, drug addicts and other debilitated travellers are free to sleep on cold streets, where they pick up TB and then spread it.

Surat has acquired the plague through poverty. ...

Mankind has lived alongside infection since time immemorial. With the onset of civilisation, bacteria and viruses multiplied to take advantage of the teeming masses and of their proximity to each other.

So diseases such as chickenpox or smallpox evolved from animal infections that spread to humans through the development of farming. In turn those human populations built up an immunity to those diseases. The populations such as the Indians of America and Polynesia who did not develop the same kind of animal

husbandry were, initially, spared those diseases. But when Columbus, Captain Cook and others finally penetrated the Western and Southern hemispheres – in ships that bore men with chickenpox and measles and so on – the local populations had no resistance.

We have seen through history the waning of many old diseases. Syphilis in Shakespeare's time was an acute disease of rapid onset. A few months were enough to debilitate the victim. Now syphilis is hardly dangerous at all, as modern man has evolved an effective immunity to it.

But Western man's real conquest of infection came through his intellect. The word 'quarantine' comes from the 17th-century Italian word quarantina, which means 40, as our forebears learnt to hold

ships for 40 days before permitting the crew to disembark.

Those 40 days were long enough to allow any latent infections to emerge. Chronicles describe how every member of the crew would die while ships waited in harbour. ...

During the 20th century, through developments in hygiene and antibiotics, we appeared to have destroyed most infectious diseases; and ten years ago it became normal to predict their ultimate destruction. Smallpox, for example, has been eradicated.

But with the collapse of social structures, with ever-increasing populations and with limitless travel, our uneasy stand-off with bacteria is being lost.

Source: *The Daily Mail*, 29 September 1994

1 Which major diseases are returning?

2 How can the author claim that the reasons are political? Give two examples of this.

3 It is said that diseases exist all the time, but only sometimes affect people. How does the article explain this?

4 Suggest one way to eliminate TB.

5 Does the author seem hopeful for the future?

Being ill

We know that less than half of people who feel ill actually visit a doctor. Although this may seem odd at first, on reflection it is obviously the truth. When we feel ill, we may decide to ignore it, to purchase a drug from the chemist, such as cough mixture or paracetamol tablets, or we may decide simply to stay in bed. Only if we regard it as serious enough, do we actually make an appointment with a GP.

In one study of over 1200 households, over 70 per cent of the people categorised themselves as in 'good' health, and a further 22 per cent said they were in 'fair' health. Yet according to the doctors who examined them, one third were actually suffering from a 'serious' medical condition. Of those who classified themselves as in good health, a quarter were actually taking some form of medicine, which they had bought in chemists. The study concluded that the number of people who actually needed medical help was 2.5 times greater than those who actually went to see a doctor.

This led sociologists to examine the reasons why people consulted a doctor or not, and what they uncovered was a complex set of factors which influence how people act if they suspect they are ill. There are three major stages:

- recognition
- decision to seek help
- response to help.

Recognition

Many of us feel ill or suffer from various pains, but we learn to accommodate these pains for a wide variety of reasons (for example, 'its just old age', or 'I always get these pains after a heavy meal'). People recognise there is pain or discomfort, but that is all. However, at a certain point, and not always when the 'illness' is at its worst, this pattern of accommodation breaks down. There appear to be different patterns of accommodation according to age, gender, social class and even ethnic group.

It may be because the person can no longer do a particular activity (run more than 20 metres to catch the bus) or fulfil certain social obligations (go to work). But at this turning point the person recognises that a particular problem exists, but goes beyond this and defines it as a possible illness.

Decision to seek help

However, there is no automatic link between deciding that you are ill and going to the doctor. At this point, people may consult friends and relatives to get their view about what to do, or whether they may be worrying unnecessarily. They may purchase medicines from the chemist, or ask the advice of the chemist. They might seek out people who have what they consider to be similar illnesses, or they might (but remember it is only one of a range of possible choices) go to seek medical advice from a doctor. Family are also approached for their opinions.

There are a number of barriers which prevent or delay people consulting doctors:

- The **perception of doctors** as busy people whose time must not be wasted by patients. This is not just a mistaken view either as numerous studies have shown that GPs are irritated by what they consider 'trivial consultations'. In fact, most GPs work very hard at limiting the amount of time they spend with individual patients.

- **Social class** Until recently there was a very significant difference between the social classes in consulting GPs, but this has almost completely disappeared now. What is more noticeable is the way in which the poorest sections of society (such as the homeless) now use the emergency departments of hospitals for GP services as they are excluded from the system.

- **Race** There is some evidence that different ethnic groups use GP services differently. This could be from different concepts of medicine or the cultural ideas regarding what is illness which we discussed earlier.

- **Gender** Women have more consultations with doctors than men, although this may reflect visits to do with children and pregnancy rather than illness as such.

Action

Once the doctor is seen, the extent and type of treatment can depend on many factors. The most important of these is the negotiation which takes place between doctor and patient. The doctor wishes to control the consultation and process patients as rapidly (and from his or her viewpoint) as efficiently as possible. Patients want the very best medical attention and to have adequate time to talk through their feelings. Middle-class patients may make greater demands upon doctors for services.

Medicine and social control

If we accept that medicine is dealing with problems which are not just physical but social as well, then medicine is involved in directing people into particular courses of action. These courses of action are regarded as 'healthy' activities, or at least the avoidance of unhealthy ones. So medical advice tells us not to consume excess alcohol, not to smoke, to eat nutritious foods and so on. In doing so, medicine is acting as a form of control over our lives. This may seem sensible to you if we are talking about physical health, but it is rather more complicated when we are discussing mental health. What forms of behaviour are 'wrong' and which are normal and correct? Some sociologists argue that an increasing range of behaviour which would at one time have been regarded as acceptable, if eccentric, has come to be regarded as evidence of illness, and that psychiatrists are controlling people not curing them, as they have nothing to be cured of in the first place!

The sick role

The best-known example of the way in which sickness is seen, not in terms of medicine, but in terms of social control is the idea of the **sick role**. According to one writer, Talcott Parsons, illness is actually a form of deviance which is threatening to society. The threat comes from the fact that anyone who is ill is unable to perform their socially-expected role. This could have serious consequences for society. If you remember, society depends upon people following a series of roles which 'interlock' to form the regular and predictable patterns of action which we call society.

Parsons suggests that illness may not be entirely random, and argues that there is often an element of conscious or subconscious desire to be sick. This is not as extreme as it sounds, as there is a close proven relationship between stress and physical illness. The problem is that if too many people were allowed to be defined as sick, and therefore unable to perform their roles, society could no longer function. Society must have a way of controlling sickness so that it does not become a threat. This form of control is the **sick role** and has two parts:

- sick individuals need not perform their normal social role requirements, but only as long as
- they agree to give themselves over to the care of the doctor and in order to try to get well again.

In other words, being sick is only allowed on condition that you try your very best to stop being sick!

The Marxist view of health and illness

A second, completely different view of sickness is that it is manipulated by those in powerful positions to control others. Marxists argue that definitions of health and illness are closely related to the needs of capitalism for a healthy workforce. So ill-health is generally regarded as the state in which a person can no longer continue to work efficiently. People are therefore checked by doctors to see if they are genuinely ill and unable to work. If the GP decides they are 'unfit to work' he then seeks to make them better, so that they can continue to work. In order to receive incapacity benefit from the government, for example, a person must demonstrate a very extreme state of long-term illness, otherwise he or she is regarded as a malingerer.

The feminist view

A further example of the Marxist view is given by feminist writers who point out the way that medical professionals have taken over control of what is regarded as normal behaviour for women. They argue that whole areas of women's lives have come to be controlled by medicine. For example, there are far higher rates of mental illness amongst women than men, and that more than twice the number of women are treated with the various anti-depressant drugs than men. What causes these higher levels of depression could be the role of women in society, argue feminists, and using anti-depressant drugs masks the real reason for depression, by turning women's depression into a medical problem.

Inequalities of health

We have seen earlier that health is not just a biological fact but a social one as well. This is true not just for how we define health, but for the causes of illness as well.

If ill-health was purely a biological game of chance, then we would expect that illness would be randomly distributed across the population with virtually everyone having a similar chance of being ill. But this is simply not the case – we know that chances of ill-health, both physical and mental, vary with such things as social class, being unemployed, gender, ethnicity and even region of the country.

Social class differences in mortality

A working man in social class V is over three and a half times more likely to die from coronary heart disease than a professional in social class I.

Source: 'Health Care Data Briefing' in *The Health Service Journal*, 7 September 1989

Mortality of men by social class and broad age groups, 1976–81

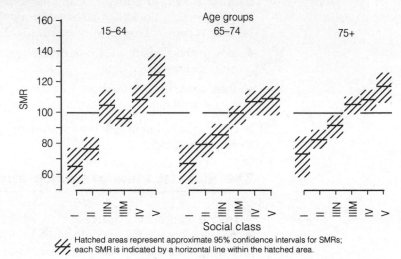

Hatched areas represent approximate 95% confidence intervals for SMRs; each SMR is indicated by a horizontal line within the hatched area.

Source: OPCS Longitudinal Study and Fox *et al.* (1986)

The standardised mortality ratio (SMR) shows the relative chances of dying at any particular age between the various social classes. The overall average chance of death in society is assumed to be 100, and a social class with an average above 100 has a higher chance of death than the average for society. Conversely, below 100 means a less than average chance of death.

1 Which social class group in each age group has the highest SMR?

2 Which group has the lowest SMR?

3 Overall what picture of the relationship between death and social class is painted by the three graphs?

4 In your opinion, why are there these differences?

5 What suggestions could you put forward to eliminate them?

Social class

The differences in the health standards of people of the different social classes are quite startling. These differences are apparent at birth, continue through a person's lifetime and are demonstrated most clearly in the difference in expectation of life of people in the different social classes.

First, you should be aware of the difference between **mortality rates**, which refers to differences in the deaths of people in different groups, and **morbidity rates**, which refers to the differences in illness of people in different groups.

Mortality

Children of parents in the lowest social classes are three times more likely to die in their first year of life. They have a much higher chance of dying from an illness or accident related to their work as well. Throughout their lives these people will live with a three times higher chance of dying, and finally they are likely to die about five years earlier on average.

Class changes and ill-health

A

Rate of decrease in mortality sharper for non-manual groups

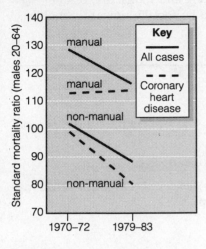

B

Perinatal death rate: class gap narrows

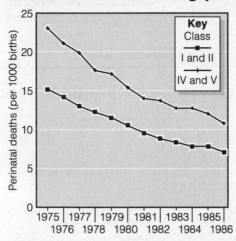

Source: 'Health Care Data Briefing' in *The Health Service* Journal, 7 September 1989

Look at **A**, which shows the decrease in mortality for manual and non-manual groups.

1 Explain in your own words the meaning of SMR.

2 What has happened to the SMR of both manual and non-manual groups?

3 Has the gap narrowed between the two groups?

4 What has happened concerning heart disease?

5 The government claims that the numbers of people dying before retirement age has declined overall. This is true, but what fact is being hidden?

Look at **B**. Perinatal mortality refers to deaths of young babies.

6 What two statements can you make about perinatal mortality rates, using the information provided in the charts?

Morbidity

Throughout their lives, people belonging to the lowest social classes are significantly more likely to suffer from such illnesses as cancer and heart disease. They are also more likely to have periods out of work through illness and to have long-standing illnesses or physical disabilities which limit their activities.

Explanations for differences in social class

Four explanations are offered by sociologists for these differences in health standards:

● the social selection approach

● the cultural approach

● the structural approach

● the artefact approach.

The first three explanations suggest that the differences are real, while the final one, the artefact approach, suggests that the statistics mentioned earlier do not tell the whole truth.

The social selection approach

This approach claims that it is not social class that causes ill-health, but it may well be ill-health that is a significant cause of social class. For example, if a person is chronically (long-term) ill, or disabled in some way, it is usually difficult for them to obtain a secure, well-paid job. The result is they are likely to have lower earnings, or be unemployed. Those who are strong and robust are, on the contrary, more likely to be successful in life, and be socially upwardly mobile.

Skin cancer – the affluent killer

Cancer of the skin, by gender (England and Wales)

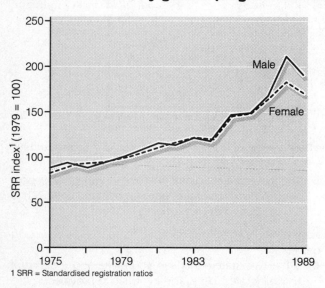

1 SRR = Standardised registration ratios

Source: *Social Trends 25* (HMSO, 1995) and Office of Population Censuses and Surveys

1 What has happened to levels of skin cancer for males and females since 1975?

2 What reasons can you suggest?

3 Give three other examples of how social factors may be related to illness.

The cultural approach

This approach argues that differences in health are affected by the sorts of exercise people do and the food they eat. Middle-class people are more likely to eat salads and fruit and less likely to smoke or eat fatty foods. Also they are more likely to do some form of sport as they get older and to be more concerned about keeping fit. This reflects the different cultural attitudes of middle-class and working-class people.

- Manual workers consume twice as much white bread, 50% more sugar, and 60% less fresh fruit than non-manual workers.
- Whereas less than 20% of professional employees smoke, 55% of male and 41% of female unskilled manual workers do.

It is not just that the social classes have differences in lifestyle which influence standards of health, but they also make different use of a wide range of medical services. For example, the different classes have different levels of usage of contraceptive devices, and of the medical services including vaccination, ante-natal and post-natal services (services for pregnant women, and for women and their babies in the first months after the birth). These different patterns of use reinforce the varying standards of health between the social classes.

Dying for Scotland

The HEA report, Escaping the Nicotine Trap, says that 37 per cent of people in Scotland are regular smokers, as are 31 per cent in the North-west and 30 per cent in the Northern and Yorkshire region. This compares to 23 per cent in Anglia and Oxford and South Thames, and 26 per cent in the South and West region.

The number of regular smokers who have succeeded in stopping in Scotland is put at 17 per cent, compared with 30 per cent in Anglia and Oxford.

The ICRF report says that one-third of all deaths in middle-aged Scots are caused by smoking. In women, the mortality rates are two-thirds higher in Scotland than in England, while in men they are one-third higher. While deaths from smoking among those aged 35 to 69 are starting to decrease in men, there has been no similar fall in women in Scotland or England.

Richard Peto, head of the charity's cancer studies unit in Oxford, who carried out the analysis, said: "If women smoke like men, they will die like men. Even in England smoking is by far the biggest cause of premature death, but in Scotland it's much worse. Scottish women have the highest death rates in the world from tobacco."

[Robert West, the author of the HEA report commented that the] failure to stop [smoking] was not due to misplaced machismo, or a rejection of health warnings, [but] the fact that living in areas surrounded by other smokers provided constant temptation, making it far more difficult to give up or remain as non-smokers.

HEA = Health Education Authority
ICRF = Imperial Cancer Research Fund

Source: *The Guardian*, 7 March 1995

1 Construct a simple table or histogram to illustrate the differences in smoking between the regions mentioned in the UK.

2 Which has the highest and which the lowest levels of smoking?

3 What decline in smoking has taken place in Scotland compared to Anglia and Oxford?

4 What explanation does the article provide to suggest why people fail to stop smoking?

Differences in cigarette smoking

Cigarette smoking[1], by gender and socio–economic group, Great Britain

Gender and socio–economic group	No. of smokers (Percentages)		
	1972	1982	1992
Males			
Professional	33	20	14
Employers and managers	44	29	23
Intermediate and junior non-manual	45	30	25
Skilled manual	57	42	34
Semi-skilled manual	57	47	39
Unskilled manual	64	49	42
All aged 16 and over	52	38	29
Females			
Professional	33	21	13
Employers and managers	38	29	21
Intermediate and junior non-manual	38	30	27
Skilled manual	47	39	31
Semi-skilled manual	42	36	35
Unskilled manual	42	41	35
All aged 16 and over	41	33	28

[1]Adults aged 16 and over except for 1972 which relates to those aged 15 and over.

Source: *Social Trends 25* (HMSO, 1995) and the Office of Population Consensus and Surveys

1 Which socio-economic group has the lowest level of cigarette smoking amongst males and females?

2 Which groups have the highest levels of smoking?

3 What percentage of skilled manual males smoked in 1992?

4 What percentage of junior non-manual females smoked in1992?

5 Which two groups in each sex had the greatest decline in smoking between 1972 and 1992?

6 Which two groups had the lowest decline?

7 What differences emerge between males and females in:
a) the percentages smoking?
b) the rates of decline?

8 What overall conclusions can we reach about cigarette smoking, social class and gender?

The structural approach

The structural approach is much more radical than the cultural approach. Whereas the cultural approach lays great stress on people from different social classes making choices about their lifestyles, as a result of their different cultures, the structural approach suggests that there is very limited choice available to people in their way of living.

People who are poor have bad housing conditions, no choice but to buy cheap, filling food, may smoke because of stress and are often unable to afford leisure facilities. So, the approach stresses that for many people an unhealthy lifestyle is all that is available to them.

There are lots of other examples of how people have relatively little choice in their types of lifestyle. One such example is that certain types of employment are more dangerous than others. Apart from the obvious ones such as the building industry, research on civil servants has shown that routine clerical workers are actually more likely to suffer from stress than more senior managers, and stress is one of the most important factors in causing ill-health. It is true also that people from the working class are more likely to become unemployed and this is closely linked to both poverty and to stress both of which are crucial factors in bringing about serious illness.

Poverty and illness

For all their good intentions, health promotion campaigns may worsen the health of the very people they are intended to help, according to a report on poverty and health launched this week.

It also says too few health authorities address the root causes of ill health in a 'systematic or strategic way' and bemoans the absence of links between organisations working in the poverty and health fields.

The report, published by the Public Health Trust, criticises

the emphasis placed on reducing health inequalities created by poverty while ignoring the role that poverty itself plays in creating them.

This, it says, leads to an over-emphasis on campaigns to change behaviour contributing to illness and blames poor people for their own ill health.

'People's behaviour does affect their health but the living conditions are far more important,' says the report.

'People need to know about the risks of smoking, alcohol and poor diet if they want to

improve their health. But there is little point in expecting people to change their lifestyle for the better if they cannot afford the healthier diets, warmer homes and exercise facilities that are recommended.

'Indeed, the worry of being lectured on how to make your family healthier while being denied the resources to do anything about it can only add to the general stress of living on little money.'

The report goes on: 'It is no wonder some people turn to smoking and drinking in

desperation. Ironically, this means the government's health messages may actually widen the health gap.

'The better off can afford to act on the advice and do improve their chances of better health, but the poorest are left powerless in the poverty sickness trap.'

The report says 12 million people in the UK live in poverty, and that there is such a close association between poverty and ill health that 'it can be assumed that for many people poverty causes much of their ill health'.

Source: M. Crail, 'Cause and effect' in *The Health Service Journal*, 27 April 1995

1 According to the extract, what is the root cause of ill-health?

2 Explain the meaning of the term 'health promotion'. (It is not in the text.)

3 How can it possibly worsen people's health?

4 Why is there a link between poverty and higher levels of smoking and drinking?

The structural approach also suggests that people (particularly young people) are strongly influenced by advertising in their choice of foods, with advertising campaigns extolling the virtues of certain types of alcoholic drinks, for example, when alcohol above a certain level is extremely bad for the health. Similarly advertisers fail to mention that in order to have a longer shelf-life, many food products are treated with additives, with little knowledge of the long-term effects on those who eat them.

The artefact approach

This final approach is one which is less an explanation of differences and more a criticism of the other approaches. Quite simply the artefact explanation claims that although the differences in mortality and morbidity between the higher and the lowest social classes are striking, they do not take into account a more important fact – that the lowest social class is shrinking rapidly in size. So, although there is a large and growing gap, the actual number of people in the lowest group is very small. A second point is that although the health of this lowest group is relatively very poor compared to the higher social classes, the overall standard of health is rising – it is just that it is rising more slowly than that of the other 80 per cent of the population.

Sex differences in health

Women are more likely to live longer than men, but that they are also more likely to visit their GPs for treatment, they have higher levels of mental illness and much higher levels of chronic (long-term) illness.

Sociologists have suggested a number of explanations for the difference in life expectancy. The first, and obvious one is the biological one that women are stronger than men. However, women may also live longer because of their social role which discourages them from violent activities (such as fast driving which is a significant killer of young men), from excess alcohol consumption, from excess smoking, and from manual work in industry.

Women are more likely to have higher levels of chronic illness, it is suggested, because they live longer, and are therefore more likely to suffer from these sorts of illnesses.

Affluence and cancer

Wealthy women are more likely to survive breast cancer than those who live in poorer areas, says a new report.

They have a greater chance of still being alive five years after treatment – and experts are trying to find out why.

Figures for the South-East reveal that the chances of long-term survival vary from 81 per cent in Mid-Surrey to 63 per cent in East London.

Professor Michael Baum, head of the breast cancer unit at the Royal Marsden Hospital, Chelsea, dismissed any suggestion of inequalities in treatment between rich and poor and said early diagnosis could be an explanation.

'More affluent women are perhaps better educated and more likely to present their symptoms,' he said. 'At the first sign of a lump they go running off to the doctor.

'Those less affluent may not be aware of a lump, or alternatively cannot afford to take time off to get advice or treatment.'

He said studies in America supported the registry's findings. 'It may be to do with poor nutrition – it's difficult to say. But it's a socio-economic issue, not a medical one.'

In areas where there was a large immigrant population, particularly Islamic, women were reluctant to see a male doctor. 'We need more female surgeons,' said Professor Baum, who is already training three.

Source: *The Daily Mail,* 29 September 1994

Age-standardised death rates for breast cancer, Europe, 1985

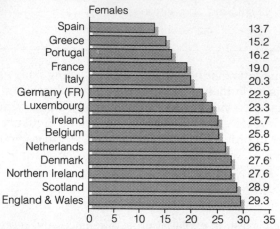

Females

Country	Rate
Spain	13.7
Greece	15.2
Portugal	16.2
France	19.0
Italy	20.3
Germany (FR)	22.9
Luxembourg	23.3
Ireland	25.7
Belgium	25.8
Netherlands	26.5
Denmark	27.6
Northern Ireland	27.6
Scotland	28.9
England & Wales	29.3

Source: Cancer Research Campaign, Factsheet 5.1, 1988

1 If illness or disease was simply a biological fact, then it could not be influenced in any way by a person's social class or wealth. What does this article tell us about cancer and affluence?

2 What proportion of women in 'affluent' mid-Surrey are more likely to be alive five years after treatment than in poorer East London?

3 Is the answer that the wealthy receive better treatment?

4 What two suggestions have been made to explain the difference between social classes?

5 Why does Professor Baum suggest that more female surgeons are needed?

Look at the table on breast cancer.

6 Which countries have the highest rates of breast cancer?

7 Which countries have the lowest?

8 How does this support the argument that levels of death from breast cancer may be influenced by social factors?

But there is an interesting division in health between different groups of women. Working-class women are more likely to be ill and to die younger than middle-class women, and working women appear to have higher standards of health than full-time housewives. It would appear that the amount of work, the social isolation and the long hours looking after the rest of the family lead to ill-health.

Differences in alcohol consumption

Consumption of alcohol above sensible[1] levels, by gender and age, 1992 (Great Britain)

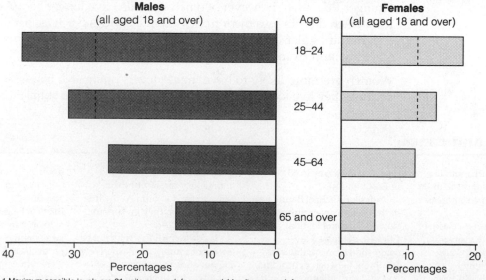

Males (all aged 18 and over) | Age | Females (all aged 18 and over)

18–24

25–44

45–64

65 and over

Percentages

1 Maximum sensible levels are 21 units per week for men and 14 units per week for women

Source: *Social Trends 25* (HMSO, 1995) and the Office of Population Censuses and Surveys

1 Which sex drinks most?

2 Which age group drinks the most alcohol? Give figures to illustrate your answer.

3 Which age group drinks the least? Give figures to illustrate your answer.

4 Can you suggest any reasons for the patterns of age, gender and alcohol consumption?

What are sensible drinking levels?

What is a unit?

Units per week

0	10	20	30	40	50	60

Women   14   35

Men   21   50

Low risk   Increasing risk   Harmful

Half a pint of ordinary strength

A small glass of wine.

A single measure of spirits.

Conduct a small survey of over 16 year olds (asking about ten people each), about smoking and drinking. What proportion of people smoke? What proportion drink alcohol? Ask them why they do so.

Gender differences in death rates

Death rates[1] for people aged under 65, by gender and selected cause of death (England and Wales)

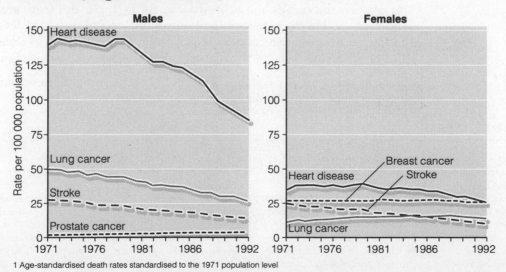

1 Age-standardised death rates standardised to the 1971 population level

Source: *Social Trends 25* (HMSO, 1995) and Office of Population Censuses and Surveys

1 The diagrams compare the reasons for death of different sexes. Which is the single biggest cause of death for men and women?

2 Is there any noticeable difference in the numbers of men and women dying of this cause? What are the figures in 1992. Has there been any change between 1971 and 1991? Could you suggest any reasons for this?

3 Look at the lines for lung cancer. What has happened to the male and female patterns over the 21 years of the charts? Can you suggest any possible reason for this?

Ethnicity and health

The relationship between health and race is very complex. The different ethnic groups have very different social customs which are reflected in the patterns of health. For example, as Asians are less likely to drink alcohol or to smoke, they tend to have lower levels of lung cancer and heart disease. However, they are more likely to suffer from diabetes. Infant death rates are higher too amongst certain groups of Asians, particularly those born to mothers who have come originally from Bangladesh or Pakistani origins. This can partially be explained by poverty, but another reason may be the short period of time between births. This reflects cultural attitudes towards contraception and the role of women. The greater likelihood of rickets amongst children of Asian origin may reflect a combination of poverty and diet. However, people of Afro-Caribbean origin do have above average rates of liver cancer and certain forms of heart disease, they also have exceptionally higher chances of suffering from strokes. At present there is no explanation for this. There is also the fact that people of Afro-Caribbean origins have higher chances of being diagnosed as suffering from mental illness. This last illness has been seen by many commentators as possibly resulting from racism.

Region and health

There are very considerable differences in levels of morbidity and mortality in the different regions of Britain. The highest chances of an early death are in Scotland, and the lowest chances of dying before retirement age are in East Anglia. There remain, however, differences across the social classes.

The further north one moves in Britain, the more common diseases are arthritis, rheumatism, bronchitis and heart disease, for example. But there are also variations within the north–south divide, with some of the worst levels of health and highest expectations of early death amongst those living in areas of Bristol and London, and some of the highest standards of health in Glasgow.

It seems that overall the levels of morbidity and mortality are related to deprivation, rather than region.

The power of stress

Divorce can seriously damage your health, new research has shown. [One Plus One, a research group, conducted a nationwide survey and found:]

- Cancer rates are significantly higher in divorced people.
- There are strong links between marital break-ups and premature death. Men aged 25 to 50 are twice as likely to die early if they are divorced.
- Divorced men are twice as likely as married men to die from heart disease.
- Divorced men and women are four times more likely to commit suicide than those who are married.
- Children of divorced parents run a greater risk of physical and psychological ill-health from the time of the break-up well into adult life.

The study even found divorced parents and their children drink and smoke more than other marital groups.

Marriage splits are accompanied by anxiety, anger and depression.

They also cause continuous stress which sparks physical problems such as headaches, chest pains, coughs, asthma, dry skin and tiredness. ...

Children of divorced parents are usually sad, depressed and angry. ...

Girls appear to show more marked symptoms than boys, though both sexes suffer profoundly and the effects can still be seen 30 years later.

One Plus One said a supportive marriage provided protection against ill health because it acted as a buffer from the effects of anxiety and stress. It found it was particularly beneficial for men.

1 Explain the meaning of the first line of the extract, 'Divorce can seriously damage your health'.

2 What is twice as likely to happen to men aged between 25–50 if they get divorced?

3 By how much does divorcing increase the risk of suicide?

4 How does divorce affect the children?

5 Apart from the serious life-threatening illnesses, what other health problems are more likely to happen to divorced people?

6 It cannot be the simple act of divorce that causes ill-health. What is the explanation put forward by the researchers?

The Holmes–Rahe life-event scale

Life event	Value
Death of partner	100
Divorce	73
Marital separation	65
Going to prison	63
Death of a close family member	63
Personal injury or illness	53
Marriage	50
Being dismissed at work	47
Marital reconciliation	45
Retirement	45
Change in health of family member	44
Pregnancy	40
Sexual difficulties	39
Gaining a new family member	39
Business or work adjustment	39
Change in financial state	38
Death of a close friend	37
Change to different line of work	36
Change in number of arguments with partner	35
Mortgage larger than one year's net salary	31
Foreclosure of mortgage or loan	30
Change in responsibilities at work	29
Son or daughter leaving home	29
Trouble with in-laws	29
Outstanding personal achievement	28
Partner begins or stops work	26
Begin or end school	26
Change in living conditions	25
Revision of personal habits	24
Trouble with boss	23
Change in work hours or conditions	20
Change in residence	20
Change in schools	20
Change in recreation	19
Change in religious activities	19
Change in social activities	18
Mortgage or loan less than one year's net salary	17
Change in sleeping habits	16
Change in number of family get-togethers	15
Change in eating habits	15
Holiday	13
Major festival, e.g. Christmas	12
Minor violations of the law	11

The Holmes–Rahe life-event scale gives an indication of how high a stress level a person may have.

1 What does it tell you?

2 How do you rank on the scale?

Divorce, by sex and age (England and Wales)

	Rate of divorce per 1000 married population			
	1961	1971	1981	1991
Males				
16–24	1.4	5.0	17.7	25.9
25–29	3.9	12.5	27.6	32.9
30–34	4.1	11.8	22.8	28.5
35–44	3.1	7.9	17.0	20.1
45 and over	1.1	3.1	4.8	5.6
All aged 16 and over	2.1	5.9	11.9	13.6
Females				
16–24	2.4	7.5	22.3	27.7
25–29	4.5	13.0	26.7	31.3
30–34	3.8	10.5	20.2	25.1
35–44	2.7	6.7	14.9	17.2
45 and over	0.9	2.8	3.9	4.5
All aged 16 and over	2.1	5.9	11.9	13.4

Source: *Social Trends 24* (HMSO, 1994) and the Office of Population Censuses and Surveys

The table shows the changes in divorce between 1961 and 1991. Using information from the article on page 348, from the Holmes–Rahe scale, and from the table, what statements can you make about health from the information in the table?

The medical professions

Doctors and nurses are regarded with great respect by most people. They are seen as professionals working for the good of the community with little thought for themselves. Medical professionals are also seen as highly-trained and competent, rarely making mistakes or errors of judgement. But these views are not shared by all sociologists. Four viewpoints have emerged:

- the medical professions as dedicated experts
- the medical professions as 'agents of repression'
- the medical professions as groups of self-interested people
- the medical professions as fallible.

Doctors as dedicated professionals

Traditionally, sociologists have stressed the need for doctors (and to a much lesser extent nurses) having a monopoly (exclusive control) over the provision of health care. This approach is associated with the **functionalist perspective** in sociology. Writers in this tradition, such as Talcott Parsons, argue that by putting very strict codes of professional conduct on doctors, patients can be certain:

- that they will receive the highest possible standards of health care – that the doctor will give the best and most appropriate treatment, no matter how difficult or expensive that may be.

- that doctors will exercise the very highest 'moral' standards – for example, a male doctor examining a female patient will treat her strictly on the grounds of being a patient and there will be no possible 'sexual' threat to her.

These are very important points because patients are very vulnerable when they are sick – they might, for example, have to undergo very significant and unpleasant surgical or drug treatment with great consequences, possibly involving the loss of limbs, organs or their lives. They therefore must have complete trust in the entire profession.

The result of this is that doctors have gained a public monopoly over the treatment of illness, because their professional standards ensure that patients are safe.

The distinction between a job and a profession

So far we have used the term 'profession' in a loose sense to mean that doctors have the highest standards. However, a (fairly) clear distinction can be made between professions and 'ordinary' jobs. For a group of workers to become professionals they need to have the following:

- **A body of systematic knowledge** This means having very high academic qualifications.
- **Professional authority** This involves people unquestioningly accepting the opinion of the expert.
- **Self-control** The professionals have the exclusive right to discipline their own members rather than being controlled by outsiders, as in most jobs.
- **Monopoly** Only the specific profession can work in the particular area. So only doctors can prescribe and engage in surgery, for example.
- **A strict code of ethics** Professionals must behave according to high moral standards.
- **A professional culture** This involves a common sense of identity and purpose.

This approach therefore sees doctors, and to a lesser extent nurses, as full professions which benefit patients.

Doctors as agents of repression

Many writers who are influenced by Marxist perspectives argue that the medical professions are really there to sell the drugs produced by the large pharmaceutical companies and to mislead people as to the real causes of illness.

The large pharmaceutical industry has some of the most profitable companies in the world. Doctors routinely prescribe these drugs to 'cure' illnesses, yet Marxists argue that many of these illnesses are caused by stress, poverty and pollution, all of which could be cured if the problem was looked at in a different way and these real causes were dealt with. The medical professions by curing and caring for ill people help to disguise the real causes of illness.

Professionals as self-interested

Another cynical approach to studying the medical professions comes from those who argue that basically professions exist to benefit the professionals themselves and no one else.

Becoming a profession has little to do with providing high standards, rather it is a way for groups of workers to get complete control of an area of work and as a result raise their own standards of living. So, for example, doctors have been particularly successful in eliminating other groups who claim to treat ill people. Historically, people chose between doctors and homeopaths, osteopaths and even faith healers, but gradually doctors eased them out and acquired legal monopoly for providing health care. The result has been high pay, with GPs for example having average salaries of over £45 000.

Medical professionals as fallible

Perhaps the strongest criticism of the medical professions is provided by Ivan Illich who argues that the medical professions seek to hide the fact that doctors are actually responsible for a large amount of the ill-health, and even death. Illich calls this **iatrogenesis** (meaning that the curer is the cause of the illness). Often, for example, doctors make inaccurate diagnoses of patients' illnesses and this can lead to worse medical problems as patients receive inappropriate drugs and often harmful surgery.

INDEX